Ontological Catastrophe

New Metaphysics

Series Editors: Graham Harman and Bruno Latour

The world is due for a resurgence of original speculative metaphysics. The New Metaphysics series aims to provide a safe house for such thinking amidst the demoralizing caution and prudence of professional academic philosophy. We do not aim to bridge the analytic-continental divide, since we are equally impatient with nail-filing analytic critique and the continental reverence for dusty textual monuments. We favor instead the spirit of the intellectual gambler, and wish to discover and promote authors who meet this description. Like an emergent recording company, what we seek are traces of a new metaphysical 'sound' from any nation of the world. The editors are open to translations of neglected metaphysical classics, and will consider secondary works of especial force and daring. But our main interest is to stimulate the birth of disturbing masterpieces of twenty-first century philosophy.

Joseph Carew
Ontological Catastrophe

OPEN HUMANITIES PRESS

An imprint of MPublishing – University of Michigan Library, Ann Arbor, 2014

First edition published by Open Humanities Press 2014
Freely available online at http://dx.doi.org/10.3998/ohp.12763629.0001.001

Design by Katherine Gillieson
Cover Illustration by Tammy Lu

ISBN-13 978-1-60785-308-4

OPEN HUMANITIES PRESS is an international, scholar-led open access publishing collective
whose mission is to make leading works of contemporary critical thought freely available
worldwide. Books published under the OPEN HUMANITIES PRESS imprint at MPublishing are
produced through a unique partnership between OHP's editorial board and the University
of Michigan Library, which provides a library-based managing and production support
infrastructure to facilitate scholars to publish leading research in book form.

MICHIGAN
PUBLISHING
www.publishing.umich.edu

O
OPEN HUMANITIES PRESS
www.openhumanitiespress.org

Contents

To the Memory of Joey Basha

Acknowledgements

Firstly, I would like to express my gratitude to two people without whom
this project would not have been possible: Dr. Antoinette Stafford and
Dr. Sean McGrath. Dr. Stafford is, in many ways, the reason why I am
doing philosophy, and it is to her that I owe my knowledge of the history of
modern philosophy and German Idealism, without which this book would
never have gotten off the ground. Dr. McGrath sparked my interest in
psychoanalysis and has been a constant source of inspiration for my reading
of Schelling. I must thank him for stressing the notion of the ambiguity of
the Real in Lacan and Žižek, which immensely shaped my own engagement
with these authors, and for all the encouragement he has given me since.

Secondly, I should thank four people who read the manuscript at various
stages of its production. Dr. Peter Trnka and the late Dr. James Bradley
read a very early version of the manuscript several years ago, and I am much
indebted to their extremely kind and useful commentary. While Dr. Bradley
gave me insight into further aspects of Žižek's philosophy—some of which
has shown up in my other work on Žižek—and encouraged me to continue
the project, Dr. Trnka's much appreciated criticism helped me avoid
conceptual imprecision at several key points, as well as general difficulties in
the presentation of psychoanalytical methodology. Specifically, Dr. Trnka's
emphasis on the conflictual relation between materialism and idealism in
many ways moulded my own views on the difficult Symbolic-Real relation in

Žižek's transcendental materialism into the form they take here. Dr. Graham Harman's comments and suggestions were of great help in stylistically improving the manuscript's quality, in increasing its overall coherence, and also in avoiding several pitfalls of argumentation. I should also thank him for his always quick responses to various questions I had while preparing the manuscript. Last but certainly not least, I thank Kyla Bruff for her laborious proofreading of the final two drafts. Her careful eye was able to eliminate innumerable ambiguities and awkward turns of phrase, thus making the book much smoother.

Thirdly, I would like to express my gratitude to the Social Sciences Research Council of Canada and Europhilosophie for their generous funding, which both directly and indirectly supported the project. I would also like to thank the Memorial University of Newfoundland's Department of Philosophy and School of Graduate Studies for additional financing in the form of fellowships and awards, which enabled me to begin the first draft.

An early version of three strands of argumentation that appear in what follows has been published as "The *Grundlogik* of German Idealism: The Ambiguity of the Hegel-Schelling Relation in Slavoj Žižek," *International Journal of Žižek Studies*, 5, no.1 (2011); "'Why is There Nothing Rather Than Something?' *Less Than Nothing*'s New Metaphysics," *International Journal of Žižek Studies*, 8. no.1 (2014); and "Denaturalizing Nature, Dehumanizing Humanity: Lacan, Žižek, and the Metaphysics of Psychoanalysis," in *Natürlichkeit und Künstlichkeit zwischen Tatsache und Ideal*, ed. Benedetta Bisol (Bielefeld: transcript, 2014).

Introduction
A Metaphysical Archaeology of the Psychoanalytico-Cartesian Subject

This book is an investigation into Slavoj Žižek's return to German Idealism in the wake of Lacanian psychoanalysis. Its thematic crux is Žižek's attempt to develop, by reading the traditions against one another by means of their mutually compatible notions of *Todestrieb*, a highly original theory of subjectivity able to explain the subject's simultaneous freedom from and dependence upon its material ground. But it does not stop there: rather than just limiting itself to a recapitulation of Žižek's account of the eruptive, ontologically devastating birth of subjectivity out of nature, it also seeks to systematize the stark metaphysical consequences of this account. The fundamental thesis of this book is that, if the emergence of the Symbolic out of the Real—the passage from nature to culture enacted by the founding gesture of subjectivity—is the advent of a completely self-enclosed, self-sustaining structural system, then not only must its founding gesture withdraw from the scene in the very act of instituting the Symbolic, but further, even to explain this act we must posit the absolute as a fragile not-all wrought by negativity and antagonism. Or, to put it in terms of Žižek's *Less Than Nothing* (his latest *magnum opus*, or "big fat Hegel book," as he says), as a series of less than nothings whose essence constitutes an ontologically incomplete field.

By means of a metaphysical archaeology of the psychoanalytico-Cartesian subject, an archaeology that is the necessary supplement to

Freud's own archaeological investigations of the emergence of mind out of the conflict of unconscious drives and their vicissitudes,[1] especially in the aftermath of Lacan's structuralist reworkings of it, what we will see is that Žižek's own ontology of the subject goes far beyond the normal constraints of psychoanalytical methodology (which is so concerned with psychogenesis and its various pathologies) and radically challenges our normal conception of self and world, a challenge summarized by the notion of *ontological catastrophe*, which I extract from it as its key operative moment. In the course of the book this concept takes on a number of different meanings.

In a first moment, it refers to Žižek's interpretation of *Todestrieb* as that which incites the passage from nature to culture, a grotesque excess of life that is unable to control itself according to its own prescribed natural logistics and thus opens up room for the possibility of experience.

In a second moment, it names the self-positing of subjectivity in nature tearing the latter apart into irreconcilable zones, which, although in a certain sense conditioned by a libidinal-material breakdown of the biological system, is ultimately irreducible to the latter as a pure act. Taken together, these two moments underlying the emergence of subjectivity demand that we delve into the naturephilosophy that this account implies, a nature that shows itself (due to the very extimate presence of *Todestrieb* and pure difference within its heart of hearts) to be predicated upon painful tension and self-sabotaging tendencies to such a degree that its very being is co-incidental not only with the existence of death, disease, and monstrosities, but also with the always possible unpredictable upsurge of disorder and complete collapse as it risks *touching the void*.

In a third moment, the metaphysical archaeology of the subject is pushed to its ultimate limits. Delving into the question of how being could sustain itself despite its rampant and devastating negativity, what we will see is how the more we move towards the most fundamental level of the universe, the latter proves to be in its depths of depths not a dense, fully subsisting reality that exists by itself by means of a self-explanatory surplus, but a series of indeterminate proto-ontological states only minimally distinguishable from the void of nothingness that serves as its contrast. Wondering how this void of nothingness could be broken so that creation itself could emerge, Žižek argues that the basic form of ontological catastrophe should be extended from that of the subject as the breakdown of nature in *Todestrieb*, or the incompletion of nature testified to by the latter's constitutive tension, to the world itself as the necessary disturbance of this void, whereby the classical terrain of metaphysics itself is inverted: "[f]or a true dialectician, the ultimate mystery is not 'Why is there something rather than nothing?' but 'Why is there nothing rather than something?': how is it that, the more we analyze reality, the more we find a void?"[2]

In broad strokes, this is the terrain we will investigate—a terrain that is not merely difficult because it is nuanced and challenging because it is new, but also primordially uncanny and traumatic, forcing us to encounter aspects of self and world that we not only normally do not acknowledge, or continually disavow, but that we even try to repress. To arrive at and evaluate this notion of ontological catastrophe, my metaphysical archaeology of the Žižekian psychoanalytico-Cartesian subject takes three paths: one that traverses the wider historical context informing Žižek's project, another that internally reconstructs its reactualization of German Idealism through psychoanalysis, and a final one that attempts to extract and problematize the intrinsic originality and daringness of Žižek's metaphysics.

The first path consists of chapters 1 through 4. Chapter 1 outlines the ambiguity of the Real in Lacanian psychoanalysis. Displaying a form of radical idealism of a linguistic structuralist variety, it proclaims that the Symbolic operates as a self-enclosed system with *no need* of any external support. This not only means that human freedom is equivalent to an ontological madness, but also appears to foreclose the very possibility of explaining this passage into madness at its basis. Chapter 2 shows how, although Žižek believes himself able to find resources to overcome this difficulty in German Idealism, he can only do so by psychoanalytically tracing and reconstructing an unconscious history of struggle with the obscure origins of subjectivity he perceives throughout the tradition. Insofar as the psychotic non-relation between the Real and the Symbolic is also a rethinking of the *cogito*, chapter 3 shows *why* Žižek feels the theoretical obligation to revitalize subjectivity in an intellectual milieu that attacks it from all sides. Chapter 4 tries to understand how the Real could have given rise to the Symbolic. Contra the early and middle Lacan, Žižek argues that the Symbolic cannot be an external parasite that attacks the Real from nowhere, but must arise from some sort of self-sabotaging tendency always already implicit within it.

The second path, which unfolds through chapters 5 to 10, comprises the substantiation of Žižek's claim that there is an identity between the founding insights of German Idealism and psychoanalysis by retroactively rewriting the former's unconscious history. Drawing upon the late Lacan's ruminations concerning the breakdown of nature as the pre-condition of the Symbolic, chapter 5 outlines how Kant finds also himself forced to posit a meta-transcendental ground of the transcendental in organic disorder, even going so far as to anticipate Lacan's mirror stage. Chapter 6 demonstrates how the early Hegel, led by insufficiencies in Kant's and Fichte's transcendentalism and Schelling's *Naturphilosophie*, attempts to reconcile idealist freedom and realist system by inscribing the subject into the fold of being as an eruptive, world-shattering event, thus radicalizing Kant's insight into the devastating origins of subjectivity. Chapter 7 then illustrates how the mature Hegel psychoanalytically recoils from the ontological catastrophe at the heart of the subject's essence by subsuming it under the self-mediation of the Notion. It is only with the middle-late Schelling, fighting against the perceived threats of Absolute Idealism, that the true kernel of truth unearthed by Kantian idealism is brought to the fore and along with it its stark, even horrifying implications for our understanding of nature, human historicity, and the absolute. Chapter 8 gives flesh to the Schellingian-Žižekian subject as the vanishing mediator between the Real and the Ideal. The symbolic universe of meaning is not a high point of evolutionary achievement, but rather a mistake, the outcome of something having gone horribly wrong in the order of things and to which it is only a defense mechanism. Given the psychoanalytical horror that is the basis of subjectivity, chapter 9 explains how Schelling, although *the* thinker of its abyssal origins, ultimately ends up recoiling just like Hegel from own great insights after coming face to face with its full trauma, which gives further support to the necessity of a psychoanalytical reconstruction of German Idealism. After this concrete exploration of Žižek's methodology, chapter 10 concludes the second path by bringing to the fore his three most significant theoretical contributions: a rich ontology of nature, a new metaphysics of the void developed through quantum mechanics, and a nuanced theory of unconscious, each of which goes beyond a mere reactualization of German Idealism or psychoanalysis.

The third and final path is summarized by the word "paradoxical" in the subtitle of the book—*Žižek and the* Paradoxical *Metaphysics of German Idealism*. Chapter 11 highlights that, instead of being opposed to metaphysics, radical idealism not only *demands a metaphysics*, for thinking in all of its intrinsic paradox and self-referentiality must be seen *as existing in the world*, but more primordially forces upon us a *new domain of metaphysics*, which first became explicit in German Idealism. Whereas all metaphysics prior to Kant is *dogmatic* insofar as it assumes thought's power to reach out and touch the truth of being in virtue of a special capacity (a gesture that is repeated by, amongst others, Badiou's and Meillassoux's elevation of mathematical formalization), what occurs in Schelling and Hegel is an intense reflection upon how the very process by which thought forms an image of being is inscribed into being as an event, whereby even the very philosophical position of theory formation is reflexively thematized both epistemologically and ontologically. What emerges is a metaphysics that can be baptized as *critical* because it is capable of developing a theory of reality that is maximally realist *and* idealist and therefore best suited to explicate the metaphysical whole of what is without falling into the downfalls of a theory that is one-sidedly one or the other.[3] Chapter 12 explores the paradoxical nature of this endeavour as it articulates itself in the intrinsically original and daring character of Žižek's own variation upon this German Idealist leitmotif and the problems it potentially poses not only for his own philosophy, but perhaps for any radical idealism seeking to break the correlationist circle.

Notes

1.   This, of course, being a constant metaphor throughout Freud's corpus, spanning from "The Aetiology of Hysteria" (1896) to "Construction in Analysis" (1937). See, respectively, *The Standard Edition of the Complete Psychological Works of Sigmund Freud,* translated from the German under the General Editorship of James Strachey, in collaboration with Anna Freud, assisted by Alix Strachey and Alan Tyson (London: Hogarth Press and the Institute of Psycho-analysis, 1953–1974) (hereafter *SE*), III, p. 192, and XXIII, p. 259.

2.   Žižek, *Less Than Nothing: Hegel and the Shadow of Dialectical Materialism* (London: Verso, 2012), p. 925.

3.   Gabriel draws a distinction between *critical* and *dogmatic* metaphysics for similar, but different reasons. See *Das Absolute und die Welt in Schellings Freiheitsschrift* (Bonn: University Press, 2006), p. 8. I take up this distinction at length in chapter 11.

I
Death Drive

Chapter 1
The Madness of the Symbolic
Transcendental Materialism and the Ambiguity of the Real

Re-interpreting Freud through structural linguistics, Lacan radically rethinks the unconscious: no longer a quasi-biological phenomenon centered in drives, it largely becomes associated with the differential system of the Symbolic responsible for the production of meaning. However, since the latter proves to be operationally closed and has no relationship to the world in itself, Lacan himself is forced to proclaim that the founding gesture of subjectivity is a passage through madness. This poses two difficulties that set up the entirety of Žižek's project. First, it points towards a *transcendental materialism* at the basis of the subject, a self-splitting of being into irreconcilable material and transcendental zones, but one that Lacan fails to systematize. Second, insofar as the Symbolic itself is self-enclosed, it seems methodologically impossible even to explain its own obscure origins, even if such is ultimately required if psychoanalysis is to find an adequate theoretical justification. In this regard, Žižek's primary task is to find a way to explain the madness of the Symbolic without overstepping the constraints of psychoanalysis.

1.1 A (Transcendental) Materialism of the Psychoanalytical Subject

Žižek's return to German Idealism is an investigation of the obscure origins of the Lacanian subject. Žižek is attracted not only to Lacanian psychoanalysis' thematization of the non-coincident "gap" in the Symbolic and its consequences for politics, but also to the conflictual relationship between mind and body that it places at the foundation of psychogenesis. If symbolic structures of language display a radical autonomy from bodily forces and can construct their own world, the essence of human being must be constituted originally by a kind of biological "short circuit" that disrupts man's complete immersion in nature, eternally separating the *Innenwelt* and *Aussenwelt* (inner world and outer world), thereby making it so they can never coincide: that is, by a mal-adaptation that "represents the minimum of freedom, of a behaviour uncoupled from the utilitarian-survivalist attitude" insofar as "the organism is no longer fully determined by its environs, that it 'explodes/implodes' into a cycle of autonomous behaviour."[4] If, as conventionally defined in Freudian psychoanalysis, psychosis or madness is taken to be a withdrawal from the objective world into an inner, self-enclosed space (a loss of reality),[5] then in Lacanian psychoanalysis psychosis or madness is paradoxically *not* a mere accidental state seen in certain "sick" individuals, but is *the irreducible ontological background of all human existence*. More disconcertingly, this is understood by Lacan not only to be the condition of possibility of human experience as such, but also that of freedom, so that the philosophical significance of the two is ultimately identified as dialectically interrelated aspects of the same phenomenon:

> Thus rather than resulting from a contingent fact—the frailties of his organism—madness is the permanent virtuality of a gap in his essence.
>
> And far from being an "insult" to freedom, madness is freedom's most faithful companion, following its every move like a shadow.
>
> Not only can man's being not be understood without madness, but it would not be man's being if it did not bear madness within itself as the limit of his freedom.[6]

For Lacan, the primary question in psychoanalysis is not how various forms of madness arise as a deviation from normal mental health, but how this more originary, irruptive state of nature as that within which freedom and madness magically emerge in a single brushstroke can be regulated so that what we regard as sanity and normality can themselves take hold.

If madness is "freedom's most faithful companion" it is precisely because madness in its most primordial sense refers to the specific ontogenetic conditions for the irreducibility of language that makes us distinctly human: that is to say, to the state of affairs by means of which language can solipsistically relate to itself as a self-enclosed differential system of signification "with no an external support."[7] Just as in clinical cases of psychosis or madness, here too the subject has "lost touch" with reality, although reality must be understood in its *natural* (animalistic) rather than its *sociopolitical* (human) meaning. It is "the price the Lacanian subject pays for its 'transubstantiation' from being the agent of a direct animal vitality to being a speaking subject whose identity is kept apart from the direct vitality of passions,"[8] that which guarantees that the subject is dominated by "non-natural" influences or which is, strictly speaking, at its zero-level *abiological* (wherein lies its freedom). This has two principal effects. First, because Lacan's self-given task is to formulate the autonomous structures that constitute human subjectivity in opposition to naturalist theories of psychiatry, his philosophy has the formal appearance of a *retour* to the modern transcendentalism of the *cogito*. The Lacanian subject is consequently haunted by similar problems as those of the Cartesian subject, both in terms of epistemology (since the relationship to the extra-conscious alterity of the world is problematized, how can we justify the propositions of science?) and the mind-body relation (what exactly is the relationship between symbolic thinking and natural processes?). Second, due to the internal constraints of his project, Lacan left unanswered how reality in itself could incite the generation of these quasi-transcendental structures that make up the universe of human meaning in its psychotic self-enclosure, with the concomitant problem of how we relate to this X that simultaneously precedes our emergence into language and forms its obscure ontologico-foundational basis. Seeing a structural identity with the immediate reactions to Kant, Žižek sees the possibility of confronting the fundamental concepts of psychoanalysis with those of German Idealism.

Žižek's metaphysics originates in his attempt to delve into the material origins preceding the psychoanalytical subject by focusing on this moment of immanent rupture in being—which he links to the *Todestrieb*—as that which, by opening up a space separating us from nature in the latter, appears simultaneously to be linked to our freedom, that is, to our madness. Refusing to buy into the claim that all is ultimately reducible to the ebb and flow of matter, he sees his own endeavour as "the necessary step in the rehabilitation of the philosophy of *dialectical materialism*."[9] Yet this designation is inherently problematic, given what we have just seen: not only does it try to make Žižek's own form of materialism approach that of Marx and Engels without drawing the necessary distinctions between them, it more importantly fails to articulate the essentially paradoxical and innovative manner in which Žižek rearticulates the materialism-idealism debate and therefore risks obscuring his own originality. Consequently, I endorse Adrian Johnston's characterization of Žižek's theory of the subject as a form of *transcendental materialism*[10] for four reasons, but differ in my own understanding in one important way that in turn distinguishes my own project from his.

First, it has the benefit of allowing the reader to have a direct intuition of what is truly at stake in Žižek's parallax ontology and its metaphysical implications. Whereas dialectical materialism traditionally views the mind-body relationship as grounded within the dynamic interpenetration of the two as a complex self-unfolding identity within difference, transcendental materialism, by focusing on the ontogenetic conditions of the possibility of the *transcendental* subject, conventionally understood as in opposition to natural conditions, already suggests the immanent emergence of an irruptive negativity *within* being, an irreducible transcendence that paradoxically shatters the former's pure immanence from within.

Second, a point not mentioned by Johnston, Fichte uses the expression in his 1794 *Some Lectures Concerning the Scholar's Vocation* to draw attention to the *impossibility* of explaining the (onto)genesis of the subject: "[i]t is certainly not true that the pure I is a product of the not-I [...]. The assertion that the pure I is a product of the not-I expresses a transcendental materialism which is completely contrary to reason."[11] Fichte's argument is simple: one cannot explain the *material* conditions of transcendental freedom insofar as that would equate two logically distinct fields irreconcilable with one another—namely, that of unbridled self-determination (the realm of acting) and that of dead contingency (the realm of being), thus causing us to lose sight of the radicality of human autonomy. Writing in a similar vein, Žižek attempts to show not only *how we can*, but more primordially *why we must* develop a metaphysical account of reality that, instead of jeopardizing the (practical) primacy of idealism, would actually found it by inscribing this very dualism of I and not-I into the fold of being as that which makes the absolute divided *within itself* and whose non-coincidence to self thereby opens up the birthplace for human freedom. Transcendental idealism *is*—or better, must be said to *always already spectrally refer to*—transcendental materialism, the difference between them being only that of a parallax shift: the two are negatively linked to one another by an impossible in-between, a disjunctive "and," the very name of which is for Žižek the subject, so that an idealism must convert itself into a materialism and vice versa if subjectivity is to be fully explained.

It is precisely at this conceptual conjuncture of the role of a disjunctive "and" that my own understanding of Žižek's transcendental materialism distinguishes itself from that of Johnston. Although Johnston is right to claim that Žižek's own descriptions of the birth of subjectivity have a propensity to focus on its process as a self-instituting fiat "analogous to the cutting of the Gordian knot" (which in a certain sense obfuscates his project insofar as one of its major questions is *how* the closed circuit of drives in the Real could result in the transcendence of subjectivity),[12] Johnston in my view has a tendency to downplay the intrinsically paradoxical nature of all such inquiry into the obscure origins of the psychoanalytico-Cartesian subject in Žižek's work in two ways. On the one hand, he emphasizes that the subject is rendered possible by a short-circuiting of its libidinal-material ground. But if an emergent breakdown in nature's inner being does *give rise to* the ontogenetic possibility of the subject, it in no way *gives birth to* the latter: nature's auto-laceration may be *necessary* for the self-positing freedom of transcendental subjectivity, but it is not *sufficient*, for there is no possible *transition* from nature to subjectivity, a point that—though also raised by Johnston—I believe must be radicalized. This is why on my reading the reference to Fichte is so important, for if Žižek's metaphysics is an attempt to show how a transcendental materialism can be developed, it nevertheless refuses to give up on the fundamental claim made by Fichte that the upsurge of the pure I in being is executed "by absolute freedom, not through a *transition*, but by means of a *leap*."[13] As a result, we can also understand why Žižek displays hesitation concerning Johnston's and Malabou's shared project of merging philosophy and neuroscience—*because there is ultimately no emergence of subjectivity possible within his parallax ontology*.[14] On the other hand, because Johnston attaches less importance than I do to the rupturing free leap into subjectivity, he is simultaneously silent concerning the necessarily *mytho-poetic* element of Žižek's transcendental materialism, which for me thus becomes central for understanding the nuance of his specific overcoming of radical idealism. This has two important consequences, one methodological and the other metaphysical. Methodologically, if the leap into subjectivity is *an ontological passage through madness*,[15] then there is an upper limit to the power of thought to explain its own emergence in being. What we need is a capacity for fabulative mythologizing, for "the need for the form of mythical narrative arises when one endeavours to break the circle of the symbolic order and to give an account of its genesis ('origins') from the Real and its pre-symbolic antagonism."[16] Metaphysically, if subjectivity is the psychotic night of the world, then any investigation into its underlying ontology simultaneously requires a metaphysical archaeology of madness, that is, a theorizing of what the ultimate structure of reality must be like so that the subject's emergence could occur. In this manner, if Johnston is perhaps more interested in the paradoxical basis of transcendental subjectivity in nature, I am more interested in what occurs methodologically and metaphysically once we inscribe radical idealism as a form of madness into being, in such a way that two similar yet different views of Žižek's system emerge.

Third, to return to the benefits of the characterization "transcendental materialism," I endorse it because it draws our attention to Žižek's philosophical relevance *outside of* the fields of cultural studies, radical politics, and film theory by placing his thinking in direct contact with a series of other contemporary thinkers rethinking metaphysics, whether it be by representatives of the analytic tradition, object-oriented philosophy, new French materialism, or various other forms of the new speculative turn. Two thinkers deserve to be mentioned here by name, since they offer a transcendental materialism radically different from that of Žižek: Iain Hamilton Grant and Rainer E. Zimmerman. Although Grant would have reservations about his thinking being referred to as a "transcendental" materialism, his *Philosophies of Nature after Schelling*[17] offers an alternative account of the materialism-idealism relationship and the immanent emergence of the transcendental subject within nature that challenges not only Žižek's reading of Schelling, but more strongly his entire metaphysics. Zimmerman, a prolific German philosopher little known in the English-speaking world, was in fact the first person to use the concept of "transcendental materialism" in a contemporary context in his 1998 book *Die Rekonstruktion von Raum, Zeit und Materie (The Reconstruction of Space, Time and Matter)*[18] and then fully develop it in his massive 2004 *System des transzendentalen Materialismus (System of Transcendental Materialism)*.[19] Zimmerman, like Grant, departs largely from Schelling, but also from Spinoza and Bloch, and offers an understanding of transcendental materialism in dialogue with contemporary science, especially physics, in stark opposition to the one presented here. For both, the thinking subject does not implicate an *ontological trembling* or *pure difference* within the field of being, and their respective accounts of the mind-body relationship can in no means be equated with what Žižek would perhaps be tempted to call a return to pre-modern cosmology. Moreover, considering how Žižek's own philosophy, similar in spirit to that of Zimmerman, does not possess mere *implications* or *consequences* for how we conduct empirical science, but directly engages with a broad range of disciplines such as quantum mechanics[20] and cognitive science,[21] by calling Žižek's philosophy a transcendental materialism I further hope to accomplish two things: to emphasize the systematic reach of Žižek's thinking and the exigence that metaphysics must also be an interlocutor with science.

Finally, it is worth mentioning that in *Less Than Nothing* Žižek also endorses Adrian Johnston's coinage of "transcendental materialism" in two passages in the last chapter on quantum mechanics, but with an important qualification that renders explicit for the first time a crucial metaphysical element of his own brand of materialism and its nuanced character. In the first instance, he claims that the key insight gained by contemporary physics is that material reality in itself does not present us with a dense field of fully constituted realities that form the ultimate building blocks of the universe, but rather with irreducibly indeterminate states lacking any substantial being and from which "hard" reality can only emerge if there is a collapse of the wave function.[22] In this sense, the micro-universe of quantum particles is strangely "less" than that of the macro-universe that constructs itself from its vicissitudes, in a way that is remarkably similar to how the Kantian subject can only construct a unified, coherent world of appearances from the inconsistent fragments of sensation. In a strange logical short circuit, it would appear that not only is there no bottom-up causality at the level of experience (transcendental constitution is more real than what Kant calls "a rhapsody of perception"[23]), but even the most fundamental level of the universe is metaphysically more chaotic than the ordered macro-level physical world that science classically described. It is as if *all reality is transcendentally constitutive,* so that the only way to break free of the correlationist circle is to push "this transcendental correlation *into the Thing itself*:" "[i]t is against this background that one can make out the contours of what can perhaps only be designated by the oxymoron 'transcendental materialism' (proposed by Adrian Johnston)."[24] The second instance adds some clarification to the metaphysical implications of this idea by stating that the "the only true consistent 'transcendental materialism' which is possible after the Kantian transcendental idealism" is one that risks the following difficult wager: "[w]hat if we posit that 'Things-in-themselves' emerge against the background of the Void of Nothingness, the way this Void is conceived in quantum physics, as not just a negative void, but the portent of all possible reality?"[25] Although Žižek here takes transcendental materialism in a different direction than Johnston by introducing it to make a metaphysical point concerning the absolute rather than a more broadly ontological one concerning the subject, part of my project in what follows will be to show that his metaphysics of the void is not only completely compatible with his older ontology of the subject, but can be seen as its organic elaboration.

If Žižek's approach differs significantly from that of Grant or Zimmerman, it is because his game is different, even though this leads him to cover much of the same thematic domains—and hence it is interesting to label all three as "transcendental materialists" for the same reasons as it is to refer to Kant, Fichte, Hegel, and Schelling as "German Idealists" insofar as subsuming such irreconcilably different thinkers under a single category reveals a dynamic, pulsating movement, a battleground of theoretical positions around a shared set of problems rather than a shared doctrine, and thus something living. What so strongly distinguishes Žižek's form of transcendental materialism from others is that, finding a fundamental structural identity between Lacanian psychoanalysis and post-Kantian idealism, he tries to illustrate the uncanny identity that exists between the psychoanalytical subject haunted by the *Todestrieb* as its constitutive basis and the unconscious, disavowed *Grundlogik* of German Idealism, with the conviction that a psychoanalytical dialogue between the two could open up a radically new possibility for metaphysics. By falling upon premonitions of the psychoanalytical experience in concepts such as Kantian unruliness, the Hegelian "night of the world," and the Schellingian notion of the *Grund*, Žižek psychoanalytically reinterprets the late German Idealist attempts to give a metaphysical vision of reality compatible with the ontological emergence of the pure I in order to make us not only rethink what is at stake in the tradition of modern philosophy, a truth repressed and haunting its very history, but more primordially what is revealed with the advent of subjectivity as such: *the notion of ontological catastrophe, the auto-disruption of reality into a painful not-all, at the origin of experience, with all the metaphysical implications that entails for our understanding of world in itself.* Although Žižek's interpretations are heterodox, he believes that he is justified in singling out and radicalizing these premonitions, which often only appear in textual margins and often officially lack the theoretical primacy that Žižek bestows upon them, by means of the methodological application of various psychoanalytical techniques to the texts of German Idealism, these enabling him to plunge into and reveal the non-coincidences internally plaguing their symbolic space and thus retroactively restructuring their surface appearance in a manner similar to the analyst-analysand relation in therapy. We must traverse the fantasy of tradition if we are to arrive at its truth—this is Žižek's provocative claim and one that we will explore throughout most of this book. Thus, if we are to gain a preliminary sense of the driving forces of Žižek's reactualization of German Idealism and the systematicity of its method in spite of its apparent self-serving selectiveness, we must briefly pass through the Lacanian subject.

1.2 The Lacanian Subject and the Irreducible Ambiguity of the Real

As the fundamental presupposition of Žižek's philosophy, the Lacanian subject is to be radically distinguished from the philosophical subject of modernity. Although the former exhibits many traits that link it to early transcendental philosophy (it grounds the symbolic structures that constitute phenomenal reality through a free idealization) it is in direct opposition to the self-conscious transparency of the Cartesian *cogito*, the self-legislation of the Kantian rational agent, or the Hegelian account of free personality. For Lacan, the freedom of the I as witnessed in phenomenological self-experience is an illusion: completely determined by cultural and linguistic influences, the ego is an *object* and is constantly trying to construct a fantasmatic narcissistic space within which it can (falsely) perceive itself as a centre of self-effectuating action. Although this does not prevent the existence of human freedom for either Lacan or Žižek, it means that freedom itself gets largely displaced from consciousness into the unconscious, in a move formally similar to the middle-late Schelling of the *Freiheitsschrift* and *Weltalter*, but with an important twist. The subject is not an energetic, productive will that precedes the constitution of phenomenal reality, but is in one of its most important modalities nothing but an impersonal abyss that, uncannily, renders possible a minimal consistency of self. In this sense, the self is infinitely split at its core: when one looks inside oneself one not only finds an "extimacy," material coming from elsewhere, where one should find one's innermost core, but if one looks long enough one only finds *a void staring back*. The Lacanian-Žižekian subject has no intrinsic content because it is pure form: the entire "plenitude" of cultural and psychological experience only emerges as a kind of defence formation against this primordial nothingness of the subject as an attempt to fill in its constitutive "gap" with false positive substantiality. But because this "gap" can never be filled in, it is ultimately repressed due to its traumatic, personality-shattering quality, so that we find traces of its disavowed knowledge in the slips and slides of speech, symbolic inconsistencies and non-coincidences in writing, the images of fantasies and dreams, and other phenomena. This creates two levels to any given (personal, ethical, political, or even philosophical) discourse: its surface movement, grounded in the narcissistic, self-deceiving orbit of the ego, and its "latent," underlying truth, which shows itself negatively within the holes and inconsistencies of the former and can only be brought forth *après-coup*. In therapy, the task of the analyst is to make the analysand encounter and appropriate the second, the Real that afflicts the analysand often to a degree of painful agony, thereby forcing them to realign the symbolic structures underlying their personality so that the latter are more in tune with that which they reject, given that this (unconscious) act of recoil and exclusion has begun to obstruct their life. After all, the repressed always returns.

To explain this complex, Lacanian psychoanalysis categorizes experience in terms of the three registers of the Imaginary, the Symbolic, and the Real. All three exist in dialectical simultaneity, so that they all depend upon and interpenetrate one another. Lacan uses a Borromean knot to illustrate this level of mutual co-existence, the point of which is to preclude the possibility of arguing for the primacy of one register over the other, as it is unclear if either can have logical priority insofar as the cutting off or isolating of one destroys the whole. The Imaginary is roughly equivalent to phenomenological experience and perception but is also related to the *cogito* and its "narcissistic" fantasy of existential self-mastery. It is identified with a necessary moment of misrecognition and irremovable untruth in one's everyday being and knowledge of self, world, and others, for it projects completion where there is lack. The Symbolic constitutes the logical fabric of language and the laws of culture that transcend and are anterior to the concretely existing personal subject. It therefore precedes the imaginary orbit of experience insofar as the individual phenomenological constitution of objects in a strong sense presupposes language. As a self-enclosed structural system capable of reproducing and propagating itself, the Symbolic displays an irreducible autonomy that displaces the role of nature in understanding human psychology and cultural phenomena because it is able to articulate itself in utter isolation from it: the "incessant sliding of the signified under the signifier,"[26] the solipsistic dance of language always in step with itself, means that the essential link between signifier and transcendent, extra-linguistic signified has been violently ruptured and that the mere chains of signifiers relating to themselves are capable of producing/ constructing meaning by themselves in an ontological void. In its simplest

form, the Real is that which does not fall under either the Imaginary
or the Symbolic, whereby its upsurge is associated with experiences of
breakdown and inconsistency not only of the transcendental unity at the
basis of phenomenological experience, but even of language or culture itself.
Lacan and Žižek therefore use a plethora of adjectives to describe it, which
attempt to capture this element of irrevocable logical and existential rupture:
"traumatic," "monstrous," "horrifying," and "impossible," to name a few.

Yet there is an irreducible ambiguity in Lacan's definition of the Real,
which serves as the starting point for Žižek's own philosophical endeavour,
for it is precisely in trying to resolve this ambiguity that his metaphysical
project gets off the ground. The Real elicits two potentially incompatible
interpretative possibilities, and we often see Lacan oscillating back and
forth between them. In its first guise, the Real is the excluded Other of the
Imaginary and Symbolic, which only truly "comes to be" when the subject
constitutes itself. In this sense, the Real is not only dependent upon the
symbolic matrix of language and the orbit of phenomenological experience
but also only shows itself negatively through their immanent obstruction.
This Real-as-lack is distinctly Hegelian: it corresponds to concepts such as
"tarrying with the negative" and the suffering that consciousness undergoes
when it runs up against non-coincidence, paradox, and limitation in social
and political action or scientific thought about the world. It has absolutely
no positive content in itself even though, as an internal limit within a given
symbolic space, it may effectuate an overhauling of the latter's structure and
possibilities as the subject attempts to overcome its deadlock so that it is
potentially productive in its very trauma. In its second guise, we could also
understand the Real as the pre-subjective life of pure *jouissance* from which
the human infant exiles itself by becoming a linguistic subject, yet upon
which the Imaginary and the Symbolic logically depend, even if they only
relate to it negatively through its primordial foreclosure from experience
and language as the founding gesture of subjectivity itself. Bruce Fink
refers to this as the Real$_1$ because it is the necessary posit of the Symbolic
despite the fact that it is inaccessible from within the latter, whose ciphering
activity doesn't merely "reconstitute" objective reality by meditating it like
a *camera obscura*. Given that this pre-subjective Real must be said to be
without *lack* (only with language can we speak of absence and presence),[27]

the idealizing process of human meaning makes it impossible to reach. As something that *overreaches* the idealizing, linguistic activity of the subject, in this modality the Real, corresponding to the Schellingian concept of the indivisible remainder (*der nie aufgehende Rest*), that pre-experiential darkness that can never be brought into light of consciousness yet upon which all consciousness rests, is the Real-as-excess. But such a free ciphering activity simultaneously creates the condition of the possibility of its own breakdown insofar as it will not always be capable of idealizing the Real in a way that enables its own autonomous, smooth functioning.[28] These "kinks" in the Symbolic correspond with the Real-as-lack or $Real_2$, something that cannot be integrated because it presents itself as intrinsically and paradoxically non-relational, as an inassimilable kernel within the self-referential matrix of the symbolic relations within which it emerged. The problem is as follows: Is the $Real_1$ a necessary, illusory construct of the Symbolic designed to give a fantasmatically fabricated sense of "positivity" to a world that exists beyond its grasp (rendering it a mere secondary effect of a solipsistically self-contained structuralist metapsychology)? Or is it, more primordially, the pre-subjective, ontological basis of the Symbolic, to which we have access *despite* the apparent impossibility of reaching the pure Real through the differential system of language (thus showing the obscure origins of the $Real_2$ in an ontology)? If the second is possible, what does this mean in terms of Lacan's declaration of the logical equivalence and interpenetration of the registers?

1.3 From Logico-Dialectical Simultaneity to the Ontogenesis of the Subject

Even if all three registers exist in a logico-dialectical simultaneity, within the development of Lacanian psychoanalysis we see a gradual shift in emphasis in the thematization of the registers largely due to internal reasons. Lacan's early work is largely an attempt to come to terms with the mirror stage and its implications for understanding psychogenesis. In the mirror stage, which happens around the age of six months, there is a recognition of an immanent blockage in nature that tears apart the organic unity of the body. The human infant lacks motor coordination—its self-experience is infinitely fragmented and lacking in any internal unity. Lacan's provocative thesis is that the only way out of this biological short circuit is a *vel*, a misrecognition of the primordial helplessness of the human organism in the "specular image"[29] of its mirror self in which the child finds a mesmerizing and captivating lie of false mastery into which it libidinally invests itself. Already at this early stage we see why Lacan is so critical of the modern conception of subjectivity and rationality. The result of the mirror stage is a reorganization of the fragmented being of the child through a virtual and therefore illusionary schema as the self becomes alienated from its real chaotic being. Yet Lacan comes to see that the imaginary beginnings of psychogenesis are themselves necessarily grounded in the Symbolic: the only reason why the child becomes tantalized by his image is because their parents provoke the response. *"Look, it's you!"* In this sense, the entire genesis of the self is preceded by a carving out of a space for the child within the symbolic universe of familial relations even before the child was born. After this "linguistic turn," Lacan turns all of his attention to the nature of the Symbolic and seems, in many respects, largely to leave the Imaginary behind.

Inspired by the work of Levi-Strauss, who argued that "[s]tructural linguistics will certainly play the same renovating role with respect to the social sciences that nuclear physics, for example, has played for the physical sciences,"[30] Lacan then begins to apply the methodology of Saussure's structuralism to psychoanalysis, accomplishing this feat largely by a *retour* to Freud. What Lacan finds so intriguing is that, despite all of Freud's attempts to ground the unconscious within a natural vitalism of the body or biological movement of instincts, his texts themselves orbit around the analyses of images and language. Lacan's fundamental thesis is that, retroactively, we can see that Freud already had an implicit idea of the importance of linguistics for understanding the unconscious but was unable fully to articulate this fundamental insight because he lacked the appropriate methodology. This in turn creates a fundamental and irremovable non-coincidence within Freud's texts as they oscillate between purely structural analyses of language and obscure vitalistic biologism. Consequently, Lacan argues that if we read Freud *against* Freud, structural linguistics can give psychoanalysis the scientific rigor that it needs by systematizing the logic of the unconscious, which is the origin of Lacan's famous saying "the unconscious is structured like a language." Linked to this linguistic turn are his critiques of ego-psychology as an attempt to strengthen the ego and post-Freudian attempts to biologize the unconscious. For Lacan, the unconscious is, strictly speaking, an irreducibly linguistic phenomenon: it only emerges *after* or *alongside* the advent of language, in the split between the subject of enunciation and the enunciating subject. It has nothing to do with deep-lying personality structures determining how the ego relates to the external world or instinctual energetics.

Although this suggests an obvious superseding of the Imaginary by the Symbolic, commentators such as Richard Boothby and Alexander Leupin warn against this, arguing that Lacan is much more complex and subtle than he may initially appear. Lacan never backs away from the claim that all registers mutually depend upon one another in order to have any efficacy at all. Even if the self-generating matrix of language and culture historically precedes and conditions the possibility of any concretely existing person, its differential network of meaning is only possible through an originary phenomenological *perception* of signifiers.[31] The colonization of the body by the transcendentally alienating structures of the Symbolic requires the activity of the Imaginary so that the various phonetic differences that allow signs to be intelligible in contradistinction from one another can be established in the first place. Moreover, the late Lacan's topological formalizations of the psyche, as already mentioned, proclaim a strict equivalency between them, so that "the symbolic order's supremacy appears as an aporia, an ethical decision that logic does not support."[32] But how can Žižek then, as a Lacanian philosopher of the Real, justify his own theoretical preference for it over the other registers where Lacan's texts seem to contradict such an approach?

Although Žižek's work holds an uncertain relation to Lacanian orthodoxy, it would be wrong to claim that this troublesome problematic is just a direct consequence of Žižek's own reading of Lacanian psychoanalysis. By the very act of embarking on a metaphysics of the Real Žižek does seem to imply that we must find a way to overstep Lacan's attempt to conserve the equivalency of the registers if psychoanalysis is to find a sufficient theoretical grounding, even if doing so means that we risk making the entire psychoanalytical edifice he constructed collapse. But Žižek's own thinking is not as radical a rupture with Lacan as it may appear, for the late Lacan too ruminates about the understanding of nature necessarily implied by his theory and therefore himself gestures towards the possibility of a metaphysics of the Real consistent with it.[33] Even as early as the seventeenth seminar, we can find Lacan proclaiming that one of the logical implications of the psychoanalytical experience is that substance is not-all (that is, nature does not present us with a spherical totality—*un tout, une sphère*).[34] Yet if the Real is only lack, and the essential link between signifier and transcendent, extra-linguistic signified has been cut, how can Lacan even legitimately make such statements? How can he philosophically justify such a "direct touching" of the Real given the epistemological solipsism intrinsic to the cybernetic ciphering of the Symbolic? Žižek's wager is that one can develop a metaphysics of the Real that not only does not jeopardize the equivalency of the registers, but even explains their emergence, thereby implying that to grasp the essence of psychoanalysis and draw out its philosophical implications we need to do two things: (i) metapsychologically explicate the ontogenesis of the subject in terms of a materialism compatible with the founding insights of a radical idealism or, in other words, explain the relation of the Real$_1$ of the apparent excess of the ontological to the linguistic to the Real$_2$ of symbolic or notional lack, since this is the great question left unanswered by Lacan and upon which his entire theoretical apparatus ultimately depends; (ii) instead of focusing on Lacan's relationship to nineteenth- and twentieth-century psychology, French structuralism, the Prague school of linguistics, or existentialism, we should return to German Idealism, since it is only in a direct dialogue with this tradition that we can find a way out of the impasses of Lacanian psychoanalysis. But to develop such a metaphysics, we must leave psychoanalysis and venture into German Idealism.

Notes

4.   Žižek, *The Parallax View* (Cambridge: MIT Press, 2009), p. 231.

5.   See Freud, "The Loss of Reality in Neurosis and Psychosis" (1924), *SE*, XIX, especially pp. 185–87.

6.   Lacan, "Presentation on Psychic Causality," in *Écrits*, trans. Bruce Fink (New York: W. W. Norton, 2006), p. 176/144.

7.   Žižek, *Less Than Nothing*, p. 77.

8.   Ibid., p. 197.

9.   Žižek, *The Parallax View*, p. 4.

10. For Johnston's justification of "transcendental materialism," see *Žižek's Ontology: A Transcendental Materialistic Theory of Subjectivity* (Evanston: Northwestern University Press, 2000), pp. 273–74.

11. Fichte, *Fichte: Early Philosophic Writings*, trans. Daniel Breazeale (Ithaca: Cornell University Press, 1988), p. 147.

12. See Johnston, *Žižek's Ontology*, pp. 80–92.

13. Fichte, *Science of Knowledge*, ed. and trans. Peter Heath and John Lachs (Cambridge: University of Cambridge Press, 1982), p. 262.

14. Žižek, *The Parallax View*, p. 214.

15. Žižek, *The Ticklish Subject: The Absent Centre of Political Ideology* (New York: Verso, 2000), pp. 33–41.

16. Žižek, *The Indivisible Remainder: On Schelling and Related Matters* (New York: Verso, 2007), p. 8.

17. Grant, *Philosophies of Nature after Schelling* (New York: Continuum, 2006).

18. Zimmerman, *Die Rekonstruktion von Raum, Zeit und Materie. Moderne Implikationen Schellingscher Naturphilosophie* (Frankfurt am Main: Lang, 1998).

19. Zimmerman, *System des transzendentalen Materialismus* (Paderborn: Mentis, 2004).

20. See Žižek, chapter 3 ("Quantum Physics with Lacan") of *The Indivisible Remainder*, pp. 189–236; and chapter 14 ("The Ontology of Quantum Physics") of *Less Than Nothing*, pp. 905–62.

21. See part 2 ("The Solar Parallax: The Unbearable Lightness of Being No One") of *The Parallax View*, pp. 145–250; and interlude 6 ("Cognitivism and the Loop of Self-Positing) of *Less Than Nothing*, pp. 715–37.

22. Žižek, *Less Than Nothing*, p. 724.

23. Kant, *The Critique of Pure Reason*, trans. Paul Guyer and Allen W. Wood (Cambridge: Cambridge University Press, 1998), A 156/B195.

24. Žižek, *Less Than Nothing*, p. 906.

25. Ibid., p. 935.

26. Lacan, "The Instance of the Letter in the Unconscious, or Reason since Freud," in *Écrits*, p. 502/419.

27. One of many possible quotes: "By definition, the Real is full." Lacan, *Le séminaire, Livre IV: La relation d'objet et les structures freudiennes, 1956–1957*, ed. Jacques-Alain Miller (Paris: Seuil, 1994), p. 218. I capitalize "the Real."

28. See Fink, chapter 3 ("The Creative Function of the Word: The Symbolic and the Real") of *The Lacanian Subject: Between Language and Jouissance* (New York: Princeton University Press, 1995), pp. 24–31.

29. Lacan, "The Mirror Stage as Formative of the *I* Function as Revealed in Psychoanalytical Experience," in *Écrits*, p. 94/76.

30. Lévi-Strauss, "Structural Analysis in Linguistics and in Anthropology," in *Structural Anthropology,* trans. Claire Jacobson and Brooke Grundfest Schoepf (New York: Basic Books, 1963), p. 33.

31. See Boothby, *Freud as Philosopher: Metapsychology after Lacan* (New York: Routledge, 2001), pp. 86–94.

32. See Leupin, *Lacan Today: Psychoanalysis, Science and Religion* (New York: Other Press, 2004), p. 27.

33. See chapters 4 and 5.

34. See Lacan, *Le séminaire, Livre XVII: L'envers de la psychoanalyse, 1969–1970,* ed. Jacques-Alain Miller (Paris: Seuil, 1991), p. 36.

Chapter 2
Grasping the Vanishing Mediator Between the Real and the Ideal
Žižek and the Unconscious Truth of German Idealism

Seeing a structural homology between the contemporary concerns of
psychoanalysis and those of late German Idealism's response to Kant,
Žižek turns to the latter to find the resources he needs to give an account
of the ontogenesis of the psychoanalytical subject. However, to do so he
not only has to go against mainstream interpretations of this tradition, but
also has to do great damage to the founding texts themselves. Outlining the
methodology behind Žižek's reactualization, what we will see is that the only
reason Žižek can apply psychoanalytical tools to restructure its symbolic
space and thereby develop his own philosophy is that this tradition itself is
haunted by a spectral history of an encounter with an underlying trauma:
namely, the subject as the vanishing mediator between the Real and the
Ideal, which both Hegel and Schelling primordially reveal in their own
manner, but ultimately recoil from and disavow. In this regard, German
Idealism presents us with an unconscious *Grundlogik* that we can only now,
with the aid of Freud and especially Lacan, reconstruct, thus giving us a
profoundly new and controversial view of its internal development and
theoretical preoccupations.

2.1 The Methodology of a Psychoanalytical Dialogue: Or, Lacan with Hegel and Hegel with Lacan

What is amazing about this psychoanalytical dialogue, however, is the heterodox readings of German Idealism and Lacanian psychoanalysis it produces. To many critics, Žižek simply shows *no* concern for textual faithfulness or the history of ideas in his readings of Kant, Hegel, Schelling, and Lacan. His methodological approach appears, if anything, to function through a deliberate misunderstanding or liberal reconstruction that purposefully overlooks key conceptual distinctions that challenge his own philosophical outlook. Although there is some superficial truth in these critiques—one must admit that Žižek focuses on often marginal selections from texts and raises them to a level of logical priority that they do not have in the original—one of Žižek's rare comments on his own methodology is very helpful for dispelling confusion on how he proceeds:

> Hegel didn't know what he was doing. You have to interpret
> him. Let me give you a metaphoric formula. You know
> the term Deleuze uses for reading philosophers—anal
> interpretation, buggering them. Deleuze says that, in contrast
> to other interpreters, he anally penetrates the philosopher,
> because it's immaculate conception. You produce a monster.
> I'm trying to do what Deleuze forgot to do—to bugger Hegel,
> with Lacan [chuckles] so that you get monstrous Hegel,
> which is, for me, precisely the underlying radical dimension of
> subjectivity which then, I think, was missed by Heidegger. But
> again, the basic idea being this mutual reading, this mutual
> buggering [chuckles] of this focal point, radical negativity
> and so on, of German Idealism with the very fundamental
> (Germans have this nice term, *grundeswig*[35]) insight of
> psychoanalysis.[36]

Even if Žižek describes his own philosophy as an act of textual violence, almost of *rape* (it is also worth mentioning that the word "bugger" originates the old French *bougre*, meaning heretic, and acquires its colloquial sense from heresy being associated with deviate, outlawed sexual practices), this quote reveals a hidden methodological presupposition that guides all of Žižek's interpretative work. The comparison of his own philosophy to that of Deleuze is of crucial importance and is not to be downplayed. It demonstrates that, even if Žižek is intentionally going against surface textual movements in his reading, he does not understand his own philosophy as in any sense arbitrary, a deliberate misunderstanding of the philosophers with whom he is engaging, or even as exhibiting any disregard for the tradition. Žižek recognizes that he is not doing traditional history of philosophy or any kind of philologico-exegetical interpretation, but is, instead, attempting to do something that is productive of new concepts by revealing their disavowed insights. But this generative activity of concept-creation can bring forth something unexpected, unsettling, even traumatic—*we may produce monsters.*

Žižek is not directly interested in what the texts of the German Idealist tradition "have to say," that is, their intended meaning, because this level of their discourse—like most discourses that fail to reflect upon the psychoanalytical conditions within which a discourse as such can take place—usually operates largely on the level of the Imaginary and its illusionary fantasy and can thus, perhaps even at most crucial junctures of conceptual argumentation, display a psychoanalytical superficiality. What therefore concerns him are hitherto unrealized textual potentialities, premonitions of which we can see in "marginal" comments or in various structures that often obstruct the general flow of a given philosophical system and consequently can be said to protrude out of its symbolic universe, negatively contorting it from the inside. Yet it is only by means of a thorough familiarity with this system and its surface affirmations that one can arrive at such unearthed possibilities and "reactualize" them. The analyst must, after all, *listen* to the analysand, even if, especially in its Lacanian mode, it often appears as if they are unconcerned or ignoring your needs and demands (for the goal of therapy is not the adaptation of the ego but rather a confrontation with unconscious, often traumatic truth). Žižek's own methodological approach to the history of philosophy, however, drastically differs from that of Deleuze insofar as it takes as its starting point the fundamental Lacanian claim that we can never say what we mean because there is an irremovable gap between the imaginary *moi* ("me" as the subject of self-conscious awareness who expresses the intention to say something, but somehow says something different and unintended) and the symbolic *je* (the elusive I as the subject that one deduces from what has in fact been said). Not only is language something that exerts control over us more than we have power over it (as an ego, rather than existing as a *speaking* linguistic subject, we are in a strong sense *spoken*), but the surface content of our own words often belies a greater (consciously) disavowed (but unconsciously known) truth, a truth that is not "hidden" in some deep, elusive place, but is so obvious that we often do not see it: "[t]he psychoanalyst is not an explorer of unknown continents or of grand depths, but a linguist: he learns to decode the writing that is already there, under his eyes, open to the look of everyone."[37] In the slips and slides of discourse, in seemingly meaningless hints and gestures, we catch a glimpse of the Real as that which cannot be said directly in discourse but around which it eternally moves, acting as a black hole drawing in everything towards it, or what Lacan refers to as its "cause" or "truth":

> Lacan's theory of interpretation is based, to some extent, on a formulation similar to that of the *caput mortuum*: an analysand speaking in the analytic setting is often unable to say, formulate, to come out with certain things; certain words, expressions, or thoughts are unavailable to him or her at a particular moment and he or she is forced to keep circling around them, beating around the bush, as it were, never enunciating what he or she senses to be at issue. The analysand's discourse traces a contour around that which it hovers about, circles, and skirts. Those words or thoughts may become accessible to the analysand in time, in the course of analysis, but they may also be introduced by the analyst in the form of an interpretation. That is what Lacan means when he says that "interpretation hits the cause": it hits that around which the analysand is revolving without being able to "put it into words."[38]

Keeping this in mind, we can easily see that Žižek's reading of German Idealism, by following its unconscious *Grundlogik*, is an attempt to psychoanalytically construct what the tradition in fact tries to say but cannot, by revealing what has been repressed in the first-level propositional affirmations of its texts. In other words, to borrow a Lacanian phrase, it tries to hit their cause. Although one can, of course, take issue with this methodology, one must admit that critics who take issue with Žižek's "selective" reading or "obvious misinterpretations" often just miss the point: they fail to see the underlying systematicity evident in his engagement with the tradition or understand why the conceptual moments he draws upon are so important.

In the spirit of Hegel and Schelling, who, in the uncertain aftermath of Kant, sought to articulate a philosophical system that could guarantee the latter's intuition of the irreducible autonomy of the subject,[39] Žižek like Lacan before him is convinced that there is something genuinely real and insurmountable in the experience of human freedom. Starting from psychoanalysis' insight into the constitutive disharmony between mind and body as a key to understanding its true essence, Žižek returns to German Idealism to see how the notion is conceptually refracted there. But in this respect Žižek's method is not a textual reconstruction of their arguments through an act of classico-philological retrieval nor is it an attempt to polish them up by using new resources at our disposal. What he notices is something primordially at odds with their surface content, which rather than rendering the texts of German Idealism logically inconsistent is more profoundly indicative of some kind of internal unconscious struggle, a struggle that is philosophically revealing and whose exploration—now made possible by the clinical tools of psychoanalysis—promises to unearth new ways of approaching its fundamental concepts. Finding premonitions of *Todestrieb* protruding out of the imaginary-symbolic space of its discourse, Žižek sees a disavowed truth lurking "beneath" the tradition's own attempts to think substance as subject by means of a dialectical interconnecting of mind and body, a disavowed truth that reduces the latter to a mere reaction formation, a defence from the true horror of subjectivity finally brought to the fore by Kant's account of transcendental freedom. After all, if German Idealism's breakthrough is the freedom of the subject, according to Žižek we must also recognize that "our experience of freedom is properly *traumatic*."[40] Consequently Žižek gives us resources to think how, if we attentively follow the tradition's conceptual movements, we can see traces of an operative logic ephemerally emerging from time to time at crucial moments only to be covered up by preceding steps, so that our task is to reconstruct retroactively this hidden *Grundlogik* constantly interfering with what the tradition takes itself to be, if we are to come to terms with the disturbing metaphysics of freedom demanded by its founding intuitions. However, the methodology of such a psychoanalytical reconstruction of philosophical trauma around which an entire tradition circulates as its unconscious cause or truth displays an important paradox that deserves to be highlighted, which we can elucidate by means of Žižek's discussion of the legend of *Eppur si muove*:

> The legend has it that, in 1633, Galileo Galilei muttered, "*Eppur si muove*" ("And yet it moves"), after recanting before the Inquisition his theory that the Earth moves around the Sun[. ...] There is no contemporary evidence that he did in fact mutter this phrase, but today the phrase is used to indicate that although someone who possesses true knowledge is forced to renounce it, this does not stop it from being true. But what makes this phrase so interesting is that it can also be used in the exact opposite sense, to assert a "deeper" symbolic truth about something which is not true—like the "*Eppur si muove*" story itself, which may well be false as a historical fact about Galileo's life, but is true as a designation of Galileo's subjective position [... B]eyond the truth of reality, there is the reality of the fiction.[41]

Likewise, the alternative history of German Idealism that I develop in the following in a strong sense *did not happen* as a historical fact. Little if any evidence points towards it, and often the philological references that I have gathered can be easily opposed by numerous counter-examples. However, this is not the point: although this account of German Idealism's failed encounter with its inner truth is in many ways nothing but a fiction, this does not prevent it from directly expressing the subjective position that each of its representatives holds (even if it falsely capitulates their conscious interpretation of what they are doing) in a manner that other philosophical methodologies cannot, for what concerns us are traces of the Real in imaginary-symbolic constructs and their logic. After all, "when truth is too traumatic to be confronted directly, it can only be accepted in the guise of a fiction."[42]

2.2 A Metaphysics of the Real: An *Hegelian* or a *Schellingian* Project?

Central to Žižek's metaphysics of the Real as a psychoanalytical reactualization of German Idealism is his stark emphasis on the indispensable significance of Hegel. In various places, Žižek characterizes his own project as strictly *Hegelian* because, like Hegel, the enigma that occupies him is the possibility of *appearance* itself: that is, how the realm of phenomenal reality could emerge from the self-actualization of substance. Hegel is said to be the first to understand this question in terms of inscribing the subject into the absolute: a subject that, in the Kantian aftermath, is understood as intrinsically irreducible to the immanent ontological field that brought it forth, and that can freely mediate the latter for itself through its own idealizing activity. In this sense, Hegel's metaphysics could structurally supply the missing principle of a Lacanian metapsychology. Through Hegel, Žižek believes he can show that subjectivity is not illusory by situating idealism into the heart of materialism as an irruptive event, the claim being that premonitions of this can be seen throughout Hegel's philosophy. Apparently arguing by means of resources found in the latter for a self-splitting or of the noumenal within the dark pre-history of subjectivity, Žižek tries to show how the only consistent way to explain why there is experience is to posit an ontological catastrophe at the basis of the subject. Consequently, it would appear that Žižek makes the following his axiomatic first principle thanks to a direct confrontation with Hegel: *Freedom is not a raw, brute fact, but an expression of the caustic collapse of material being, a brisure in the heart of Real, which is synonymous with the subject itself*; "it designates [...] the primordial Big Bang, the violent self-contrast by means of which the balance and inner peace of the Void of which mystics speak are perturbed, thrown out of joint."[43]

But the overtly Hegelian nature of Žižek's project does not go without saying. In one essay, Žižek makes a claim that to many readers must appear out of place insofar as he gives it no qualification: "Hegel's 'overcoming' of Schelling is a case in itself: Schelling's reaction to Hegel's idealist dialectic was so strong and profound that more and more it is counted as the next (and concluding) step in the inner development of German Idealism."[44] What is more, this claim is repeated almost verbatim in *Less*

Than Nothing.[45] The effect of this comment is twofold: not only does it strike
those immersed within "conventional," textbook accounts of the history of
philosophy as essentially wrong (which, it must be said, are losing credibility
as Fichte and Schelling research has finally gained an autonomy of its own),
but it also highlights a fundamental difficulty at the core of Žižek's reading
of German Idealism and by consequence his own philosophy, insofar as his
parallax ontology is perceived as a reactualization or continuation of this
movement. This problem is only amplified when one engages with Žižek's
major works on German Idealism. In both The *Ticklish Subject* and *The
Parallax View*, for example, there are praises of Schelling as the greatest
philosopher of the pre-symbolic Real, of the nature of the impossible X, the
je ne sais quoi, which precedes consciousness as the most central theme in
post-Kantian philosophy and whose problematic uncannily reappears in the
wake of the Lacanian subject. Žižek even goes as far as to say that Schelling
was "the first to formulate this task"[46] and the philosopher who "gave the
most detailed account of this X in his notion of the Ground of Existence,"[47]
which is why *his* philosophy and not that of Hegel is "at the origins of
dialectical materialism."[48] Given that Žižek in *Less Than Nothing* describes
"the key question" of philosophy as that of "how thought is possible in a
universe of matter," so that we should focus our efforts on "the very rise of
representation or appearing out of the flat stupidity of being" if we are to
avoid "the very rise of representation or appearing out of the flat stupidity
of being" if we are to avoid "a regression to a 'naive' ontology of spheres or
levels,"[49] the issue of whether this project is most radically accomplished
by Schelling or Hegel is more than a matter of intra-textual consistency or
classico-philological accuracy, but touches the very heart of what Žižek takes
to be the program of speculative philosophy.

On account of this ambiguity, Žižek's own project of describing this
process of the auto-disruption of the Real displays an undeniable oscillation
between the characterization of this project as a *Schellingian* or a *Hegelian*
one, even though he claims outright that Schelling is the culmination of
this line of thought. Not only does it potentially suggest that Žižek tries to
disavow too strong a relationship between a Lacanian-inspired metaphysics
of the Real and Schelling, but it also shows that he might downplay the
role that Schellingian notions play (or undermine possible roles that others

could) in such a metaphysics, in terms of either our understanding of
ontology (the universal), natural sciences (the particular), or politics (the
singular), the trinity that constitutes the conceptual fold of *The Parallax
View*, his first theoretical *magnum opus*. In other respects, however, it appears
that Žižek may have recently changed or distanced himself from his earlier
interpretation of Schelling, perhaps precisely for these reasons. Although
Žižek, despite his constant insistence that his fundamental question is a
"properly Hegelian one: *how does appearance itself emerge from the interlay of
the Real?*,"[50] oscillates in his early major theoretical works *The Ticklish Subject*
and *The Parallax View* in his descriptions of who most adequately answers
this question, in his new masterpiece *Less Than Nothing* this oscillation
suddenly stops. While this project is again and again characterized as
Hegelian,[51] the former glory once bestowed upon Schelling as the great
thinker of the "phenomenalization of being"[52] is not just downplayed, but
apparently completely forgotten, with Žižek even going so far as to say that
thinking the emergence of appearance is "what at his most radical Hegel
does,"[53] thus contradicting himself. However, despite appearances to the
contrary, the ambiguity does not thereby disappear. Not only does Žižek
claim that "[t]he minimal definition of materialism hinges of the admission
of a *gap between what Schelling called Existence and the Ground of Existence*,"[54]
but the ambiguity of the Hegel-Schelling relationship in fact gets radicalized
in the middle of the second chapter on Hegel, when Žižek describes the
latter's dialectic as "the science of the gap between the Old and the New,"
and then without explanation jumps into a two-and-a-half page discussion
of Schelling's theosophic odyssey of the emergence of "the cosmos (of fully
constituted reality, ruled by *logos*) out of the proto-cosmic pre-ontological
chaos."[55] Although to many readers this may appear as just another "typical"
Žižekian digression with no inner logic, the argument that I develop in this
book attempts to show that it is anything but that. Insofar as Žižek himself
claims that the only way to avoid mystification is not to abandon the project
of the *Weltalter* but rather "to reformulate it so as to avoid the mystification
of the theosophic mytho-poetic narrative,"[56] it appears that the proximity of
his reading of Hegel and Schelling, when coupled with this brief and rare
methodological elaboration, points to the core of his heterodox reading of
German Idealism and thus to the core of his philosophy itself. Rather than

being purely Hegelian or purely Schellingian, Žižek's philosophy thus proves to be a hybrid of the two, an attempt—in some as yet unidentified way—to use Hegel to formalize Schelling's thinking, "saving" it from its theosophic commitments, and to use Schelling to radicalize Hegel, allowing him to draw out implicit but disavowed moves in his own philosophy and thus in German Idealism as a whole. But why does this ambiguity exist in the first place?

Immediately after his remarkable and provocative reading of Schelling in the first chapter of The *Indivisible Remainder*, Žižek goes on to argue for the supremacy of Hegelian dialectics over Schellingian metaphysics. For him, although there are premonitions of a radical breakthrough in works such as the *Freiheitsschrift* and the *Weltalter*,[57] Schelling remains philosophically inferior to his great rival because *Grund* and existence ultimately remain distinct from one another only by being founded within absolute indifference, which itself "is not a product of opposites, nor are they contained in it *implicite*; rather it is a being of its own, separated from all oppositions, on which all oppositions are broken, which is nothing other than their very non-being, and which therefore has no predicate except predicatelessness."[58] Indeed, Schelling claims that "from this neither-nor, or from this indifference, duality [...] immediately breaks forth, and *without* indifference, i.e., *without* an unground, there would be no twofoldness of the principles."[59] For Žižek, however, this means that "the [Schellingian] Absolute is primarily the 'absolute indifference' providing the neutral medium for the coexistence of the polar opposites" of the Real and the Ideal[60] and, as such, is at odds with the potential latent in his middle-late philosophy, a potential Žižek sees in its articulation of the eruptive logic of *Grund* and its relationship to existence at the basis of subjectivity. In this regard, Hegel provides a superior logic in which there is no need for a principle of meditation exterior to *Grund* and existence as two reflective pairs that determine themselves through their internal dynamic, which in turn allows us to internally restructure Schelling's own descriptions of the interrelation of the two. In Hegel the very category of "and" changes—it becomes, in essence, *tautological*, thereby enabling us to identify *Grund* and existence instead of rendering them mere opposites or dual principles founded in something external to their own inner movement. In the logical process of the dialectic, the third term is already the second, understood as a negativity or internal limit inscribed in the first, insofar as it has merely taken over, *usurped*, the primary position from which the movement began by asserting itself as such. In terms of substance and subject, this means that "*this very reversal is the very definition of subject*: 'subject' is the name for the principle of Selfhood which subordinates to itself the substantial Whole whose particular moment it originally was."[61] Nothing at the level of content changes: it expresses a purely formal change at the level of structure due to the tension generated by the contorting presence of negativity. The dialectical movement that goes (i) immediacy → (ii) negation → (iii) negation of negation is superior because there is no genuine return movement to the first, although it all takes place in a single, logically immanent field. The beginning and end do not overlap because something irreducibly different emerges within the first moment (negativity now being made foundational to identity), namely, to take the example that concerns us here, an "out of joint" spirit that has a degree of notional self-reflexivity in opposition to its ontogenetic ground, the whole within which it gave birth to itself. There is no need to posit a state of "originary health" of which the devouring restlessness of the negative cannot be predicated (absolute indifference as that which stands *in the difference* between *Grund* and existence and thus is equally in one as in the other) in order to explain the dialectical movement of reality and its relation to the absolute.

As we shall see, Žižek's criticism of Schelling gets more complicated because it does not universally apply to the entirety of Schelling's work, since for Žižek the latter is not characterized by an organic unity or continuity, but rather by a series of irreconcilable ruptures. He draws a distinction between a Schelling₁ of the period of quasi-Spinozism (the philosophy of indifference), a Schelling₂ of the radical ontology of freedom as seen in the second draft of the *Weltalter* and the *Freiheitsschrift*, and a Schelling₃ of the philosophy of mythology and revelation, which he qualifies—very violently—as a return to pre-modern essentialism. For Žižek, what distinguishes the middle-late period of Schelling's thinking is, strictly speaking, the articulation of an ontogenetic emergence of self-positing freedom in a manner remarkably similar to the Hegelian dialectical movement from abstract immediacy to notional self-reflexivity, which goes against the surface-level theosophic inclinations of the texts. It protrudes out of them and makes them non-coincidental with themselves in such a way that we can psychoanalytically reactualize their fundamental movement by "tarrying with the negative"—that is, by encountering the Real within them. What this means is that even if the self-operative logic of the *Grund* contains premonitions of a radical transcendental materialism, Schelling is at the same time the father of "New Age obscurantism."[62] Expressing a reliance upon and indebtedness to Schelling would, in essence, open up a possible connection between Žižek's own thinking and everything he denies—the non-Freudian unconscious (in its Bergsonian, Jungian, Deleuzian, and other forms), "pre-modern" cosmology, Romantic theories of nature, theosophy and even its pop-culture descendant, New Age spirituality. In this sense, the very act of placing the logic of the *Grund* at the heart of the psychoanalytic subject appears to risk "destabilizing" the primacy of the Lacanian mode of the unconscious insofar as it opens up the possibility of interpreting it through a different account of one's relation to the pre-subjective life of the Real; covering up the pivotal importance of Schelling would seem to be nothing but a certain ideological act on Žižek's part. But here two remarks must be made. First, although it is perhaps a bit underhanded on Žižek's behalf to downplay the importance of Schelling for the development of his transcendental materialism, it must be added that this obfuscation is consistent with his overall interpretation of Schelling, for he rejects most of the latter's philosophy and needs recourse to Hegel even to reactualize the logic of the *Grund* that he sees as its breakthrough. But second, and more importantly, such an explanation does not solve the problem of the Hegel-Schelling relation insofar as this emphatic shift is simultaneously ambiguous, given the fact that Žižek does not distinguish *which* Schelling he is arguing against or justify *how* he is able to read the second draft of the *Weltalter* as an ephemeral breakthrough.

In this regard, by characterizing his own philosophy again and again as a *Hegelian*, but never a *Schellingian* project Žižek belies his overt reliance on texts such as Schelling's *Freiheitsschrift* and the *Weltalter* for his project. What I propose, therefore, is to read Žižek *against* Žižek not only to demonstrate the implicit, complex intertwining of Schellingian ontology and Hegelian logic throughout his thinking, wherein I perceive the nuance of his theoretical philosophy, but also to show how by unravelling this ambiguity we can find new resources to explore the obscure origins of the psychoanalytical subject and the fundamental structures and essence of the world within which it emerges. Yet if embarking upon a reconstruction of the Hegel-Schelling relation within Žižek's work can achieve this, it is only because Žižek sees his own work as an attempt to culminate the *Grundlogik* of German Idealism itself, which gestures towards the hypothesis that the intra-textual ambiguity of the Hegel-Schelling relation within his thinking is perhaps less expressive of an internal inconsistency in his philosophy than of *a fundamental problem inherent in the self-unfolding of that tradition itself* in its endeavour to overcome radical idealism; so that, if by a dialectical reversal we turn an epistemological limit into a positive ontological condition, apparent textual confusion into a real feature of the movement itself in its historical development, the ambiguity will prove itself in a second moment to be a side effect of a sustained methodological engagement with the fundamental insights of German Idealism which thus deserves to be investigated in its own right. As we will see, this ambiguity is in fact due to a single traumatic kernel of truth that both Hegel and Schelling, attempting to ground the Kantian subject, bring to the fore in different ways, but ultimately have to repress or force into the unconscious, a fact that therefore requires us to use a mode of inquiry that goes beyond philologico-exegetical interpretation if we are to penetrate it:

> The notion of Schelling's *Grundoperation*—the "vanishing mediator" between the two poles (the Real and the Ideal, B and A)—opens up the possibility of establishing a connection with Hegelian dialectics: the founding gesture "repressed" by the formal envelope of the "panlogicist" Hegel is *the same* as the gesture which is "repressed" by the formal envelope of the "obscurantist" Schelling, yet which simultaneously serves as its unacknowledged ground. [...] Does the gesture of "vanishing mediation" not point, therefore, towards what, following some German interpreters, one could call the *Grundoperation des Deutschen Idealismus*, the fundamental, elementary operation of German Idealism?

> It is our endeavour to articulate clearly the *Grundoperation*
> of German Idealism which necessitates reference to Lacan;
> that is to say, our premiss is that the "royal road" to this
> *Grundoperation* involves reading German Idealism through the
> prism of Lacanian psychoanalytical theory.[63]

In this manner, to raise the question of whether Žižek's project is
Schellingian or *Hegelian* is misleading, for what interests Žižek is not
Kant, Schelling, or Hegel as particular historical thinkers per se, but a
psychoanalytically retrievable unconscious truth self-unfolding throughout
their works, a truth inaugurated by the Cartesian *cogito* but from which
the entire tradition of modern philosophy has been repelled because of its
horror, but to which we can now have access thanks to Freud's and Lacan's
groundbreaking work on the original trauma of the human subject. In
short, my wager is that Žižek forces us to consider that what makes German
Idealism so singular in the history of philosophy is that it is haunted by an
unconscious history that is nothing other than one of the sustained encounters
with the ontological catastrophe at the very basis of human subjectivity in
human thinking, this concept thus presenting itself as a Lacanian cause or
truth around which the surface structures of its great epics circulate as their
repressed traumatic Real and whose movement demand being systematically
reconstructed retroactively.

But the ambiguity of the Hegel-Schelling relationship has another
advantage: it not only allows us to construct an original and perhaps
controversial understanding of German Idealism and its legacy by
articulating its unconscious history, a dynamic spectral history of
repression and the return of the repressed, but it also allows us to evaluate
the philosophical significance of Žižek's work by situating him directly
within its concerns. Žižek is able to rely upon Hegel and Schelling to
explicate the origins of subjectivity and their metaphysical implications
because he sees them as embarking upon a metaphysics from within a
self-grounding transcendental framework, whereby German Idealism and
the psychoanalytical tradition in its Lacanian legacy become uncannily
close due to their underlying epistemologies and the need to make sense of
them ontologically. In this respect, unpacking the ambiguity of the Hegel-
Schelling relation is of profound methodological importance, for it brings to

the fore and deals explicitly with the critical difficulties posed by attempting to give an account of the emergence of the Ideal out of a Real that has been, from within the former, always already lost. The psychoanalytical fusion of Schelling and Hegel implicit in his thinking—a fusion which points towards a certain unconscious struggle inherent to German Idealism itself—either reveals or resolves a potentially fatal ambivalence in the conception of the Real, an ambivalence that risks jeopardizing not only Žižek's project, but also the development of any form of metaphysics from within a radical idealism. According to Lacan, the Symbolic exhibits what may be called a form of *ontological solipsism* insofar as it is an irreducibly self-referential matrix of signifiers whose relation to an external, extra-ideal world has been utterly cut off. Yet to give a theoretical grounding of our inability to access objective reality we must describe its dark pre-history in the orgasm of forces that is the pre-symbolic Real. Is the Real that which *precedes* and *exceeds* consciousness, or a pure lack that only presents itself through the breakdowns of the Symbolic? Can these two modalities be reconciled *within a metaphysics*? If so, can a hybridization of Hegel and Schelling help us conceive of the emergence of the Symbolic out of the Real *from within the Symbolic* by overcoming the opposition between materialism and idealism? But before we answer these questions, we should step back and ask: why would we even want to proclaim such a Cartesian dualism of mind and body, nature and spirit, the Real and the Symbolic, especially since such a form of subjectivity has been criticized for so long in the contemporary intellectual scene as no longer sustainable? What are its theoretical advantages?

Notes

35. Neither this word nor a comparable one appears to actually exist in modern or old German. A simple Google search is enough to be suspicious: it only comes up with this quote.

36. Žižek, "Liberation Hurts: An Interview with Slavoj Žižek (with Eric Dean Rasmussen)." Retrieved Feb. 23, 2010, from http://www.electronicbookreview.com/thread/endconstruction/desublimation.

37. Lacan, "Clefs pour la psychoanalyse (entretien avec Madeleine Chapsal)." Retrieved May 16, 2010, from http://www.ecole-lacanienne.net/documents/1957-05-31.doc.

38. Fink, *The Lacanian Subject,* p. 28.

39. Žižek, *Less Than Nothing,* p. 266.

40. Ibid., p. 265.

41. Ibid., pp. 3–4.

42. Ibid., p. 24.

43. Žižek, *The Ticklish Subject,* p. 31.

44. Žižek, "Fichte's Laughter," in *Mythology, Madness and Laughter: Subjectivity in German Idealism* (New York: Continuum, 2009), p. 122.

45. Žižek, *Less Than Nothing,* p. 137.

46. Žižek, *The Parallax View,* p. 166.

47. Žižek, *The Ticklish Subject,* p. 55.

48. Žižek, *The Indivisible Remainder,* p. 11.

49. Žižek, *Less Than Nothing,* p. 905.

50. Žižek, *The Parallax View,* p. 106.

51. See, for instance, Žižek, *Less Than Nothing,* pp. 13f. and 642ff.

52. See Žižek, *The Indivisible Remainder,* p. 14; and Žižek, *The Abyss of Freedom,* in *The Abyss of Freedom/Ages of the World* (Cambridge: MIT Press, 2008), p. 15.

53. Žižek, *Less Than Nothing,* p. 239.

54. Ibid., p. 912.

55. Ibid., p. 273.

56. Ibid.

57. Žižek, *The Indivisible Remainder,* p. 8.

58. Schelling, *Philosophical Investigations into the Essence of Human Freedom and Other Related Matters,* trans. Priscilla Hayden-Roy, in *Philosophy of German Idealism,* ed. Ernst Behler (New York: Continuum, 2003) (hereafter *Freiheitsschrift*), p. 276.

59. Ibid., p. 278.

60. Žižek, *The Indivisible Remainder,* p. 105.

61. Ibid., p. 106.

62. Žižek, *The Abyss of Freedom,* p. 4.

63. Žižek, *The Indivisible Remainder,* p. 92.

Chapter 3
Psychoanalysis and the Enigma of Transcendental Subjectivity
Towards a New Materialism

Žižek's reactualization of German Idealism represents an avid attempt to revitalize Cartesian transcendental subjectivity. In the face of a contemporary discourse that attacks from all sides the very possibility of a non-material I that stands in its own autonomous register, Žižek's philosophy aims to articulate the theoretical currency still implicit within the groundbreaking intuition that heralds modernity. But what warrants this repetition/resurgence of such an apparently "outmoded" idea? What kind of explanatory efficacy could it still exhibit in a theoretical field that believes itself to have largely overcome its shortcomings? By exposing the various theoretical holes revealed in the contemporary intellectual scene by Lacanian psychoanalysis, Žižek rethinks the modern materialism-idealism debate by showing how movements such as those in current phenomenology of the body, postmodernism, and neurobiology are philosophically insufficient and thus force us to reconceptualize transcendentalism radically.

3.1 Postmodernism and an Uncanny Defence of Transcendentalism

Although phenomenologists like Merleau-Ponty and more recently Michel Henry and Jean-Luc Marion argue for the primordial unity of consciousness and the lived body or the self's immanent auto-determination from the unfolding of givenness of the flesh (which indicates the disappearance of a radical subject-object distinction by the interpenetration of both in embodiment), Žižek makes the claim that such descriptions are intrinsically lacking insofar as they fail to take account of the experience of the monstrous and the traumatic irrevocably tied to the essence of human being. One cannot merely replace classical subjectivity with a more organic theory of experience that intertwines consciousness with a phenomenological auto-affection of the flesh. The rift between the spiritual and the material uncovered by the I destabilizes the very possibility of such a primordial union or identity: if we take transcendental reflexivity seriously we see, according to Žižek, a *pure self-positing* that tears itself away from any kind of immersion within the field of corporeal activity. The very possibility of the psychoanalytical experience as that which reveals a split between the energetic dynamics of the body and subjective, experiential reality presupposes an irreducibly antagonistic interrelation, a discordant dichotomy, between mind and body, which proclaims that the human subject must in some sense "protrude" out of its carnal materiality and be understood on its own terms. The claim is that the modern subject not only paves the way for the psychoanalytical discourse of the unconscious, but also sets up the possibility of a genuine encounter with what it means to be a human subject existing with an intrinsic relation to a bodily substrate that paradoxically presents itself as Other. We cannot just think the self that comes after the subject in a way that does away with the latter, for transcendental subjectivity brings to our attention a primordial truth of what it means to be a free human being that, in many ways, we have yet to come to terms with: *that of a structural conflict between mind and body which divides our being into two incommensurate spheres.*

However, the implications of Žižek's reactualization of German Idealism are not just limited to the phenomenology of the body. Arguing against postmodern theorists like Derrida and Foucault, who claim that the subject itself is merely an empty, accidental construction that arises out of the flux of historical experience, Žižek contends that by forgetting the ontological schism between mind and body that enables the self to be determined according to linguistic and political forces in the first place, they lose sight of the very formal structure of the I that is required even to speak of the endless temporal variations of selfhood within the contingent upsurge of sociopolitical activity. The unceasing play of cultural difference, the non-finite proliferation of identities and discourses, can only be adequately understood through the transcendental framework offered by Cartesian subjectivity because, as that which prevents human activity from being explicable through solely natural or biological grounds, it supplies the formal-universal structure through which such change is rendered possible. The *cogito* is necessary for deciphering not only human embodiment, but also human historicity insofar as it gives us a clue to what kind of *ontological* event could have led to the emergence of something like a symbolic universe in contrast to the "cyclical" movement of nature. Here we see another advantage of the *cogito* that transcends its theoretico-explicative currency, or more strongly, *coincides with it*: as the transcendental condition of the possibility of historical contingency, the pure I always stands above all fixed, particular sociopolitical constellations and thus presents the always possible basis of ideological critique and political revolution.

But perhaps the greatest threat to subjectivity comes from contemporary cognitive science. In light of decades of groundbreaking research in neurobiology, there is a growing tendency to turn towards scientific models of explanation to explain away the uniqueness of human subjectivity. Researchers are not just constantly downplaying the role of systematic self-observation and autonomous discourses that deny the supremacy of experimental science; rather, what is increasingly coming into question is the infinite array of material offered by self-consciousness and the meaning of philosophical investigations into its culture and politics as structurally free from biological concerns. Instead of having recourse to first-person experience as it shows itself to us in the irreducibility of its complex dynamics as the site of personality (phenomenology), or the labyrinthine network of the symbolic universe of discourses informing our sense of self and other (postmodernism), they are able to explain the entire range of emotional and social characteristics through the nonconscious, asubjective pulsation of brute matter, the mere non-personal movement of neurochemico-electrical activity wherein the I becomes an epiphenomenal illusion created by a closed biological system of response mechanisms predetermined by genetic code.

Žižek's argument here is twofold. Firstly, founding itself upon classical biology, contemporary cognitive science presupposes that every organism is a self-contained system in harmony with itself seeking homeostasis and self-preservation, which prevents it from coming to terms with the psychoanalytical concept of *Todestrieb*. Representing a malfunction in biology, whereby a person no more strives for pleasure and satisfaction, for the minimal possible level of distress and affliction, but rather for pain and even self-destruction, psychoanalysis identifies this apparently negative moment of short circuit within the biological machine with one of the defining traits of human subjectivity and thus of culture itself.[64] Instead of being a mere haphazard disorder or a contingent feature of a sick mind, *Todestrieb* comes to represent a necessary feature of the singularity of our being: the condition of the possibility of psychopathological self-destruction is ultimately linked to our very freedom because the two are structurally homologous. Secondly, what Žižek adds to this argument for the supremacy of psychoanalysis over reductionist biology is the following insight: if there were nothing but the self-contained, deterministic system of the neuronal interface of the brain, then why is there (self-)experience at all?[65] Why is there not just blind existence, a mere mechanism that auto-develops according to its own laws? Why does the nonconscious trembling of brute matter in its dynamic pulsations need to be aware of itself? Since the category of subjective experience is *superfluous*, *unnecessary*, to the materialism displayed by science, the mere fact of experience proclaims that neurobiological activity is not-all—that there is a gap, a series of interstices, which arise within its logical fold as a kind of unpredictable short circuit to which, perhaps, phenomenal reality arises as a response. Naming the place of this rupture the subject itself, Žižek's own work on cognitive science consequently tries to underline the inherent difficulty that the discipline has (for this very reason) to explain the emergence of consciousness, insofar as it points to a limit-situation within which the discourse itself breaks down.

Neither the phenomenology of the body, postmodernism, or cognitive science can just dispel the "myth of subjectivity" because all three of them, in distinct ways, need it to account for the very subject matter they take as their own. If the phenomenology of the body is to understand the very field of the (self-)appearing of phenomena to consciousness as embodied, then it has to come to terms with the breakthrough of transcendental reflexivity as a form of pure self-positing that institutes a subject-object schism rendering the very body that we live in Other to ourselves: "the subject (Self) is [...] immaterial: its One-ness, its self-identity, is not reducible to its material support. I am precisely *not* my body: the Self can only arise against the background of the death of its substantial being, of what it 'objectively' is."[66] Postmodernism needs to presuppose the pure I as something over and above the contingent field of non-finite cultural difference that it sets up even to talk about the complex network of discourses irreducible to naturalistic influences. Lastly, cognitive science cannot discard the subject if it is to explain the very possibility of how a gap in (material) being could emerge so that there is the basic distance from self that is necessary for the phenomenalization of reality. If we are to understand the true nature of the human being, Žižek's contention is that we must reread transcendental philosophy through the psychoanalytical category of *Todestrieb*, for both seem to cover the same theoretical set of problems in an uncanny manner; this unholy marriage of German Idealism and psychoanalysis aims to reconfigure the contemporary intellectual scene by offering a comprehensive system that is able to respond to the intrinsic limitations of all three disciplines.

However, although Žižek's retrieval of subjectivity thus superficially appears to be an attempt to assert the unshakeable supreme position of the human subject against the various de-centerings that it has undergone in the twentieth century, this is an overt *vel*. Whereas most defenders of the transcendental ego return to Descartes, Kant, or Hegel to regain and unpack their conviction in the self-grounding ipseity at the core of human activity in face of its dissipation within flux of radical historicism, the all-engulfing force of structuralism, or the brute determination of mechanical nature, what intrigues Žižek are the various ways in which the *cogito* fails at its own task and the implications of this failure for our understanding of self and world. Instead of presenting an intuition of a self-positing substantiality that persists behind all representational content of thought while being co-given, co-equal, and ultimately fully coinciding with my own personal self, what we truly find in the thinkers of subjectivity according to Žižek is the affirmation of a negatively charged *void* that holds together the sedimentations of personality through its sheer self-reflexive nothingness. Whether this be Descartes' inability to establish the positive characteristics of the I that necessarily thinks,[67] Kant's failure to penetrate into the kernel of the subject *an sich* that makes experience possible,[68] or Hegel's early account of the night of the world,[69] what is obvious to Žižek is that the impervious, vacuous core of subjectivity is simultaneously its condition of possibility and impossibility. Consequently, what interests Žižek are two things: (i) the traces of this abyssal nature of subjectivity that can be found in modern philosophy, which immanently problematizes all attempts to ground experience in the intuition of a self-positing substantial core of existential familiarity and transparency; and (ii) how this grounding insight into transcendental reflexivity and the deadlocks it generates are schematized under the textual surface in different modalities by Kant and his followers, yet in such a way that they display in them a hidden logic implicitly working itself out throughout the entire tradition that can be retroactively constructed and used today in order to combat a range of theoretical problems that plague us.

3.2 Idealism and its Shadow: Materialism in the Cracks

However, to return to German Idealism and its "rampant" transcendentalist inclinations with the intention of retrieving a conception of the subject able to respond to perceived dead ends in contemporary intellectual discourse presents an immediate problem. In order to articulate an account of experience that can combine psychoanalysis and modern subjectivity in a manner capable of combating the phenomenology of the body, postmodern discourse theory, and cognitive science, Žižek must fight against the anti-materialistic tendencies evident in the German Idealist tradition itself. Žižek's fundamental thesis is—perhaps counter-intuitively—that it is the latter's very descriptions of the non-material, purely spiritual I that point the way. The nothingness of the *cogito* reveals more than a form of ontological dualism, the horrifying split nature of subjectivity that forever haunts psychic life: not only is the *cogito* unable to find an existential or ontological interiority at the heart of one's own most personal being—being a mere formal void that guarantees the self-sameness of identity through phenomenal time, the I is an empty set—but the very gesture of a self-grounding idealism that it sets into play shows itself to be structurally incomplete and riddled with holes. In modernity's irreversible establishment of the primary function of the *cogito* (as a synthesizing activity that idealizes our contact with the world in such a way that we lose contact with real entities non-mediated by mind) Žižek argues that we immediately come face to face with the internal limitation and contradiction of idealism as such, insofar as absolute mediation is not possible for the subject. Instead of exhibiting a smooth transcendentally constituted fabric of experience freely brought forth by the subject on its Godlike throne, idealism generates in and of itself irremovable and unpredictable moments of blockage and obstruction that infringe upon the subject's totalizing claims for autocratic autonomy and a complete, undisturbed idealization of experience. In other words, every attempt of idealism to affirm itself as "all," to set the stage for the transcendental constitution of phenomenal reality as an almighty, full-blown "hallucination," fails: within idealism there is always something uncannily more than ideal, an extimacy that corrodes it from the inside and cannot be explained from within its free idealization of the world.

Taking the inevitable failure of self-grounding idealism to fully posit itself as a guide, Žižek's reading of German Idealism focuses on what he perceives as an ambiguous relationship in its texts: between such a self-grounding idealism, and the spectral presence of what appears as a form of materialism within its ideal-synthetic fold that must somehow be posited as theoretically more fundamental and primordial *après-coup*. The agonizing tension within ideality as it tries to constitute the world of experience suggests that, although a non-mediated, purely material reality has been forever lost due to the idealizing activity rendered possible by the subject, we can still, *through the very limitations, blockages, and obstructions of this activity*, negatively catch a glimpse of it, the very inconsistency of thought guaranteeing that we gain knowledge of reality "outside" our representations. The figure of Fichte is of utmost importance in this context for comprehending the conceptual contours of Žižek's position. Instead of being a contradictory, deficient concept within the internal trajectory of German Idealism that automatically reveals Fichte's inconsequentiality and impotence as a thinker, the concept of *Anstoß* manifests the truth of the materialism-idealism relation expressed within the tradition, albeit in a manner that he does not explicitly thematize.

In Fichtean subjective idealism, the I is the axiomatic starting point of philosophy. Even the not-I, the entire sphere of everything that presents itself within consciousness as "extra-subjective" content, is freely posited and brought forth by the self-grounding activity of the absolute subject, in effect robbing it of any alterity that it would possess in itself as a material, non-mediated being with its own interiority that thrusts itself upon consciousness. In other words, the not-I does not affect the I through a form of causality. Yet because of the double meaning of *Anstoß* as a hindrance *and* impetus, as something that obstructs *and* incites our activity, one cannot just say that the *Anstoß* is a mere obstacle created by the subject so that it can have the necessary degree of resistance needed in order concretely to assert and actualize its own freedom. Although the not-I depends upon the pure I for its meaning, the former of itself cannot be reduced to the idealizing activity set up by the latter: it is not "like the games the proverbial perverted ascetic saint plays with himself by way of inventing ever new temptations and then, by overcoming them, confirming his strength." For if this were so, "it would present a case of the hollow playing of the subject with itself, and we would never reach the level of objective reality."[70] There is therefore an element of speculative truth in Fichte that Žižek wants to bring to the fore: even if the circle of idealism is a self-enclosed, free creation rendered possible by the subject, due to the painful curvature of this space we must nevertheless speak of a *negative materialism* in Fichte's thinking.[71] Here, we encounter a paradoxical coincidence of internal-external limitation and inside-outside: "*Anstoß* thus designates the moment of the 'run-in,' the hazardous knock, the *encounter* of the Real in the midst of the ideality of the absolute I: there is no subject without *Anstoß*, without the collision with an element of irreducible facticity and contingency—'the I is supposed to encounter *within* itself something foreign,"[72] some inassimilable body that sticks in its throat like a bone. According to Žižek, this truth is then later radicalized by Hegel's and Schelling's own response to Fichte's thinking insofar as they realize it gives us the necessary resources we need to develop a metaphysics *while never leaving the transcendental idealist framework.*

Žižek's own theoretical position is therefore a rather precarious one. It contends that it is only from *within* the deadlock and limitations of a full-blown idealism asserting the ultimate irreducibility of mind and subjectivity to matter—here we must think of Žižek's philosophy as a turning inside-out of Jacobi's challenge that idealism must become a *speculative egoism* by following it to its logical conclusion: "[t]he transcendental idealist [...] must have the courage to assert the strongest idealism that has ever been taught, and not even to fear the charge of speculative egoism"[73]—that we can develop a truly speculative materialism up to the task of explaining the emergence of experience, for it also suggests that only a full-blown idealism is truly capable of disclosing crucial facts about the nature of materiality. However, such a materialism rests upon the apparently paradoxical claim that it is the very auto-collapse of idealism that is epistemologically capable of overcoming itself and describing the world in itself. As Adrian Johnston says, "materialism [...] formulates itself vis-à-vis the deadlocks internal to radical transcendental idealism. On this account, materialism is philosophically tenable solely as the spectral inverse of idealism, accompanying it as the shadow cast by idealism's insurmountable incompleteness."[74] But the stark consequences of this thesis must be brought to the fore: it claims that all forms of radical idealism always already contain traces of materialism in their blind spots, *even if they do not recognize this.* Yet how are we to grasp this overlapping of the Real and the Ideal, this contradictory mode of inclusion/exclusion, internal/external, presence/absence, from within a logical space that by its very essence proclaims to exclude it? How can this impossible feat of a materialism within the cracks of idealism be accomplished?

3.3 A Metaphysics of the Disjunctive "and"

By zoning in on the limitations of idealization, the experiences of internal resistance within its own self-enclosed phenomenal space (experiences that reveal a difficult truth concerning the impotence of self-positing idealist freedom), Žižek tries to construct his own metaphysics. Only able to sustain itself from within the cracks of transcendental synthesis, his parallax ontology functions within the impossible in-between of spectral materialism and full-blown subjective idealism. But Žižek does not just claim that the latter is wholly untenable because its internal tension proclaims that there is necessarily an extimate, spectral presence of the Real within the Ideal haunting it due to its impotence to hallucinate its own world. What is more, the very nature of idealizing activity *must tell us something about the nature of the world as it is in itself* and this in two ways: firstly, we cannot just understand our own inability to grasp the Real as a mere limitation due to the finitude of human cognition, but must see this inability as revelatory of an ontological state of affairs—the subject is, after all, an event in the world, such that our entrapment in the solipsistic circuitry of ideality is always already minimally revelatory of that which we are searching for once we make a parallax shift in perspective. Secondly, the very inconsistency of our notional apparatus points to the fact that there can be no absolute constructionism, which appears to epistemologically justify the possibility of using the internal limitations and obstructions of ideality to overcome ideality's very self-enclosure. The goal of Žižek's materialism is to seek to understand the precise philosophical status of the free ideal constitution of the world and *how* and *why* this autonomous register could collapse. In other words, its defining feature is that, although it strives to maintain the ontological significance of the irreconcilable difference between materialism and idealism, it searches for a way to overcome this absolute opposition at the epistemological level so that the conflict between them does not infringe upon knowledge. If the self-grounding gesture of idealism expresses a constitutive opposition to materiality, and its failure is indicative of the phantom-like presence of the latter in the former, then this disharmonious non-relation must reveal a method of explaining it.

The underlying question guiding Žižek's ontology is therefore the following: What do the internal obstructions in idealization and the fact of ideality itself tell us about the mind-body relation: that is, our connection to the vital movement of being? Whereas there have been for some time in the contemporary intellectual scene two options for understanding the relationship of consciousness and world—their dynamic interconnectivity and unity in phenomenological accounts of the lived body or the outright rejection of the importance of lived first-person experience as a mere epiphenomenal effect due to the mechanical movement of nature or the structures guiding discourse, both of which comprise a disavowal of the primordial self-reflexive ipseity of the subject—Žižek opts for a third. What is noticeable in all of these approaches is not only an inability to grasp the true insight unveiled by a transcendental freedom, but also the latter's direct consequence: namely, the experience of idealistic disintegration and failure, the two types of experiences being so crucial in Lacanian psychoanalysis for our understanding of psychopathologies and psychogenesis that for Žižek they demand the rehabilitation of the ontologically schismatic duality opened up by Cartesian subjectivity. These are not merely revelatory of the structure of an individual psyche lost in disarray, but rather reveal a basic metaphysical truth of subjectivity by presenting a world where "the mind and body are, so to speak, negatively related—oppositional discord is, obviously, a form of relation."[75] Pointing towards the subject being more than the matter it inhabits, insofar as the symbolic structures constituting psychic life display a quasi-absolute degree of freedom from purely naturalistic activity, the psychoanalytical experience proclaims that these two zones must resist, *must be in perpetual conflict with*, one another, so that the structure of psychoanalytical subjectivity is brought close to an archaic form of modern dualism while calling for a radical reconfiguration of the latter's split between mind and body. Accordingly, Žižek's attempt to think materialism *and* idealism requires a far-reaching remodulation of the logical conjunctive between the two into a form of psychotic non-relation, insofar as transcendentalism implies a kind of negative space isolated unto itself and alienated from external reality, an isolation that is simultaneously the logical structure of normal and pathological subjective reality. But what exactly is this disjunctive "and"? Žižek's answer is unequivocal: the place of non-coincidence between mind and body, the break or rupture between these two zones of independent activity, is *nothing but the subject itself*, where the subject is transformed from a mere transcendental-epistemological construct grounded through concerns in a theory of knowledge into some kind of self-positing negativity in material being, a bone in substance forever holding apart materialism and idealism. The lacuna in contemporary thinking is therefore immense: by failing to take into account the experience of psychopathology whose possibility coincides with that of freedom (as that which institutes an infinite conflict between mind and body) its representatives fail to see the terrifying truth intrinsic to our very relation to the world: something that proclaims the need for a new paradoxical form of materialism developed within idealism to be able to combat phenomenological accounts of embodiment, postmodern theories of discourse, and cognitive science, a materialism that would be at the same time a metaphysics of the disjunctive "and."

Since it is Lacanian psychoanalysis that most strongly brings forth this disjunctive "and" as an irreducible element of human experience, Žižek's controversial thesis is not merely that Lacan brings to the fore something previously underdeveloped or neglected in other theories of subjectivity. Rather, it is much stronger—he claims that Lacan constitutes a true breakthrough in the history of thought that irreversibly restructures the field within which we can do philosophy, in a gesture that rivals that of Kant. Yet the great downfall of Lacan is that he is only interested in the systematization of the breakdowns and structural inconsistencies that define psychoanalytic experience, the antagonistic interaction of the three registers as the condition of the (im)possibility of phenomenal reality, and largely leaves unanswered the ontological question of the subject. Realizing that the Lacanian subject is lacking any explicit account of its genesis—which leads many commentators to argue that Lacan is a transcendental idealist or linguistic phenomenalist—Žižek is driven back to German Idealism to do away with this theoretical deficiency.

But if German Idealism, alongside Lacanian psychoanalysis, is able to help us elucidate the paradoxical "and" negatively linking together materialism and idealism, it is because there must be something homologous in their attempts to think the subject that would allow them to be creatively read through one another. By drawing out various passages that link the basis of subjectivity in late modern philosophy to fundamental concepts of psychoanalysis, Žižek gives flesh to this disjunctive "and" by showing how the very fact of the existence of the field of ideality illustrates the necessity of the existence of the former, a fact from which many recoil. In this respect, if the Symbolic cannot assert itself as all, it is not only because of the ever-present pressure exerted from the inside upon its constitution of phenomenal reality, but also because the very "and" that precedes and sets the stage for the autonomous universe of meaning prevents the latter from being able to posit itself as a self-sustaining, total positivity. Idealization always collapses upon itself, and it is due to its self-foundering that we are led to see that there is a disharmonious relationship between mind and body that requires a new materialism to complement its internal limitations. The fundamental problematic guiding Žižek is consequently the following: what is the relationship between (i) this abyssal void of the I; (ii) the pre-symbolic, material X; and (iii) the mediating activity of conscious ideality? What are the "meta-transcendental" conditions of possibility for the emergence of the subject that could explain the systematic discord that persists between mind and body? Can the psychoanalytical notion of the *Todestrieb* as a form of biological malfunction and its avatars in the tradition tell us something about the extra-ideal state of affairs logically preceding experience? But in order to grasp the stakes at hand in this endeavour, we must first understand the problem of nature bequeathed by Lacan and how it sets up the coordinates of his own procedure.

Notes

64. Lacan, "A Theoretical Induction to the Functions of Psychoanalysis in Criminology," in *Écrits*, p. 127/104.

65. Žižek, The Parallax View, p. 168.

66. Žižek, *Less Than Nothing*, p. 905.

67. As Žižek points out, as soon as Descartes makes the breakthrough to the *cogito*, he is forced to conclude: "[b]ut I do not yet understand sufficiently what I am—I, who now necessarily exists." What follows is a discussion that prevents the confla-tion of the *cogito* with any specific experiential content—in short, the recognition of its intrinsic vacuous nature. However, Descartes is unable to hold onto this groundbreaking insight and quickly ends up reifying the subject into a *res cogitans*. See *Meditations on First Philosophy*, trans. Donald A. Cross (Indianapolis: Hackett Publishing, 1993), pp. 18ff.; and Žižek, "Cartesian Subject versus Cartesian Theater," in *Cogito and the Unconscious*, ed. Slavoj Žižek (Durham: Duke University Press, 1998), pp. 259–61.

68. On Žižek's reading, not only is any intimate self-relation in Kant precluded in-sofar as the self qua phenomenal is denied any experience of its "true being," but subjectivity is reduced to a positive void: the ground of self-reflexive consciousness becomes a mysterious "this I or he or it (the thing) that thinks" that strangely guarantees the condition of possibility of experience. See Kant, *The Critique of Pure Reason*, A346/B404; and Žižek, *Tarrying with the Negative: Kant, Hegel, and the Critique of Ideology* (Durham: Duke University Press, 2003), pp. 12–18.

69. This concept will be explored in detail in chapter 6.

70. Žižek, *The Abyss of Freedom*, p. 45.

71. See Johnson, *Žižek's Ontology*, pp. 16–20.

72. Žižek, *The Abyss of Freedom*, p. 45.

73. Jacobi, "Idealism and Realism," in *Kant's Early Critics: The Empiricist Critique of the Theoretical Philosophy,* ed. Brigitte Sassen (Cambridge: Cambridge University Press, 2000), p. 175.

74. Johnson, *Žižek's Ontology,* p. 19.

75. Ibid., p. 56. This is Johnston's thesis about the nuance of Lacanian-Žižekian subjectivity.

Chapter 4
The Problem of Nature in the Lacanian Subject
The Obscure Origins of the Symbolic

In this chapter I will lay out various theoretical problems plaguing Lacan
that serve as the starting point for Žižek's own endeavour. Beginning
with a precursory analysis of Žižek's identification of the Cartesian and
psychoanalytical subjects, I move on to a discussion of the intrinsic
limitations of Lacan's psychoanalytical methodology for understanding
the ontologico-foundational basis of subjectivity. By focusing on the self-
grounding, non-natural function of images and words, especially the
transcendental reflexivity underlying both, Lacanian psychoanalysis has a
tendency to perceive them as an external parasite that derails the substantial
unity of the body. But this tendency renders problematic any account of
how images and words could successfully implant themselves, thus leaving
the Symbolic itself potentially without theoretical justification. Seeing an
uncanny structural homology here between post-Kantian idealism and the
legacy bestowed upon us by Lacan, Žižek returns to Hegel and Schelling
with the conviction that a combination of psychoanalysis with late German
Idealist metaphysics could help us articulate the paradoxical emergence of
subjectivity.

4.1 An Uncanny Pair: The Cartesian and Psychoanalytical Subjects

Lacan's and Žižek's situating of the psychoanalytical discourse within the trajectory of modern transcendental philosophy could appear surprising. Following the works of Freud, it is clear that the father of psychoanalysis understands the psychoanalytical subject as intrinsically *anti*-Cartesian. Whereas the *cogito* conjures forth the idea of an untouchable conscious freedom, of complete self-mastery and perfect self-transparency as guaranteed by our capacities of reason, ratiocination, and deliberation, the Freudian unconscious does not merely haphazardly obstruct existential self-familiarity like some kind of accidental feature of human being, but rather puts all conscious activity in the clutches of a mysterious, obscure Other that by definition resists all ideational (re)presentation. The goal of modern philosophy as the articulation of a sound foundation for systematic philosophy through the free mediation/idealization of the world by means of the rational, self-grounding activity of consciousness is by definition foreclosed, for the very process of (re)constituting reality by the I rests upon a structurally *non*-representational process, a process that constantly risks interfering with the subject's synthetic mediation of self and world. It is no longer the subjective I that "thinks," but the impersonal, non-subjective *Es* (the id): the "it" thinks in the same way that "it" rains. So how can "the subject of the unconscious [be] none other than that of the Cartesian *cogito*"?[76]

Although this may be true it is evident that, despite the qualitative remodulation that subjectivity undergoes in Freudian psychoanalysis, especially in terms of the nature and scope of conscious personality, there is nevertheless a series of homologous structures at the heart of both the psychoanalytical and modern Cartesian subjects. Most fundamentally, both rely on the splitting of being into two separate zones, the mental and the material, and the inability to reduce one to the other. Even if Freud's later theoretical works exhibit a propensity to reduce psychic processes to the vital force of biological activity, this very attempt self-destructs (as Lacan makes clear) in the face of the brute autonomy of images and words in his analyses over and against their subsumption within the pulsating activity of nerves or the movement of instincts. There always remains a chasm separating human psychological life from the mere flux of corporeal or instinctual energetics, because ideality and materiality are operationally different registers in terms of their inner articulation or logical makeup. For Žižek, it is not a question of the actual doctrine espoused by Descartes with respect to his own doctrine of the *cogito* and the essence of consciousness it entails, but rather of various theoretical potentialities and possibilities exhibited by *the very structure inherent in his concept of subjectivity*, which come to the fore in the aftermath of psychoanalysis.

Consequently, what Žižek perceives in the Cartesian subject and its various reworkings is the possibility of extracting theoretical resources from it that could be used to help explicate the enigma of human freedom and the essence of personality as revealed in the psychoanalytical experience of the conflictual (non-)relation that holds between mind and body. In Cartesianism and psychoanalysis, we do not come across a mere conceptually regulative difference between the arena of human subjective activity and the raw processes of brute material nature, which would enable both to enjoy a strong degree of epistemic autonomy insofar as both could self-actualize themselves in terms of a standalone language game with the appearance of being intrinsically incommensurate to one another despite being on the ontological level fundamentally one. Žižek is unwilling to reduce this difference to the level of useful "working distinctions" that have the status of an "as if," for consciousness refuses to be completely naturalized. In a similar vein, in contradistinction to a theory of monism according to which both are merely seen as attributes of a single, overarching whole (however it may be conceived) and whereby both would offer differing expressions of an ultimately identical self-same reality, Žižek wants to bestow ontological heft upon the difference. The claim is that any account of subjectivity that attempts to reduce conscious experience to the register of a pure material or substance caught within self-sustaining laws, whether it be the neuronal Real, vitalistic energetics, or nature as all, not only does not take heed of the radical metaphysical implications of the psychoanalytical experience, but is also by consequence unable to propound a satisfactory account of what it is to be a human and our relation to the world.

In Žižek's view, the theoretical advantage of Cartesianism and psychoanalysis is their defence of the profound ontological difference between the registers of objective material corporeality and (inter)subjective cultural and psychic experience. Difference is just another word for an irresolvable two-way resistance that constitutes a battleground of conflicting, oppositional systems and thereby sets the very stage for the experiential reality that we find ourselves thrown into. To speak in Freudian parlance, one cannot understand consciousness merely in terms of the id-forces that comprise the bodily substrate of the libidinal-material basis of human existence. Although they may serve as the ontologico-foundational basis for all psychic and ultimately phenomenological life, they are philosophically inadequate to explain the full essence of personality and its pathologies insofar as the latter are constituted through the antagonistic interaction of forces that emerge within the tripartite field of id, ego, and superego. None of these alone would be able to articulate what it is to be a human subject, but must be implicated within an intricate psychological trinitarian logic if we are to hope to come to terms with ourselves and our world of experience. Even though the ego and superego arise out of the pre-subjective activity of the id—the id immanently generates the ego out of itself as a way to cope with its own organic insufficiency and primordial *Hilflosigkeit* to deal with the demands of its external environment—they are not dependent upon it for their being, their very vitality, each constituting a self-subsisting system enjoying a level of genuine autonomy and irreducibility to the other. This very structure of independence is also hinted at in the breakthrough that is the Cartesian subject, which argues that although we could attempt to understand the ideality of spirit by recourse to the mechanics of nature, this attempt would ultimately collapse upon itself because something essential would be lost. It is not that the mechanical externality that forms the causal determinacy of the body's extensive field as the obscure ground of mind and its sensations is a mere underdetermination of mental activity. Descartes' claim is much stronger: it is ultimately incapable of helping us establish the nature of subjectivity, even if some kind of paradoxical non-relation must nevertheless be said to hold between the two; the *cogito*'s founding gesture exhibits an irreducible self-grounding that rejects mechanical externality in all of its modes (or however it may be reworked by reinterpreting it as nature, vitalistic energetics, the neuronal Real, etc.) in a process that not only makes it distinctively non-natural in terms of its inner structuration, but also thereby guarantees its capacity for transcendental self-determination and its incommensurability with other logical registers. The question is how we can explain this ontological difference opened up by Cartesianism with the aid of psychoanalysis, and vice versa.

4.2 Lacan, *antiphusis*, and the Parasite of Images and Words

In order to expand upon this problematic, two comments can be made that will enable us to uncover the conceptual limitations inherent to the psychoanalytical theory of subjectivity and that allow us in turn to draw out its similarities with the central conceptual problems plaguing post-Kantian German Idealism as bestowed upon it by its Cartesian heritage. First, for psychoanalysis, the language that we use mediates our very experience of the biological constitution of the body in such a way that there is a radical degree of separation between the idealization of the givenness of the flesh and its objective, extra-subjective existence in itself. Freud speaks of people who suffer from paralysis of a certain part of their body, although scientifically speaking the paralysis does not coincide with where the nerve anatomically ends, and when this is pointed out the pain ceases. Here it is the common, everyday belief of where a nerve ends and begins that structures the symptom. Thus, understood as a complex cultural phenomenon and not just grammatical structures of syntax and morphology, language shows itself as an irreducible element of experience and points to a discordant relationship between mind and body. Second, as arising from the facticity of cultural, historical experience, language appears to emerge out of a symbolic interpersonal network of meaning that operates according to its own intrinsic and self-unfolding logical matrix. Even if it has a *basis* in our physiology (vocal folds) and neurology (language centres in the brain), words themselves appear to exist in an autonomous world of their own that, in many ways, shows itself as a kind of external parasitic attachment to the biological unity of the body. Taken together, these two points assert more than the fact that both registers, the Symbolic and the corpo-Real, exist in disunion: the former even appears to manifest itself as a "psychotic" withdrawal from the latter into some kind of self-enclosed sphere. What is obvious from this is not only the intrinsic Cartesian structure of the psychoanalytical subject—here the deadlock of ontological dualism is amplified, brought to its extreme, by the *advocation* of a constitutive dissonance—but that the latter's philosophical legitimacy depends upon the precise articulation of the delicate relation between these two mutually incommensurate spheres. Although these zones are infinitely conflictual and never to be harmonized, they must nevertheless be somehow related if the system is to be held together. The Cartesian problem of the mind-body relation is consequently inverted: the issue at hand is not how both can be in unison with one another through some kind of occasionalism, but how the conflictual gap that separates them emerged in the first place so that there can never be a harmony or overlapping of each sphere.

Both Freud and Lacan spend the majority of their careers elaborating this field of disparate spheres whose interaction generates and constitutes personality. Rereading Freud through contemporary developments in linguistics and structuralism and even drawing upon cybernetics, Lacan attempts to reconfigure our understanding of the self in what he believes to be a more scientific manner than Freud could by excavating the strict logical structures constituting the condition of the possibility of the psychoanalytical subject: that is, the irreducibly non-natural basis of experience and the mind-body discord it reveals. There is something intrinsically transcendental about the project, even if the end result is apparently quite removed from the Kantian analysis of consciousness in the *Critique of Pure Reason*, Fichte's *Wissenschaftslehre*, or later attempts such as Husserl's transcendental idealism. Any project that advocates the autonomy of subjectivity over materiality and a form of self-grounding idealization or symbolization of reality must at some level seem so, for the question of the condition of the possibility of experiential reality does not pose itself in more "realist-inclined" philosophies insofar as experience is here seen as just the effect or another instantiation of a large set of dynamic relations between objects in the world. As a consequence, fighting against Freud's attempt to biologize/naturalize the unconscious by highlighting that one can never escape the ultimate primacy of *images* and of *words* in psychoanalysis, Lacan relentlessly maintains what he perceives as the Cartesian essence of subjectivity. Just as the Kantian, the Fichtean, and even to a certain extent the Husserlian transcendental ego grounds itself and the fabric of the world of its experience in a moment of absolute freedom that establishes an insurmountable rupture between reflexive self-consciousness and the causal mechanics of nature, within Lacanian psychoanalysis we encounter the same logical move, but merely displaced. In the latter it is not a subject in any traditional sense, but rather the self-generating play of signifiers within the web of the Symbolic that expresses the impossibility of articulating a comprehensive, satisfactory psychological theory of the self only by recourse to the pulsations of neurological activity or biological instincts. There are two principal reasons for this. First, the Symbolic constitutes the possibility of the orbit of the Imaginary within phenomenological experience in such a way that it autonomously mediates *all* contact with the outside world, thus diminishing the latter's importance; second, as a consequence, it represents the predominance of *non-natural* (= irreducible to the ebb and flow of the material-objective world) influences in the explanation of the essence of psychic life. It is in this precise manner that the ciphering activity of the Symbolic can be said to obey its own self-grounding transcendental logic and be that which sustains the primordiality of the real-ideal divide: "subjectivity has no relationship to the Real, but rather to a syntax which is engendered by the signifying mark."[77]

Accordingly, one can now understand why Lacan defines the object of psychoanalysis in "The Direction of the Treatment and the Principles of its Power" as "*antiphusis.*"[78] With this terminological choice he is drawing our attention to the fact that what analysis deals with is not something natural in any sense of the nature investigated by science or understood by our common sense. Analysis operates at a level that is, by definition, incommensurate with natural laws. The effect of this designation is much greater than it may initially appear, for the human subject is characterized as "non-natural" not only insofar as the structural fabric forming the base of conscious experience enjoys a freedom over and above, or an ontological heft irreducible to, the flux of nature, but also because it transcendentally alienates us from the immediacy of the corpo-Real of our body, the ground of our objective substantial being, as the very condition of our possibility of what we call experience. Images and words not only *precede* us historically in terms of the temporal genesis of our identities (we are often *named* before we are *conceived*: a space is always already carved up for us in the symbolic universe before we can be said to exist in the Real) but also structure the logico-formal space that makes personality possible in such a way as to prevent us from having a genuine access to the brute reality of our own "intimate" being as it is *an sich*. After the I is spoken, that is, after self-reflexive subjectivity emerges, an experience of the Real is only possible through the ideational (re)presenting capacity of a symbolic network of signifiers, thus becoming *impossible*: a mysterious, ever-elusive X. As soon as we enter language, the Real as a time of "fullness," "immediacy," and "complete immersion," if ever there was one, is subsequently lost forever, leaving us trapped within the fragmented, ontologically solipsistic world opened up through the Symbolic-Imaginary matrix.

Insofar as the symbolic network simultaneously constitutes the underlying structural support of experience *and* mediates all our contact with an external, subject-independent reality, Lacanian psychoanalysis appears to be a completely self-grounding transcendental idealism in the spirit of Kant. Whatever the human subject is, it is *not* natural in the same sense as other objects within phenomenal reality, even those that appear to have some kind of spontaneous connection with that which they find around them. Indeed, according to Lacan even animals have a kind of *knowledge in the Real*[79] that is missing in us due to the Symbolic. Although language is intimately linked with "our" freedom—and "our" *madness*, we must never forget, the two being structurally identical—nevertheless it thus appears as some kind of alien, foreign presence that cannot be understood in terms of the categories of the world because it has no analogue within it. But then the question arises: where do these transcendental structures come from? How and why do they irredeemably separate the human subject from the vital ebb and flow of nature? As a science of the symbolic network that constitutes the nature of personality and self-conscious experience, if psychoanalysis is unable to articulate the origins of these non-natural structures and the process of their genesis, it itself rests groundless insofar as the object of its inquiry remains unable to explain its own theoretical, ontogenetic basis: that is, how it itself is possible as a discourse.

As Fichte, Schelling, and Hegel looked upon Kant's critical philosophy, they themselves were taken by a similar problem concerning the heritage bestowed upon them. They asked themselves how the transcendental structures of subjectivity could be explained in a more comprehensive manner, how and why they emerged in the first place, and why they were as such necessary for the very possibility of experience. They held the brute givenness of the categories of understanding to be philosophically unacceptable and took it upon themselves to explore the Achilles' heel of the entire critical system. Their guiding intuition was that by undertaking an explanation of their genesis they would not only save the Kantian breakthrough, but also delve into the wider implications of the subject as propounded by it. Similarly, there is a brute givenness in Lacan's account of the transcendentality of the symbolic matrix because he never gives an account of its origins. When one reads his early and middle works, one is consequently struck by the impression that images and words are a purely external force that attacks the raw unity of the body and devastates it from the outside, thereby creating a denaturalized human subject out of a preexisting substantial whole. There is a movement from uncontaminated instinctual being within the positive order of the Real—the oneness of the body, the immediacy of an organic nature—to a being that speaks, to words as intruders that radically split the subject, destroying its immersion in objective being. The network of the Symbolic comes from an infinite elsewhere ravaging the unity of substance and precluding the possibility of a biologically closed libidinal economy as an inborn, innate movement of energy defined by materially articulated, instinctual schemata. Whereas in the animal kingdom this schema directs bodily energy towards various objects that it needs within its immediate environment through a kind of immanent causal push, language eternally obstructs the dialectic of need and satisfaction, fullness and lack, by instituting an ontological going-haywire in being. Preventing the flow of the search for homeostatic constancy, the subject is thrown into the endless deferral of desire and structurally loses the possibility of attaining its object. Instead of predetermined, biological goals, we are left with the *objet petit a*:

> [T]he standard Lacanian theme in the 1950s and 1960s was the unsurmountable opposition between the animal universe of imaginary captivity, of the balanced mirror-relationship between *Innenwelt* and *Aussenwelt*, and the human universe

of symbolic negativity, imbalance. Lacan thereby fully participates in the line of thought that begins with Hegel, according to which man is "nature sick unto death," a being forever marked by traumatic misplacement, thrown "out of joint," lacking its proper place, in contrast to an animal which always fits into its environment, that is to say, is immediately "grown into" it. Symptomatic here is Lacan's "mechanistic" metaphorics: an almost celebratory characterizing of the symbolic order as an automaton that follows its path, totally impervious to human emotions and needs—language is a parasitic entity that battens on the human animal, throwing his or her life rhythm off balance, derailing it, subordinating it to its own brutally imposed circuit.[80]

Within this advocacy of a split between the cyclical, balanced world of nature and the derailed being of man, the following theoretical concerns immediately emerge: how does the symbolic-imaginary matrix give rise to itself through a transcendental act of self-positing? How is it able to take control of and infiltrate the body, apparently lacerating its objective unity? If the symbolic order is really an external force, an alien blow, that in some way tears apart or obstructs the body's knowledge in the Real, how is it able to sustain itself in face of the corpo-Real of the biological organism? To put it another way, why is it not "rejected by this economy in a manner analogous to failed organ transplants"?[81] The problem of the psychoanalytical constitution of human experience opens up unto the extra-psychological/meta-transcendental conditions or state of affairs that must have preceded the emergence of the subject if we are to give a complete account of the psyche as such. Psychoanalysis must explain its own beginnings in a lost ontological time in a move similar to how the categories of the understanding must not be taken as mere elementary facts liberated from the theoretical exigency of explaining their genesis. Just as the history of the reception of Kantian idealism has shown that it must open up onto a comprehensive metaphysics that is inclusive of it, so too we must try to develop a metaphysics in the wake of psychoanalysis.

4.3 German Idealism, Psychoanalysis, and the Quest for the Birthplace of the Transcendental

Yet after the 1950s and 1960s, we see within Lacanian psychoanalysis a developing preoccupation with the ontologico-foundational basis of the subject. After the period of Lacan's "The Direction of the Treatment and the Principles of its Power" (1958), which defines the object of psychoanalysis as "*antiphusis*," there is a profound shift in the meaning of this concept that is highly significant for the development of a metaphysics capable of explicating and thus justifying the psychoanalytical subject. Whereas the early to middle Lacan focuses on the derailing capacity of images that set the stage for words as that which parasitizes the corpo-Real of the body, which makes the human subject radically non-natural by preventing its immersion in the autopoietic, self-regulating unity of positive organic being by creating an alienating self-distance within it, we encounter in the late Lacan a reconceptualization of the problematic. His new emphasis on the Real proclaims that one must radicalize this notion of self-distance. The object of psychoanalysis and by consequence the human subject are not *antiphysical* because images and words are an infinite Other to nature, an external alterity that arises *ex nihilo* only to penetrate into its secret chamber   like a vandal and deface its sacred inviolability. The incommensurability lies elsewhere: images and language cannot be the *cause* of the denaturalization of the human subject; there must be something in nature itself that *immanently* moves it toward denaturalization. In short, *nature itself is antiphusis, self-sabotaging, self-lacerating.*

Although this represents a fundamental change in the meaning of the category of the non-natural, it only serves as a beginning. Insofar as the psychoanalytical experience is engulfed by images and words, which means that it is predominately ridden by non-biological influences, the only way to philosophically ground the primacy of psychoanalysis is to elaborate an underlying ontology that could explain how the subject could have emerged out a biological field that it presents itself as *irreducible to.* The theoretical merit of the Lacanian project is dependent upon the articulation of the workings of substantial reality that renders possible the birth of a more-than-material subjectivity out of its material *Grund* (to borrow an expression from Adrian Johnston), a paradoxical *ontologization* of the transcendental structures that constitute and found experience by separating themselves from and effacing their ontological foundation. It is exactly this problematic that thematically binds together the theoretical concerns of the psychoanalytical and German Idealist traditions, for according to the latter the only way to save the breakthrough of the Kantian critical system is to find a way, from within the self-founding idealism that it advocates, to reach out into the extra-subjective Real, or to speak in its parlance, the field of noumena, and ground it within a system that does not represent a *return* to previous modes of thinking (naïve dogmatic realism) but rather somehow manages to reach the Real through the Ideal despite the self-enclosed, self-subsistent ideal activity of consciousness. But how? The very trap in which we find ourselves proves to hold the way out:

> We can now see in what sense Hegel's logic remains "transcendental" in the strict Kantian sense—that is, in what sense its notional network is not merely formal, but constitutive of reality itself, whose categorical structure it describes. Hegel's *Logic* is the inherent tension in the status of every determinate/limited category: each concept is simultaneously *necessary* (i.e. indispensable if we are to conceive reality, its underlying ontological structure) and *impossible* (i.e. self-refuting, inconsistent: the moment we fully and consequently "apply" it to reality, it disintegrates and/or turns into its opposite). This notional tension/contradiction is simultaneously the ultimate *spiritus movens* of "reality" itself: far from signalling the failure of our thought to grasp reality, the inherent inconsistency of our notional apparatus is the ultimate proof that our thought is not merely a logical game we play but is able to reach reality itself, expressing its inherent structuring principle.[82]

Looking back at the history of the inner development of modern transcendental philosophy, Žižek sees a structural homology to his own task of searching for the ontogenetic condition of the possibility of the psychoanalytical subject, a question left unanswered by Freud and Lacan, in the tradition's attempt to find a way to construct a metaphysics *from within the internal deadlock of transcendental idealism*. If our generation of experience proves itself to be unable to posit itself as an absolute and unbridled hallucination of objects, then we must encounter some kind of paradoxical limit to our autonomous ciphering and constitution of phenomenal reality from within; the impasses obstructing the self-grounding idealization of the world demonstrate that, although we are forever stuck within ideality, we are not simply prisoners of the completely solipsistic sphere of the self-referential, masturbatory play of thought within thought and that a metaphysics of the Real, an account of the noumenal, appears to be theoretically possible. The inassimilable kernel of the Real within our notional, symbolic code points to the paradoxical negative coinciding of inside with outside, the Real and the Ideal, *within* thinking: the cracks of ideality cast an abyssal shadow that opens up onto the materiality of being, albeit only as refracted through the impossibilities of the Ideal, in such a way that tarrying with the latter offers a way to develop idealism into a science of the Real. Idealism has been overcome because the materialism-idealism distinction has become intra-discursive, that is, internal to idealism itself. In this sense, we should not understand Žižek's proclamation of Hegel's "transcendentalism" to say that Hegel, like Kant, remains at the level of a pure subjectivism: due to the constitutive movement of notional tension intrinsic to the concept of dialectics, not only is idealism prevented from being *subjective*, but, more strongly, "[t]he opposition between idealistic and realistic philosophy is therefore without meaning," which is why idealism can be said to be *absolute*.[83] Embracing the paradox of the critical system, its breakthrough articulation of the irreducible idealizing activity of consciousness, the mediative structures that freely transcendentally constitute the fabric of experience, Hegel's philosophy is a daring attempt to rethink the possibility of a metaphysics in the wake of the Kantian revolution, to carve a space between idealistic ontological solipsism and a speculative materialism *within the former*. It is only within such a space that the question: "What is the transcendental subject's relation to nature?" or, in Lacanian parlance, "What is the Symbolic's relation to the pre-symbolic Real?" can be asked.

Žižek's retrieval of the *cogito* and his reactualization of German Idealism are therefore irrevocably caught up in his own attempt to develop a metaphysics of the Real able to explicate the obscure grounds of the psychoanalytical subject. Attempting to excavate the ontological edifice implied by the latter, his more overtly theoretical works pass through modern to late modern philosophy by means of an intuition of a basic structural parallelism binding together such seemingly different traditions. Although the starting point is *always* psychoanalysis—"psychoanalysis is ultimately a tool to reactualize, to render actual for today's time, the legacy of German Idealism"[84]—it is clear that Žižek does not understand his work as an intrusion or unmethodological tearing apart of the tradition according to extrinsic philosophical principles he is imposing upon it. In fact, for him, the psychoanalytical subject is not merely a direct consequence of German Idealism's grounding insights—there is actually something intrinsically *identical* in these traditions, so much so that it seems that the *only* way to fully realize the former is to supplement it with the latter and vice versa, insofar as they are both really dealing with the same central issues that each fail in their own way to adequately thematize. Describing his own project, Žižek says:

> If you were to ask me at gunpoint, like Hollywood producers who are too stupid to read books and say, "give me the punchline," and were to demand, "Three sentences. *What* are you really trying to do?" I would say, Screw ideology. Screw movie analyses. What really interests me is the following insight: if you look at the very core of psychoanalytic theory, of which even Freud was not aware, it's properly read *death drive*—this idea of beyond the pleasure principle, self-sabotaging, etc.—the only way to read this properly is to read it against the background of the notion of subjectivity as self-relating negativity in German Idealism. That is to say, I just take literally Lacan's indication that the subject of psychoanalysis is the Cartesian cogito—of course, I would add, as reread by Kant, Schelling, and Hegel.[85]

By zoning in on this basic identity, Žižek's philosophy doesn't lose methodological rigor, as if it made him blind to other, more broad-reaching concerns in the tradition, thereby reducing his thinking to a mere haphazard picking out of various conceptual structures and ideas that are useful for his own project to the neglect of others. Rather, it enables him to show

how there is an unconscious, disavowed *Grundlogik* that repeats and self-unfolds throughout modern transcendental philosophy and finally comes out into the open with the advent of psychoanalysis, which shows itself as the culmination of this entire lineage. Because Žižek perceives some kind of self-developing truth inherent within the tradition that binds it together with psychoanalysis, his reading is pushed on by a sense of fidelity to the movement as such so that his return to German Idealism resembles Fichte's, Hegel's, and Schelling's return to Kant[86] just as much as Lacan's return to Freud: what is at stake is never merely textual faithfulness, but a hidden kernel of truth that has been simultaneously opened up and obscured by the tradition itself.

The effect here is twofold: while psychoanalysis allows us to reconstruct retroactively the *Grundlogik* inherent in the German Idealist account of subjectivity by bringing to the fore the relevance of previously underemphasized concepts and textual moves, this reconstruction of its fundamental concepts also allows us to elaborate our understanding of the psychoanalytical subject. It is not merely that psychoanalysis reveals a hidden unconscious logic at work throughout tradition; the backward retroactive glance is simultaneously a forward-looking task that tries to pave the way for the new. Žižek's investigation into the history of philosophy is never a mere activity of philological exegesis, the retrieval of the "primordial" meaning of a text, but a creative generation of new concepts that, paradoxically, must be said to have been already present in the now lost factical past, yet to have existed there in the paradoxical temporality of a *futur antérieur* ("I will have been") whose contours are now first visible in the *après-coup* reconstruction of said past. A repetition is always the establishment of a difference, so that the legitimacy of Žižek's reading rests not so much upon his apparent "lack" of faithfulness to the words or the spirit of the great German philosophers, but how this temporal intersection of philosophico-psychoanalytical interpretation, the space within which Žižek effectuates his reactualization, functions and realizes itself. But what *is* the true breakthrough of the German Idealist and psychoanalytic traditions and why can only a psychoanalytical dialogue between the two enable us to see the conceptual impetus underlying the former's unconscious *Grundlogik* and also to come to terms with the ontology of the subject? Žižek's answer

not only questions our conventional reading of this movement, but more
fundamentally challenges our very conception of ourselves and the world.

Notes

76. Žižek, *Less Than Nothing*, p. 632.

77. See Lacan, "Seminar on 'The Purloined Letter,'" in *Écrits*, p. 51/38. I capitalize "the Real" for consistency.

78. Lacan, "The Direction of the Treatment and the Principles of Its Power," in *Écrits*, p. 615/514.

79. Knowledge in the Real (*savoir dans le réel*) refers to the fact that "it is as if there is a knowledge of the laws of nature directly inscribed into the Real of natural objects and processes—for instance, a stone 'knows' what laws of gravity to obey when it is falling." Žižek, *How to Read Lacan* (New York: W. W. Norton, 2007), pp. 74–75.

80. Žižek, *The Indivisible Remainder*, p. 218.

81. Johnston, *Žižek's Ontology*, p. 271.

82. Žižek, *The Ticklish Subject*, pp. 98–99.

83. Hegel, *The Science of Logic*, trans. George di Giovanni (Cambridge: Cambridge University Press, 2010), p. 124.

84. Žižek, "Liberation Hurts."

85. Ibid.

86. "The Kantian philosophy needed to have its spirit distinguished from its letter." Hegel, *The Difference between Fichte's and Schelling's System of Philosophy*, trans. H. S. Harris and Walter Cerf (Albany: SUNY Press, 1977), p. 79. Fichte's says the same thing: Kant should be "studied, not as the Kantians without exception have studied him (holding on to the literal text [...]), but rather on the basis of what he actually says, raising oneself to what he does not say but which he must assume in order to be able to say what he does." Fichte, *The Science of Knowing: Fichte's 1804 Lectures on the Wissenschaftslehre*, trans. Walter E. Wright (Albany: SUNY Press, 2005), p. 30.

II
Nature Torn Apart

Chapter 5
Kant, *Todestrieb*, and Beyond the Pleasure Principle
The Unruly Basis of Transcendental Freedom

In this chapter I begin an examination of Žižek's metaphysics by showing how the thematic intersection between German Idealism and psychoanalysis allows him to develop a highly original approach to the transcendental. Beginning with a brief discussion of Adrian Johnston's summary of Lacan's passing remarks on nature in largely unavailable seminars stemming from the late period, I then precede to analyze how these remarks lay the foundation for Žižek's own radical rethinking of the Symbolic-Real relationship. Trying to comprehend the emergence of the Symbolic, Žižek attempts to demonstrate that the very fact of its existence must be revelatory of some ontological process that set the stage for its immanent genesis out of the Real as an extimate Other, even if, in turn, it makes the very Real from which it arose an impossible concept. Perceiving the key for understanding this paradoxical point of discordant (non-) relation between the pre-subjective Real and the transcendental matrix of the Symbolic in the *Todestrieb*, and following Lacan's claim that "Kant's practical philosophy [is] the starting point of the lineage culminating in Freud's invention of psychoanalysis,"[87] Žižek reactualizes the legacy of German Idealism in order to articulate his own parallax ontology through an intuition of a fundamental identity between Kantian transcendentalism and psychoanalysis as established in the former's concept of the primordial unruliness and diabolical evil at the core of subjectivity.

5.1 From the Rottenness of Nature...

Although Lacan lacks an explicitly developed philosophy of nature as a complement to his structuralist metapsychology, throughout his career we see a growing interest in and appreciation for the underlying ontology implied by his theory of the subject. Adrian Johnston succinctly describes the theoretical situation plaguing the late Lacan in his shift from the primacy of the Symbolic to that of the Real, a problematic of utmost importance for understanding the deficiency in Lacanian psychoanalysis that guides Žižek's own project:

> A psychoanalytically influenced theory of the subject that fails to furnish a basic delineation of human nature as the precondition for the genesis of subjectivity is groundless, incapable of explaining a foundational dimension of its object of inquiry.
>
> In the later seminars of the 1970s, a series of somewhat cryptic remarks testify to Lacan's awareness of the need to redefine nature itself in order to account for why human nature is predisposed to being thoroughly altered by the denaturalizing mediation of socio-symbolic structures. In both the twenty-first and twenty-fourth seminars, Lacan contends that nature is far from being entirely natural. However, this isn't just a slightly reworked reiteration of his earlier remarks from the 1950s about humanity's denaturalized nature. Rather than grounding his assertions here by invoking the externally imposed intrusion of images and signifiers as the ultimate cause of the denaturalization involved in subjectification, Lacan takes the additional step of pointing to something within nature itself that inclines it in the direction of its own effacement.[88]

What is missing in Lacan, however, is a fully worked out account of the consequences of this shift, a detailed investigation into the paradoxical ground of the subject intrinsic to the very gesture of psychoanalysis. Yet he makes a crucial advance by suggesting that the Real is not to be, despite the fact that we can only posit its existence from within the differential network of signifiers, merely taken as that which must be said to *logically* precede the emergence of the linguistic subject, but also as that which *renders the latter in a certain sense possible* by virtue of a self-destructive tendency always already within it that opens up the space for its infinite loss to self through the colonizing activity of images and words. We encounter a metaphysical thesis: subjectivity does not come on the scene as a scar inflicted upon an otherwise harmonious nature, as a disturbance of its symphonized order by means of a haphazard intrusion into its sphere of non-natural influences that produce an accidental zone of ontological non-coincidence. The psychoanalytical experience is, rather, revelatory of something much more primordial: namely, that *nature itself must be always already antiphusis, self-sabotaging, self-lacerating, and responsible for its own demise in the human being's denaturalized essence*. But why?

> Lacan provides only a few hints. At one point, he identifies "liberty" (*liberté*) with "the non-existence of the sexual relationship," which, in light of the above, can be understood as indicating that the freedom enjoyed by the autonomous subject is made possible by the lack of an integrated organic foundation as the grounding basis of the subject's being. Similarly, several years later, Lacan speaks of nature as not all that natural due to being internally plagued by "rottenness" (*pourriture*), by a decay or defect out of which culture (as *antiphusis*) bubbles forth (*bouillonner*). Viewed thus, human nature is naturally destined for denaturalization. Put differently, more-than-material subjectivity immanently arises out of the dysfunctionality of a libidinal-material ground.[89]

Yet it would perhaps be erroneous to say that this theoretical awareness is limited to the late Lacan's move from the primacy of the Symbolic towards that of the Real. As early as 1949 in his work on the Imaginary and the mirror stage, Lacan had already said that "these reflections lead me to recognize in the spatial capture manifested by the mirror stage, the effect in man, even prior to this social dialectic, of an organic inadequacy of his natural reality—assuming we can give some meaning to the word 'nature,'" an inadequacy that points to "a certain dehiscence at the very heart of the organism, a primordial Discord betrayed by the signs of malaise and motor uncoordination of the neonatal months"[90] which is, in fact, responsible for the alteration we see in our relationship to nature in comparison with other animals insofar as it represents "the shattering of the *Innenwelt* and *Umwelt* circle"[91] and thus functions as the true "intersection of nature and culture."[92] Here it is noteworthy to mention that the French word *stade* does not completely map onto the English *stage*. Although it does correspond in one of its principal meanings to the latter (a distinct stage in a process of evolution: *les stades de la vie*) it also means *stadium* (a terrain or area where something takes place) and thus signifies a primordial scene constituting the foundation or arena within/through which an activity unfolds. Consequently, Lacan's thesis is that the mirror stage can never be subsumed in a later phase of development, forcing us to conclude that, even in the early period, it must necessarily refer to some kind of self-effacing force immanent within nature that gives rise to and simultaneously sustains the ontogenetic condition of the possibility of the paradoxical emergence of a more-than-material subject. This force thereby institutes the infinitely denaturalizing process of flirtation with images and symbolic castration, so that organic discord in the motor coordination of the body is not a mere failure of the biological system but also a "positive" support that persists in its very non-naturalness even after the Imaginary and the Symbolic have taken hold as their dark origin. If the quasi-experience of dismemberment is to be taken as originary, as that which incites the libidinal investment of the captivating mirror picture the human infant sees of itself as the beginning of psychogenesis by letting itself be alienated by the Otherness of images and words, then nature here must also be seen—at least in the case of human being—as a festering, half-living corpse. The shift of emphasis in the late seminars is already contained within the founding texts of Lacanian psychoanalysis, which not only suggests their central thematic unity, despite the stark differences that they may exhibit, but more strongly a historical unfolding that follows an internal development conforming to the model of the Hegelian movement from the in-itself to the for-itself.

But we should avoid looking at the various hints and suggestions in the late Lacan that gesture towards the character of the material edifice upon which the subject rests as a mere immanent elaboration of the implications of his previously laid out position, given that there are important changes of position in the development of his thinking. What is important is not the unity or disunity of Lacan, but rather the radicality and nuance inherent in his thinking of the subject as brought to the fore when we focus on this very specific constellation of problems hovering around the obscure relation between nature and the essence of human being, a constellation that proposes a frightening metaphysical conception of the world, albeit only implicitly. Synonymous with the irrevocable organic inadequacy of its biological prematurity at birth, and functioning as such as the basis for full-fledged subjectivity, the primordial *Hilflosigkeit* of the human infant already points toward a vision of the world that exceeds the constraints of psychoanalysis as a mere investigation into psychogenesis and its pathologies as to be dealt with in the psychiatric setting. Driven by its own concerns, psychoanalysis—indeed, perhaps like any strong theory of subjectivity— offers a metaphysics, or at least *must become a metaphysics*, since we can never safely isolate the subject under investigation from the greater scheme of ontology within which it is inscribed as a thing, process, or event. The subject *is*. What Lacan proclaims about its modality of "being" is that subjectivity can no longer be perceived as unnatural in the sense of an external-parasitical *invasion* into the vital movement of nature through the alienating effects of flirtatious images and castrating words, which somehow spoil or disfigure its pure unity by disrupting the smooth functioning of its immanent laws. The necessary theoretical posit of an originary rottenness of nature contends that there was never a realm of innocence, a pre-symbolic whole whose peaceful in-itself precluded division, a self-pervasive oneness whose unbroken energetic flow was then interrupted through the advent of language, which would be said not only to forever ideally fragment and lacerate it through artificial categories, but more disconcertingly to upset the very positivity of its movement, the cyclical repetition of things in the Real of nature, by short-circuiting the body's self-determining laws striving after homeostatic balance by giving rise to desire. No: it is not that it is *only here* that we see a snag, a breakdown, in the natural flow of things. Lacan's claim is much stronger: nature, in some sense, was *never completely natural* (it is in this spirit that we should interpret Lacan's hesitation in "The Mirror Stage as Formative of the Function of the I as Revealed in Psychoanalytical Experience" of being able to "give some meaning to the word 'nature'"[93]).

For Žižek, it is precisely this intuition of a necessary moment of negativity, which simultaneously rots nature from the inside out and gestures towards its constitutive weakness, that allows us to come to terms with the Symbolic-Real relation in Lacanian psychoanalysis. It alludes to the necessity of a metaphysics of the Real to explicate what the subject truly is and sketches its contours. Yet due to his conceptual reworking of Lacan, Žižek is led to part ways with and challenge many conventional ways of understanding this relation. Bruce Fink, for example, says:

> So too, Lacan's Real is without zones, subdivision, localized highs and lows, or gaps and plenitudes: the Real is a sort of unrent, undifferentiated, fabric, woven in such a way as to be full everywhere, there being no space between the threads that are its "stuff." It is a sort of smooth, seamless surface or space which applies as much to a child's body as to the whole universe. The division of the Real into separate zones, distinct features, and contrasting structures is a result of the symbolic order, which, in a manner of speaking, *cuts into* the smooth facade of the Real, creating divisions, gaps, and distinguishable entities and laying the Real to rest, that is, drawing or sucking it into the symbols used to describe it, and thereby annihilating it.[94]

For Žižek, if we are to understand how language emerges out of/within the Real, this pre-symbolic, pre-logical Real *sans fissure* does not go far enough and must be argued against for two reasons, even if traces of it can be found in Lacan. First, it is a necessary posit created by the Symbolic at the moment of its free self-instituting, just as the transcendental subject posits the notion of a pure noumenon as a consequence of its (re)constitution of phenomenal reality. In this sense, the idea of the extra-subjective Real as an undifferentiated "mass" exhibiting no absence and negativity, just like the noumenon, risks being a mere fantasy of some kind of positive state of ontological completion outside of symbolization and idealization, which psychoanalytical experience (the mind-body discord) disproves. The Real prior to language may not possess linguistic and conceptual determination into a system of *strict* symbolic differences, but it cannot be said to be a substantial reality fully existing unto itself in such a way that language "pierces" its smoothness by "cutting into it" it like a flesh wound, which such presentations of the problematic appear to imply. This means that the above reading (represented by Lacanians such as Fink) is not *false*, but must be qualified. The Real *sans fissure* and the noumenon represent a compensation for the impossibility of an intimate experience of the Real within the Symbolic by claiming that, outside the reach of this synthetic (re)constitution of reality, it can still be said to persist in a state lacking contradiction and antagonism. It safeguards us from the realization that the Real itself is *morcelé*: it does not merely get itself into traps, producing monsters that disrupt the flow of knowledge in the Real by making the latter howl under ontological pain (chaotic states such as black holes, wherein the laws of physics seem to break down, or states in which animals, misreading meteorological conditions, perceive warm days in winter as the beginning of spring and act accordingly, "not only rendering themselves vulnerable to later onslaughts of cold, but also perturbing the entire rhythm of natural reproduction"[95]) but is always already riddled with internal differences, in such a manner that symbolic categories, due to a certain kind of "family resemblance," cannot be said to be some kind of lacerating agent that *first* cuts up the stuff of the world into a system of divisions. Speaking of quantum mechanics (which Žižek is interested in precisely because it gives us resources that prevent us from having recourse to "a 'naive' ontology of spheres or levels"[96] and challenges our understanding of nature and culture/the Real and the Symbolic), he says:

> According to [our] "spontaneous ideology," nature stands
> for the primacy of actuality over potentiality, its domain is
> the domain of the pure positivity of being where there are no
> lacks (gaps) in the strict symbolic sense; if, however, we take
> the ontological consequences of quantum physics seriously,
> then we have to suppose that the symbolic order pre-exists in
> a "wild" form, albeit in what Schelling would have called a
> lower potency.[97]

Žižek outlines four precise ways in which the symbolic order unexpectedly "pre-exists" in the Real as according to quantum mechanics, which deserve to be paraphrased in full in this context:

1. *Possibility as such possesses actuality, that is, has effects.* Just like parental authority imposes itself all the time despite the fact that it is normally only virtually and not actually present, understanding a particle's trajectory at the quantum level presupposes that we already know its possible trajectories within its wave function, which have a "being" of their own. What is more, the actualization of one of these latter does not do away with the rest: similar to the case of parental authority, as various phenomena of guilty conscience arising from an act or thought that no parental authority (or their stand-in) could ever find out or demonstrate, "what might have happened continues to echo in what actually happens as its virtual background."[98]

2. *Both possess knowledge in the Real.* As the now (in)famous double-slit experiment testifies, if we observe a particle to see through which slit it will pass, it will always behave as a particle, but if we do not observe it, it will always behave as a wave; it is as if the particle *knows* when it is and when it is not been watched by scientists. We display similar behaviour in the Symbolic—often, for instance, when others project certain roles on us, we act appropriately, being aware of the projection and assuming it.

3. *Each exhibits the phenomenon of registration.* In the symbolic universe of meaning, an event only truly occurs when the surrounding "external" environment *takes note of* or *registers* it, that is, if it *can leave a trace*. In order to explain the phenomenon of the collapse of the wave function, physicists must also resort to such metaphors: even at the quantum level, an event only "fully actualizes itself only through its symbolic registration, its inscription into a symbolic network, which is external to it."[99] For this reason, particles can pop into and out of existence, just as long as the universe does not notice—like it is possible to cheat a banking system if one does not violate normal functioning.

4. *Both exhibit an irreducible openness.* In the Symbolic, there is always a delay between an event and its symbolic registration. The rise of a new master signifier that rewrites the entire logical field

within which it occurs is not a substantial, fully constituted and self-unfolding process that was determined from the get-go, like a plant growing from a seed: it was not until the precise moment when it fully actualizes itself (when it inscribes itself into its surroundings as a master signifier) that it comes to be that which it retroactively always already was, thus *rewriting its own entire past*. Similarly, in the double-slit experiment, when a particle is observed, it "will not only (now) behave as a particle, its past will also retroactively become ('will have been') that of a particle,"[100] so that beforehand it could be said to have only existed as a form of proto-reality.

Secondly, if we try to understand the pre-logical Real as in itself an *undifferentiated "mass"* or *ontologically complete*, we just cannot comprehend the possibility of the emergence of the Symbolic in the first place. If something like the human subject is to emerge, then nature must be self-divided, wrought with tension-ridden zones of inner laceration, for otherwise we cannot account for its ontogenesis in any adequate manner, insofar as the subject, intrinsically exhibiting an originary ontologico-natural discord, could not be inscribed into the world. The subject and its linguistic capacities must be seen as expressive of the underlying ontological status of the Real, even if they represent within Lacanian metapsychology the loss and impossibility of such a non-mediated, pre-symbolic reality: the Symbolic is not merely some kind of extraneous, self-unfolding construct (a self-generating matrix of "meaning" that can assert itself in complete freedom from the Real as such) for the mere fact that we are entrapped within it must be revelatory of the essence of objective reality at some level since it must have given birth to it. The meaning of this is twofold: firstly, descriptions of the Symbolic-Real relation such as Fink's risk obfuscating what is for Žižek of essential importance for understanding what is at stake because they describe language as "encrusted upon the living,"[101] thereby reducing language to an external reflection upon substance and rendering the task of explicating its obscure origins impossible; secondly, the apparently self-grounding idealism of Lacanian psychoanalysis—the autonomous, self-positing ciphering of the Real by the Symbolic—already points to a way of explaining its emergence, and thus of breaking free from its correlationalist prison, by zoning in on that very feature that seems to prohibit such an inquiry: that is, *its ontological solipsism now understood as an ontological event*. It is necessary to explain how the Real can open itself up and give rise to a force seemingly Other to itself, to explain how images and words can "colonize" being from within, but this process forces us to include a moment of non-coincidence and antagonism with the Real. Although it may be without meaning to say that in the Real there is lack—lack only being brought forth in the reign of the Symbolic—it would nevertheless be erroneous to deduce from this that there is no negativity or difference within it. Yet how are we to understand this element of negativity in the all-pervasive fabric of the pre-symbolic Real, this self-sabotaging moment in the very heart of being?

5.2 …to a Denaturalized Monstrosity

We can now begin to see why the psychoanalytical experience of the infinite dichotomy between the structures underlying personality (subjectivation, culture) and the vital flow of energy sustaining us in objective being (nature, the corpo-Real of the body) is so pivotal for Žižek. The two registers of the Symbolic and the Real may function without any degree of reciprocal interaction or mutual interconnectivity, but the simple declaration of this unstable Cartesian bipolarity actually belies a third element that subsists throughout the discord and, in fact, paradoxically ties them together in their very antagonistic dialectical (non-)relationship. Here, following another hint given by Lacan—

> While psychoanalysis cannot, since its experience is limited to the individual, claim to grasp the totality of any sociological object or even the whole set of forces currently operating in our society, the fact remains that it discovered in analytical experience relational tendencies that seem to play a basic role in all societies, as if the discontent in civilization [*das Unbehagen in der Kultur*] went so far as to lay bare the very meeting point of nature and culture.[102]

—Žižek writes:

Furthermore, is not the object of psychoanalysis precisely this gap between first and second nature—the insecure position of a human subject who, after losing his footing in the first nature, can never feel fully at case in the second: what Freud called *das Unbehagen in der Kultur*, the different way the subject's passage from first to second nature can go wrong (psychosis, neurosis ...)? There is thus a core that resists the subject's full reconciliation with his second nature: the Freudian name for this kernel is drive, the Hegelian name for it is "abstract negativity" (or, in more poetic terms of the young Hegel, the "night of the world").[103]

The conceptual contours of this passage are much more complex than they may originally appear. Žižek is saying that central to any psychoanalytical theory of psychogenesis and psychopathology is the claim that the subject is *out of joint* with both the biological needs of the corpo-Real of its body (the anorexic eats nothing, the romantic is willing to die for love) and the symbolically constituted "second" nature that is created to compensate for the primordial *Hilflosigkeit* of human organic insufficiency. Understood in the context of seeking the obscure origins of the Symbolic in the Real, the subject, as the very gap between first nature (Real) and second nature (Symbolic), *cannot be said to fit into either*: it is a paradoxically self-standing space of non-relation that protrudes out of and obstructs both. Strictly speaking, the subject is *neither* Real *nor* Symbolic—it is a pure logical non-coincidence that possesses no place in either, so that the question of its upsurge within being must also go beyond a mere exploration of the breakdown of the libidinal-material fold of its biological nature as that which sets the stage for its emergence by opening up a liberating space within nature's hold.

What is crucial and groundbreaking here is the outlining of the ontological edifice that grounds human subjectivity qua *cogito*: we see the articulation of the "site" or "juncture" from which transcendental freedom and spontaneity emerge and take told. Self-positing autonomy, as both freedom from the laws of a closed libidinal-material economy *and* the relatively closed structural determinism of the symbolic law of culture, rests upon the subject as a self-relating point of infinite negativity, a *positively charged, excessive void,* but it can only beget itself if there is first of all a short circuit, a breakdown, in the dynamic flow of energy constitutive of nature's rhythms as that which carves up room for its more-than-materiality. Full-fledged subjectivity is rendered possible by a devastating ontological violence and is consequently nothing but a *denaturalized monstrosity* (*Todestrieb*) logically existing above and beyond the flux of being (due to its non-coincidence with the latter) while never able to leave its immanent plane within which it is primordially inscribed as out of joint: representing the failure, the collapse, of a self-enclosed biological system based upon the homeostatic self-preservation of the organism, it is an extimate inassimilable body in nature that exhibits the double feature of inclusion/exclusion, internal/external, presence/absence so characteristic of the Real in Lacan, which simultaneously demonstrates why the pre-symbolic Real must be said to be *morcelé*. In other words, set up as *nature turned against itself*, the first dull stirrings of the human subject refer to some kind of trauma that eventually incites the growth of individual ego life and culture in such a way that the latter exhibit the structural form of a reaction formation against this dysfunctionality in being and thus can never prevent themselves from being a negative, symptomatic expression of their basis in an ontological crisis, no matter how they may try to occult this fact. The psychoanalytical experience by definition presupposes an emergent schism in the fabric of the world between substance and subject, matter and mind, the Real and the Symbolic. But how can psychoanalysis—explicitly a theory of psychogenesis and its pathologies—explain where this denaturalization comes from, since such an investigation by principal must be external to its theoretical field and methodology?

Using Lacan's gesture towards an originary rottenness plaguing nature as a theoretical starting point, Žižek seeks to expand this structuralist metapsychology in order to secure the means of articulating the ontogenetic possibility-conditions of the Symbolic in the Real. Seeing psychoanalysis as conceptually unable to fulfill this task, he expands its horizon by recourse to modern philosophy, seeing therein a certain homology that enables him to draw upon its resources.[104] Following Lacan's claim that "Kant's practical philosophy [is] the starting point of the lineage culminating in Freud's invention of psychoanalysis," Žižek's project could be described as having two goals.[105] First, because the Lacanian subject is lacking any account of its ultimate origins, Žižek turns to German Idealism to develop a transcendental materialism insofar as there exists a structural parallelism in the underlying problematic plaguing both post-Kantian idealism and contemporary psychoanalysis. Second, and more strongly, Žižek's claim is that this parallelism is more than a mere shared set of theoretical concerns hovering around the grounding of the subject. If we read Kant, Schelling, and Hegel through Freud and Lacan, we actually see that there is a fundamental identity between the psychoanalytical subject haunted by the *Todestrieb* as constitutive of its very existence and the unconscious *Grundlogik* of German Idealism. We just have to look at how the latter's key representatives have recourse to various concepts (unruliness and diabolic evil in Kant, the night of the world in Hegel, or the *Entscheidung* in Schelling) that indicate a necessary disruption, breach, or violence at the very basis of the founding attributes they bestow upon the subject (self-legislative reason, the irreducibility of spirit, or freedom as the capacity for good and evil). It is exactly this paradoxical connection between real discord and ideal freedom throughout both traditions that enables Žižek to develop a new metaphysics by working in the intersections of both traditions, a metaphysics whose first conceptual contours we already see in Kant.

5.3 Kant, Unruliness, and the Cry of the Newborn

Lacan's claim that the beginning of psychoanalysis is in Kant's practical writings appears, at first, counter-intuitive. Especially given Lacan's structuralist bent, one would perhaps expect the clearest elaboration of the subject to be found in Kant's philosophical treatises on the mediating structures of consciousness. What do we see by delving into his practical philosophy except an attempt to found the ethical in the self-legislative spontaneity of human reason through articulating the self-imposing impetus of the categorical imperative and a listing of the a priori duties that automatically follow from its law? How could such a cold, machine-like way of determining the legitimacy of existential action be the immediate origin of psychoanalysis? Although we do encounter traces here of the irrevocably split nature of subjectivity in the tension between reason and sensible inclination, Kant's practical philosophy appears to have absolutely nothing to do with the unconscious in the Lacanian sense; on top of that, it displays great hope in the modern Enlightenment project of establishing the self-transparency and powers of reason—albeit through reason's own self-critique—as a means of historical progress and concretizing man's perfectibility. However, even if this might be the image of Kant's practical philosophy that always comes to mind, the matter at hand is far more complicated.

Kant's practical philosophy is of central importance because it is an expression and systematization of the experience of *freedom* in its irreducible essence, freedom understood as the self-legislative spontaneity at the core of human subjectivity, a faculty that separates us from the rest of mechanical nature insofar as we generate and obey our own laws. One must also remember that, for Kant, the *Critique of Pure Reason* is an attempt to make room for faith by *limiting* knowledge and reason, a point that directs the entirety of the critical enterprise from beginning to end by penetrating into the originary self-positing of human liberty at all costs, something that the late German Idealists were retroactively convinced revealed a decisive deficiency present in all the great thinkers in the history of philosophy. It is not the Copernican revolution—indeed, Schelling's[106] and Hegel's[107] projects are founded upon an attempt to escape its consequences—which forces us to rethink the very possibility of philosophy, but rather *Kant's account of freedom*.[108] This is also true of Žižek: "Kantian practical reason provides a glimpse into the abyss of freedom beyond (or beneath) the constraints of traditional metaphysical ontology."[109]

It is all a matter of how one understands the Kantian breakthrough. Even if it is true that it is a response to specific epistemological and scientific concerns that emerge out of modern philosophy (the [im]possibility of universal and necessary knowledge, the nature of the correlation of our ideas to reality in the genesis of concepts, etc.) it is clear that Kant's revolution cannot merely be reduced to his innovative way of rethinking the question of the subject-object relation, for the radical reflexivity of the *cogito* that imposes upon us the task of reconceptualizing what it is for an object to be present in the field of experience *is also at the basis of what it means to be a practical subject.* The movement goes both ways: if we read the *Critique of Pure Reason* through the later ethical, pedagogical, and religious writings,

Kant appears to be making the self-legislative freedom we witness in concrete, existential situations the very basis of theoretical philosophy—instead of a passive thinking subject that receives external reality as a kind of inert receptacle, a mere spectator, we have a reflecting subject that spontaneously and freely generates the very fabric of its own experience into a continuous, unitary whole through an activity of synthetic integration in a way similar to how it gives itself its own laws. The theoretical subject that is unearthed in transcendental apperception is ultimately identical with the practical subject of self-legislative freedom—or in other words, one cannot speak of one without the other, because they form a dialectical whole: if one wants to plunge into the labyrinthine depths of subjectivity, one should not read the *Critique of Pure Reason* in isolation from later works such as *Lectures on Pedagogy* and *Religion within the Limits of Reason Alone.*

In a similar vein, Žižek locates the true Kantian breakthrough in Kant's practical thinking on subjectivity instead of his epistemologico-transcendental destruction of metaphysics insofar as it is in the former that we most directly see the abyss of freedom at the obscure origin of subjectivity. But *what* is so primordial in the former that could bestow upon Kant's pedagogical writings such a privilege for understanding the radicality of critical philosophy, while also enabling us to shed light on the basis of the Cartesian-psychoanalytical subject? Finding numerous textual traces of the death-drive understood as a self-sabotaging tendency in nature as logically prior to subjectivity in both Kant, Fichte, Schelling, and Hegel, what interests Žižek in Kant's pedagogical writings is how they set the stage for what he claims to be the unconscious *Grundlogik* of German Idealism: that is, its founding intuition of the passage from nature to culture centred around a disturbing moment of irreducible negativity inscribed within the palpitating heart of being, which suggests that what first appears as a mere homology in conceptual structure between psychoanalysis and German Idealism is in fact a strict identity. What they bring to the fore is a thematization of the subject as some kind of disjunctive "and":

> The key point is thus that the passage from "nature" to "culture" is not direct, that one cannot account for it within a continuous evolutionary narrative: something has to intervene between the two, a kind of "vanishing mediator," which

is neither nature nor culture—this In-between is silently presupposed in all evolutionary narratives. We are not idealists: this In-between is not the spark of *logos* magically conferred on *Homo sapiens*, enabling them to form his supplementary virtual symbolic surroundings, but precisely something that, although it is also no longer nature, is not yet *logos*, and has to be "repressed" by *logos*—the Freudian name for this In-between, of course, is the death drive. Speaking of this In-between, it is interesting to note how philosophical narratives of the "birth of man" are always compelled to presuppose such a moment of human (pre)history when (what will become) man is no longer a mere animal and simultaneously not a "being of language," bound by symbolic Law; a moment of thoroughly "perverted," "denaturalized," "derailed" nature which is not yet culture.[110]

According to Žižek, within Kant this "in-between" finds its expression in the necessity to discipline the excessive "unruliness" (*Wildheit*) of human nature, the "wild, unconstrained propensity to insist stubbornly on one's own will, cost what it may."[111] What is to be emphasized here is the drastic nature of this claim: if we do not tame this primordial rawness (*Rohigkeit*) that presents itself as the zero-level of human spontaneity, not only do we fail to become full-fledged, fully adjusted subjects in the sociopolitical field of the world, but our freedom even threatens to devour itself in its frenzy in such a way that we become *failed* subjects: we are not born as humans, but rather *become* human—or, as Kant says, "[m]an only becomes man by education,"[112] which leads him to contend that "with education is involved the great secret of the perfection of human nature"[113] insofar as it is only through the principles offered by this act of disciplining, a means of schematizing our originary unruliness, that a "second nature"[114] can emerge as a response to the grounding ontological dilemma of human being, "nature ha[ving] placed no instinct in [man] for that purpose."[115] Even if the dysfunction of nature, this ontological abortion that is a monstrous, uncontainable excess of life, can in a second dialectical moment serve as a "positive" foundation or support, it can also collapse upon itself like a dying star. Yet this "unruliness" cannot be equated with the brute reality of animal existence—even if it exists *within* nature, it is strictly speaking something non-natural:

> The love of freedom is naturally so strong in man, that when once he has grown accustomed to freedom, he will sacrifice everything for its sake [...]. Owing to his natural love of freedom, it is necessary that man should have his natural roughness smoothed down; with animals, their instinct renders this unnecessary.[116]

For Žižek, this extract shows that the enigma of the emergence of subjectivity in German Idealism cannot be reduced to a mere dichotomy between nature and culture, as if in order to conform to the symbolic law of our own making we must first tame the blind, egotistical pleasure-seeking principles of our animal nature. The self-creative, logically autonomous milieu of culture is only possible through a prior, infinitely uncontainable freedom that acts as the "vanishing mediator" between brute animal reality and structured human intersubjective existence. The passage to culture does not consist in a sublimation of animalistic needs, but rather in a disciplining or symbolic re-articulation of a monstrous and logically irreducible unruliness that marks the essence of the human being, a disciplining that, *when it succeeds* (the possibility of neurosis always lurks in the air), simultaneously functions as that which once and for all separates us from nature by causing this denaturalized *Grund* (our ontogenetic "origins") to withdraw from the scene.

It is worth pointing out that Žižek strangely overlooks an important passage on the *first* page of the transcript we have of Kant's *Lectures on Pedagogy*, the very text that he makes use of at such a crucial point in his argument, which actually further supports his own Lacanian-inspired and ontologically oriented rereading of the vision of practical freedom it offers. In a perhaps unexpected move, Kant defines the human neonate as *non-natural*, claiming that, if an animal came to the world crying as a human does, it would merely attract attention to itself as potential prey, thus establishing that there is something off, primordially non-advantageous from a biological point of view, about the obscure ontogenetic beginnings of human subjectivity. In this context, we only need to cite a passage from the

Anthropology from a Pragmatic Point of View to show how *explicitly Lacanian* Kant's point is:

> The cry of a newborn child is not the sound of distress but rather indignation and furious anger; not because something hurts him, but because something annoys him: *presumably because he wants to move above and his inability to do so feels like a fetter through which his freedom is taken from him.*—What could nature's intention be here in letting the child come into the world with loud cries which, in *the crude state of nature,* are extremely dangerous for himself and his mother? For a wolf or even a pig would thereby be lured to eat the child, if the mother is absent or exhausted from childbirth. However, no animal except the human being (as he is now) will *loudly announce* his existence at the moment of birth [...]. One must therefore assume that in the first epoch of nature with respect to this class of animals (namely, in the time of crudity), this crying of the child at birth did not yet exist; and then only later in a second epoch set in, when both parents had already reached the level of culture necessary for *domestic* life; without our knowing how, or through what contributing causes, nature brought about such a development.[117]

Not only does Kant relate the dark unruliness that sets the stage for full-fledged human freedom to some kind of ontologically disjointed state of natural being, but he more radically links the cry of the newborn to the infinite dis-coordination of the corpo-Real of the human neonate, its feeling of utter dismemberment so central to the mirror stage in Lacan, and even suggests that this direct expression of painful negativity immanent in the fold of material being *is fundamental to the passage from nature to culture.*

These passages could be further drawn out by supplementing them with a number of possible citations from *Religion within the Limits of Reason Alone,* the first book in which Kant attempts to deal with the insurmountable propensity to evil that lies at the core of human subjectivity and ethical action. It argues two major points: (i) "the ground of this evil cannot be placed, as is so commonly done, in man's sensuous nature" and (ii) "neither can the ground of this evil be placed in a corruption of the morally legislative reason."[118] As such, this diabolic evil can neither be linked to the corpo-Real of the body and its pleasure-seeking tendencies or to the self's being within the law of a criminal or coercive symbolic order, but must itself be a foundational, constitutive part of the subject insofar as, being an infinitely self-asserting activity irreducible to and incommensurate with either zone, it articulates this same paradoxical structure of the in-between. Protruding out of nature and culture and failing to be understood except by its own self-positing, self-determining logic, the diabolic evil at the basis of freedom can only appear as an uncontrollable urge threatening to devour everything, even itself, in its self-destructive forward thrust. But here we see one crucial difference: whereas before we were at the strict level of ontogenesis (the "origins" of transcendental subjectivity) we now encounter full-fledged speaking subjects acting in a world (the ambiguity of freedom). Linking this consuming fire at the core of subjectivity to the perverse truth hidden in the Cartesian gap between mind and body, nature and culture, we already see in Kant the outlines of a radical materialist ontology, for it is as if in the movement from the former to the latter we see unruliness positing or owning itself in its own attempt at self-domestication, the structural consequences of which have profound metaphysical consequences for our understanding of reality as a substantial whole or totality. Since the ontogenetic origins of the subject are linked to a denaturalized unruliness and a full-fledged subject only comes on the scene when the latter posits itself as such in this endeavour of schematizing itself, which in turn institutes a pure difference in being by forever sustaining the gap it attempts to fill in, subjectivity exhibits an insurmountable propensity to evil *because its very founding gesture is structurally evil.* It is a radical, egotistical "No!" that reverses the order of the world according to its own self-assertion and cannot be undone without undoing itself. What is more, not only did Kant identify the intrinsic break from the order of substantial being that sets the stage for the *cogito*'s very autonomy and sketch this movement, he also already saw the paradox at the heart of subjectivity. That is to say, he implicitly understood that we can only grasp the latter as a pure act non-deducible from the obscure libidinal-material grounding that renders it possible (after all, for Kant evil is intrinsically enigmatic insofar as once as it is understood, it fails to be evil and becomes misguided good).

Kant's breakthrough is the following: if human subjectivity is to be *truly* self-legislative, at its zero-level there can be no formal distinction between a good and evil free act insofar as both are self-chosen in a non-disciplinable frenzy that has no definitive (real or symbolic) status and knows no influence exterior to its own self-asserting, self-positing activity. In itself, freedom is *indifferent* to both: there is no intrinsic difference between a will that wills evil and a will that wills good in terms of the pure act itself insofar as both are merely following their own self-given causality, an unconstrained self-legislation that tears apart the very fabric of nature in its self-imposition.[119] A will that wills evil is *not* merely giving itself over to the animalistic impulses of the body, nor is it expressing its ignorance or even corruption of the symbolic fold of cultural laws; it is merely forcefully upholding its own diabolical evil for the sake of it, basking in its own self-grounding tyranny, even when it has complete knowledge of its nature and repercussions. What is so difficult to come to terms with in the theoretical positing of this state of unruliness, and the ambiguity at the core of the self-positing of the subject, is its proclamation that the good itself is only possible through the gentrification or *taming* of evil. In order for good to be truly good, it too must present itself as a non-deducible act that breaks free from any order within which it could be contained by refusing all inscription within a field of heterogeneous, external forces that could impose itself upon the absolute originarity of its uncompromising self-assertion. The Yes of union depends upon the No of separation, but the process of converting the latter into the former can never be complete, since this would reduce freedom to a mere moment of cultural law as a kind of quasi-natural immersion within a pre-given logistics, thereby robbing human spontaneity of its untouchable autonomy in face of everything else that may be said to have influence upon it. Posited as that which transcendentally precedes and even conditions the possibility of its (logico-symbolic) articulation, at the very heart of the good there paradoxically lies evil as its extimate Other and menacing ground, threatening at any moment to erupt and disturb its smooth surface. Evil and good are not infinitely different and opposed, but merely two logical modalities of freedom, a freedom that in and of itself knows no law except its own uncontainable upsurge. If subjectivity is evil and the subject is an event in the world, then the world must not be understood as not-all, for the latter is not incapable of subsuming the former within its smooth touch.

It is precisely for this reason that Žižek, along with Lacan, believes that Kant's practical philosophy is the beginning of the lineage that culminates in psychoanalysis, the latter being understood as the second great revolution in philosophy that inflicts upon us the task of radically reconfiguring how we view ourselves and our relation to the world. Not only can we already therein see its *traits principaux* being thematized in an implicit way, but paradoxically one could even say that it in any uncanny manner develops them in different directions from Freud or Lacan so that bringing psychoanalysis and the German Idealist tradition together promises to produce something new. Just as Kant asserts an ultimate identity between the theoretical and practical ego, Žižek argues for the interpenetration of modern transcendental philosophy and psychoanalysis through the Kantian notion of the original "unruliness" of human nature. *Todestrieb* becomes a synonym for the transcendental "I," the *cogito*, by giving expression to the pre-subjective conditions of the possibility of freedom as some kind of non-masterable excess in nature that must be "tamed" if full-fledged subjectivity is to come on the scene. Exposing an activity uncontainable within positive being, it alludes to an ontologically self-violent "wildness" that serves as the ontogenetically constitutive basis of the subject's self-positing, in such a way that makes the late Lacan's passing remarks over the ontology of the psychoanalytical subject ("the rottenness of nature") come strikingly close to those of Kant ("[w]hat could nature's intention be here [...] ?"). In Kant, however, just as in Lacan, the actual status of the subject remains ambivalent and theoretically undetermined, even if there are various suggestions littered throughout their texts that programmatically outline how to proceed if one were to develop a materialism of transcendental freedom, despite the insurmountable problem that such gestures surpass the very constraints imposed upon the epistemology that they develop. The exact same set of theoretical questions is brought to the fore by both thinkers but remains unsolved: why does transcendental freedom develop? What is its exact relation to the "unruliness," synonymous with the excess of life presented by the *Todestrieb*, at the core of our being that appears to logically precede it? Insofar as transcendental spontaneity is just as related to the synthetic powers of the imagination as it is to self-legislative reason in Kant, what role does the former play in this picture (or, in a Lacanian parlance, how can the Symbolic emerge as that which [re]constitutes the fold of experience)? It is only in Kant's successors that such concerns will be addressed in a more explicit manner, and it is through a psychoanalytical reactualization of their thinking that the transcendental materialist ontology at the heart of Kant's breakthrough can finally come to light.

Notes

87. Žižek, *The Ticklish Subject*, p. 48.

88. Johnston, *Žižek's Ontology*, p. 272. Here Johnston is referring to *Le Séminaire de Jacques Lacan, Livre XXI: Les non-dupes errent, 1973–1974* (unpublished typescript), pp. 2, 21, and 74; and *Le Séminaire de Jacques Lacan, Livre XXIII: Le sinthome, 1975–1976,* ed. Jacques-Alain Miller (Paris: Éditions du Seuil, 2005), pp. 5, 17, and 77 (untranslated).

89. Ibid., p. 273. Following Johnston's bibliography, the first quote comes from *Le Séminaire de Jacques Lacan, Livre XVIII: D'un discours qui ne serait pas du semblant, 1971* (unpublished typescript), pp. 2, 17, and 71, while the second seminar he makes reference to is (as in the previous footnote) *Le Séminaire de Jacques Lacan, Livre XXIV: L'insu que sait de l'une bévue s'aile à mourre, 1976–1977,* ed. Jacques-Alain Miller, in *Ornicar?* 12-18, pp. 5, 17, and 77.

90. Lacan, "The Mirror Stage as Formative of the *I* Function," *Écrits*, p. 96/77.

91. Ibid., p. 97/78.

92. Ibid., p 100/80.

93. Ibid., p. 96/77.

94. Fink, *The Lacanian Subject*, p. 24. I capitalize "the Real" for consistency.

95. Žižek, *Living in the End Times* (New York: Verso, 2011), pp. 350–51.

96. Žižek, *Less Than Nothing*, p. 905.

97. Ibid., p. 921.

98. Ibid., p. 920.

99. Ibid.

100. Ibid., p. 921.

101. Fink, *The Lacanian Subject*, p. 12.

102. Lacan, "A Theoretical Induction to the Functions of Psychoanalysis in Criminology," *Écrits*, p. 127/104.

103. Žižek, *The Ticklish Subject*, pp. 81–82.

104. Žižek, "Liberation Hurts."

105. Žižek, *The Ticklish Subject*, p. 48.

106. The founding gesture of Schelling's entire project *begins with* an attempt to surmount the Copernican revolution. Only the modalities of his response differ: whether it be through an attempt to give a genesis of the categories from the I as the first principle, a daring naturephilosophy, or eventually by a theosophic mytho-poetics of creation, one thing is clear—we must go "beyond simple representation." *Einleitung in die Philosophie,* ed. Walter E. Ehrhardt (Stuttgard-Bad Connstatt: Frommann-Holzboog, 1989).

107. Although people are wont to speak about the tight relationship between Kant and Hegel, one must point out that in the *Lesser Logic* Hegel badmouths Kant by by throwing upon him the ultimate insult one could give to a systematic philosopher (except, of course, that their absolute is a dead dog)—namely, *that he was just too lazy to think through what he says and therefore completely misses the point:* "[i]n dealing with this highest Idea [teleological causality], however, the laziness of *thought,* as we may call it, finds in the 'ought' an all too easy way out." *The Encyclopedia Logic (with the Zusätze),* trans. T. F. Geraets, W. A. Suchting, and H. S. Harris (Indianapolis: Hackett Publishing, 1991), p. 101 (§55A).

108. See chapter 6.

109. Žižek, *The Ticklish Subject*, p. 48.

110. Ibid., p. 36.

111. Ibid.

112. Taken from Kant, *Kant on Education,* trans. Annette Churton (Boston: D. C. Heath, 1900), p. 6; for a more easily findable edition, see *Lectures on Pedagogy,* trans. Robert B. Louden, *Anthropology, History, and Education,* ed. Günter Zöller and Robert B. Louden (Cambridge: Cambridge University Press, 2007), p. 439.

113. Ibid., pp. 7 and 439.

114. Ibid., pp. 9 and 440.

115. Ibid., pp. 13 and 442.

116. Ibid., pp. 4–5 and 438; quoted by Žižek, *The Ticklish Subject*, p. 36.

117. *Anthropology from a Pragmatic Point of View,* trans. Robert B. Louden, *Anthropology, History, and Education,* p. 423. First set of italics is my own.

118. *Kant, Religion within the Limits of Reason Alone,* trans. T. M. Greene and H. H. Hudson (New York: Harper & Row, 1960), p. 30.

119. Žižek & Daly, *Conversations with Žižek* (Cambridge: Polity, 2004), p. 124.

Chapter 6
From Transcendental Philosophy to Substance as Subject
Hegel and the Psychotic Night of the World

This chapter comprises a Žižekian-inspired interpretation of the philosophical movement from Kant to Hegel by focusing on Kant's thematization of freedom and how it radically reconfigures the possibility of metaphysical inquiry. In the aftermath of critical philosophy, what is clear is that any philosophy unable to think system *and* the irreducibility of the human subject is to be rejected. By following certain premonitions within Kant's pedagogical writings that appear to link transcendental spontaneity to the psychoanalytical concept of *Todestrieb*, Žižek gives us resources to read Hegelian Absolute Idealism against standard interpretations by claiming that Hegel's attempt to think substance as subject implies the ontogenetic emergence of freedom through a self-sundering of being, the immanent advent of a devastating ontological non-coincidence, which forces upon us the necessity of a new kind of metaphysics: *a metaphysics of the not-all*. This enables us not only to rethink the Kant-Hegel relation in a provocative manner, but also to explain how Žižek is able to draw upon post-Kantian idealism to lay the foundation for the logic of his own transcendental materialism.

6.1 Fichte and the Frailty of Freedom

Within the trajectory of modern philosophy, the inheritors of the legacy of the critical system all agree that it is with Kant that we see the *first* truly penetrating account of the essence of human freedom.[120] Although much of what he says concerning freedom is already laid out in Descartes' thinking on the *cogito*, it was Kant who gave it a full, profound expression. For Žižek, this means that it is here that the principal intuitions that heralded forth modernity—the ontologically shattering schism between the thinking mind and extended substance and subjectivity's irreducible reflexivity as that which institutes this very split—are radicalized and find an overpowering degree of theoretical articulation. After Kant, there is just *no* going back, for this would be to give up on what it means to be an infinitely self-standing, autonomous subject, to turn one's back on one's own freedom, whose apparently indemonstrable existence *has been proven once and for all*.[121] Any system that regresses into a "primitive," "pre-critical" way of philosophizing is in effect merely recoiling from the difficulty that is the burden of freedom, "our experience of freedom [being] properly *traumatic*, even for Kant himself."[122] Herein lies the fundamental undecidability intrinsic to the Kantian breakthrough: not only is the freedom of human subjectivity *liberating*, but it is also (and perhaps more originally) *monstrous*, insofar as we are infinitely given over to it and therefore responsible for it, yet can only comprehend it according to the frenzy that is its own self-positing essence. In the wake of the Kantian system, there is only "the uncanny abyss of freedom without any guarantee in the Order of Being":[123]

> in Kantian ethics, the true tension is not between the subject's idea that he is acting only for the sake of duty, and the hidden fact that there was actually some pathological motivation at work (vulgar psychoanalysis); the true tension is exactly the opposite one: the free act in its abyss is unbearable, traumatic, so that when we accomplish an act out of freedom, in order to be able to bear it, we experience it as conditioned by some pathological motivation. Here I am tempted to bring in the key Kantian concept of schematization: a free act *cannot be schematized*, integrated into our experience; so, in order to schematize it, we have to "pathologize it."[124]

Immediately following the birth of transcendental idealism, however, there is an overall ambiguity as to how to proceed. Although there is some general consensus concerning the various ways that the critical system is by itself incomplete, internal discord quickly arises. Leaving aside Reinhold's and Maimon's own responses to its perceived insufficiencies, Fichte, Schelling, and Hegel, despite all agreeing that (i) the categories of the understanding are dogmatically asserted (they lack a genetic deduction grounding their necessity and universality) and ultimately too static (there is no clear articulation of their systematic interconnectivity) and (ii) concepts such as the thing-in-itself in their Kantian mode are internally contradictory or at least theoretically unnecessary, each offer different strategies to think through the deadlock of Kant's legacy to retain its grounding insights.

The early Fichte of the Jena period—the only Fichte who had a significant impact on the internal development of German Idealism—proceeds by removing the extra-subjective alterity of the thing-in-itself, often referred to as the residual trace of a materialism in Kant, by reducing its status to a mere generated effect of subject's purely autonomous activity that knows no outside. Taking as his starting point the immanent field of absolute actuation presented by the subject's radical freedom, whose self-manifestedness is revealed in the unavoidable transcendental reduction of any given fact of consciousness to its activity and most primordially demonstrated by intellectual intuition, and which is best exemplified in the infinite thetic judgement *I am*,[125] subjectivity, as uncontainable freedom, cannot be trumped. Groundless, nothing can get beyond it: it is the ultimate, self-explanatory condition of experience. Yet, although a wondrous fountainhead of activity, the theoretical and practical unconditional beginning that is the I is paradoxically lacking. Not only is its essence (an essence that is its very act of existing) indistinguishable from nothingness insofar as it knows no bounds; more disconcertingly, it is also immensely fragile and immediately threatened by a not-I that risks destroying its very omnipotence *from within its own sphere*. In the face of the "not-I," which is transcendentally simultaneous with the "I," freedom cannot be simply restricted to the undetermined nothingness of the *I am*, but it must upsurge in an attempt through our very actions and finitude to overcome that which opposes it. In order to truly sustain its theorectio-practical firstness, to assert its own primordiality against the not-I that "desires" its annihilation, the subject must bring forth the freedom that is its own capacity for absolute actuation in the natural and sociopolitical field of the world, since as soon as the pure act of freedom tries to posit itself as such, it runs up against the impossibility of asserting itself as an autarchic all. In this conflict-ridden battle, the not-I proves to be more than a pure alterity wreaking havoc on the subject's freedom. Instead, it becomes a determined other, an *Anstoß* (an obstacle and impetus). Through encountering this *Anstoß* there can be a continual overcoming of the menacing not-I and a never-ending perfecting of the I's own savage freedom by attaining an ever greater degree of concrete autonomy. In this sense, consciousness emerges from the shock of the not-I on the immanent field of actuation that is the unconscious I in its pure freedom and the latter's defiant cry and refusal to submit when confronted with the possibility of its own demise. The victory of this freedom is never ontologically guaranteed, but can only ever be won again and again in the onslaught of time, whose basic structure is described by the total theoretico-practical syntheses of divisibility opened by the third principle, thus making all principles simultaneous in experience.

In this picture there is *nothing* outside of the pure immanence of the I as freedom and the dynamics of its subjectification as necessitated by the opposition it encounters to its raw, unconditional power. Due to this internal opposition, the I is divided between the absolute I (which is less an egological pole than a faceless, even inhuman activity that only warrants the title of I because it is always spoken of in relation to persons amongst whom it incarnates itself, thus making it in its very essence *cryptic*[126]) and the finite (which in turn is divided into passive and active aspects wherein the absolute totality of reality as expressed by the I is never completely annihilated). There is no need for a hard, impenetrable remainder left over from the transcendental constitution of reality: that which threatens to destroy the subject if not gentrified through the syntheses of divisibility, the not-I, is a mere negative magnitude, even if its contorting effects upon the subject can never be predicated and could potentially upsurge as traumatic events. We do not need to go beyond this logical role of an internal pressure proclaiming the possible implosion of the I as freedom to explain experience. Thus, to say that the thing-in-itself becomes a theoretical posit of the subject is to say that its irreducibility to conscious, finite subjectivity and thus its apparently extra-subjective status have been deduced from the self-manifestedness offered by subjectivity as a first principle: its function is to underline the paradoxical simultaneity of radical spontaneity *and* fragility in the free constitution of phenomenal reality as it continually comes upon an alien presence *within its very intimacy*: namely, the irresolvable contradiction that exists in subjectivity between the groundlessness of consciousness as a radically self-grounding idealist freedom and the necessary realist contingency that continually jeopardizes it.

For Fichte, the removal of an extra-subjective reality is a necessity imposed upon us not just by Kant's radical articulation of freedom, but more broadly by idealism as such. From within the latter, there can be no coherent assertion of a self-subsisting thing-in-itself which, existing outside of the closed idealist circle of phenomenality in an infinite elsewhere, causes our representations. This would be to transgress the epistemological constraints imposed upon us by the very confines of the idealization of the world; any assertion of the thing-in-itself would constitute a return to the worst kind of dogmatism. The *Anstoß* is therefore not merely the true limit of idealism, but contains the necessary resources to synthesize idealism and realism into a greater unity:[127] instead of proclaiming that all our idealizations are first caused by a foreign intruder pushing in upon subjectivity, it says that *if* there are immanent obstructions from within the mediating activity of the Ideal, if phenomenal experience is plagued by internal inconsistencies, we can legitimately say that these knots negatively point to some extra-subjective, inassimilable body in subjectivity itself forcing it partially to negate itself and transfer its power to that which is extimately Other in order to save itself from complete collapse.[128] Giving the immanent intruder reality is a way to appropriate it: in short, to *idealize* it. In this way, one of the major tasks of Fichte's 1794 *Wissenschaftslehre* is to draw our attention to the radicality of this conditional: if we take idealism seriously then we can without difficulty account for realism, for the realist character of our everyday experience can be entirely explained by the very movement of the Ideal itself. Idealism does not infringe upon the freedom of the objective world, since it is clear that the latter can in some way make itself known through the very obstructions of our idealizations of it. The epistemic priority of the Ideal is not to be equated with the unknowability of the world, since its autonomous operational self-closure is precisely that which enables us to have a world at all.

For Fichte, however, the most decisive consequence to draw from the removal of the thing-in-itself is not a rethinking of the realism-idealism debate. He never takes an interest in the resources that this new way of philosophizing would offer for developing a new form of spectral materialism. The reason is simple: taking the unbridled freedom of the I as his starting point, Fichte agrees with Kant's prohibition on searching for the ontological origins of the subject because, even if it seemingly becomes methodologically possible in Fichte, he argues that it is a futile project, the Ideal being self-explanatory without recourse to the Real. That the subject has no need for the thing-in-itself signifies that the subject is characterized by a constitutive groundlessness: transcendental spontaneity demonstrates that it is totally engulfed within a self-unfolding practical world of its own making, so that what is of primordial importance is never an extra-subjective reality, but the unconditioned freedom of our concrete activity. Fichte does not need to embark upon a metaphysical archaeology of the subject, instead focusing all of his attention on the dynamic inherent in the process of subjectification itself, which inflicts upon us a frightening realization ridden with stark ontological and political implications. Not only are all our actions—and thereby the identities and the collectives that we construct through them—irreducible in themselves insofar as they have *no* foothold in objective reality, but they become, as it were, mere parts of the free play of an infinite imagination so engrossed by its own self-composing stories that it almost lacks the power to know its self-narrating fiction as a fiction:

There is no being. *I myself* do not know at all and don't exist. There are *images*: they are all that exists and they know about themselves in the manner of images—images which drift by without there being anything by which they drift; images which hang together through images; images which do not represent anything, without meaning and purpose. I myself am one of these images. No, I am not even that, but only a distorted image of these images. All reality is transformed into a fabulous dream, without there being any life the dream is about, without there being a mind which dreams; a dream which hangs together in a dream of itself. *Intuition* is the dream; *thought* (the source of all being and all reality which I imagine, of *my* being, my power, my purposes), thought is the dream of this dream.[129]

Subjectification is nothing more than a spinning in the positively charged void of freedom. In the latter's aftermath, we become irrevocably lost in a series of dream-like images, a rhapsody of sociopolitical phantasmagoria, which give a transcendental structure to the fabric of our experience and thus to our ethical striving, thus even making our own self just one image amongst others, *but without having any basis in the world at large.* If we take Freud's definition of psychosis as a loss of the causal impact of the world upon the self—a "loosening of the relationship to reality"[130]—due to a radical withdrawal into primary narcissism, whereby object cathexes are libidinally cut off and the primary process slowly takes over psychic reality, we could venture the claim that the founding gesture of the Fichtean subject is a form of psychosis (the I "posits itself absolutely, and is thereby complete in itself and closed to any impression from without"[131]), justified in the name of autonomy. Here, just as in the illusionary, image-filled world of the psychotic, the "objective" world is reduced to a mere haphazard obstruction to a self-unfolding and self-sustaining tale creative of its own experiential reality (which for Fichte, "*absolutely creates itself* [...] in a genesis out of nothing"[132]), a mere haphazard obstruction that is to be overcome and integrated within the tale if the latter is to sustain its very consistency. What is more, in the same manner that the psychotic must continually refuse new perceptions so as to "autocratically" construct an external and internal world that pleases the id's wishful impulses,[133] the Fichtean subject, struggling to subsist as a pure I due to the contemporaneous emergence of the not-I and its violence with its self-positing, strives to rid itself of all influence of the not-I in the syntheses of divisibility and thereby actualize the sphere of absolute self-positing at the empirical level. In this respect, its ideal is a *full-blown psychosis,* an "alloplastic"[134] creation of its own experience, which, though technically impossible (without the influence of the not-I, the I would lack determination), is a structural tendency *in all experience,* the paradoxical basis of practical freedom. From within this originary psychosis at the heart of subjectivity, there is no escape "except" accepting it and taking the path it opens up to its end by the self-conscious creation of fabulous, imaginative identities (criticism) that can be used to give the subject the resources it needs to actualize itself through the formation of an absolutely free identity liberated from all external causality (dogmatism). What this means is that "the human being is originally nothing:"[135] it is free to strive, and should strive, to absolutely create itself according to its own transcendental self-positing/primary narcissism.

For both Schelling and Hegel, however, this complete removal of the problematic of the grounding of the subject is not satisfying on two accounts. First, although Fichte's notion of the *Anstoß* in the 1794 *Wissenschaftslehre* does allow us to develop something like a spectral materialism, Fichte does not use his own real-idealism/ideal-realism to investigate the obscure origins of the subject, rejecting any transcendental materialist account of the emergence of the I out of the not-I as contrary to reason.[136] Transcendentalism must remain purely immanent—we need not investigate its ontological origins, since these will never suffice. But this does not necessarily mean we cannot embark on such an inquiry (a "pre-history" of the Ideal). Second, Fichte himself, despite his remarks concerning its impossibility, like Kant cannot refrain from commenting on the paradoxical ground of the subject's freedom, as if to say that the matter at hand *cannot be limited to* the transcendental structures at the heart of the self-unfolding conceptual-imaginative fabric underlying subjectification, but must also include the *birthplace* of the I as *causa sui*:

> Every animal, a few hours after its birth, moves and seeks nourishment at the breast of its mother [...]. To be sure, the human being has a plant-like instinct, but he has no animal instinct at all in the meaning given here. He needs the freely given assistance of other human beings, and without it would die shortly after birth. When the human offspring has left its mother's body, nature withdraws her hand from it and cuts it loose, so to speak [...]. For it is precisely nature's abandonment of him that proves that the human being, as such, neither is nor should be nature's pupil. If the human being is an animal, then he is an utterly incomplete animal, and for that very reason he is not an animal.[137]

What is striking about this quote is not only that Fichte, like Kant before him, draws attention to the utter helplessness of the neonate as an indication of some kind of ontological indeterminacy within nature as that which sets the stage for subjectivity and freedom, an indeterminacy that is non-natural ("nature withdraws her hand"), but also that he is forced to do so *from within the confines of a self-grounding idealism.* To account for the very transcendental unity of experience, there is a point during the deduction of its laws that something *meta-transcendental* must be posited whose very existence appears to be responsible for the subject's groundlessness. That there is no possible explication of the leap from not-I to I appears now shaken, for a certain relation between the two has been established despite the fact that such a relation would seem to jeopardize the I's self-standingness. What is at stake is not that Fichte creates an unacceptable subjective idealism within which knowledge of the world is lost and even precluded through being constructed, but that his philosophy ultimately lacks the resources to tie together an ontology of nature with the spontaneity of the I, though such an impossible link has been immanently deduced. Although Fichte too outlines a transcendental materialist ontology of the subject, he, like Kant before him, cannot answer the question "How does appearance itself emerge from the Real?," even if he stumbles upon the solution.

If Fichte and Kant are right in these intuitions in the same way that Lacan could be said to be right in his late musings on the status of nature in light of the psychoanalytical subject, the task facing Hegel, Schelling, and Žižek is thus remarkably similar: how can being and thinking, the Real and the Symbolic, be reconciled to one another, for surely the latter must exist in the former? For the early Schelling, what is necessary is a theoretical project that supplements the ontologically solipsistic Fichtean subject with an account of its emergence out of an unconsciously creative nature, which would implicate the interpenetration and ultimate identity of the Real and the Ideal, so that such a problem is shown to be ultimately moot.[138] Interestingly, though he is initially satisfied with Schelling's response to the deadlock of Fichtean idealism,[139] Hegel later breaks from what Schelling himself refers to as a "real" or "objective idealism,"[140] claiming that by attempting to solve the internal contradictions of Fichte's idealism, Schelling unknowingly becomes its inverted opposite, a mere reactionary form spurred on by the inconsistencies of the former that ultimately fails because of its one-sided countermove.[141] But *what*, then, exactly drives Hegel to part ways from Schelling and develop his own way of balancing idealism (radically self-positing freedom) with a philosophy of nature (a system of the world)? And why is this juncture so important for understanding Žižek's own metaphysics of the disjunctive "and"? To answer this question, we must first make a brief detour through the development of modern philosophy.

6.2 Metaphysics in the Aftermath of Freedom: The Case of Spinoza

A common critique of Schelling and Hegel as they attempt to think through the problems bequeathed by Kantian idealism is that they ignore the basic breakthrough of the *Critique of Pure Reason*: that is, the recognition of the insurmountable finitude of human reason and its inability to grasp the absolute structure of reality. In face of its debilitation of a priori enquiry by pure reason, they return to a metaphysical thinking that has already been debunked. According to the canonical reading, while Schelling talks of the interrelated poles of subject and object in his attempt to balance transcendental idealism with a naturephilosophy, and then of their ultimate identity in the absolute as indifference by developing an account of absolute reason, Hegel supposedly attempts to show that the *logical* structures that the thinking subject uses to constitute the world transcendentally are actually one with its *ontological*, that is, its extra-conscious structure. What Hegel does is dialectically "fix up" Schelling by revealing that reality in all its facets (mind and matter, nature and subject) is merely an expression of the rational self-actualization of the absolute as a logical self-unfolding totality, which does away with the Schellingian indifference as an indeterminate void lacking genuine philosophical content, "the night in which, as the saying goes, all cows are black."[142] Žižek, however, refuses this interpretation, calling it "the standard cliché according to which German Idealism pleads the 'pan-logicist' reduction of all reality to the product of the self-mediation of the Notion."[143]

Žižek gives us material that allows us to shed new light on the movement from Kant to Hegel by showing that this conventional reading of German Idealism levels off the daring character of the post-Kantian gesture by making it look like just another classical metaphysical system. Not only

are Hegel and Schelling attempting to demonstrate how it is still possible
to do metaphysics *within* the very breakthrough of critical philosophy
without denying any of what they consider to be its necessary/essential
presuppositions, but also, and most importantly, *why it is necessary to do so*:

> Here, however, a gap between Kant and his followers occurs:
> for Kant, freedom is an "irrational" fact of reason, it is simply
> and inexplicably given, something like an umbilical cord
> inexplicably rooting our experience in the unknown noumenal
> reality, not the First Principle out of which one can develop
> a systematic notion of reality, while the Idealists from Fichte
> onwards cross this limit and endeavour to provide a systematic
> account of freedom itself. [... F]or the Idealists [this is] just an
> indication that Kant was not yet ready to pursue his project to
> the end, to draw all the consequences from his breakthrough.
> For the Idealists, Kant got stuck half-way.[144]

Although this may mean a vigorous rethinking of transcendental spontaneity
and imagination, noumena and the status of nature, ultimately neither Hegel
nor Schelling wants to give up on Kant's descriptions of freedom in order to
substitute transcendental idealism with just another classico-metaphysical
system. Yet for this endeavour to be successful, they realize that they need to
fight against the *Critique of Pure Reason*'s own prohibition of pure ontological
inquiry; they deny one of the major claims of critical philosophy in the hope
of saving it from itself.

This becomes clear when we realize that for both Hegel and Schelling,
Spinoza is the very emblem of a philosopher. His rationalist system is
admirable not only for its depth and beauty, but for its self-consistency,
clarity, and comprehensiveness. In terms of an expression of metaphysics,
each looks up to him and sees something fundamentally askew in Kant's
preclusion of its possibility—or, as Hegel says "[i]t is therefore worthy
of note that thought must begin by placing itself at the standpoint of
Spinozism; to be a follower of Spinoza is the essential commencement of all
Philosophy."[145] Not only did Kant not show trust in the capacities of human
reason, more problematically his critical system was lacking any foundation
insofar as it left the origins of the transcendental subject, the very object
of its thematic, a mystery and even went so far as to put a ban on their

investigation. They reject this for two reasons: first, it seems arbitrary, and, second, it threatens to destabilize the very Kantian edifice. Although both Schelling and Hegel believe that metaphysical knowledge of an objective reality is still possible, they are at the same time unwilling to abandon idealism insofar as they are not willing to back down from its articulation of freedom, which leads them to see both questions as intimately intertwined and refuse to separate them as Kant does in order to make room for faith and human autonomy. Schelling, for instance, bemoans the fact that "idealism," whose founding intuition he identifies in the *Freiheitsschrift* with the principle of freedom, "is not a work of reason," and that consequently "the supposedly sad honor of being a system of reason remains only for pantheism and Spinozism."[146] Even if Kant's systematization of freedom is of irreducible importance for the late German Idealists, it must be stressed that of itself it remains theoretically *negative* in a strong sense: largely remaining at the level of *formality*, it never really manages to get off the ground and provide a thoroughly developed basis for itself.[147] We must provide the missing link between system (Spinozism, absolute determinism) and idealism (Kantianism, the true philosophy of freedom) by showing that freedom itself is a *metaphysical possibility*. But what does it mean for system if freedom is inscribed within it?

Amongst other things, Spinozistic metaphysics represents an avid attempt to rethink the ontological splitting of mind and matter by reconceiving the very notion of substance so that the two categories no longer represent a schismatic split but are subsumable under a single, unified substrate of which they are merely different attributes, all the while preserving as much as possible the basic intuitions of Cartesianism. Mind and matter, the brute material Real of the universe and the self-reflexive powers of ideal spirit, are merely differing "perspectives" on the same, unchanging substance,[148] a kind of epistemic parallax shift between two of the countless logical modalities of an all-pervasive "weave" that encompasses all things within its vital ebb and flow. Although they succeed in manifesting the infinite power of substance through different refraction mediums irreducible to each other, they ultimately must be said to interpenetrate one another insofar as they articulate the same content: there is no possible rupturing chasm between them, but only an untouchable oneness.[149] But

this oneness is not some kind of undifferentiated, static whole, an abyssal
metaphysical void that devours all difference within its cruel awesomeness,
like Chronos who eats his own offspring, but rather a pure power or force
that is capable of expressing itself in an infinite variety of ways,[150] and indeed
is only one insofar as it does so. If "nothing exists except substance and
its modes,"[151] it is because the two constitute one another in an immanent
pulsating field teeming, overflowing, with immanent life. Substance is a
raw, pulsating activity, an unconstrained upsurge of a dynamic, quivering
freedom that is at the very core of the flux that is perceived reality and
circulates through its most minute and insignificant features: "God's power
whereby he and all things are and act, is his very essence."[152] Substance
exists *absolutely* as a harmonious play of forces even in its most seeming
conflict, tension, and struggle. It is a wondrous ballet of cosmic energy
whose dance is something peaceful and inspiring, sometimes macabre and
dreadful, for us mortals who without choice are engaged in its spectacle.

Although this may appear to preclude human liberty, it actually
proclaims that human beings *are* in a certain sense free insofar as they
directly participate in the self-actualizing movement of substance (God,
nature) as *causa sui*. In Spinozism, however, there is a crucial modification
of the underlying logic of modern subjectivity already seen in Descartes:
the intuition of *irreducible* subjective freedom is said to arise out of a
misrecognition of our fundamentally determined character as egos. By
locating freedom within the kernel of my being, my will, I am merely
misperceiving its notion, for real spontaneity lies in the impersonal self-
writing symphony of the universe, the self-creative flow of life and difference
("we are in God's power as clay in the hands of the potter"[153]), in which I
also play a constitutive part insofar as its energy expresses itself through
me, animates me, *constitutes me*, so that any radical distinction disappears.
The cause is fully in its effect, for it itself is immanent. Spinoza's account of
human freedom, instead of being a pure cancellation of the significance of
concrete human ethical striving by its submission to the total system of the
world in its self-imposing oneness, is an attempt to show its greater truth,
meaning, and role by its inclusion in the intimate life of God or nature:
in short, its function within the autonomous and infinitely inventive self-
actualization of substance. It is precisely for this reason that metaphysics

is an *ethics*: the whole endeavour of Spinozism is meant to show how, by coming to this realization step by step through clear and precise reasoning, one can liberate oneself from the bondage of one's passive emotions and see how one directly takes part in the freedom of the self-unfolding cosmos, overflowing with uncontainable energy. *Showing* the structure of the world *forces* us to act differently—logical proofs are equivalent to opening the mind's eye to the dynamics of substance as totality.[154] For the late German Idealists working in the aftermath of Kant, however, this vision reduces the apparent autonomous essence of subjectivity to a mere epiphenomenon, a false appearance, of the vital flux of a more primordial life force that runs through and simultaneously is the universe, thus leaving nothing untouched and no room for a transcendence within its omnipresent pull. This "direct participation" can only be paradoxically interpreted as a *passive* participation, a forced enactment, which befalls us. We see this most unsettlingly in Spinoza's stone:

> Furthermore, conceive, if you please, that while continuing in motion the stone thinks, and knows that it is endeavouring, as far as in it lies, to continue in motion. Now this stone, since it is conscious only of its endeavour and is not at all indifferent, will think it is completely free, and that it continues in motion for no other reason than that it so wishes. This, then, is that human freedom which all men boast of possessing, and which consists solely in this, that men are conscious of their desire and unaware of the causes by which they are determined. In the same way that a baby thinks that it freely desires milk [...].[155]

For the late German Idealists, if this is freedom, it is a grotesque joke: instead of being liberating, it is *claustrophobic*, for our infinite strivings are reduced to a mere puppet show for an impersonal God *sive* nature whose power drowns any hope we may have for true self-standing independence in its might. Whatever freedom is here, it is distant from us: "[i]n the mind there is no absolute, or free, will. The mind is determined to this or that volition by a cause, which is likewise determined by another cause, and this again by another, and so ad infinitum."[156] It is without a doubt Fichte who most succinctly expresses the German Idealist disdain at this picture.

What repels him is that freedom is "not *my* freedom at all but rather that of *an alien force outside me*:"[157] "[t]o stand there cold and dead and merely to look at the change of events an inert mirror or fleeting forms—that is an unbearable existence and I disdain and deplore it. I want to love, I want to lose myself in taking an interest, I want to be glad or sad. [...] Only in love is there life; without it there is death and annihilation."[158]

At this juncture, a Spinozist may argue that the German Idealist misgivings of Spinoza's naturalistic pantheism are false. Is not the *Ethics* itself a profound celebration of life rather than death, love rather than indifference, a text that itself can be read as a quasi-psychotherapeutic intervention that aims, with the aid of its geometrical proofs, to liberate one from the passivity of the passions and in so doing find a new manner of radically asserting the (limited, though existent) freedom of one's own conatus? As Spinoza says, the *Ethics* "concerns the method, or way, leading to freedom."[159] By demanding that we build a new organ of sight,[160] it asks us to undergo a profound change in our relationship to self and world, *to become a new species*, by giving up ill-founded politico-theological ideals and conceptions of humanity (mere fictions),[161] which we can only accomplish by giving into and working with the relational dynamics at the heart of what it means for to be singular essence insurmountably inter-bound with the infinity of other essences. Substance as a causal network of complete interpenetration wherein each being attains its life force reveals the immanent "potentials" of existence: that is, how it can achieve more power, more strength, more force in this or that existent. However, even if in this respect Spinoza does allow for the mind to have some power over the body and thus a certain degree of spontaneous activity (for surely the *Ethics* is emancipatory for the subject only because it is a work of ideas), according to the German Idealists this does not come close to articulating the irreducibility of freedom attested by Kant.[162] Spinoza fails to see the true kernel of human liberty, a failure that not only makes the Spinozistic system insufficient in terms of the lived essence of freedom, but also thereby takes away life and richness from its ontology. Without inscribing the *difference* announced by subjectivity *into substance*, we miss something essential about the life of the absolute, a critique raised by Schelling in his *Freiheitsschrift*:

> The error of his system lies by no means in the positing
> of things in God, but rather in that there are things in the
> abstract concept of the world's being, instead of infinite
> substance itself, which in fact is also a thing for him. Thus
> his arguments against freedom are entirely deterministic, and
> in nowise pantheistic. He treats the will, too, as a thing, and
> then naturally proves that it must be determined in its every
> action by another thing, which, in turn, is determined by yet
> another thing, etc., into infinity. Hence the lifelessness of his
> system: the mindlessness of its form, the impoverishment of
> its concepts and expressions, the unyielding acerbity of its
> definitions [...]. One could view Spinozism in its rigidity as
> Pygmalion's statue: it needed to be given a soul by the warm
> breath of love.[163]

Hegel makes a similar point in his *Science of Logic*:

> Of course, substance is the absolute unity of *thought* and being
> or extension; it therefore contains thought itself, but only in
> its *unity* with extension, that is to say, not as *separating* itself
> from extension and hence, in general, not as determining and
> informing, nor as a movement of return that begins from itself.
> For this reason, on the one hand substance lacks the principle
> of *personality*—a defect that has especially aroused indignation
> against Spinoza's system.[164]

Humans are not mere passive players in the self-unfolding drama of the universe, but constitutive writers of it, dominating it from the inside out, to such an extent that they even present a *challenge* to the autonomy of substance. In the face of man, the very fabric of substance appears lacerated, for it encounters a transcendent Other within its heart of hearts that makes it non-coincident to itself, infringes upon its oneness and thereby renders it not-all. According to Žižek, what both Hegel and the middle-late Schelling find unsatisfactory about Spinoza is that he is unable to articulate the *ontogenetic condition of the possibility of the emergence of a freely existing transcendent(al) subjectivity out of the purely immanent plane of being and its implications for understanding the metaphysical nature of reality.* The problem is that freedom—in its very specific articulation in German Idealism—is

not compatible with substance qua devouring totality. How, then, are we to think substance *and* subject/system *and* freedom if we are to retain the spontaneity first brought to light, albeit for the most part formally, by Kant? For Žižek, the answer is clear: "[t]he passage from the Spinozan One *qua* the neutral medium/container of its modes [to] the One's inherent gap is the very passage from Substance to Subject."[165] But the recognition of this gap has to be intrinsically traumatic, terrifying—it demonstrates a radical shift in our understanding of the world as some sort of harmonious cosmos that holds itself together in its infinite rational majesty to a world that, lacking totalizing order, must be predicated upon disruption and upheaval. If such an intuition did arise in the history of German Idealism, we would expect to see a series of psychoanalytical defence mechanisms against a conscious acknowledgment of its truth, which in turn obstruct its texts. It is a direct confrontation with this Real of the tradition that will enable Žižek to bring forth the true *metaphysical horror* of subjectivity that he thinks Descartes had already glimpsed and that has been haunting philosophy like a spectre ever since.

It is this specific spin on the dialectical "union" of system and freedom that is of utmost importance for understanding Žižek's psychoanalytical reactualization of German Idealism. It has two functions. First, it demonstrates the heterodox character of Žižek's appropriation of the tradition insofar as he proclaims that its real truth has always been this disjunctive, parallax relationship between the two terms.[166] It clearly shows us how and why Žižek challenges our normal preconceptions of German Idealism's internal historico-theoretical concerns and puts us in a position to evaluate Žižek's own readings more clearly. Second, it demonstrates that Žižek's own specific take on its unconscious *Grundlogik* is grounded in an extremely coherent reading of the stakes at play in post-Kantian philosophy, even if these have been drastically reformatted along the way according to a perceived and unrealized textual possibility. This makes reading Žižek a strange experience because there is an irreconcilable tension between Žižek's account of German Idealism and what its representatives on the surface appear to accomplish with their systems. Yet through this productive clash, Žižek is trying to create a space of "therapeutic" interplay between German Idealism's surface content (what it takes itself to be in the narcissistic orbit of the Imaginary that often tells itself lies to cover up its dirty spots) and various symbolically non-integrated elements visibly existing in its fold (the ephemeral flickering of a traumatic Real interrupting its normal discourse pointing to its repressed truth), whose integration would demand a radical reconfiguration of its own self-perception (in the spirit of *Wo Es war, soll ich werden*). Žižek seeks to understand what the role played by this disavowed knowledge could teach us about this crucial turning point in the history of philosophy, the nature of subjectivity, and, ultimately, the very ontological structure of the world we live in.

6.3 The Suffocating Deficiency of a *Naturphilosophie*

The immediate problem facing the late German Idealists is that the Kantian affirmation of transcendental freedom must be grounded in an ontological edifice that can rival Spinozism, for otherwise a Spinozist could argue that freedom is merely the *misrecognition* of the absolutely free self-unfolding oneness of substance, of man's subsumption within the positive order of being driven by a divinely energized and productive nature as its immanent cause. While both the early Schelling and Hegel offer their own solutions, Hegel remains unsatisfied with the results of his onetime colleague and friend, both in terms of the former's naturephilosophical response to the early Fichte and his quasi-Spinozistic attempts to ground transcendental subjectivity and creative nature in a point of absolute indifference that is neither subjectivity nor nature, but possesses both equally within it. Both projects seem to miss the mark, but why this would lead to a break between Hegel and Schelling is not clear. As hinted by Žižek's vision of Hegel and the middle-late Schelling, Hegel must have implicitly recognized here that Schelling fails to grasp the true radicality of Kantian freedom and its implications by adhering too much to a unitary view of the absolute, the seamless oneness of all that is. Consequently, Hegel tries to save the breakthrough of the critical system by thinking substance *as* subject, by thinking how the positive order of being *ex-ists* (*existere* in the sense of stepping or standing out) in the mode of subjectivity, instead of merely tying two apparently different yet complementary areas together into a precarious, "dead" harmony in indifference, wherein all qualitative difference between subjectivity and objectivity becomes secondary, unimportant, and ultimately lost. As Hegel himself says in his *Philosophy of Nature*:

> The cause of [*Naturphilosophie*'s] aberration lay in the fundamental error of first defining the Absolute as the absolute indifference of subjective and objective being, and then supposing that all determination is a merely *quantitative* difference. The truth is rather, that the soul of absolute form, which is the *concept* and living reality, is solely qualitative self-sublating differentiation, the dialectic of absolute antithesis. One may think, in so far as one is not aware of this genuinely infinite negativity, that one is unable to hold fast to the absolute identity of life, without converting the moment of difference into a simply external moment of reflection. This is of course the case with *Spinoza*, whose attributes and modes occur in an *external* understanding; life must then completely lack the *leaping point* of selfhood, the principle of autonomous movement, of internal self-diremption.[167]

This citation clearly shows the task Hegel believes must be accomplished: a full actualization of the primordial insight underlying the *cogito* by instituting the I and the schism it evokes into the very immanent activity of the absolute. For if we follow Fichte's intuition that the subject emerges in being "by absolute spontaneity alone," that is, "not through a *transition*, but by means of a *leap*,"[168] in the wake of the subject the life of substance must be said to undergo a process of *internal self-diremption*. Accordingly, Hegel's project is an attempt to *ontologize* the Kantian framework by exploring conditions of the possibility of the emergence of the subject out of a ground that remains Other to it (its "pre-history"), insofar as its self-positing must be identical to a liberating self-caused separation from substance that leaves the latter *bleeding* in its ontological fold. Hegel's goal is to balance Spinoza and Kant by creating a metaphysical system that *renders possible* rather than *precludes* freedom in such a way that his "transcendentalism" reaches far beyond the conditions of theoretical knowing or practical action and directly opens up to a metaphysics of the ontological rupture that presents itself as the extra-subjective condition of human autonomy.

The issue is to explain how a true freely existing subject can arise from within the internal mechanics of substance. Žižek's heterodox and challenging claim is that the only way to do this is by taking the split announced by Cartesian subjectivity and pushing it to its limits by inscribing the non-coincidence of mind with matter *into the very heart of being*. If human freedom is *irreducibly* self-reflexive and self-legislative it cannot be understood in terms of the basal energetic pulsating of the absolute. Reading the Hegelian response to Schelling remodulated through psychoanalysis, Žižek suggests that what provokes the movement from transcendental philosophy to Hegelian substance as subject is how Spinozism and the Kantian articulation of freedom reciprocally expose each other's intrinsic limitations, which simultaneously force us to rethink our understanding of ourselves and our relation to the world. While the latter lacks a metaphysics, the former misses the irrevocable (ontological) disturbance of/in nature at the basis of the *cogito*, which signals that human spontaneity cannot be contained in the positive order of being, something also missed in Schelling's own early *Naturphilosophie*. For Žižek, the true breakthrough of Kantian idealism, made explicit for the first time in Hegel and in the middle-late Schelling and then most acutely in psychoanalysis, is the proclamation of transcendental freedom as linked to *Todestrieb*, an excess of being that breaks from all externally given laws, dirempts being from the inside out, and thereby produces a tension-stricken not-all bursting at the seams from inner turmoil. Because of the value Žižek accords to the psychoanalytical experience of the discord between mind and body, he arrives here at a conditional: *If* freedom exists, substance cannot be all. Substance's auto-disruption is the first-level condition of the possibility of the subject. Although this is perhaps a tenuous claim to make within the context of post-Kantian idealism (it exhibits an abundance of *other* ways of understanding the substance-subject relation), we should be wary of dismissing Žižek for purely "historico-contextual" reasons. He himself is more interested in another possibility of understanding German Idealism he sees hinted at behind the scenes of its texts. The fact that his reading is not a mere line-by-line commentary is no reason to proclaim that it is outright wrong. As a Lacanian, Žižek does not share the presuppositions that would make such a reading possible in the first place—and to apply external

methodologies and constraints of truth for evaluating his interpretation would, in fact, merely do to Žižek what his critics accuse him of doing. In this respect, their critiques are a performative contradiction.

What intrigues Žižek in Hegel's articulation of the subject as self-relating negativity is its connection with the Kantian pedagogical concept of "unruliness" and "diabolic evil." Insofar as self-relating negativity indicates that human subjectivity is *non-natural*, it shows that, if we follow the internal course of German Idealism, many of Hegel's concepts such as the "night of the world" or "the activity of dissolution [which] is the power and work of Understanding"[169] appear to be nothing other than an elaboration of the subject's origins within an ontological disruption from the closed circuitry of nature's homeostatic laws as already alluded to but not fully developed by Kant. Žižek proclaims that we normally overlook something crucial in Hegel, for what Žižek's Hegel adds to the Kantian notion of the transcendental constitution of experience and rational self-determination is a gesture towards their dark commencement, a glimpse into how the spectral pandemonium of the pre-logical Real we see in "unruliness" precedes and makes possible the autonomy of the *cogito* and its originary "diabolic evil," thus drawing a more explicit link between notions whose interdependence Kant merely suggested:

> The human being is this night, this empty nothing, that contains everything in its simplicity—an unending wealth of many representations, images, of which none belongs to him—or which are not present. This night, the interior of nature, that exists here—pure self—in phantasmagorical representations, is night all around it, in which here shoots a bloody head—there another white ghastly apparition, suddenly here before it, and just so disappears. One catches sight of this night when one looks human beings in the eye—into a night that becomes awful.[170]

Prior to the self-legislative laws of practical reason and the synthesis of transcendental imagination constituting the unity of phenomenal reality, we must posit some kind of ontological going-haywire that represents a savage *tearing apart* of the flow of vital being ("here shoots a bloody head—there another white ghastly apparition") as that which opens up their logical possibility. If practical reason and transcendental imagination go hand in hand, it is because both are a response to subjectivity itself, a radicalization of this denaturalizing tendency, to a nature whose fold has been disrupted and thus demands re-articulation ("a night that becomes awful"):

> The pre-synthetic Real, its pure, not-yet-fashioned "multitude" not yet synthesized by a minimum of transcendental imagination, is, *stricto sensu, impossible*: a level that must be retroactively presupposed, but can never actually be *encountered*. Our (Hegelian) point, however, is that this mythical/impossible starting point, the presupposition of imagination, is already the product, the result of, the imagination's disruptive activity. In short, the mythic, inaccessible zero-level of pure multitude not yet affected/fashioned by imagination is nothing but *pure imagination itself*, imagination at its most violent, as the activity of disrupting the continuity of the inertia of the pre-symbolic "natural" Real. This pre-synthetic "multitude" is what Hegel describes as the "night of the world," as the "unruliness" of the subject's abyssal freedom which violently explodes reality into a dispersed floating of *membra disjecta*.[171]

This chaotic aggregate of ghastly forms and shapes making up the quasi-phenomenological self-experience of the night of the world is the pure expression of the unruliness/biological short circuitry of the human organism, the German Idealist variation upon Lacan's mirror stage.[172] As in the latter, this moment is not to be taken in isolation, but to be supplemented with what it ontogenetically makes possible, namely, the ideal-symbolical realm of ordered experience. What we see here is *quasi-phenomenological* because, in actuality, there is no fully developed I that stands in relationship to an alterity over and against which it can stand (rather than there being well-defined *Gegen-stände*, there is nothing but a fragmentary field lacking coherence). This I can only emerge *après coup* after a free act of synthesis of this initial state of chaotic dispersion, that is, its ideal-symbolic re-articulation. As a result, the unruliness of the human organism is nothing other than another logical modality of transcendental imagination, its ontological zero-level as a disruption in/of the circuitry of nature's laws that demands its recombination, a recombination that can only be done in a non-natural (virtual) register; and reading this insight in light of Kant's pedagogical writings on the necessity of disciplining unruliness for the emergence of culture, we can thus further say that the epigenesis of the categories[173] as that which bestows upon experience its form cannot be limited to the logico-scientific structure that the latter assumes, but must also extend to the sociopolitical code underlying culture itself. The out-of-control freedom of the subject is intimately linked with the power of imagination (*Einbildungskraft*) precisely because it is only by means of the latter that the subject is capable of producing images (*Bilder* or schemata) by which it can give structure to this ghastly state of chaos in the Real, a quasi-phenomenal field lacking subject-object articulation since, although the subject itself has emerged in a primordial sense, as of yet there are no conceptual structures and no symbolic network necessary to mould reality into an integrated, smooth fabric (a process of transcendental *Bildung*, a schematization of the night of the world). The paradox lies in the following: we can only explain the order of experiential reality in its multifarious modes by presupposing an originary, impenetrable pandemonium that we can only glimpse, but never know (it being always already "overcome" as soon as experience has come on the scene), a pandemonium that logically precedes and ontologically renders possible the consistency of full-fledged subjectivity and psychic life.

The I itself as an irreducible core of transcendental reflexivity can only emerge out of this chaos, this macabre seizure of forms that represents ontological mayhem/madness at its finest, which in turn signals that, at its zero-level, the subject is *nature in the mode of auto-denaturalization*. Hegel's horrifying ontologization of transcendental imagination in the night of the world, however, goes a step further. The night of the world does not merely indicate a radical breakdown in the flux of materiality in the Real; it is also the beginning of an infinite withdrawal of being into itself that cuts all ties with the outside world through obeying its own self-given law. Consequently, if this ontogenetic mayhem/madness is that which renders possible the absolute spontaneity of the I, then it shares an uncanny structural identity with Hegel's definition of evil in the *Jenaer Realphilosophie* as an "internal reality, absolute certainty of itself, the pure night of being-for-itself."[174]

Just as Kant demonstrates in *Religion within the Bounds of Reason Alone*, the basis of subjectivity for Hegel is inherently ambiguous, insupportably undecidable: not only does it necessarily bring our own understanding of freedom dangerously close to that of evil, where the difference between them threatens to dissipate, but more disconcertingly it points to the ancestral past of the subject as entangled in some kind of unfathomable *ontological crime*.[175] Whereas early post-Kantian philosophy, namely that of Reinhold and the early Fichte, sought to unify the critical project through elementary philosophy and the absolute self-positing of the I, respectively, Hegel came across something disquieting in his own endeavour to escape its impasses: *theoretical and practical reason coincide in a chasm in being that testifies to an unspeakable extra-subjective violence.* What both Kant's pedagogic writings and Hegel's night of the world reveal is that in order for idealization/ symbolization to occur as a purely autonomous activity, there must be something in nature that leaves it lacerated, wounded, *bleeding*, this being the only way that a zone freed from its hegemony could arise. In other words, even if we take the breakthrough of Kantian idealism to be the priority of the symbolic-conceptual categories whereby the subject engenders experience rather than its account of freedom (a move that also assures that culture is always of our own making because not subject to natural determination) even on this reading, this is the dark horizon within which ideality and, by implication, the sociopolitical as a logically autonomous milieu can operate: *the death of nature in us.* In this respect, if the major insight of German Idealism and psychoanalysis is that "the passage from 'nature' to 'culture' is not direct,"[176] then one of its major implications is that the Symbolic is not only a "kingdom within a kingdom" (*imperium in imperio*), but more radically one that has won its way to ontological sovereignty through a destructive, murdering force, thus establishing the avid anti-Spinozism of both traditions.[177]

The pure I inaugurated by transcendental philosophy exposes a bone in the throat of substance, a snag in natural causality, proclaiming that the absolute as nature or the physical universe cannot be all. What must be taken from this is one of the key principles of Žižek's ontology: *freedom is not a raw, brute fact, but depends upon the caustic collapse of the vital fold of being, a brisure in the heart of the Real; the chaotic aggregate of ghastly forms that constitutes the zero-level of human freedom represents an ontological catastrophe, a catastrophe that is synonymous with the subject itself:* "it designates [...] the primordial Big Bang, the violent self-contrast by means of which the balance and inner peace of the Void of which mystics speak are perturbed, thrown out of joint."[178] In this sense, the Žižekian appropriation of the Hegelian attempt to think substance as subject readdresses what really differentiates Hegel from Schelling the *Naturphilosoph* and sets the stage for his own philosophical career. Although the early Hegel does support Schelling's project to develop a rich teleological account of nature (as various sketches in the Jena period demonstrate), he must be said to have come to some kind of recognition of the inherent limitations of Schelling's endeavour. It is this vital hemorrhaging of nature that, preventing the ideality of the subject from being subsumed within the self-actualizing of the absolute, pushes Hegel away from Schelling: before the transcendental (re)constitution of reality by the I can occur, an internal ontological short circuit, a metaphysical breakdown of substance, must be posited, which not only renders impossible a complete immersion of subjectivity within a natural evolutionary narrative, but declares the ultimate discontinuity between nature and spirit instead of their peaceful identity and mutual interpretation in nature as "the unconscious poetry of spirit."[179]

6.4 The Night of the World/A Monism Bursting at Its Seams

Hegel makes a crucial step towards elaborating the paradoxical ground of the subject by demonstrating that it is this going-haywire, this *dysfunctioning* of substance that makes subjectivity incommensurable with material being and renders possible freedom in the truly "idealist" sense of the word. It is Hegel's account of the advent of the I in nature that is the first to truly explicate the eruption of the subject as an extimacy that cannot afterwards be resubsumed within the oneness of the self-integrating unity of the absolute. There is no smooth union, no ultimate self-penetrating identity within the fabric of all-pervasive being, for we encounter an infinite breakdown, an internal tension, that causes irrevocable havoc in the life of the absolute: "Subject designates the 'imperfection' of Substance, the inherent gap, self-deferral, distance-from-itself, which forever prevents Substance from fully realizing itself, from becoming 'fully itself.'"[180] The subject, therefore, has no *positive* ontological substrate, so that in Hegel the German Idealist attempt to supply a foundation for freedom strangely backfires on itself. But in its very failure, this attempt stumbles upon a great truth: the zero-level of human freedom is a blockage, an obstruction in the mechanics of nature, for the ontological status of the transcendental expresses its dependence upon *a self-destructive negativity in substance itself.* The Žižekian thesis is that without the articulation of this paradoxical site of excessive negativity (*Todestrieb*) as emerging immanently within being, all metaphysical accounts of human subjectivity and freedom risk their reductionist-monistic cancelation—otherwise we cannot explain the leap constitutive of the latter without risking their subsumption within an evolutionary transition. If we are to defend the *fact* of freedom, we must assume it and go all the way, which leads us to a single coherent conclusion: *"either subjectivity is an illusion, or reality itself (not only epistemologically) is not-All."*[181]

Here we see again how Žižek's reactualization fights against textbook accounts of German Idealism. If Hegel is to be a philosopher of freedom, his metaphysical articulation of the absolute *must* pass through the Kantian critical system, which means it cannot just be a simple *retour* to Spinozistic metaphysics; we must witness some kind of *brisure* within the absolute that disrupts the blind, immanent movement of natural laws and thereby enables the possibility of a freely existing subject. Although this is a rather controversial claim to make in the context of German Idealism, Žižek believes it allows us to reconceptualize its attempt to think substance as subject in such a way that it does not fall into conventional platitudes that smother its theoretical potential: platitudes such as comprehending the absolute as a cosmic subject-like agency that remains constant through all determinate change, preceding and (sub/con)suming the freedom of concrete existence by autonomously actualizing itself from a safe distance from the flux and contingency of reality, thereby guaranteeing the movement of history.[182] The subject only emerges from an accidental blockage, an irrevocable moment of self-division, which means that substance and subject are in themselves diremt and caught in finitude:

> "Substance is Subject" means that the split which separates
> Subject from Substance, from the inaccessible In-itself beyond

> phenomenal reality, is inherent to the Substance itself. [...]
> The point is not that Substance (the ultimate foundation of
> all entities, the Absolute) is not a pre-subjective Ground but
> a subject, an agent of self-differentiation, which posits its
> otherness and then reappropriates it, and so on: "Subject"
> stands for the non-substantial agency of phenomenalization,
> appearance, "illusion," split, finitude, Understanding, and so
> on, and to conceive Substance as Subject means precisely that
> split, phenomenalization, and so forth, are inherent to the life
> of the Absolute itself.[183]

Not only does the transcendental reconstitution of reality depend upon a
prior upsurge of pure ontological violence, but the very phenomenalization
of experience is co-incidental with this rupturing, the not-all, of substance.
In other words, *subject is substance in its mode of self-alienation: the
transcendental reconstitution of reality is nothing but an immanent attempt by
the absolute as nature to overcome its split by filling in the gap opened up in the
core of its vital being*, whereby ego development and concrete experience are
reduced to a reaction formation, an attempt to suture a wound. Substance
is *not* subject (as a proclamation of identity): substance *becomes* subject (in a
moment of trauma). The very fact that there is experience demonstrates this
for Žižek, for there is no intrinsic reason for experience within the "smooth"
self-articulation of substance.

But here we should make another addition. When we say that the
subject is a transcendent Other created from within the immanence of
being, we must be careful. It is not that substance creates or produces
another substance, in which case the enigma concerning how one could
explain the genesis of one out of the other would remain unsolved. Rather,
the subject is nothing but the void of substance, the minimal difference of the
absolute to itself,[184] which creates a metaphysical vacuum that is able to
have devastating effects in the fabric of the Real of nature from which it
emerged as soon as it develops the capacity to paradoxically relate to itself
(movement from "unruliness" to "diabolic evil," from the *tearing apart* of
the flow of vital being to its radicalization in "the night of the world"). In
this sense we should understand late German Idealism, and by consequence
Žižek's own metaphysics, as attempts to think system and freedom as a

critique of Propositions 12 and 13 of Part I of the *Ethics*, which argue for the absolute indivisibility and untouchable oneness of substance, but in such a way that we do not fall into the logical conundrum outlined in Propositions 2 through 6, whose goal is to show the impossibility of two substances having nothing in common being able to have an effect upon one another or to produce one another, all the while paradoxically without violating Propositions 14 and 15, which argue that all things must be within one substance. What idealism reveals to us is that freedom expresses something *operatively new that has emerged within being and is irreducible to its ebb and flow, yet that does not exist outside of it,* a transcendence in immanence that indicates some kind of split within substance itself infringing upon the logical hegemony of its infinite power by means of its internal breakdown. The subject "is not a new name for the One which grounds all, but the name for the inner impossibility or self-blockage of the One."[185] In man, negativity, having attained notional self-reflexivity, shows itself to be foundational to identity rather than a mere subcategory of positivity of the absolute used in the determination of finite things, so that it possesses its own monstrous logic that colonizes the immanent field within which it has emerged from a place that can only appear, from within that field, as an infinite elsewhere. However, what do we see here except the beginnings of a systematic ontologization of Lacanian metapsychology, centred in the mirror stage as a primordial organic disharmony indicative of a disjunctive "and" inscribed within being? Doesn't Žižek imply here that the only possible way to answer Miller's famous question: "Lacan, what's your ontology?" is by a passage through German Idealism, because of the distinctly "psychoanalytical" themes omnipresent in the latter once we psychoanalytically reconstruct its *Grundlogik*?

Yet one other thing should be clear at this juncture. Although Žižek's Hegel glimpses into the ontologico-foundational basis of human spontaneity preceding the transcendental constitution of experiential reality, he is unable to account for two things. First, *the immanent generation of this negativity within the material flux of substance* that sets the stage for subjectivity by enacting the first lacerations upon substance. How does the vital flow of being itself rupture? How does this extimate core germinate within the Real and incite a violent explosion that forever precludes the ontological life of

the Real, thus making it barred, nothing but a series of *membra disjecta*?
Second, the *absolute spontaneity of the very founding gesture of subjectivity* that
depends on nothing but itself for its own self-positing, a self-positing that
presents itself as a fiat that of itself institutes a pure difference in being:

> the problem for us is how we are to conceive of the founding
> gesture of subjectivity, the "passive violence," the negative
> act of (not yet imagination, but) abstraction, self-withdrawal
> into the "night of the world." This "abstraction" is the abyss
> concealed by the ontological synthesis: by the transcendental
> imagination constitutive of reality—as such, it is the point of
> the mysterious emergence of transcendental "spontaneity."[186]

To answer these questions, we will need to delve into Žižek's oft-neglected
work on Schelling, for it is Schelling who delved most profoundly into the
obscure origins of subjectivity.

Notes

120. In the *Freiheitsschrift,* for instance, Schelling says that it is idealism that "we
have to thank for the first perfect concept of freedom" and then situates the true
Kantian breakthrough in its revolutionary articulation. See pp. 231ff. Hegel also
praises Kant's theory of freedom. See *Encyclopedia Logic,* p. 101 (§54Z). The same
applies to Žižek: "No wonder Kant is *the* philosopher of freedom: with him, the
deadlock of freedom emerges." Žižek, *The Parallax View,* p. 9. But all this was
stressed by Kant himself, who declares that freedom "constitutes the *keystone*
of the whole architecture of the system of pure reason and even of speculative
reason." *Critique of Practical Reason,* in *Practical Philosophy,* trans. and ed. Mary J.
Gregor (Cambridge: Cambridge University Press, 1999) p. 139.

121. In this sense, both Hegel and Schelling are following Fichte: "I live in a new world
since I read the *Critique of Practical Reason;* it destroyed theses that I thought were
irrefutable, proved things I thought indemonstrable, like the concept of absolute freedom." Johann Gottlieb Fichte, *Gesamtausgabe der Bayerischen Akademie
der Wissenschaften,* Division III: Briefe, vol. I, ed. R. Lauth, Hans Jacob, and H.
Gliwitzky (Frommann: Stuttgart-Bad Cannstatt, 1964–), no. 63, p. 168.

122. Žižek, *Less Than Nothing,* p. 265.

123. Žižek, *The Parallax View,* p. 93.

124. Ibid., p. 92.

125. Fichte, *Science of Knowledge,* p. 114.

126. Maldiney, *Penser l'homme et la folie* (Paris: Gillon, 2007), p. 114.

127. Fichte, *Science of Knowledge,* p. 247.

128. Ibid., p. 152.

129. Fichte, *The Vocation of Man,* trans. Peter Preuss (Indianapolis: Hackett Publishing, 1987), p. 64.

130. Freud, "The Loss of Reality in Neurosis and Psychosis," *SE,* XIX, p. 183.

131. Fichte, *The Science of Knowledge,* p. 243.

132. Fichte, *Wissenschaftslehre 1805,* ed. H. Gliwitzky (Hamburg: Felix Meiner, 1984), pp. 127–28.

133. Freud, "Neurosis and Psychosis," *SE,* XIX, p. 151.

134. Freud, "The Loss of Reality in Neurosis and Psychosis," *SE,* XIX, p. 185.

135. Fichte, *Foundations of Natural Right,* ed. Frederick Neuhouser, trans. Michael Baur (Cambridge: Cambridge University Press, 2000), p. 74.

136. Fichte, *Fichte: Early Philosophic Writings,* p. 147.

137. Fichte, *Foundations of Natural Right,* p. 76. Also compare p. 74.

138. See Schelling, *System of Transcendental Idealism,* trans. Peter Heath (Charlottesville: University Press of Virginia, 2001), p. 232.

139. See Hegel, *The Difference between Fichte's and Schelling's System of Philosophy,* pp. 143 and 168.

140. Schelling, *Darstellung meines Systems der Philosophie, Schellings sämmtliche Werke,* ed. K. F. A. Schelling, division I, vol. 4 (Stuttgart and Augsburg: J. G. Cotta'scher Verlag, 1856–1861), p. 109.

141. In his "mature period," Hegel declares Schelling as merely Fichte's *successor,* ironically going against the spirit of his early work on the insurmountable *difference* between them. Cf. *Lectures on the History of Philosophy: Medieval and Modern Philosophy,* trans. E. S. Haldane and Frances H. Simson (London: University of Nebraska Press, 1995), p. 529.

142. Hegel, *The Phenomenology of Spirit,* trans. A. V. Miller (London: Oxford University Press, 1977), p. 9.

143. Žižek, *The Ticklish Subject,* p. 55.

144. Žižek, *Less Than Nothing,* p. 266.

145. Hegel, *Lectures on the History of Philosophy: Medieval and Modern Philosophy,* p. 257.

146. Schelling, *Freiheitsschrift,* p. 231.

147. Ibid., p. 232.

148. Spinoza, *Ethics and Selected Letters,* ed. Seymour Feldman and trans. Samuel Shirley (Indianapolis: Hackett Publishing, 1982), II p7 (p. 66).

149. Ibid., I p13c (p. 39).

150. Ibid., I p16 (p. 43).

151. Ibid., I p15 (p. 40) and I ax1 (p. 31).

152. Ibid., I p34 (p. 56).

153. Ibid., Letter 78 to Henry Oldenburg (p. 254).

154. Ibid., V p23s (p. 216).

155. Ibid., Letter 58 to G. H. Schuller (p. 250). Compare with I p24 (p. 49), I p26 and 27 (p. 50), and I p33 (p. 54).

156. Ibid., II p48 (p. 95).

157. Fichte, *The Vocation of Man*, pp. 21–22.

158. Ibid., p. 24.

159. Spinoza, *The Ethics*, p. V pref (p. 203).

160. Ibid., V p23s (p. 216).

161. Ibid., I app (pp. 57–62).

162. Schelling, *Freiheitsschrift*, p. 227.

163. Ibid., pp. 230ff.

164. Hegel, *The Science of Logic*, p. 472.

165. Žižek, *The Parallax View*, p. 42.

166. See Žižek, *The Abyss of Freedom*, pp. 11–14.

167. Hegel, *Hegel's Philosophy of Nature*, vol. 3, pp. 142–43 (§359A). Translation modified.

168. Fichte, *Science of Knowledge*, p. 262.

169. See Hegel, *Phenomenology of Spirit*, pp. 18–19.

170. See Hegel, *Frühe politische Systeme* (Frankfurt am Main: Ullstein, 1974), p. 204; quoted in Donald Philip Verene, *Hegel's Recollection: A Study of Images in the Phenomenology of Spirit* (Albany: SUNY Press, 1985), pp. 7–8, whom Žižek takes it from. For a discussion, see *The Abyss of Freedom*, pp. 4–14; *The Ticklish Subject*, pp. 26–48; and *The Parallax View*, pp. 43–45.

171. Žižek, *The Ticklish Subject*, p. 33.

172. Kant knew this very well. See Kant, *Anthropology from a Pragmatic Point of View*, p. 423.

173. Kant, *The Critique of Pure Reason*, B167.

174. Hegel, *Frühe politische Systeme*, p. 262.

175. Žižek and Daly, *Conversations with Žižek*, p. 126.

176. Žižek, *The Ticklish Subject*, p. 36.

177. Compare Spinoza, *The Ethics*, III pre (p. 103).

178. Žižek, *The Ticklish Subject*, p. 31.

179. Schelling, *System of Transcendental Idealism*, p. 12.

180. Žižek, *The Abyss of Freedom*, p. 7.

181. Žižek, *The Parallax View*, p. 168; *Less Than Zero*, p. 725; and Žižek & Woodard, "Interview," *The Speculative Turn: Continental Materialism and Realism*, ed. Bryant, Levi, Nick Srnicek, and Graham Harman (Melbourne: re.press, 2011), p. 407. My italics.

182. See Žižek, *Less Than Nothing*, pp. 234–35 and 286–92.

183. Žižek, *The Ticklish Subject*, pp. 88–89.

184. Žižek, *Less Than Nothing*, p. 905.

185. Ibid., p. 380.

186. Žižek, *The Ticklish Subject*, p. 61.

Chapter 7
The Logic of Transcendental Materialism
Schelling and the Spectral Other Side of German Idealism

Žižek needs to go beyond Hegel to articulate a crucial dialectical moment of transcendental materialism: the emergence of an ontological violence within being that prohibits the indivisibility of the absolute as an infinitely powerful, self-sustaining whole and creates room for irreducible freedom and ideality. To demonstrate this, I will outline the inherent limitations in Hegel's attempt to think substance as subject by focusing on Žižek's criticisms of the mature Hegelian *Encyclopedia*, thereby showing the theoretical hole simultaneously opened up and concealed by Hegel. Spurred on by the perceived threat of Absolute Idealism to human freedom, what we will see is how Schelling's investigation of the abyssal origins of subjectivity presents us with a passionate attempt to rethink the grounding of the subject and its role in being so that the former is never reducible to the latter. In this regard not only can Schelling's "materialist" response to Hegel be seen as the culminating, concluding step in what Žižek takes to be the unconscious *Grundlogik* of German Idealism, but it puts us face to face with the spectral Other Side of that tradition which it previously recoiled from to varying degrees: the insurmountable tension between the Real and the Ideal, which imposes a new conception of a never-to-be-reconciled *quadruple* dialectics with stark consequences for our understanding of nature, human historicity, and the absolute.

7.1 The Hegelian Recoil, The Schellingian Breakthrough

In order to explicate how substance auto-disrupts into a chaotic series of *membra disjecta*, the ontological zero-level preceding the synthetic modality of transcendental imagination, we have to move outside Žižek's reading of Hegel and confront his works on Schelling. The night of the world is merely a profile portrait of the disarray and pandemonium that pave the way for the transcendental constitution of reality into a (relatively) unified fabric of experience. It does not of itself explain the originary moment of withdrawal from organic immersion in the positive order rendered possible by *Todestrieb* as the obscure birthplace of an irreducible more-than-material subjectivity; comprehending this event requires us to first plunge headfirst into the immanent pulsation of the vital ebb and flow of being itself if we are to see how it sets the stage for the latter—a project that Žižek explicitly says is most acutely developed in Schelling:

> Kant was the first to detect this crack in the ontological edifice of reality: if (what we experience as) "objective reality" is not simply given "out there," waiting to be perceived by the subject, but an artificial composite constituted through the subject's active participation—that is, through the act of transcendental synthesis—then the question crops up sooner or later: what is the status of the uncanny X that *precedes* the transcendentally constituted reality? F. W. J. Schelling gave the most detailed account of this X in his notion of the Ground of Existence—of that which "in God Himself is not yet God": the "divine madness," the obscure pre-ontological domain of "drives," the pre-logical Real that forever remains the elusive Ground of Reason that can never be grasped "as such," merely glimpsed in the very gesture of its withdrawal.[187]

This, however, creates an internal problem for Žižek's work insofar as he describes his own project time and time again as Hegelian and *never* as Schellingian. If it is Schelling who is the philosopher who most fully describes the material ontogenetic conditions for the emergence of the subject rather than Hegel and thus more predominantly influences Žižek's metapsychology and ontology, then the fact that his own overt reliance upon Schelling remains largely behind the scenes potentially demonstrates some kind of error, inconsistency, or sleight of hand. Not only does Žižek fail to give any systematic argumentation for the superiority of Schelling over Hegel in terms of the obscure origins of the I out of its pre-subjective *Grund*, he also levels off the differences between the two insofar as he appears, as will become clear, to read them reciprocally through one other. Here I am thinking specifically of his endeavour in *The Parallax View* to show that, "far from posing an irreducible obstacle to dialectics, the notion of the parallax gap provides the key which enables us to discern its subversive core. To theorize this parallax gap properly is the necessary first step in the rehabilitation of the philosophy of *dialectical materialism*."[188] But this quote is suspicious: remarking that Schelling was "the first to formulate the post-idealist motifs of finitude, contingency and temporality,"[189] and is even thus "at the origins of dialectical materialism,"[190] it is clear that Žižek associates Schelling with the beginning of this tradition rather than Hegel; Schelling occupies an "immediate" place, acting "as a kind of 'vanishing mediator' between the Idealism of the Absolute and the post-Hegelian universe of finitude-temporality-contingency, [such] that his thought—for a brief moment, as it were in a flash—renders visible something that was invisible and withdrew into invisibility thereafter."[191] It is Schelling, not Hegel, who supplies us with the premonitions of a new radical way of philosophizing, a new dialectics. Moreover, the very idea of an insurmountable internal limit (a gap) as constitutive of (onto)logical movement—the necessity of positing the non-coincidence and tension of its moments to one another in order for it to function—has a more manifest affinity with Schelling's middle-late philosophy, which, developed as a response to the absoluteness of the Hegelian self-mediating Notion, bases itself on the idea of the indivisible remainder, *der nie aufgehende Rest*, as an irremovable snag in every system that guarantees its very vitality. Žižek in many ways appears to be interpreting Hegel retroactively through Schelling, which would explain why the irreducibility of the parallax between moments in contradistinction to their organic interpenetration in the notional structure of any given phenomenon is the "perverse" truth of Hegelian dialectics.[192] What is more, in a key passage in *Less Than Nothing* that describes dialectics as "the science of the gap between the Old and the New," Žižek abruptly and without

explication jumps into a discussion of the middle-late Schelling, going so
far as to say that to avoid mystification properly we should not abandon
his project from this period of his thinking, but rather "reformulate it so as
to avoid the mystification of the theosophic mytho-poetic narrative,"[193] in
such a way that it appears that the proximity of his reading of Hegel and
Schelling when coupled with this brief and rare methodological explanation
points to the core of his heterodox reading of German Idealism and thus his
philosophy. This suggests that the core of Žižek's philosophy is a hybridism
of Schellingianism and Hegelianism, so that exploring this intersection
puts us face to face with the theoretico-ontological stakes underlying his
entire project.

Yet the following question imposes itself: at what point is Žižek's own
metaphysical archaeology of the subject *Schellingian* or *Hegelian*? The
very posing of this question is relatively misleading within the context of
Žižek's reactualization of German Idealism, considering that what interests
him is not Kant, Schelling, or Hegel as particular historical thinkers
whose respective philosophies often display insurmountable differences
to one another, not to mention incompatible concerns (to such a degree
that one could even question whether German Idealism constitutes a
coherent tradition with a single logical nucleus). What he finds alluring
is a psychoanalytical truth self-unfolding throughout their works, a truth
inaugurated by the Cartesian *cogito* and ultimately culminating in Freud
and Lacan, but that they are unable to articulate fully due to its traumatic
nature, "our experience of freedom" being, after all, "properly *traumatic*."[194]
However, even if what intrigues Žižek is the disavowed *Grundlogik* implicitly
driving the movement as an unconscious formation—something that
appears in a flash only to withdraw again into the abyss from which it
came—we can nevertheless demonstrate a certain dominating influence of
Schelling by showing how the latter fills in a theoretical void opened up by
Hegel and thereby radicalizes the founding insight of German Idealism.

According to a Žižekian narrative of the untold history of German
Idealism, the essence of that impossible X that eternally precedes the birth
of consciousness remains underdeveloped in the Hegelian attempt to think
substance as subject. Although the Hegel of the night of the world hints at
the disturbing metaphysical paradoxes that arise out of the ontologization of

transcendental imagination and its concomitant concept of freedom, in *The Ticklish Subject* Žižek expresses outright dissatisfaction with Hegel's most systematic undertaking to inscribe the subject within a dialectics of nature as propounded in the various versions of *The Encyclopedia of the Philosophical Sciences*. Since this book is written after *The Indivisible Remainder*, it would appear that Žižek's critical engagement with Hegel's mature system and its account of the passage to culture is based on the presuppositions that guide his own transcendental materialism as worked out in this vehement work on Schelling published only three years earlier. In other words, his admitted disapproval is an implicit proof of the prioritization given to Schellingian ontology for the theorization of the parallax as a metaphysics of the disjunctive "and."

Pointing to an ambiguity persisting within the movement from self-contained Notion to nature and then to spirit in his mature system, Žižek suggests that Hegel was unable to bring into conceptual fullness the earth-shattering realization that he was on the verge of.[195] What is left aside is, strictly speaking, the night of the world that Hegel's earlier *Realphilosophie* had uncovered. In the *Encyclopedia*, it is uncertain how this radical negativity, this moment of irremediable ontological breakdown haunted by sanguinary spirits, truly fits in. Instead of the precarious, never-to-be-complete "reconciliation" between nature and finite spirit brought forth by the subject, culture itself becomes a closed circuit, a complete return of the Idea to itself out of its infinite self-outsidedness in nature, a move that, by rendering culture a self-sufficient, self-contained all, completely does away with the unruliness that is the zero-level of freedom as revealed in psychoanalytical experience and potentially jeopardizes the irreducibility of the practico-concrete in Kant and made explicit for the first time in Fichte. The issue is that the Idea is nothing other than this very act of its own returning to itself, nothing but the *attempt* at reconciliation, so that not only is this very movement generative of that to which the movement returns, but more drastically the self-alienation of the Idea is a condition of its returning to itself.[196] If the ontological zone wherein the fabric of the world is torn apart ("here shoots a bloody head—there another ghostly apparition") disappears, the claim is stronger than simply the subject as the irreconcilable in-between of nature and culture, the bone in the throat of substance and the snag in the machine of the Symbolic, loses all currency: we would paradoxically lose the very condition of free spiritual activity, for a complete sublation of nature into culture would herald the destruction of culture as a process of building an artificial, second nature where one is missing. *Losing the obstacle causes us, in turn, to lose the goal; dialectics needs its own inner impediment to get off the ground.*

Corresponding to the reality/Real distinction in Lacanian psychoanalysis, we may thus venture that there are two forms of Hegelian dialectics: either we have the perfect dialectical *triad* of the mature system (Logic → Nature → Spirit) or a non-closed *tetrad* that signals the self-collapse of dialectical logic itself as seen in the *Realphilosophie* (Logic → Nature → finite Spirit → objective/naturalized Spirit).[197] The triad is, strictly speaking, not merely inconsistent with Hegel's—and ultimately Kant's—true earlier insight, but self-defeating: it robs dialectics of its own energy, energy that can only be mobilized due to the structural impossibility of completing the task it sets out to complete. At the most basic level, culture can never utterly sublate the excessive kernel of human being and simply make it a moment of the self-meditation of the Notion as it seeks to actualize itself: there must always be a minimal, insurmountable distance between the unruliness of human nature, the withdrawal into the nocturnal *Innenwelt* of the world that is the founding gesture of subjectivity, and the symbolic, cultural network that attempts to form and discipline this non-natural violence into a new order after subjectivity has posited itself as such. The two can never overlap within an all-pervasive totality, insofar as for Žižek this overlapping would not merely level out the singularity that marks the subject (namely, the fact that it cannot be fully explained by either material or cultural determinations) but also in the same breath radically preclude the condition of the possibility of human freedom and the exploration of its larger metaphysical implications.

The difference between traditional accounts of Absolute Idealism and the quadruple dialectic of the *Realphilosophie* thus enables us to demonstrate the logic Žižek wants to defend both in terms of his own transcendental materialism and the unconscious *Grundlogik* of modern philosophy that he psychoanalytically constructs. Whereas the former articulates itself according to a series of upward-moving spirals wherein each new turn completely encompasses the previous one in an act of subsumption (so that we encounter a completely self-enclosed, organic oneness that slowly articulates itself in increasing complexity) the very self-unfolding operation of the later precludes the possibility of such a self-totalizing activity. While Absolute Idealism itself does move forward on the basis of fundamental non-coincidence or immanent contradiction (there is conflict internal to the system), it is always productive of new, evermore comprehensive unity, but in such a manner that its innate teleological push towards greater order and self-coherence is able to project an upper limit. Since it knows no radical inner impediment, the ever-expanding series of upward spirals predicts a point in history when the Idea would attain perfection by returning to itself and in turn overcome its prior self-alienation, that is to say, when nature and culture would become reconciled in a moment of ontological jubilation. Here, understood as the self-development of the structure of the world, the absolute is seen as an immanent processual movement from self-externality to absolute self-mediation: by making itself into the Idea, nature (as a realm of *pure contingency*) would have succeeded by coming to a complete grasp of itself in the *freedom of thought*, whereby the end of the movement would see itself in the beginning, thus closing the circle of circles. Within transcendental materialism, however, the passage from nature to culture does not reveal a struggle of notional transmutation as culture endeavours to rid itself of its basis in nature in the onslaught of history with the promise of completion, but rather reveals a standstill in the heart of being that cannot be brought into a higher moment of truth of free spirit that would bring the circle of circles to an end: the ebb and flow of substance ontogenetically incites the birth of a freely existing subject only through a self-sabotaging, self-destructive movement that defies perfect reconciliation, because this unruliness inheres in all culturally achieved unity and disrupts it from within. Conflict, though here too internal to the system, articulates at this juncture of the passage from nature to culture an irrevocable place of rupture, devastation, or laceration in the absolute, which points to a dialectical residue that can never become a vehicle of internal growth of the structure of the world, yet that simultaneously sustains culture as the very attempt to overcome it. With culture, we see that nature had immanently produced an eruptive, shattering transcendence (the subject) that bursts the seams of any monistic wholeness and gets in the way of the immanent self-development of the absolute by instituting a new age of the world that can never be reconciled with that which came before, in a moment of ontological triumph. As a consequence, if we inscribe culture into the fabric of the universe according to the second model of dialectics, we are forced to conclude that the absolute is open, precarious, and necessarily incomplete, for the symbolic universe is not only constitutively out of joint with nature, but as the always doomed attempt to reconcile itself with the latter, is constantly forced to reinvent itself.

The process of subjectification (culture) emerges out of the ontological chasm opened up by the pure I and holds a position of infinite difference with respect to nature insofar as it operates within a zone of logical non-coincidence that has been carved out from within the laws of the latter. Instead of a self-enclosed spiral or circle of circles, we see an immanent "break" that prevents the next dialectical phase of self-appropriation from occurring and by means of which another level of autonomous activity irreducible to the first can take hold. The image is of two cones—one ontologically positive, the other immersed in a virtual zone of nonbeing—linked together by a black hole that is the pure I, the night of the world, whereby nature and culture self-actualize in isolation to one another, but are nevertheless negatively tied together by the abyssal void of subjectivity—that which "protrudes" out of both as an impossible in-between non-explicable in either. The subject stands for the bone in the throat of substance that prevents it from being a devouring all following its own immanent laws (nature's non-coincidence to self) just as much as it stands for that snag in the cultural machine (the non-all of the symbolic Other) that can never be filled in or completely overcome, and that thus constitutes the impetus for all subjectification as a series of reaction formations *and* the infinite proliferation of the forms it can take on due to its necessary failure of covering up, schematizing, the primordial trauma. In this regard, transcendental materialism presents a radically different view of dialectics as Absolute Idealism, going so far as to claim that what the latter misses is that it is, at best, a mere compensation in fantasy for the traumatic truth of the former. Here we have a rich account of the emergence of two zones of activity wherein, although the second is dependent upon the first that constitutes its genetic ground, it remains entirely free. To anyone familiar with the *Freiheitsshcrift* or the *Weltalter*, this demonstrates the manifest *Schellingian* character of Žižek's criticism of Hegel, while at the same time locating the germ of the former's logic of the *Grund* within Hegel's early *Realphilosophie*:

> But dependence does not annul autonomy or even freedom. It does not determine essence, but merely says that the dependent, whatever it might be, can only be as a consequent of that upon which it is dependent; it does not say what it is, and what it is not. Each organic individual, as something which has become, has its being only through another, and to this existent it is dependent in terms of becoming, but not at all in terms of being. It is not incongruous, says Leibniz, that he who is God is at the same time begotten, or vice versa; as it is no more a contradiction to say that he who is the son of a man is himself a man.[198]

7.2 The *Weltalter* and the Systematization of Freedom

One of the most interesting aspects of Žižek's reactualization of German Idealism is its claim that the middle-late Schelling's "departure" from the throes of reason and "descent" into theosophical obscurantism does not demonstrate a break from modern rationality as inaugurated by Descartes' search for a self-evident Archimedean starting point for all philosophy (famously developed further in Kant's transcendental conditions of the possibility of knowledge, and ultimately epitomized by Hegel's self-mediating Notion).[199] On the contrary, Žižek's reactualization states that Schelling actually makes explicit for the first time the perverse, unconscious truth that remains hidden throughout the entire tradition, but only appears ephemerally through the distortion of its imaginary-symbolic universe: his attempt to present a system that would be able to combat the perceived threat posed by Hegel's horrifying "pan-logicism" presents a radicalization, a *completion*, of modernity's fundamental insight into the paradoxical origins of subjectivity, an insight that Hegel himself was unable to follow through in his own endeavour to solve the impasse bequeathed by Kant's critical philosophy. In this sense, Žižek implies that it is philosophical orthodoxy that got it wrong: it is not Schelling who is the misfit, but rather *Hegel*, for it is he who turns away from the abyss brought forth by the idealist account of freedom after gazing too deeply into its traumatic core. After the *Realphilosophie*, something prevents Hegel, holds him back—there is a recoil, a hesitation.

What is so compelling for Žižek about works such as the *Weltalter* is *not* their anti-Hegelian character, but their ability to penetrate into the breakthrough heralded by modern philosophy and to bring it to a new, higher level. It is Schelling who gives the complete articulation of its underlying but disavowed core insofar as it is he who most fully outlines the principles of a *quadruple* dialectical logic, whereas Hegel, going against his own initial tendencies, falls back into a triad at a crucial moment and loses sight of the "deontologized being" of the subject. What thus characterizes the passionate fury of the middle-late period is its embrace of the paradoxes surrounding subjectivity. This is what makes Schelling that which is in Hegel more than Hegel himself, the extimate core deeply entrenched within the body and soul of Hegel's philosophy that he could not own, as if Schelling were the real spectre haunting and destabilizing his mature system. Consequently Schelling, more than anyone else, is the culmination of German Idealism: it is he who most passionately tarries with its Real, for, in their "very failure, [the *Weltalter* drafts] are arguably the acme of German Idealism and, simultaneously, a breakthrough into an unknown domain whose contours became discernible only in the aftermath of German Idealism";[200] "Hegel's 'overcoming' of Schelling is a case in itself: Schelling's reaction to Hegel's idealist dialectic was so strong and profound that more and more it is counted as the next (and concluding) step in the inner development of German Idealism."[201]

In the context of the Žižekian reactualization of German Idealism, the fundamental assertion to be made is that to understand the movement towards the middle-late period in Schelling we must at some level say that Schelling himself came to realize the deficiencies of his previous philosophical endeavours, perhaps either through a rethinking of the Kantian critical system or by being spurred on by Hegel. Although, for instance, in the *Naturphilosophie* Schelling is also interested in the dark side of nature, the project forecloses the possibility of *Todestrieb* as an emergent and infinitely disruptive force in being. In this sense, Žižek's rejection of the early Schellingian attempts to balance transcendental idealism with materialism follows the same line of argument as his denial of the theoretical weight of contemporary evolutionary models of self-reflexive consciousness,[202] for both share the same fault: the ultimate identification of mind and matter instead of the articulation of their ultimate irreconcilability to one another. From the standpoint of the immanent laws of the pre-symbolic Real (as avowed by Spinozistic monism or reductionistic materialism), Žižek's claim is that the Ideal cannot be explained either on the basis of a teleological or purely naturalistic emergence. The Ideal *explodes* from within the vital throes of positive being,[203] rather than just being one specific (albeit complex) mode of physical organization, for it names an alienating distance to self, a non-coincident split that literally short-circuits the world. Rather than inhering in matter as its implicit structure, mind can only emerge within the void of this ontological scar, thus making it impossible to reconcile with matter.

Written in the aftermath of the birth of the Hegelian system with the publication of the *Phenomenology of Spirit* in 1807, which contains a famous explicit criticism of the Schellingian philosophy of absolute indifference as an attempt to balance the two poles of realism and idealism,[204] the *Freiheitsschrift* (1809) and the *Weltalter* (1810–1815) radically restructure the problematic that had occupied Schelling's philosophical career. But what complicates the issue at hand is the fundamental ambiguity of the Hegel-Schelling relationship in Žižek's own thinking, which is brought to an extreme at this crucial juncture: while one could say that much of the young Schelling's work is an attempt to rethink the subject's relation to the noumenal thing-in-itself that haunts its representations or to explicate the androgynous complementarity of the ideal-real poles, the middle-late Schelling's problematic, on Žižek's reading, is the one he erroneously attributes to Hegel: "the true problem is not how to reach the Real when we are confined to the interplay of the (inconsistent) multitude of appearances, but, more radically, the properly Hegelian one: *how does appearance itself emerge from the interplay of the Real?*"[205] Although Žižek does oscillate between calling this problematic Hegelian and Schellingian, what should be clear is that it is more accurately *Schellingian*, insofar as it is the latter—

according to Žižek's own words—who most fully develops the quadruple logic of the passage from the pre-logical Real into the Symbolic as the unconscious *Grundlogik* of German Idealism, whereas Hegel recoiled at the most crucial moment.

Interpreting the Weltalter through this theoretical framework, Žižek is then able to interpret its ontology as an attempt to articulate a transcendental materialism capable of grounding the psychoanalytico-Cartesian subject by thematizating the vanishing mediator between the Real and the Symbolic. He can do this, perhaps surprisingly, because first and foremost the *Weltalter* manuscripts present themselves as a theosophic exploration of creation. Perceiving Hegelian logic as a purely conceptual artifice that suffocates the freedom under the self-articulating necessity of the Notion, Schelling puts his philosophical prowess to use to give his own account of the emergence of temporality and finitude that could rival the dialectics of his great adversary. His basic thesis is that, although Hegelian logic can express notional necessity (what something ideally is) it ultimately fails to grasp the *fact* of any being, the *thatness* of its existence, especially if that being has its primordial basis in the brute, raw reality of freedom, something that forever eludes the self-mediation of conceptuality.[206] For Schelling, however, this failure of pan-logistic dialectics in the face of a freely deciding being (the emergence of the subject) does not amount to a mere admittance of the intrinsic limitations of knowledge and human reason. It must be distinguished from a merely negative constraint upon philosophizing because this dialectical dead end we come across in explicating freedom does not arise due to the limited synthesizing activity of the subject and the finite conditions of the possibility of knowledge, but rather through an (onto)logically disruptive and yet productive metaphysical activity: to say that the *fact* of a specific being that possesses freedom as its essential predicate cannot be *conceptualized* according to an a priori dialectics is to point to the uncontainable act constituting its very self-positing, which is therefore capable of continually heralding forth the new and tearing apart any given causal matrix in which it finds itself,[207] thereby making itself only graspable *après-coup* in the wake of its own self-instituting revelation in the world. The inability to conceptualize the advent of eruptive subjectivity in substance through pure reason transcends mere epistemological constraints and reaches out unto the ontological: it is not merely that we must be agnostic concerning the existence of a totalizing principle that holds being together, but more disconcertingly, *freedom proclaims that there is not any*. The subject is an unpredictable event in being that rewrites what we consider to be possible. Thus, in trying to systematize freedom in a way to escape the perceived threat of Hegelian Absolute Idealism, Schelling reaches a contradiction, a contradiction that paradoxically becomes the very vitality of his system itself, insofar as it declares that the totality of being must be understood in terms of a constitutive yet conflict-ridden relation with an immanent Other: "[w]ere the first nature in harmony with itself, it would remain so. It would be constantly One and would never become Two. It would be an eternal rigidity without progress."[208] Both the *Freiheitsschrift* and the *Weltalter* give expression to the necessary snag in the dialectical machine, the primordial, unruly excess of the Real over the Ideal that prevents any system of thinking from being self-enclosed unto itself and in the same breath guarantees the dynamic character of the latter by making it inclusive of freedom as an irrepressible, self-rupturing event at its very core.

In order to situate ourselves more firmly within the dialectical nuance of the *Weltalter* and show how, in relation to Žižek's ontology, Schelling holds a position of theoretical primacy over Hegel, we can use the problem of evil as an entry point, since it is perhaps in their respective theories thereof that they most strongly distance themselves from one other. Whereas for the mature Hegel evil becomes a mere sublated moment in the self-development of the good, a necessary phase for its establishment, for Schelling evil remains at its very core irrational and illogical. By definition it cannot be sublated as a moment within a higher dialectical standpoint because it is, at its primordial basis, the effect of an irreducible act of will. There is something spontaneous about evil that forever eludes conceptualization, something insurmountable about the wildness of a soul that insists on that which it wants and will sacrifice whatever it can to achieve it. Evil has something crazed and frantic about it: it is the capacity to say "No!" with the full knowledge of the implications of one's action. As soon as evil is *understood*, it fails to be *evil*; it becomes, rather, misguided good in the Platonic sense that no one does wrong willingly. Hence Schelling's articulation of freedom as the capacity for good *and* evil: freedom in itself must rest intrinsically incomprehensible, that which *cannot be dialectically mediated*, which means that its pure self-positing can only resemble madness insofar as it *precedes* and *makes possible* any articulation of a table of values that could be used to comprehend it. It of itself knows no order, no rationality—if it did, it would be explicable in terms of the principle of sufficient reason and at risk of being thrown into a subordinate position within a greater self-articulating whole of which it is a mere functional part. There is therefore something always essentially impenetrable in every good *and* evil act done out of freedom, something always irreducible and violent in each act of self-positing: without this intuition, we lose the breakthrough of the critical system as revealed most poignantly in Kant's pedagogical writings and succumb to another form of determinism (dogmatism) that cancels out the primordial meaning of autonomy within a logic of overarching and self-unfolding reason. Insofar as the act itself is concerned, both the modalities of good and evil as expressions of freedom are *formally identical*; they involve an act logically distinct at its zero-level from any set of values—or in other words, an act done *without any guarantee and without any external determination or influence*. More radically, this testifies that evil is itself at the core of every good act, *that evil is actually more primordial than the good*. In order for an act to be truly good and authentically free at the same time, it must "pass" through evil, discipline it, and use it as the tamed Grund for its own expansive power—any Yes (adherence to rationally determined ethical principles) must first be a No (an egoistic self-assertion) if it is to be *utterly* self-determined and not just a blind following of laws: "the day lies concealed in the night, albeit overwhelmed by the night; likewise the night in the day, albeit kept down by the day, although it can establish itself as soon as the repressive potency disappears. Hence, good lies concealed in evil, albeit made unrecognizable by evil; likewise evil in good, albeit mastered by the good and brought to inactivity."[209] In this respect, a priori dialectics *must* fail: if all birth is a birth from darkness to light, there is always something in the emergence of rational order that remains impervious to the latter.[210]

From this it becomes clear that the Schellingian concept of freedom is an explicit rethinking of the Kantian notion of diabolic evil and its co-related concept of the original "unnatural" unruliness of the human organism, so that these original insights become an intrinsic part of his own logic of the *Grund* as the indivisible remainder, the "incomprehensible basis of reality," which is missing in mature Hegelian dialectics. As a full-fledged ontologization of Kant's declaration of the radical spontaneity at the basis of human practical activity,[211] Schelling's philosophical impulse initiated by the *Freiheitsschrift* is an attempt to develop a system wherein freedom is irreducible to notional necessity, for "[o]nly he who has tasted of freedom can sense the desire to make everything its analogue, to spread it throughout the whole universe."[212] What intrigues him is the fact that there is an insurmountable enigmatic blind spot at the core of *every* action, *every* decision, a blind spot that not only presents the truth, mystery, and potential horror of human freedom, but more primordially reveals a deep *hole* that has been carved out in the flesh of being, making it tremble from within, for the unpredictable has emerged in its core. It is this strong conviction in freedom that leads Schelling into the abyssal labyrinths of self-exploration that constitute the conceptual fabric of the *Weltalter*, in the same way the intuition of freedom made Kant limit knowledge in order to make room for faith and embark down the path where he would eventually articulate the necessity of diabolic evil and unruliness in his pedagogical writings after years of original investigation into the essence of self-legislative practical reason. For Žižek, it is not an accident that Schelling's own project in the *Weltalter* ends up radicalizing Hegel's descriptions of the night of the world or Kant's account of unruliness, which in turn proves that his response to Hegel is the concluding step of German Idealism: all are driven by an attempt to give a philosophically adequate bedrock to freedom,[213] with Schelling merely following its intuition right to the metaphysical conclusions it forces upon us in a way other representatives in the tradition were unable to do. What distinguishes Schelling is that he, propelled by an immense energy to battle against what he perceived as the threat posed by Hegelian dialectics on human freedom, had the strength to go further than the others in the symbolization of the unconscious *Grundlogik* inherent in the tradition. If his best-known work is called *Philosophical Investigations into Human Freedom*, which in many ways spends more time speaking of God/nature than of humanity, it is because it is a work that delves into the *ontological* implications of the freedom revealed by idealism.

7.3 The Problem of the Beginning Itself: Schelling's Uncanny Response to Idealism

Just as in the *Freiheitsschrift*, and using the operative logic that it had already programmatically developed as a guide, Schelling in the *Weltalter* embarks upon a specific form of introspective analysis with the aim of developing a theosophy, the founding intuition of which is that the same process underlying the birth of human subjectivity is fundamentally structurally identical to God's creation of the world (as exhibited in the alchemical principle "so above, so below").[214] In another vein, the idea is that *psychological* experience is in some sense directly revelatory of the absolute drama of divine being in all its vicissitudes, *even if* it must pass through the meditating filters of self-reflexive consciousness: the experience of the relationship of dependence and autonomy that holds between one's pre-subjective, material *Grund* and free personality is primordially disclosive of an ontological event that is a symbol of God's relation to the finite created world. In this way, the theosophic odyssey of the birth of God out of that which in God is not God himself, is irrevocably intertwined with a parallel investigation into the ontogenesis of subjectivity out of a nature that presents itself as Other to and irreconcilable with its free self-standingness. Since the methodological starting point is similar to the psychoanalytical experience of disharmony between mind and body as the obscure basis of freedom (which hints at the vanishing mediator between them), Žižek is led to discard the entire theosophic scope of the work as ultimately accidental to its "true" philosophical core, so that Schelling's narration of the painful process of the self-begetting of God and the decision of divine creation presents itself as a mere "*metapsychological* work in the strict Freudian sense of the term."[215] Whether or not Žižek himself is justified in completely removing the theosophic scope from Schelling's argument, one must at the very least admit that Žižek's wager follows the spirit of Schelling's middle-late philosophy *to the letter*, for Schelling himself declares in the *Freiheitsschrift* to "have established the first clear concept of personality."[216]

What makes Žižek's appropriation of Schelling at times so provocative and compelling is his profound ability to penetrate into the fine details of the conceptual structures that make up the operative logic of the *Freiheitsschrift* and the *Weltalter* in a way no one else has. What interests him is how Schelling advances the descriptions in the tradition of the status of the elusive X, which simultaneously haunts transcendentally constituted reality, precedes it, and appears to set the stage for its condition of possibility. These three conceptual aspects of this *je ne sais quoi* map directly unto the three modalities of the Real: (i) the Real as a "kink" in the Symbolic, which pressurizes phenomenal reality; (ii) the Real as pre-symbolic "immediacy" that is lost through the advent of language; and (iii) the barred Real ($\cancel{R}$) now understood as an auto-disruptive substance ($N \neq N$) whose self-laceration creates the necessary room within which the transcendental constitution of reality through the Symbolic-Imaginary matrices underlying self-experience can take place, thus drawing attention to the interconnection of each aspect. Prior to these middle-late works, as we have seen, our relation to this mysterious X had already been partially "schematized" by a list of concepts (from Kantian transcendental freedom, diabolic evil, and unruliness to the Hegelian accounts of the night of the world and substance as subject). However, for Žižek, it is only with Schelling's own additions that we move away from the paradoxes of the ideal representation of the extra-subjective world or from a mere haphazard glimpse into the self-effacing ontological catastrophe that precedes the very possibility of free idealization. With him, we completely plunge into the auto-disruptive logic of the pre-symbolic Real at the basis of subjectivity so that the unconscious *Grundlogik* plaguing the German Idealist tradition, which had already from time to time appeared only to fall back into the darkness from which it came, finally comes clearly into light, becoming now minimally subjectified, as it were. The major difficulty, however, is how to articulate a philosophical system that can synthesize the various aspects of the Real together into a stable whole insofar as the very ontological space whose exploration would enable it *retreats the very moment that conscious experience begins and is only visible in its very gesture of self-withdrawal.*[217] It is no accident that the problem that haunts the entirety of the middle-late Schelling of the *Freiheitsschrift* and the *Weltalter* is, as Žižek emphasizes:

the *problem of the Beginning itself*, the crucial problem of German Idealism—suffice it to recall Hegel's detailed elaboration of this problem and all its implications in his *Science of Logic*. Schelling's "materialist" contribution is best epitomized by his fundamental thesis according to which, to put it bluntly, *the true Beginning is not at the beginning*: there is something that precedes the Beginning itself—a rotary motion whose vicious cycle is broken, in a gesture analogous to the cutting of the Gordian knot, by the Beginning proper, that is, the primordial act of decision. The beginning of all beginnings, the beginning *kat' exohen*—"the mother of all beginnings" as one would say today—is, of course, the *"in the beginning was the Word"* from the Gospel according to St John: prior to it, there was nothing, that is, the void of divine eternity. According to Schelling, however, "eternity" is not a nondescript mass—a lot of things take place in it. Prior to the Word there is the chaotic-psychotic universe of blind drives, their rotary motion, their undifferentiated pulsating; and the Beginning occurs when the Word is pronounced which "represses," rejects into the eternal Past, this self-enclosed circuit of drives. In short, *at the Beginning proper stands a resolution, an act of decision which, by differentiating between past and present, resolves the preceding unbearable tension of the rotary motion of drives*: the true Beginning is the passage from the "closed" rotary motion to "open" progress, from drive to desire—or, in Lacanian terms, from the Real to the Symbolic.[218]

What Žižek refers to as "Schelling-in-itself: the 'Orgasm of Forces'"[219] is the remarkable capacity Schelling's philosophy possesses of being able to descend into the immanent driving forces governing the extra-subjective, material Real, the elusive, obscure phase of darkness that precedes and sets the stage for the birth of the light that is the openness of self-reflexive consciousness. But what fascinates Žižek is the depth of his *materialist* response to Hegel, which still remains immersed in the fabric of transcendental idealism, a response that is "at the origins

of dialectical materialism."[220] This is why Žižek describes Schelling as a
vanishing mediator between classical philosophy and the contemporary
discourse of finitude: Schelling stands in a position of irreconcilable
contradiction between the two, a tension that Žižek takes upon himself
to further develop insofar as Schelling, according to him, is unable to
endure his own breakthrough and recoils.[221] If, onto the ground/existence
distinction propounded in the *Freiheitsschrift* and systematically laid out in
the *Weltalter*, we superimpose the real(ity)/ideal(ity) distinction operative
within modern philosophy from Descartes onward, we perceive a nuance in
the ontologization/grounding of Cartesian subjectivity: this split announced
between mind and matter, which makes them non-reconcilable to one
another, *occurs "within" or "on the side of" the material Real through an
ontologico-metaphysical deadlock, a schismatic rupture.* The standard debate
between idealism (ideality precedes and structurally makes possible the
positive order of physical being and is thus the insurmountable metaphysical
zero-level as in Platonism and textbook Hegelianism, or constitutes
completely self-grounding and self-justifying transcendental conditions or
normative values that make discourse possible as in Kantianism or much
linguistic philosophy) and materialism (there is nothing but the ebb and flow
of brute matter, the rest being reducible to an epiphenomenal production of
nature's self-enclosed laws, as in the Greek atomists, conventional cognitive
science, and logical positivism) is thus stood on its head in Schelling:

> idealism posits an ideal Event which cannot be accounted for
> in terms of its material (pre)conditions, while the materialist
> wager is that we *can* get "behind" the event and explore how
> Event explodes out of the gap in/of the order of Being. The
> first to formulate this task was Schelling, who, in his *Weltalter*
> fragments, outlined the dark territory of the "prehistory
> of Logos," of what had to occur in pre-ontological proto-
> reality so that the openness of Logos and temporality could
> take place.[222]

This quote expresses Schelling as one of the most crucial figures (if not *the*
most crucial figure) in the history of dialectical materialism for Žižek, and
thus establishes once and for all the pivotal role Schelling's ontology plays
in his own philosophical development, despite his own characterizations

of his project as Hegelian. So how, then, do the vicissitudes of pure, raw materiality open up unto the irreducible event of the Ideal and the transcendentally constituted reality of phenomenological (self-)experience?

7.4 *Grund* and Existence: The Pulsating Heart of Nature and the Upward Spiral of Human Temporality

Schellingian nature is more than a mere symbol or paradoxical representation of the eternal Past that precedes consciousness: it *is* that elusive, impossible X, that *je ne sais quoi* in the modality of the pre-symbolic Real prior to conceptual-linguistic mediation. Yet when we move from the world of human meaning and into the circuitry of nature's vital ebb and flow, we see that "[e]verything that surrounds us points back to a past of incredibly grandeur. The oldest formations of the earth bear such a foreign aspect that we are hardly in a position to form a concept of their time or origin or of the forces that were then at work,"[223] in such a way that the task of philosophy becomes to reconstruct this ancestral trajectory of the immemorial into a system of times:

> We find the greatest part of [its formations] collapsed in ruins, witnesses to a savage devastation. More tranquil eras followed, but they were interrupted by storms as well, and lie buried with their creations beneath those of a new era. In a series from time immemorial, each era has always obscured its predecessor, so that it hardly betrays any sign of an origin; an abundance of strata—the work of thousands of years— must be stripped away to come at last to the foundation, to the ground.[224]

It is at this very juncture in the *Weltalter* that Žižek invites us to risk a daring thesis. If we draw our attention to its operative logic, we see that Schelling's system of times does something more radical than displace the primordiality of the human subject by illustrating its subsumption within the tenebrous pulsating heart of nature's productive potency, whose own self-unfolding takes place in the abyssal dregs of an immemorial time that threatens to engulf they who look into it. The crucial observation to be made here is that nature *does not* have a history that evolves by means of an activity of internal self-transmutation that leads to man, so that he is ultimately included within it. The reason for this is not that nature, instead of being characterized by a smooth teleological development, is plagued by unpredictable catastrophism, irruptive disharmonies of widespread murder and extinction that cover up their own traces, so that the history of the world *cannot* be subsumable under a single, all-pervasive trajectory that, preceding from simple to more complex organizations in the unimaginable passage of aeons and aeons, would crown man as the summit of an unconscious yearning for the Word, that is, the structured *logos* of the symbolic world (contra the surface structure of Schelling's thinking[225]). This would effectively prevent nature from being motivated by an unknowing search for the light of self-consciousness from within the darkness of its raw, productive potency,[226] but the reason lies elsewhere. There are, of course, differing stages, periods, and epochs in nature—and ones that have been lost forever, never to be recovered—due to varying levels of dynamic evolution and growth within its immanent activity, even if there is always unforeseeable violence risking to wreak havoc. Yet when we look around, we cannot find the subject within the system of nature. *It just does not fit*, a fact that has stark metaphysical implications: the progressive, transformative time of nature presents itself as radically Other to the distinctiveness of human (spiritual) temporality because it does not display the same intensity of uncontrollable dialectical self-sublation. In nature, beginning and end for the most part coincide: in the darkness of the soil, the seed gives birth to the plant, which, after reaching the life-giving light of the radiant sun, finally dies, leaving behind its fruit and thereby returns to itself, only to burst forth again in an eternal recurrence of the same. Change can only transpire in the span of incomprehensible ages: unmeasurably dilatory, dialectical movement is here "enchained" within the unbreakable spurious infinity of endless circularity and does not display the same frantic upward-moving spiral of human temporality, the never repetitious onslaught of history, where beginning and end exist in a productive non-coincidence that is the very vital force of its unimaginably fast paced metamorphosis and unending creation of nuance.[227] A new era of culture displaces and supersedes the previous one, going in an unfathomable number of conflicting directions at once, so that no return to the beginning is even possible: the beginning, the origin, is always out of place in the inaccessible residue that is the past. The end, the result, is a qualitative break rewiring the plethora of human thoughts, expressions, and emotions, *and even the past itself*,[228] thus setting up a new beginning to be surmounted in its own right. As Žižek succinctly puts it, "[h]ere we encounter the key feature of the Symbolic: the fundamental 'openness' it introduces into a closed order of reality,"[229] in such a manner that saying nature *yearns* for humanity in its depths as the solution to its enigma[230] merely covers up the fact that humanity is an irreconcilable *break* from it. But if the subject is a break from the system of times that constitutes nature and its catastrophism by bringing forth a new age of self-unfolding activity, this does not mean that we are liberated from all dismay by being brought into the luminous sphere of holy spirit. Instead, bound by the erratic and excessive life of freedom that overflows itself, *we face our own non-natural catastrophes.*

We also encounter traces of this paradoxical upward spiralling and uncontrollable linear time in Kant and Hegel, which establish its integral place within founding intuitions of the tradition. Kant's account of unruliness as the ontogenetic starting point of transcendental freedom not only establishes the non-natural basis of human sociopolitical activity—not only is the human being "the only creature that must be educated," but due to his unruliness, man "has no instinct" and is therefore separated from the vital throes of nature[231]—but, what is more, it demands to be disciplined if it is not to devour the subject in its frenzy. Due to this exigence of discipline, there is an intrinsic link between what Kant calls moral education and the historical destiny of man that institutes a new form of temporality driven forward through a productive non-coincidence at the core of what it is to be man. Although presenting itself as an excessive energy whose domestication/schematization will enable us to attain terrestrial perfection, the very ground of our progress is in actuality its own inevitable obstacle: the meta-transcendental condition of subjectivity, while it opens up a distinctly human sphere within which progress is possible, at the same time tarnishes it with the inevitability of eventual collapse, misfire, failure. But this is not a mere proclamation of defeatism, resignation, and forfeit: the very impossibility of our task *is* the impetus for action, that which provokes an infinite plurality of new ways of "purifying" the insupportable surplus of our being, so that man is forever spurred on in the course of history to reinvent himself because of the insurmountable ontological violence preceding all acts of subjectification: "[t]he human being must therefore be *educated* to the good; but he who is to educate him is on the other hand a human being who still lies in the crudity of nature and who is now supposed to bring about what he himself needs. Hence the continuous deviation from his destiny with the always repeated returns to it."[232] But the consequence of this is that man is *nothing more* than this perpetual deviation from his destiny, that "man only becomes man"[233] by continually (re)creating his own identity by means of education through the construction of a second nature within the forward onslaught of history, its fragile movement of contraction and expansion, history itself thus circulating around an ideal sociopolitical point that it posits by its very activity as necessary to it but which it can never reach, for beginning and end can never coincide as in the realm of nature. In other words, the impossibility of reaching our destiny is that which constitutes its very possibility, that which gives us a destiny in the first place. *Due to this impossibility, we have historical time.*

This idea of a sharp distinction between the natural and the spiritual in terms of time is also taken up by the mature Hegel, even if, on Žižek's reading, he misses the radicality of the vanishing mediator—the night of the world—that enacts the passage from the former to the latter. There are two sides to the story. First, Hegel's starting point in the philosophy of nature is nature as "the Idea in the form of otherness."[234] This means that nature cannot exhibit the characteristics Hegel associates with the Idea, such as development qua self-unfolding activity, whose image we see in the growth of plants from seeds, wherein we encounter a purposive causality guiding all change and movement. "The abstract universality of nature's self-outsidedness"[235] demonstrates that nature lacks any inner structuration that would enable it to realize itself freely according to a pre- or self-given *telos*. In this sense, there is no teleological activity intrinsic to nature: its zero-level is a deterministic mechanics ruled by the contingency of its relations that are always external to themselves. Exclusively determined by the conditions that engulf them, the bodies emerging here do not display any capacity for self-reproduction, but merely stumble against one another due to empirical laws, whereby nature presents itself as a dead husk and time is nothing other than a meaningless giving birth to and destruction of its own offspring.[236] Second, at the level of organic life, although nature has sublated this prior staleness and intrinsic lack of purposiveness within its ebb and flow, it nevertheless exhibits a kind of claustrophobic immanence wherein the freedom distinctive of spiritual temporality is foreclosed by the eternal repetition of sameness within nature's cycle of life and death, fullness and lack, for there is a suffocating coincidence between the birth of one individual and the death of the other. Even though there is teleological self-unfolding explicit within organic living being—there is a universal genus that concretizes itself by constituting itself within the series of particulars that it generates and that generates it in turn, a complex unity that sustains itself within difference throughout the dispersion of time—there is no real difference and thus no *history* possible, even if we are allowed to speak of gradual sedimentations of change over the course of living being's activity. To put it crudely (borrowing one of Hegel's favourite animal examples) in nature we see nothing but one damn parrot after another,[237] which ultimately makes nature uninteresting for him: nature remains immensely poor with regard to its notional reflexivity, for in contrast with historical existence, it is not capable of the faster-than-light transformations constitutive of the latter's essence. Hegel refers to this deficiency as the "impotence of nature,"[238] insofar as it is incapable of the power of self-relating negativity and therefore displays a spurious infinity.[239] Consequently, we must assert the following "distinction between the spiritual and the natural worlds: that, whilst the latter continues simply to return into itself, there is certainly a progression taking place in the former as well."[240] As such, it is thus only with the rise of human spirit that we see contradiction posited as such, and with it, the possibility for real metamorphosis: "[s]pirit is posited as contradiction existing for itself, for there is an objective contradiction between the Idea in its infinite freedom and in the form of singularity, which occurs in nature only as an implicit contradiction, or as a contradiction which has being for us in that otherness appears in the Idea as a stable form."[241]

In German Idealism, a human subject is not merely born and then, by dying, proliferating his progeny in an endless repetition of the same. During man's slow march towards his oblivion, a frenzy of naturally uncontainable and unfathomable activity articulating itself emerges, a difference representing an irreconcilable *rupture* with the autopoiesis of nature, a self-legislative spontaneity that defines itself in direct opposition to its self-organizing totality, even if it must rely upon it as a dark, inaccessible ground. Human history begins with a *cutting off* of immemorial natural history, a tearing itself away from the natural cycle of life and death. Although our biology falters and brings us to our end, we die as *men*, not as mere creatures immersed in the world of substantial being. Schelling testifies to this insight, and advances it further than other representatives of the tradition (despite the fact he simultaneously recoils from, *represses*, the radicality of his own thematization of it[242]) insofar as, when we examine the genealogy of natural history in the *Weltalter*, we realize that nature is not the unconscious proper. Strictly speaking, nature is *nonconscious*.[243] In it, we only encounter a pulsation of matter, an annular rotary movement of contraction and expansion that follows its own automatic rhythm—what we see knows no pure upsurge of the irrevocable forward march of time, no dynamic linear temporality, as first witnessed in the human symbolic universe, even if its constitutive openness already appears in a "wild" form at lower levels of being. Nature eternally repeats itself in an infinite, relatively self-enclosed cycle of life and death, day and night, fullness and lack, wherein change sediments excruciatingly slowly over inscrutable eons and eons through a sluggishly self-developing, self-growing activity. Outside of it, there is nothing—*everything* is caught within an agonizing deadlock insofar as there is no room for completely free movement, for there is nothing but a symphonized flow of energy within the indivisibility of nature that is at the same time, from our perspective, a "blind" oscillation because our singularity is there lost. When one looks into nature as that impossible X, that *je ne sais quoi*, which sustains our life as subjects, one is almost forced to collapse: in face of the all-encompassing immanent laws of substance, one is pushed into an infinitely claustrophobic space. For Žižek we get a sense of this all-devouring, all-consuming force when we look inside the body and specifically the skull—"the realization that, when we look behind the face into the skull, we find nothing; 'there's no one at home' there, just piles of grey matter—it is difficult to tarry with this gap between meaning and the pure Real."[244] This raw flow of biochemical and electrical energy is so "terrifying" for two reasons. First, it is faceless, personless—*it has absolutely nothing to do with either the orbit of phenomenal experience or the human universe of meaning.* There is no indication of any genuine human quality: we are only confronted with anonymous, dull palpitations, which resemble the industrial buzzing of automatic machinery, a machinery that may amaze us with its complexity and dynamism (the plasticity of the neuronal network) but that nevertheless exists as a matrix of closed circuitry locked within its own self-enclosed, self-sustaining movement, a movement that is not only greater than us but also thereby appears to "threaten" our very existence as free subjects at every step. Second, the passage from the pure, senseless Real of nature in its mechanism to the absolute spontaneity of the I—the rupturing advent of a dialectical leap—is *stricto sensu* inexplicable, for given our inability to locate the full-fledged human subject in nature, there is always a moment of arbitrariness and fiat.

In the contemporary scientific scene, however, these menacing dimensions of the writhing, pulsating material of the *Grund* and its irreconcilable tension with free existence are constantly being brought into a new power, because *neuroscience puts the very gap itself in question*: the neuronal *Grund*, as a seething, all-devouring force, comes closer and closer to annihilating the distance from nature necessary for the autonomous transcendental constitution of reality, insofar as the fact of experience here risks being reduced to a mere epiphenomenon of a complex biological interface that uses the I as a system of representation to mediate itself to the world. As Žižek reiterates time and time again, "there are two options here: either subjectivity is an illusion, or reality itself (not only epistemologically) is not-All."[245] That being said, Žižek's reactualization of Schelling's revamped Cartesian positing of the difference between nature (cyclical time, body, ground) and human being (dialectical temporality, mind, existence) allows him to rethink the significance of contemporary neuroscience. The divide between our world of experience and the mechanisms of the natural world does not proclaim the irrelevance of the latter for our understanding of human subjectivity in face of the pure power of scientific explanatory models, their efficacy and statistical guarantee, as perhaps various representatives of phenomenological psychiatry or even psychoanalysis would advocate. On the contrary, according to Žižek, these models adequately describe the Real of our lives *with a rigorous vigor and precision never before imaginable by penetrating into the true ontologico-foundational basis of experience.* Žižek criticizes attempts to respond to the threat announced by neuroscience that merely assert the irreducible character of the subject, seeing instead the only feasible way to find a solution being to "develop one approach to its extreme, radically abstracting from the other—to develop the logic of brain science, for instance, at its purest."[246] The question is how a parallax gap could emerge *from within* the self-regulated biochemical and electrical activity inside the skull, how "the 'mental' itself explodes within the neuronal through a kind of 'ontological explosion.'"[247] The question and problematic here is distinctly Schellingian: what is the nature of the copula in judgement?[248] *Grund is* existence in exactly the same way that the neuronal *is* the mental: the copula here does not primordially distinguish a relation of identity or pure equivalence, so that the latter is entirely subsumable under the former (ground = existence; the neuronal = the mental). It represents an activity that, through the logical self-withdrawal of its pervasiveness and primordiality, results in the production of irreducible difference (ground *generates* existence; the neuronal immanently *gives rise* to the mental), wherein each exists as opposite and therefore autonomous to one another, although the unpredictably new—a pure difference—that emerges nevertheless retains an internal thread of logical dependence upon that which gave birth to it at an originary level of theoretical investigation: that is, one of ontogenesis, whereby a *productive* or *creative (schöpferisch)* identity emerges between the irreducibly different terms.[249] But one must be careful. *Grund* and existence are just as much "contemporaneous" logical relations as stages of historical development. Although the emergent split institutes two autonomous zones of activity—or, to speak in the parlance of the *Weltalter*, although the divide in being created by the irreducible spontaneity of the unconscious decision or de-scission (*Entscheidung* as *Ent-Scheidung*) sets the stage for the irreconcilability of the Present and the Past as epochs or ages in nature that forever alter it—they both exist simultaneously *after the act of separation*, despite the fact that the *Grund* also represents the dark "pre-history" of existence. It is in this way that the body as an independent entity existing in infinite contradistinction to mind can still follow its own laws, even if mind ultimately proves itself to be superior to its ontogenetic origins by existing in its own free register only in the aftermath of its hegemonizing self-positing or usurping of the primacy of body—or, to put it differently, natural cyclical time can still exist *alongside*, albeit in tension with, the out-of-joint dialectical temporality of spirit in the same creature. The neuronal interface can subsist in two paradoxical times, in the non-coincident two-way pull of the parallax as a multistable figure, the eternal "Past" of nonconscious material pulsation and the eternal "Present" of self-consciousness, both being "held" together in the positively charged void that is the subject as the impossible in-between (the vanishing mediator) generated within/by the negativity of being, so that the gap that sustains the subjective consistency of the universe of meaning can be maintained without denying the autonomy and power of cognitivism to describe the pure Real of biochemical and electrical activity that is the brain. The two zones are not to be confounded with one another, even though in a certain sense there is only the brute matter of the neuronal interface. Here we must recognize an implicit wordplay in Schelling: the copula in judgement (*Urteil*) is not merely an act of mind, a mental synthesis bringing a subject and predicate into relation with one another, but the expression of an act of primordial ontological division (*Ur-Teil* as *ursprüngliche Teilung*) exhibited by the thing in question with itself.[250] The principle of identity should be able to explain eruptive breaches in the fold of being instead of being doomed to subsume everything under the dead univocity of a claustrophobic immanence: "[t]his principle does not give expression to an unity which, revolving in a circle of sameness, would be unprogressive, and thus insensitive or unalive. The unity of this law is immediately creative."[251] The copula in judgement is, in this sense, one of Schelling's many expressions for a metaphysics of the disjunctive "and." But what does this moment of the breaking of existence out of *Grund*, of the explosion of the Ideal out of the Real, look like? This leads us into a detailed analysis of the role of ontological catastrophe in the emergence of experience in being.

Notes

187. Ibid., p. 55.

188. Žižek, *The Parallax View*, p. 4.

189. Žižek, *The Indivisible Remainder*. Taken from the book description.

190. Ibid., p. 11.

191. Ibid., p. 8.

192. The other important figure here is, of course, Lacan. Since Lacanian psycho-analysis declares that the Symbolic is never all, it is only natural that dialectical logic for Žižek would necessarily include an irremovable moment of irreconcilability. After all, for Lacan "when one gives rise to two, there is never a return. They don't revert to making one again, even if it is a new one. The *Aufhebung* is one of philosophy's pretty little dreams." *The Seminar. Book XX. Encore, On Feminine Sexuality, The Limits of Love and Knowledge, 1972–3,* ed. Jacques-Alain Miller, trans. Bruce Fink (New York: Norton, 1998), p. 86. Yet insofar as Žižek's project rests on the claim that psychoanalysis is the culmination of a lineage that begins in German Idealism, to assert that he merely reads Hegel through Lacan does not suffice, especially given the similarities between his own dialectics and his reading of Schelling.

193. Žižek, *Less Than Nothing,* p. 265.

194. Ibid.

195. See *The Ticklish Subject,* pp. 79–86.

196. Žižek, *Less Than Nothing,* pp. 234–35.

197. Žižek, *The Ticklish Subject,* p. 82.

198. Schelling, *Freiheitsschrift,* p. 227.

199. Žižek, *Less Than Nothing,* p. 922.

200. Žižek, *The Abyss of Freedom,* pp. 3–4.

201. Žižek, "Fichte's Laughter," p. 122.

202. See, for instance, *The Parallax View,* pp. 197–99.

203. Žižek, *The Parallax View,* p. 197 and 210.

204. Hegel, *The Phenomenology of Spirit,* p. 9.

205. Žižek, *The Parallax View,* p. 106 (repeated in *Less Than Nothing,* pp. 13f. and 642ff.). Contrast this with what he says of Schelling at ibid., p. 166;*The Ticklish Subject,* p. 55; *The Indivisible Remainder,* p. 14; and *The Abyss of Freedom,* p. 15.

206. This stays the same in the late philosophy. See *The Grounding of Positive Philosophy,* trans. Bruce Matthews (Albany: SUNY Press, 2007), p. 207.

207. Žižek, *Less than Nothing,* p. 265.

208. Schelling, *The Ages of the World: Third Version (c. 1815),* trans. Jason M. Wirth (Albany: SUNY Press, 2000) (hereafter *Weltalter III*), p. 219.

209. Ibid., p. 217.

210. Schelling, *Freiheitsschrift,* p. 239.

211. Ibid., p. 232.

212. Ibid.

213. Žižek, *Less Than Nothing,* p. 266.

214. Schelling, *Ages of the World*, in *The Abyss of Freedom/Ages of the World*, trans. Judith Norman (Ann Arbor: University of Michigan Press, 2008) (hereafter *Weltalter II*), p. 121.

215. Žižek, *The Indivisible Remainder*, p. 9.

216. Schelling, *Freiheitsschrift*, p. 281.

217. Schelling, *Weltalter II*, p. 6.

218. *The Indivisible Remainder*, p. 13.

219. Ibid.

220. Ibid., p. 11.

221. Ibid., pp. 35–39. I take up this point in chapter 9.

222. Žižek, *The Parallax View*, p. 166.

223. Schelling, *Weltalter II*, p. 121.

224. Ibid.

225. Schelling, *Freiheitsschrift*, pp. 241–42.

226. Ibid., p. 239.

227. Žižek, *Less Than Nothing*, p. 233.

228. See Žižek, *The Parallax View*, pp. 201–4.

229. Žižek, *Less Than Nothing*, p. 558.

230. Schelling, *Freiheitsschrift*, p. 239.

231. Kant, *Kant on Education*, p. 1; *Lectures on Pedagogy*, p. 437. For my discussion, see chapter 5.

232. Kant, *Anthropology from a Pragmatic Point of View*, p. 420.

233. Kant, *Kant on Education*, p. 6; *Lectures on Pedagogy*, p. 439.

234. Hegel, *Hegel's Philosophy of Nature*, vol. 1, p. 205 (§247).

235. Ibid., p. 223 (§254). Translation modified.

236. Ibid., p. 257 (§257A).

237. This example comes from my first Hegel teacher and philosophy mentor, Toni Stafford.

238. Hegel, *The Science of Logic*, p. 536.

239. Hegel, *The Encyclopedia Logic*, p. 293 (§221Z).

240. Ibid., pp. 302–3 (§234Z).

241. Hegel, *Hegel's Philosophy of Nature*, vol. 1, p. 206 (§247Z).

242. Žižek, *Indivisible Remainder*, p. 92.

243. The full argument for this will be spilled out in chapter 10.

244. Žižek, *The Parallax View*, p. 7.

245. Ibid., p. 168 (again in *Less Than Zero*, p. 725; and Žižek & Woodard, "Interview," *The Speculative Turn: Continental Materialism and Realism*, p. 407).

246. Ibid., p. 175.

247. Ibid., p. 210.

248. Schelling, *Freiheitsschrift*, pp. 223–25.

249. Ibid., p. 227.

250. Hegel draws upon the same wordplay in his Logic. Cf. *The Encyclopedia Logic*, p. 244 (§166A); and *The Science of Logic*, p. 552.

251. Schelling, *Freiheitsschrift*, p. 227.

Chapter 8
When the World Opens its Eyes
The Traumatic Fissure of Ontological Catastrophe

Žižek's quadruple dialectics sets forth a conception of the absolute that is incomplete, insofar as it has split itself through a moment of primordial division into two irreconcilable zones of activity: body and mind, nature and spirit, the Real and the Symbolic. However, to explain this moment of self-sundering, Žižek must reappropriate various elements from Schellingian ontology to articulate the pre-conditions of subjectivity in the throes of being, something that the mature Hegel, recoiling from his *Jenaer* night of the world, fails to do. Žižek's provocative claim is that if we attentively read Schelling's account of the eruption of a freely existing subjectivity out of a nature that becomes infinitely Other, we encounter two startling insights. First, the emergence of desire in being as the ontogenetic condition of the possibility of subjectivity and phenomenalization displays a structural parallel to Schelling's own theory of disease and evil. Second, we must follow the implications of this to the end: rather than exhibiting a great triumph at the end of the odyssey of being, self-consciousness is merely the possible aftereffect of a cancerous negativity in being, an *ontological catastrophe*, which points to an irreversible fracturing of the very essence of the world. We will also explore the consequences of this for evolutionary theory and contemporary philosophy of mind.

8.1 Desire, the Disease-Stricken Body of Being

Following Schelling's descriptions of the eternal Past forever anterior to
consciousness and language, a concern immediately arises: when we look
at the elusive X of nature in the immemorial epochs of cosmological and
geological time or the evolutionary strata of biological auto-development,
we encounter an all-encompassing/all-consuming whole that precludes
the *absolute* freedom of the subject. Insofar as this self-totalizing causality
immanent in nature represents a relatively closed circle, how is this
deterministic "deadlock" surpassed so that autonomy is possible? How
exactly can the *Grund*/neuronal interface act in the self-effacing yet world-
giving mode of existence/the mental? Although Žižek's own descriptions
of the passage in *The Indivisible Remainder* and *The Abyss of Freedom*
focus on the founding gesture of subjectivity as a self-instituting fiat, this
is not enough. It is only one side of the story. The question is how the
undifferentiated circuit of drives that constitute the pre-logical Real could
paradoxically ground—give rise to or help incite—the irreducible self-
positing act of decision. As Adrian Johnston argues, although this self-
positing *is* ultimately an arbitrary, groundless act "analogous to the cutting
of the Gordian knot"—which, as Žižek himself says, "can be described
(narrated) only *post festum*, after it has already taken place, since we are
dealing not with a necessary act but with a free act which could also not
have happened"[252]—Schelling himself searches for a way to inscribe the very
condition of the possibility of the act itself within the material palpitations
of nature, in works that Žižek for the most part does not discuss.[253] In this
sense, Žižek's own account is not satisfactory because it has a tendency
to present the drives as an irrevocably closed and blind system without
explaining how of themselves they could short-circuit, a theoretical point
that would be advantageous to his overall project.

As Johnston points out, within the Schellingian ontogenetic narrative,
the self-positing of the subject is first possiblized by the emergence of *desire*
(*Begierde*) within being. Desire marks the first juncture of some kind of
primordial blockage in the heart of blind necessity that upsets the automatic,
unbridled oscillation of drives by shattering their pure immanence. This
has two effects. First, in psychoanalytical terms, it means that instead of a
relative homeostasis as the inner *telos* guiding the entirety of an organism's

biological life, we see for the first time a relative short-circuiting within the pleasure principle, an inability to find satisfaction through the mere repetition of the same constitutive of the movement of instincts. Second, in place of a smooth, determined relation to the environment wholly programmed by instincts (the coincidence of *Innenwelt* and *Aussenwelt* through a predetermined set of biological schemata that hardwire the organism into its "exterior" surroundings) we get a degree of liberation from the various sense data of perception that normally mechanically determine an organism's actions as it enters into a state of *denaturalization* that is contemporaneous with an act of withdrawing from its immersion in being, and thereby the first stirrings of a free creation of a world of experience. Desire in its Schellingian mode is thus an intermediary stage between nature and the violent unruliness that is the dark birthplace of the transcendental I. But what must be noted here is how desire, as the beginning of the idealization of reality, is essentially identical to the conventional definitions of psychosis as withdrawal from objective reality into self, but here *at the ontological level instead of that of sociopolitically structured reality.* Consequently, it is Schelling and *not* Hegel who most succinctly describes the ontological passage through madness insofar as it is the former and not the latter who describes *how* the night of the world could disrupt the world into a series of *membra disjecta.* In this respect, when Žižek in *The Ticklish Subject* and *Less Than Nothing* proclaims that it is Hegel who is the most radical philosopher of the abyss of madness at the core of subjectivity and the minimal paranoia at the basis of order itself,[254] he appears to be completely unaware of how strongly his reading of Schelling influences his own reactualization of German Idealism. On his own account, not only is the Schellingian concept of the erratic oscillation of drives that precedes fully constituted reality *the* expression of the abyss of madness at the core of subjectivity, which Schelling himself supplements with the emergence of desire/ontological madness in being, but at the end of the first chapter of *The Indivisible Remainder* Žižek discusses Schelling's great insight into the necessarily paranoiac structure of universality as such, a point made explicit for the first time by Lacan, thus establishing a link between the two.[255]

In this sense, in both Žižekian and Schellingian ontology we can speak of *something like* a spectrum of subjectivity or ideality inherent within nature. Following this claim literally, we must say that we come across traces of desire within other organisms to varying degrees: there is a kind of quantitative accumulation of desire (an evolutionary genesis) that may lead to a complete qualitative break with nature (the splitting act of *Ent-Scheidung*) but in such a way that the possibility of the latter is not logically contained within the former as a kind of hidden, self-unfolding kernel—rather, the former can only incite it, so that only after the fact can we establish a "relation" between the two. There is no guarantee for freedom in the realm of mere being. Yet, what desire shows us is that the pure Real is *not* completely all-consuming: it is teeming with crevices within its positive fold, interstices within its being, which present a restless negativity tearing it apart. However, these sites of negativity are to be distinguished from human subjectivity insofar as despite expressing a minimal level of liberation from nature's cycles, they are unable to completely liberate themselves from nature's biological hardwiring and thus seek a new form of non-natural (virtual) organization. In this respect, they would only *resemble* the primordial unruliness prior to the advent of the Symbolic insofar as they would not exhibit a violent process of utter denaturalization, although we must nevertheless speak of a tension-ridden trembling of the organic system as it begins to quiver under its own weight.

It is for this reason that Žižek can adopt Heidegger's claim in *The Fundamental Concepts of Metaphysics* that animals feel "the 'poorness' of their relating to the world" in such a way that we see "an infinite pain pervading the whole of living nature."[256] As Žižek points out, this shares common ground with Schelling's notion of "the veil of despondency that spreads itself over nature."[257] But we must understand this pain or despondency in nature in two separate but interrelated ways. First, one could say that in desire as the beginnings of the idealization, that is, *of the world's psychotic replication of itself within itself*, animals have a kind of implicit yet nonconscious "knowledge" that they are unfree because they exist in a mode of unfathomable tension between the Real (instinctual-deterministic schemata) and the Ideal (desire as a blockage), but without this distinction being posited as such, as if here the Ideal has begun to inhere/persist within the Real, disrupting it from the inside, without yet being autonomous. *The Real rules supreme*—and not only has full-fledged ideality not yet emerged in being, but what we encounter here may only be referred to as a form of ontological proto-ideality once ideality in its freedom has come on the scene, that is, retroactively. By consequence, the slightest tinge of desire within the biological system that is supposed to determine the animal's reaction with its environment in advance through a pre-set logistics gives it, as it were, a taste of its own possible, but unreachable freedom, the animal being liberated yet confined in its movement. It is this simultaneous nonconscious "dreamlike" premonition of subjective freedom and its ultimate ontological foreclosure that constitutes nature's despondency or melancholy (*Schwermut*). But it must be noted that the "despondency" or "melancholy" of nature is not a moment of mere poetical rhetoric or uncalled-for anthropomorphism. As Henri Maldiney points out, Heidegger's descriptions of living beings as plagued by a constitutive *Benommenheit* (captivation, dazedness) coincide with that "mode of being of the type *melancolicus*" elaborated by Tellenbach.[258] If nature is overcome by a veil of despondency, it is because non-human life is wrought by a structure that is, for us, distinctively pathological: it is as if it is held back, stuck in its tracks, because it is incapable of a truly effective willing. Second, with emergence of desire, the self-sustaining circuitry of nature becomes disturbed by the interruptive presence of an extimacy, an inassimilable Real, within its very ebb and flow, causing its relatively balanced rotation to fall into a painful deadlock, an erratic oscillation of conflictual tendencies that become more and more uncontrollable as desire increases. If the animal gets its first taste of freedom in desire, then nature in the same moment gets the first taste of the madness that awaits it if this freedom were to fully actualize itself (the night of the world). Nature's pain is the unsteady, unpredictable palpitation of its heart of hearts threatening to explode in one excessive outburst as *Todestrieb* begins to awaken itself, but because it has yet to self-accumulate to a great intensity, and nothing has arisen to tame this propensity, there is a bleak darkness of antagonism. What is at issue here is the state of nature that precedes and sets the stage for humanity *as a response*; the emphasis is not on us, but rather on ontogenetic conditions, so that the apparent anthropomorphization of nature is coincident with the dehumanization of humanity, for inscribing desire into being is identical with taking it away from us as a privileged attribute.

The Žižekian night of the world emerges as the nonconscious drives of nature for the first time liberate themselves from their blind rotation in being through an immanently generated pandemonium within the corpo-Real of the body. Properly speaking, desire is an impasse within the ontological life of substance—"[s]ince there is consequently an unremitting urge to be and since it cannot be, it comes to a standstill in desire, as an unremitting striving, an eternally insatiable obsession with Being"[259]—that prevents substance from encompassing all, for the organism now obeys its own non-natural logic. It stands for the irremovable and impenetrable kernel of the Real qua logical paradox/internal limit that disturbs the annular circulation of drives through its own self-assertive violence. Here, the analogue with the body again proves to be useful to perceive the radicality of Žižek's reactualization of Schelling. Although the biological unity of the corpo-Real can astound us with its organic dynamism and systematic efficacy, the very awe-inspiring force of this self-organizing totality can cast a shadow over its dark underbelly, whose traumatic fact is often attested by nature's production of monstrosities, degenerative diseases, the mindless proliferation of cancerous tumors, or even the emergence of various forms of mental illness and psychosis caused by pure organic dysfunction, a fact that demonstrates how, from within the closed totality of a determinist system, a part can assert itself from within and hegemonize the organic whole, restructuring it according to its own "unruly" whim and thereby perturbing its harmonious, symphonized flow. Even if everything is logically pre-determined (the ebb and flow of matter can only follow certain paths carved out by genetics, the neuronal interface of the brain, and various different autopoietic systems), the laws that normally regulate the body can by themselves immanently generate a (bio)logical short circuit, thereby opening up a negative space within the body's corpo-Real that can assert itself and wreak havoc over its self-governing unity through a glitch in its programming. That which guarantees the placid functioning of everyday life and the health of body can suddenly turn into a ghastly apparition of true terror. Like an illness or disease within Schellingian ontology, desire does not stand for a positive ontological unity, but for an internal scrambling of the biological system that does not follow its supposed path within the whole and instead stubbornly asserts its own self at all costs—*even its own dismal downfall by obstructing its own life source.* A false unity, it simultaneously represents an ontological perversion and a metaphysical distortion: freedom is a devouring black hole, a mere disturbance, in the vital throes of being. In this context, Žižek talks of Jacques-Alain Miller's remarks on an unsettling rat experiment mentioned in one of Lacan's unpublished seminars, where it is only through a kind of neurological *mutilation* that a rat can be made to behave like a human. Formally, the specific character that distinguishes human freedom and separates it from the rest of the world is identical to rampant malfunction, a violent ontological disfiguring.[260]

As the force of desire is raised to a higher and higher degree of ideality, matter enters into a self-lacerating rage (*sich selbst zereißende Wut*) like a cancer-ridden, disease-stricken body howling under its own out-of-control energy.[261] Desire is a self-destructive mania that *tears apart* the smooth fabric of the world. This is why Žižek finds Schelling's "Wagnerian" vision of God so terrifying. It depicts a being that, by means of the painful, crippling amplification of desire into *Todestrieb*, becomes *completely* denaturalized and can thus posit itself as distinct from the anonymous, faceless pulsation of substance by the carving up of a self: "[t]he horror of the rotary motion resides in the fact that it is no longer impersonal: God already exists as One, as the Subject who suffers and endures the antagonism of drives," "a state of an endless 'pleasure in pain,' agonizing and struggling with Himself, affected by an unbearable anxiety."[262] The primordial unruliness of human nature and its coequal term diabolical evil are therefore synonymous with this grotesque excess of life that we witness in the breakdown of the corpo-Real in times of illness, with what occurs when the self-enclosed logic of nature auto-disrupts through pure dysfunction. In this regard, the freedom of the subject—that anarchic state that precedes the birth of the Symbolic as a form of retroactive damage control—is not a positive characteristic or attribute: it is the failure of the auto-actualization of the essence of nature, its inability to contain itself within its own preset logistics, which causes an ontological catastrophe.[263] As Žižek makes clear in an interview, when viewed from the standpoint of the natural world we can only even understand the peculiarity of (self-) consciousness and human intelligence by positing something going horribly wrong in its internal development:

Žižek. What I am currently engaged with is the paradoxical idea that, from a strict evolutionary standpoint, consciousness is a kind of mistake—a malfunction of evolution—and that out of this mistake a miracle emerged. That is to say, consciousness developed as an unintended by-product that acquired a kind of second-degree survivalist function. Basically, consciousness is not something which enables us to function better. On the contrary, I am more and more convinced that consciousness originates with something going terribly wrong—even at the most personal level. For example, when do we become aware of something, fully aware? Precisely at the point where something no longer functions properly or not in the expected way.

Daly. Consciousness comes about as a result of some Real encounter?

Žižek. Yes, consciousness is originally linked to this moment when "something is wrong," or, to put it in Lacanian terms, an experience of the Real, of an impossible limit. Original awareness is impelled by a certain experience of failure and mortality—a kind of snag in the biological weave. And all the metaphysical dimensions concerning humanity, philosophical self-reflection, progress and so on emerge ultimately because of this basic traumatic fissure.[264]

8.2 Malfunction, Mal-adaptation, Breakdown: Žižek and the Sciences

We should pause for a moment and consider this Žižekian notion of a "snag in the biological weave" in order to draw out its full meaning and implications for our understanding of the sciences, which will simultaneously allow us to show that such an ontogenetic account of the emergence of *Todestrieb* is not enough to explain the emergence of subjectivity. Taken at a purely formal level, both standard accounts of evolution and Žižek's theory of the ontogenesis of the subject appear to share a fundamental presupposition. Functioning through random mishaps in the self-replication of genetic code producing new, unforeseeable ontological differences in living being, neo-Darwinian evolution is rendered possible by a moment of malfunction, error, the always possible upsurge of inconsistency in the "rhythmic" flow of nature. Irreversible *mutations* form the basal and primordial stuff from which life gains its mercurial character. Consequently, for modern-day biology, nature too is not-all insofar as there is no eternal, overarching unity in the vital energetics of substance, no all-inclusive weave with a preset structure, plan, or predictable movement: there are constant slips and slides in positive reality, glitches and functional disturbances. Evolution is nothing other than nature encountering its own real limit, which proves to be the actual driving force of material creation and change: its weakness does not prove to be a mere limitation, a deficiency, but is often even *its strength*, allowing its forms to endure by adaption. However, what we could call the biological movement of the negative is only able to ground this transformative activity insofar as it sets up a new "dialectic" between organism and environment. As malfunction slowly and contingently gives rise to new characteristics by the sedimentation of small changes over the sluggish march of evolutionary time, an automatic rubric of natural selection occurs: those who are, by pure chance, more "fit" for their particular niche survive and pass on·the biological glitch that, paradoxically, shows itself retroactively to have been a source of force and power, making those that were not struck by accident with the given mishap of self-replication in question disadvantageous, leading them to die out. Though here the possibility of monstrosities coincides with the possibility for new natural forms, a new emergent logistic is able to subsume both within a greater system of the struggle for life and death, even if this struggle is, in and of itself, non-teleological.

For Žižek, however, this naturalistic account of biological "negativity" within being at the level of the self-reproduction of organisms does not go far enough. Although he agrees with its fundamental presuppositions— nature as not-all, as driven forward by an internal yet productive inconsistency—he believes that the mechanism of neo-Darwinian evolution is unable to explain the emergence of subjectivity because it falls back into the trap of an organic theory of nature. Even if it does not posit an indwelling, necessary tendency for progression, a forward-moving advancement towards more sophisticated life-forms, the "dialectic" between organism and environment is all-inclusive: the law of self-preservation and homeostasis becomes so primordial that even a mishap in reproduction becomes ultimately subsumed under a species' attempt to assert itself and stay alive, so that the moment of the negative retroactively posits itself as being always already a teleologically guided, rational development. In other words, we can always give reasons as to why this or that evolutionary feature benefited the organism as a being immersed in the natural cycle of life and death. Even if within the naturalistic viewpoint nature/substance is in a certain respect not-all—there is nothing guaranteeing its completion—it does not go far enough, for nothing transcends its grasp. There may be conflict and negativity *within* the system, but this in no way poses a problem to the inner algorithm of its biological "dialectics." The problem with this theoretical position is that it fails to see how the subject, haunted by *Todestrieb*, demonstrates that there is *no* single overarching principle of explanation, that there is a "place" in nature that is, strictly speaking, *non-natural* and *defines itself against the rhythm of life and death, fullness and lack*: the negativity that opens up the space for self-consciousness cannot be, even retroactively, subsumed within an evolutionary narrative of survival. Scientific methodology cannot explain the human, for the zero-level (= unruliness) of experience not only provides no functional advantage in nature, but even disturbs the dialectic of organism and environment because it *cuts the link between* Innenwelt *and* Aussenwelt. As Žižek says, "we should bear in mind the basic anti-Darwinian lesson of psychoanalysis repeatedly emphasized by Lacan: man's radical and fundamental *dis*-adaptation, *mal*-adaptation, to his environs,"[265] a point not only argued for by Lacan, but also by Kant and Fichte at the beginning of the German Idealist tradition.[266]

In his own work on cognitive science, Žižek attempts to show for this very reason how a variety of cognitive scientists and neurophilosophers falter at the enigma of consciousness and thereby create a plurality of approaches at odds with one another. He divides the latter into four groups, which cover the logical possibilities of explaining consciousness in terms of the standard natural model (sadly, the details of each on the Žižekian reading must be left aside here):

I. *eliminative/reductive materialism*: the proclamation that there is
no such thing as consciousness and qualitative experience is a
"naturalized" illusion (Patricia and Paul Churchland);

II. *the antimaterialist position*: the necessity of positing a
new fundamental force of nature yet to be discovered
(David Chalmers);

III. *the inherent inexplicability of consciousness*: given the "cognitive
closure" limiting knowledge, we must assert that the birthplace
of conscious awareness is unknowable, even if it did arise out of
materiality (Colin McGinn, Steve Pinker);

IV. *an "as-if" non-reductive materialism*: consciousness exists, and we
can use teleological language to describe it, but it has emerged
entirely due to natural laws and can ultimately be completely
subsumed within them (Daniel Dennett).[267]

What remains common to each of these approaches, according to Žižek,
is the failure of a purely scientific account of consciousness. In typical
psychoanalytical style, it is the places where these discourses reach an
impasse, where their symbolic space is internally obstructed, that are the
most revealing; paradoxically, this occurs *whenever they face the essentials of
the very object of their investigation.* Whether it be (i) the outright dismissal of
self-consciousness reflexivity as a pseudo-problem, (ii) the thesis that the
only way to inscribe the singularity of consciousness within nature is to posit
a new force comparable to gravity or electromagnetism, (iii) entirely giving
up any possible material explanation of consciousness, or (iv) the forced
attempt to understand conscious reflexivity as a purely natural phenomenon,
*the closed loop of infinite self-relating that is the condition of the possibility of self-
consciousness is itself the impasse of each discourse,* for consciousness cannot be
naturalized. This leads Žižek to say: "I am therefore tempted to apply here
the dialectical reversal of epistemological obstacle into positive ontological
condition: what if the 'enigma of consciousness,' its inexplicable character,
contains its own solution? What if all we have to do is to transpose the gap
which makes consciousness (as the object of our study) 'inexplicable' into
consciousness itself?"[268] Either by trying to bypass the problem by fiat ([i]
completely eliminating the object, "consciousness," or [iv] stripping it of

its singular character as ideal self-reflexivity—both an attempt to show the theoretical prowess of materialism) or by tackling it head-on ([ii] declaring the irreducibility of mind or [iii] making a possible materialist explanation disappear—both an attempt to demonstrate the necessity of idealism), what each option shows, positively or negatively, is that the self-reflexivity constitutive of consciousness is a disruption of natural laws that demands a new metaphysical vision of the world.

For these reasons, Žižek does not locate the moment of malfunction constitutive of the subject at the level of genetic mutation and, in a second step, he refuses to equate it completely with a breakdown of the libidinal-material ground of nature. It goes beyond a scientifically measurable "unit of change" (even if is ultimately incited by a certain series of genetic mutations) insofar as it breaks with all totalizing, homogenizing principles or laws. As a *closed loop* of infinite self-relating, consciousness can only be made possible by a prior psychotic withdrawal of the world into its nocturnal, ontologically solipsistic self, the primordial rupture dividing *Innenwelt* and *Aussenwelt*. It is this founding gesture that sets an internal limit to scientific models because it obstructs the "dialectic" of organism and environment: the self-organizing, instinctual schemata offered by our genetic code go haywire in the life of the organism, so that we are no longer immersed in the world through a preset logistical program, but open up a space within which we are able to freely relate to it as an Other. The point is not to search for how the raw immediacy of the brute Real of neurons and their ancestral history in immemorial time dissipates the primordiality of self-experience, but how the irreducible reflexivity that sustains consciousness itself emerges from within the brute, faceless abyss of asubjective brain matter in such a way that the former remains incommensurate with latter, even if the latter is its obscure birthplace. Relying upon John Taylor's theory of consciousness, Žižek locates this primordial act of ontological division at a very specific point: through the relation of past working memory to present input, present experience spontaneously acquires the ability to relate to itself *through a detour through the (its) past*, the condition of which is "bubbles" of neuronal activity in local cortical regions establishing complex feedback systems. It is this direct self-instituting short-circuiting that allows for free, infinitely self-standing thought, the ease, energy and speed of mental operations, in contradistinction to the complex mediative channels of neuronal activity that produced the organism as a biological system, for it allows present experience to liberate itself radically from a mere attachment to input.[269] In a flash, the organism stops being determined through external conditions, but creates a zone within which it can relate to itself as a self so that bit by bit this self-relation takes charge of instinctual schemata. For Žižek, this "short circuit" or "(bio)logical glitch" between various faculties within the brain—a kind of naturally inexplicable overlapping that creates the possibility of psychotic self-relation, which, just like Schelling's account of the self-begetting of God, "can be described (narrated) only *post festum*, after it has already taken place, since we are dealing not with a necessary act but with a free act which could also not have happened"[270]—as a meta-transcendental condition of consciousness is related only in a derivative or secondary sense to the "malfunction" so fundamental to the process of neo-Darwinian evolution. This is true for two reasons. First, it makes itself superior to the natural basis that paves the way for it and thereby elevates itself above it. Second, it is not predictable from the mere level of genetic mutation. In this sense, not only is it a pure self-positing that depends on nothing but itself (even if it is *incited* by a genetic mutation, it remains irreducible to and logically distinct from it: it is a mere neuronal mishap, a disruptive emergence in the interstices of the logical network sustained by the biochemical and electrical interface of brain matter), but this capacity for self-assertion also allows it to liberate itself from its immersion/imprisonment in the natural world (the generated closed loop of self-relation breaks the interpenetration of *Innenwelt* and *Aussenwelt* in such a way that it cannot be retroactively subsumed within a survivalist narrative of newfound functionality, even if it does manage to acquire a second-degree survivalist function). Genetic mutation, the "dialectics" of organism and environment, and with it the breakdown of the libidinal-material ground of the organism, may be necessary for explaining the origins of subjectivity, but they are not sufficient. For full-fledged subjectivity to emerge, natural breakdown must paradoxically *double itself.*

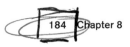

8.3 Terror, Perplexity, and the Awakening of the World

Situating his own philosophical project within the heritage of German Idealism, Žižek's psychoanalytical reactualization of the Schellingian eruptive logic of the *Grund* is an attempt to show how the subject is not external to the absolute. In other words, the gaze of the subject in Žižekian ontology must be seen as the material universe finally "gaining" the power to look upon itself through an internal reflection: "the whole domain of the representation of the world (call it mind, spirit, language, consciousness, or whatever medium you prefer) needs to be understood as an event within and of the world itself. Thought is not at all opposed to being, it is rather being's replication within itself."[271] As the dense, closed circuitry of nature dissolves under the impact of the *Todestrieb*, it gives way to the possibility of the "miracle"[272] of human thinking and its free idealization of the world as immanent in the latter. However, this moment of parallax shift from mere being to thought must be taken for what it is. Within the ancestral genealogy of forgotten, phenomenologically inaccessible time, the system of nature slowly and contingently grows in complexity, eventually reaching its autopoietic apotheosis in the structure of the brain, which, because of its some one hundred billion neurons possessing a total of at least one hundred trillion synaptic connections, thereby displaying one hundred times more synapses than the estimated number of stars in our galaxy, is unable to hold itself together according to its own immanent, self-regulating laws. Unintended loops and gaps in its processes become visible as they writhe under the infinite pressure of their own labyrinthine intricacy, nature failing to find its own way in its own production. Substance falls into deadlock: with the emergence of the complex neuronal interface of man, it can no longer successfully posit itself as a fragile all, and it breaks into a series of *membra disjecta*, which opens up the space within which the self-enclosed loop of experience asserts itself out of nowhere, further intruding upon and obstructing its activity from within. All at once and as if in a cosmic flash, through an accident of overlapping in the neuronal network, material being encounters its own internal limit amplified to the maximum *and the world opens its eyes*: with the rise of subjectivity it appears that an unsolvable glitch in the smooth functioning of its own inward-dwelling logic posits itself as such, enabling the world for the first time to find the distance to self necessary for its own self-phenomenalization by virtue of a shock, a blow, a violence, for which it itself is responsible. The claustrophobic immanence that drowns everything in the blind void of non-experience is finally shattered—yet when the world finally opens its eyes for the very first time in the mode of subjectivity it does not rejoice, it does not celebrate, nor does it feel a passive, grateful joy from the beauty surrounding it and bask in the bliss aroused by the wonder and amazement of the brute fact of its existence. It whimpers under its own weight, hearing its own inarticulate cry as it experiences itself in a moment of unbearable agony and catastrophic self-diremption, "a mixture of terror and perplexity" that Žižek compares to the atrocity of sexual abuse and the horrific pictures of children dying from radiation exposure in Chernobyl:

> Although one of today's main candidates for the figure of Evil is child sexual abuse, there is nevertheless something in the image of a hurt, vulnerable child which makes it unbearably touching: the figure of a child, between two and five years old, deeply wounded but retaining a defiant attitude, his face and poise remaining stubborn, although he is barely able to prevent an outburst of tears—is this not one of the figures of the Absolute? One thinks here about the photos of children dying from exposure to radiation after the Chernobyl accident, or—also from Ukraine—one of the photos on a child-porn website showing a really young child, no more than four years old, confronting a big ejaculating penis, face covered with fresh sperm. Although the shot probably plays on the link between the penis ejaculating sperm and the mother's breast full of milk, the expression on the child's face is clearly a mixture of terror and perplexity: the child cannot make out what is going on.[273]

What the world first sees is not its own awe-striking unity and oneness, the spiritual fullness of a self-seizing, self-actualizing centre that holds everything together in an all-encompassing totality. All it discerns is the tumultuous uproar of erratic pulsation, an insurmountable, non-masterable chaos resulting from the degradation or collapse of its own positive, autopoietic activity. The self-awareness of the world, its self-experience in the first person as made possible by the existence of subjectivity and thus *all* experience as such, is necessarily preceded by this irreducible and irreversible auto-disruption that must be seen as catastrophic. The ontogenetic basis of subjectivity is the trauma of primordial loss, where nature is forever alienated from itself through complete breakdown (N ≠ N), so that we must say that the subject is paradoxically that which has survived its own death, for "the past traumatic loss of substance [...] is constitutive of the very dimension of subjectivity"[274]—or as Schelling himself puts it, "[p]ain is something universal and necessary in all life, the unavoidable transition point to freedom [...]. It is the path to glory."[275] But this is no mere rhetoric on behalf of Žižek: as his Schellingian-inspired argument makes clear, this psychosis-inducing auto-disruption of being is a *necessary* theoretical posit if free experience is to be possible instead of a blind experiential void:

> We cannot pass directly from nature to culture. Something goes terribly wrong in nature: nature produces an unnatural monstrosity and I claim that it is in order to cope with, to domesticate, this monstrosity that we symbolize. Taking Freud's fort/da as a model: something is primordially broken (the absence of the mother and so on) and symbolization functions as a way of living with that kind of trauma.[276]
>
> In short, the ontological necessity of "madness" resides in the fact that it is not possible to pass directly from the "animal soul" immersed in its natural life-world to "normal" subjectivity dwelling in its symbolic universe—the vanishing mediator between the two is the "mad" gesture of radical withdrawal from reality that opens up the space for its symbolic reconstitution.[277]

The implication of this is that the Symbolic (the reconstitution of reality, the world's self-replication within itself) is nothing but an attempt to tame, to gentrify this constitutive mayhem/madness in the immanent fold of being. But it must be insisted that this can only be accomplished at the level of the virtual: "[t]he third moment which 'resolves' the contradiction is by definition 'prothetic' (virtual, artificial, symbolic, not substantially natural)."[278] When the world "perceives itself" as lost to self and infinitely dirempt (N ≠ N as the originary [onto]logical violence preceding and possibilizing transcendental imagination) in the mode of subjectivity, it recoils into culture as a defence mechanism to try to sublate this gap in its being, to fill in this hole in its depths and thereby posits itself as such as a full-fledged subjectivity.[279] In short, the passage from darkness to light *only occurs at the level of the Symbolic*: in the Real, nothing changes, unruliness (our break from nature) is left untouched. It is this aspect of the *intrinsic madness* of culture, language, and phenomenal reality, its psychotic *lack* of contact with the world, that Žižek claims we forget, that we *must necessarily forget*, if the transcendental misrecognition of reality necessary to subjectification as a reaction formation is to be a successful "compensation." All our discourses, all our "truths," are nothing but the deluded ravings of the asylum unaware of their true origin within the founding gesture of subjectivity as a recoil spurred on by the brutal trauma of violently awakening up into a dismembering hemorrhaging of being, the ultimate ontological catastrophe. All the beauty of the world merely belies its true, unbearable horror: "[i]f we take into consideration the many terrible things in nature and the spiritual world and the great many other things that a benevolent hand seems to cover up from us, then we could not doubt that [the ego] sits enthroned over a world of terrors."[280] In this respect, "the true point of 'madness' [...] is not the pure excess of the 'night of the world,' but the madness of the passage to the Symbolic itself, of imposing a symbolic order onto the chaos of the Real. If madness is constitutive, then *every* system of meaning is minimally paranoid, 'mad.'"[281] Paradoxically, the world can only become known to itself—being can only replicate itself within thought—if its medium of self-disclosure operates "with no external support of its truth,"[282] without ever touching the Real.[283]

Accordingly, Schellingian desire must be said to be the beginning of being's withdrawal into its nocturnal, irreal self and that which opens up the space necessary for ego development as symptom formation (a defence). Following various hints and gestures in the middle-late Schelling, Žižek takes premonitions of the psychoanalytical experience of mind-body discord and brings to the fore their underlying eruptive logic. This leads him to the idea of *Grund* and existence as a dialectically irreconcilable pair emerging through the caustic collapse of being as it gains notional self-reflexivity, this being the fundamental logical moment for understanding how his own parallax ontology can bring together a materialism and a self-grounding idealism. It is not the mediating filters of language that are primordially responsible for our lack of access to extra-subjective reality due to some internal limitation—rather, *it is reality itself that renders impossible its own access to itself.* The Symbolic is always already revelatory of the nature of the world, albeit in an intrinsically negative manner: the prison house of language, our inability to "transcend" it and grasp reality as it is in itself,[284] necessarily refers to the material processes that gave birth to the alienating linguistic-conceptual structures that permanently rob us of the immediacy of being. Psychosis is not the feature of a single isolated subject lost in disarray—it is the rite of passage of becoming a subject, a point explicitly brought to the fore by Lacan[285] and that justifies rereading Schelling through Lacanian psychoanalysis. It is no accident that both Schelling's *Stuttgarter Privatvorlesungen* and the third draft of the *Weltalter* contain at a crucial point a meditation on the relationship between subjectivity and madness and the latter's irreducibility (in the former when discussing the soul's higher faculties, in the latter at the very end of the book of the Past): "[u]nderstanding, if it is to be an actual, living and active understanding, is therefore properly nothing other than a coordinated madness";[286] "[f]or in what does the intellect prove itself than in the coping with and governance and regulation of madness? [...] Without continuous solicitation of it, there would be no consciousness."[287]

The difficult paradox of Žižek's metaphysical archaeology of the subject is that it is *only* through this ontological catastrophe that the true "miracle"[288] of human thinking can emerge, so that there is a speculative identity between the highest (that which sustains and creates the autonomous sphere of spirit in its dialectical creativity) and the lowest (the irrevocable alienation of being to itself, its schismatic auto-disruption that produces a non-natural excess). As that which thereby negatively binds together materialism and idealism, the impossible in-between that is the subject is neither Real nor Symbolic insofar as it dialectically coincides *with both modalities simultaneously*, yet is also outside of them, thus rendering its status as a vanishing mediator undecidable. In both, it is internally contained as external, present as absent, included as excluded. The subject is therefore infinitely non-coincidental and contradictory: having no place in either mind or body, it can only show itself as the caustic breakdown of substance $(N \neq N)$ or in the fleeting, ephemeral distortions of symbolic space between signifiers (\$), but these two traces fail to grasp its essence in its purity, for the subject is more than the material collapse of being and the limits of discourse. But what is more, not only is the subject outside the Symbolic because it is minimally non-coincident with it, but insofar as it is at its very origin and must withdraw in order for the Symbolic to take hold, *we need a new form of language even to discuss its genesis out of pre-logical antagonism*, since not even the inconsistencies of our notional apparatus could thus aid us to explain its pure upsurge. The subject is "a non-provable presupposition, something whose existence cannot be demonstrated but only inferred through the failure of its direct demonstration."[289] As a result, the metaphysical archaeology of the subject I have been executing contains a necessary moment of *speculative fabulation* to fill in the unavoidable gaps of the narrative of how thought arises within the flat plane of being.

Here, however, we encounter a major methodological difficulty. Drawing upon Schellingian ontology to embark upon such a mytho-poetic articulation of how substance could act in the self-effacing, self-sundering mode of subjectivity presents an immediate problem to those who are familiar with the texts upon which Žižek relies, for the *Freiheitsschrift* and the *Weltalter* display the structure of a quaternity, with a principle exterior to the dynamic of *Grund* and existence that ties them together as androgynous opposites in a point of absolute indifference, an *Ungrund*, whose conceptual contours appear to have starkly different consequences for human self-consciousness and culture, namely, that humans participate in the theo-cosmogonic drama of God's search for self-manifestedness in creation, or to put it differently, in the emergence of "the cosmos (of fully constituted reality, ruled by *logos*) out of the proto-cosmic pre-ontological chaos."[290] According to this picture, ontological catastrophe (the subject) is less a cataclysmic breakdown than part of the inherent negativity in the intimate life of God that makes His personality truly alive. Only through the preclusion of a theosophic philosophy of nature as the illusion that there is "a secret, invisible, all-powerful agent who effectively 'pulls the strings' behind the visible, public Power... [an] obscene, invisible power structure acts the part of the 'Other of the Other' in the Lacanian sense, the part of the meta-guarantee of the consistency of the big Other (the symbolic order that regulates social life),"[291] can Žižek ground his reading of the ontogenesis of the subject by identifying the act of decision—the pure self-positing of the I that separates *Grund* from existence for the first time—with the self-assertive violence of evil and disease. Because there is no God who needs a being like Himself in order to recognize Himself as Himself through a mirror that is His Other, the irreducible freedom of the human subject can only be seen as an ontologically narcissistic disturbance of the relatively ordered whole of nature: there can be no internal teleology guided by divine understanding and will whereby man participates in the divine drama of being's search for self-disclosure. Nature is not the primordial, first revelation of God,[292] but the obscure basis of subjectivity, that against which it defines itself by a self-caused break. Rejecting the theosophic *Ungrund* central to Schelling's middle-late texts, Žižek sees traces of a disavowed analytic of finitude within them that, wrought with self-destructive, self-sabotaging tendencies, can paradoxically efface itself in the production of an extimate kernel of negativity, which then, in another moment, hegemonically takes over. In this sense, Žižek's own ontology—just like his work on Hegel—must be understood as an attempt to psychoanalytically construct the unconscious truth of Schelling's thinking by demonstrating how "his thought—for a brief moment, as it were in a flash—renders visible something that was invisible beforehand and withdrew into invisibility thereafter," and how this tension constitutes the central difficulty of his theosophic epic.[293] What, then, motivates and philosophically founds Žižek's violent "reactualization" of the Schellingian subject? To come to terms with this, we will have to explore the psychoanalytical conflict omnipresent in the *Weltalter* project.

Notes

252. Žižek, *The Indivisible Remainder*, pp. 22–23.

253. See Johnston, *Žižek's Ontology*, pp. 80–92.

254. Žižek, *The Ticklish Subject*, p. 78; and *Less Than Nothing*, p. 331.

255. Žižek, *The Indivisible Remainder*, p. 76.

256. Žižek, *The Fragile Absolute: Or, Why Is the Christian Legacy is Worth Fighting For?* (London: Verso, 2008), pp. 86–89.

257. Schelling, *Freiheitsschrift*, p. 271.

258. Maldiney, *Penser l'homme et la folie*, p. 270.

259. Schelling, *Weltalter III*, p. 232.

260. See Žižek, *The Indivisible Remainder*, pp. 219–20.

261. Schelling, *Weltalter III*, p. 322.

262. Žižek, *The Indivisible Remainder*, p. 24.

263. Or, as Johnston succinctly puts it, "[t]he surplus of autonomy is made possible by the deficit of heteronomy. Freedom emerges from the dysfunctioning of determinism." *Žižek's Ontology*, p. 114.

264. Žižek and Daly, *Conversations with Žižek*, p. 59.

265. Žižek, *The Parallax View*, p. 231.

266. See chapters 5 and 6.

267. Žižek, *The Parallax View*, pp. 177–78.

268. Ibid., p. 241.

269. See ibid., pp. 210–14, for a rather interesting, detailed discussion.

270. Žižek, *The Indivisible Remainder*, pp. 22–23.

271. Gabriel and Žižek, "Introduction: A Plea for a Return to Post-Kantian Idealism," in *Mythology, Madness and Laughter*, p. 3.

272. Žižek and Daly, *Conversations with Žižek*, p. 59.

273. Žižek, *The Parallax View*, p. 73. Strangely enough, this passage is omitted in the French translation. Cf. *La Parallaxe* (Paris: Fayard, 2008).

274. Žižek, *Living in the End Times*, p. 312.

275. Schelling, *Weltalter III*, p. 335.

276. Žižek and Daly, *Conversations with Žižek*, pp. 64–65.

277. Žižek, *The Ticklish Subject*, p. 35.

278. Žižek, *Less Than Nothing*, p. 314.

279. Žižek, *Living in the End Times*, p. 398.

280. Schelling, *Weltalter III*, p. 291.

281. Žižek, *Less Than Nothing*, p. 331.

282. Ibid., p. 77.

283. Ibid., p. 959.

284. Žižek, *The Ticklish Subject*, p. 33.

285. Lacan, "Presentation on Psychic Causality," in *Écrits*, p. 176/144.

286. Schelling, *Stuttgart Seminars*, in *Idealism and the Endgame of Theory*, trans. Thomas Pfau (Albany: SUNY Press, 1994), p. 233.

287. Schelling, *Weltalter III*, pp. 338–39.

288. Žižek and Daly, *Conversations with Žižek*, p. 59.

289. Žižek, *Less Than Nothing*, p. 730.

290. Ibid., pp. 273ff.

291. Žižek, "The Big Other Doesn't Exist," *Journal of European Psychoanalysis*, Spring-Fall 1997. Retrieved Jan. 7, 2013, from www.lacan.com/zizekother.htm.

292. Schelling, *Freiheitsschrift*, p. 284.

293. Žižek, *The Indivisible Remainder*, p. 8.

Chapter 9
The Abyss of Unconscious Decision
Schelling's *Weltalter* and Psychoanalytical Horror of
Substance as Subject

Since Schelling's own account of the *Grund* has theosophic tendencies
in contradiction with the Lacanian subject, and by consequence with the
disavowed yet formative *Grundlogik* of German Idealism, Žižek is only able
to reactualize Schelling by "formalizing" its content. By elaborating Žižek's
psychoanalytical methodology, I will show how Žižek is able to legitimate
such a violent overhauling of Schelling insofar as he sees an inability to
assimilate an encounter with the Real within key conceptual moments,
a maddening struggle that simultaneously causes the "failure" of his
middle-late philosophy *and* testifies to his prowess as the greatest thinker of
subjectivity, thus presenting us with a nuanced and controversial reading of
Schelling's philosophical development and his relation to German Idealism
as a whole. What is more, reconstructing this "therapeutic space" will enable
us to not only come to a greater understanding of the systematic rigour of
Žižek's approach in opposition to what his critics want us to believe, but
also bring us face to face with the psychoanalytical horror of the founding
insight of modernity—the ontologically catastrophic nature of the subject
as the vanishing mediator between the Real and the Symbolic—and the
mechanisms by which even the greatest thinker of subjectivity can be
seduced by fantasies as he tarries with its essence.

9.1 Into the Void: The Frenzy of God's Self-Diremption

The ambiguity of the Hegel-Schelling relationship within Žižek stems from his critique of Schellingian metaphysics. Even if Žižek's own transcendental materialism is founded upon a notion of emergent ontological catastrophe at the origin of subjectivity, a notion he largely derives from the *Freiheitsschrift* and the *Weltalter*, Žižek is quite adamant in distancing himself from these texts, even if in the same breath he praises Schelling's profound ability to penetrate into the pre-symbolic material of the Real.[294] Indeed, immediately after his remarkable and provocative reading of Schelling in *The Indivisible Remainder*, Žižek argues for the supremacy of Hegelian dialectics. Despite the ephemeral moments of genuine breakthrough that emerge "as it were in a flash,"[295] Žižek insists that Schelling remains philosophically inferior to his great rival: he ultimately fails to conceive the radicality implicit in the self-positing act of separating *Grund* from existence and tries to cover up the non-coincidence in being it indicates by making the two distinct from one another only by being founded within absolute indifference, which itself, as Schelling says, "is not a product of opposites, nor are they contained in it *implicite*; rather it is a being of its own, separated from all oppositions, on which all oppositions are broken, which is nothing other than their very non-being, and which therefore has no predicate except predicatelessness."[296] The eruptive logic of the *Grund*, intrinsic to the notion of ontological catastrophe, is thereby completely lost: "from this neither-nor, or from this indifference, duality [...] immediately breaks forth, and *without* indifference, i.e., *without* an unground, there would be no twofoldness of the principles,"[297] in such a way that "the [Schellingian] Absolute is primarily the 'absolute indifference' providing the neutral medium for the coexistence of the polar opposites" of the Real and the Ideal.[298] As such, it provides a way out of the abyss of freedom as a kind of metaphysical violence: the act of unconscious decision, the vanishing mediator that mediates between the real and ideal poles, "'repressed' by the formal envelope of the 'obscurantist' Schelling," becomes relegated to a mere secondary position in a theosophic drama that subsumes it.[299]

Although Hegel's mature ontology as outlined in the *Encyclopedia* suffers, in Žižek's view, from a similar deficiency by articulating the complete return of the Idea to itself in a manner that attempts to get rid of the psychotic night of the world, nevertheless Hegel develops a superior logic because within it there is no need to leave the internal dynamic of *Grund* and existence and posit some transcendent principle. All can be done at the level of (a self-destructive, negativity-wrought) immanence. What Hegel fails to bring to full conceptual expression is how in dialectics the very category of "and" changes, along with the full range of implications this presents for any metaphysical system of the world: through the paradoxical identification of *Grund* and existence "and" becomes, in essence, *tautological*,[300] which not only prevents *Grund* and existence from being mere opposites existing alongside one another through their foundation in something external to their own movement, but also excludes the possibility of any self-totalizing activity. In the logical process of the dialectic, the third term is the second, understood as a negativity or internal limit inscribed in the first, but only insofar as it has successfully taken over, *usurped*, the originary position from which the movement began by asserting itself as such—that is, the passage from the second to the third is that of an emergent extimacy within the first moment, which renders it non-coincident to itself, and thereby not-all, by owning itself and taking over its originary position to which it was once held at bay through an uprising. In terms of substance and subject, this means that "*this very reversal is the very definition of subject*: 'subject' is the name for the principle of Selfhood that subordinates to itself the substantial Whole whose particular moment it originally was."[301] Nothing at the level of content changes: it expresses a purely formal self-relationality giving birth to itself from within the radical non-coincidence of the absolute with itself, a self-begetting that resets the latter's logical hardwiring in an unpredictable way from within an unforeseeable self-posited zone of operation. The dialectical movement from (i) immediacy → (ii) negation → (iii) negation of negation is superior to Schellingian metaphysical narrative because there is *no genuine return movement to the first*, for everything takes place within a self-effacing, yet productive immanent field: the beginning and end do not overlap because something irreducibly different emerges within the first moment (negativity being now made foundational to identity): namely, an "out of joint" spirit that has a degree of notional self-reflexivity. In other words, *the tautology indicated by the category of "and" is, in fact, revelatory of a monism bursting at the seams*: to say that *Grund* and existence are identified is to say that *Grund* can only attain to existence, can only subsist in the modality of existence, insofar as it has erased itself, withdrawn from the scene. In this way it makes itself identical to the latter through the institution of its very difference from it, a difference that at some level is always a self-difference, a self-sabotaging, for there is no outside.[302] We come across a "self-enclosed" immanence that has produced a transcendence that persists in its heart of hearts in the paradoxical mode of the double feature of inclusion/exclusion, internal/external, presence/absence, so characteristic of Lacan's descriptions of the Real, but in such a way that what is excluded, external, absent, has a power over that from which it has emerged. Negativity means that the indivisibility and power of substance is shattered from within, because it is colonized by its own parasites like a madman is terrorized by his own hallucinations, but with the added effect that there is no need to posit a state of "originary health" of which the devouring restlessness of the negative cannot be predicated to explain the dynamism inherent to reality.

Because of the theosophic structure of the middle-late Schelling, Žižek's own appropriations of concepts such as *Grund* and *Entscheidung* in the development of his own metaphysics put him in a delicate situation. The issue at hand is further complicated by Žižek's division of Schelling's philosophy into three distinct and irreconcilable stages, which he finds reflected in the three existent drafts of the *Weltalter*.[303] Schelling₁ largely coincides with his quasi-Spinozistic philosophy of absolute indifference, where freedom is completely subsumed under the positive order of being. In the first draft this is seen in terms of the explication of freedom as a logical mode of necessity within the inner articulation of substance, its subsumption within the self-harmonizing genesis of the latter's rational structure and order. In the Schelling₂ of the second draft of the *Weltalter* and the *Freiheitsschrift*, we see an interesting twist with regard to the concern with how the contraction of material being itself is made possible. By conceiving the act of contraction as ultimately free and self-positing, here Schelling is able to think the will-to-contraction (the No) and the will-to-expansion (the Yes) as identical and therefore internal to the dynamic of freedom, which makes his thinking approach that of Hegelian dialectics and secures his position as the concluding step of the unconscious *Grundlogik* of

German Idealism whose lineage culminates in the advent of psychoanalysis. For Žižek, this brief period of breakthrough was quickly left behind by the Schelling₃ of the philosophy of mythology and revelation, where we see a return to a pre-modern "essentialism," traces of which he claims are already hinted at in the third draft of the *Weltalter*, where Schelling posits another principle of synthesis external to the movement of contraction and expansion within which freedom and determinism are grounded as opposites.

It is because of these tendencies (which explain why Žižek qualifies the revolutionary character of Schelling's philosophy by describing him as the father of "New Age obscurantism" just as much as the father of contemporary philosophy of finitude)[304] that Žižek so quickly changes tone in the second chapter of *The Indivisible Remainder*. Yet while consistent with his overall interpretation of Schelling, this emphatic shift is simultaneously ambiguous insofar as Žižek does not distinguish *which* Schelling he is arguing against or justify *how* he is able to read the second draft of the *Weltalter* as an ephemeral rupture in Schelling's thought "which goes farthest in the direction of Freedom."[305] Given that the only way for freedom to exist according to Žižek is through the space opened up by the caustic collapse of being, and that both Hegel's ontology and Schelling's logic fail in their own fashion to come to terms with this insight,[306] even if each encounters it in a significant manner, how exactly is Žižek able to retrieve this concept from the second draft without falling into the pitfalls of Schelling's own thinking, insofar as it is evidently against its letter and spirit even as he presents it? How is he able to maintain that the *Weltalter* and the *Freiheitsschrift* are the most sustained confrontation in the entire tradition with the frightening origins of subjectivity and its metaphysical implications, that they reveal the most profound penetration into the "perverted" core of the *cogito* that lurked latent in itself since the very founding gesture of modernity?

What specifically interests Žižek in the middle-late work of Schelling is its frantic and uncertain nature. For all its intense, uncontrollable passion, for all its feverish outpouring, it does not get off the ground. Schelling's masterpiece, the *Weltalter*, never gets finished. Although this is not an outlier in Schelling's long philosophical career—his entire corpus is ridden with rapidly written sketches of systems and allusions to publications on the horizon that never appear—there is an undeniable hesitation saturating this period. The trunk of stillborn, abortive drafts of the first book of the *Weltalter* found in the library of Munich, of which only three remain today due to the fires that wrought havoc in the city in the aftermath of Allied bombings (but of which there were more than twelve different handwritten versions) is enough to demonstrate that this work haunted Schelling in a manner and with an intensity that others did not, as does the fact that after the 1809 *Freiheitsschrift* he refrained from publishing another major work, and largely withdrew from the German intellectual scene where he was once the rising star. Aside from scattered lectures—for instance, an 1827 and an 1833 course on the *System der Weltalter*—he would not return to the public eye with any sustained vigor until he was called to Berlin in 1841. At that time, assuming Hegel's chair ten years after the latter's untimely death, addressing an audience that had eagerly awaited him to break his silence for decades (an audience that included both Engels and Kierkegaard) and whose final reappearance was exacerbated by the uncertain fate of Hegelianism, he gave lectures on the philosophy of mythology and revelation. But the *Hörsäle*, first overflowing with excited, enthusiastic students of philosophy anxious to hear the words of Hegel's old rival, were quickly abandoned in utter disappointment, leaving only a handful of devoted students, Fichte's son Immanuel Hermann von Fichte among them.

But what explains this sudden change in Schelling's career, this lack of desire to publish, to engage in dialogue, to spread his philosophy over the European landscape that had eagerly welcomed it? Jason Wirth hints at something that comes to mind for anyone who knows Schelling's life story:

> Yet 1809 marked a turning point in Schelling's zeal to
> publish. Already Schelling's reputation had been injured by
> Hegel's unwarranted dismissal of the intellectual intuition
> as the "night when all cows are black." [...] More seriously,
> however, Schelling's wife, Caroline, had become very ill. It is
> hard to read the Freedom essay, published in May 1809, with
> its analogy between sickness and evil (sickness is to Being
> as evil is to human being), without thinking of Caroline. In
> the treatise, Schelling claimed that the "veil of melancholy
> [*Schwermut*] that is spread out over all of nature is the

profound and indestructible melancholy of all life." Caroline
died on September 7, 1809. Schelling was devastated. In
a letter written less than a month after Caroline's death,
Schelling claimed that "I now need friends who are not
strangers to the real seriousness of pain and who feel that
the single right and happy [*glücklich*] state of the soul is the
divine mourning [*Traurigkeit*] in which all earthly pain is
immersed." A year later, Schelling began work on *Die Weltalter*,
a philosophical poem about the rotatory movement of natality
and fatality, pain and joy, comedy and tragedy within God,
that is, within the whole of Being, itself.[307]

Žižek allows us to offer a new, interesting, and controversial spin on this
enigma. If we follow and reconstruct his implicit methodology, we see
that he refuses the claim that Schelling's "retreat" was spurred on by
the tragic death of his true love and great muse Caroline in 1809 just
before the publication of the *Freiheitsschrift*, or for that matter even by the
overwhelming influence of the Hegelian system that could also be seen
as leaving him in a state of philosophical and existential paralysis. What
Žižek invites us to argue is that, when one looks at the very structure of the
Weltalter drafts themselves, one is confronted with an uncanny struggle of
composition that reveals something primordial concerning what its texts
give witness to and attempt—*but ultimately fail*—to bring forth. This painful
unrest is not to be reduced to the mere level of personal dissatisfaction, as if
there were a conscious recognition by Schelling that his own "masterpiece"
could never hold its own as a rival of Hegelian logic, nor could it just
boil down to some personal trauma that began to cloud Schelling's own
philosophical capacities through a devouring melancholy that made the
world during these years an agonizing repetition of bitter grey upon bitter
grey. Instead, it provides the key to understanding both the self-deploying
historico-dialectical (Lacanian) cause of German Idealism at work in
Schelling's thought and ultimately dividing it into the three distinct stages
as outlined by Žižek *and* establishing its true greatness in this fragmented
second stage, whereby we can open up a legitimate space in which to
reactualize it and let it come to terms with that which, by itself, it was
not able to do.

After Hegel's critique of the Schellingian absolute indifference[308] in *The Phenomenology of Spirit*, and recognizing the strength of Hegel's dialectics, Schelling is forced to rethink the philosophical foundation of his thought and its attempt to balance transcendental idealism with an organic philosophy of nature in such a way that he can at the same time fight against the perceived threats of Hegel's philosophy. He puts his own prowess to use in articulating his account of the emergence of temporality and finitude that does not succumb to the claustrophobic subsumption of human freedom within the self-mediation of the absolute. Arguing that Hegel can only show the notional necessity of things and never their brute reality, he embarks on a theosophic exploration of the creation of the world that would not only challenge, but hopefully put a stake in the heart of the philosophy of his now adversary and former friend. Yet Schelling's middle-late philosophy is not just a theo-cosmogonic odyssey of the vicissitudes of divine being in its restless search for self-revelation. Following reason by analogy and identifying a structural parallel between God's speaking of the Word by which he becomes a full person and the birth of self-experience out of the eternal darkness that precedes it,[309] Schelling's philosophy simultaneously functions on two levels, that of the theo-cosmological and that of the metapsychological, in such a way that Schelling is able to say, at the end of the *Freiheitsschrift*, that we "have established the first clear concept of personality."[310] It assumes that we can pass from the lowest to the highest, from the known to the unknown, by a careful, methodologically guided introspection, insofar as there is "a system of times [...] for us, of which the human system would be just a copy, a repetition within a narrower sphere."[311]

What is so intriguing about Schelling's attempt to describe the emergence of finitude from eternity and human subjectivity out of nature is the conceptual restlessness evident in the existent drafts of the project, each of which oscillates around an insurmountable deadlock located in the movement from the Past to the Present: that is, how the divine and human subject could emerge from the non-experiential void that precedes them. Schelling remains unable fully to explicate the meaning of what Žižek calls the "breach of symmetry," God's contraction of finitude, and in the same vein the emergence of a free, deciding being (the subject) in a manner that leaves him at ease. In the first draft the abyss of freedom contracts materiality out of *necessity*, so that both divine and human freedom are subsumed within the self-unfolding of substance, while the second declares that the very contraction itself is an act of *freedom*, a self-positing, which not only renders the two opposed principles of the Yes and the No *identical* in the internal dynamic of freedom, but also (and more disconcertingly) results in a structural homology with sickness and evil as an unpredictable negative reversal of established ordered and wholeness from within. The third merely complicates the picture insofar as it breaks from the "Spinozistic" determinism and closed systematicity of the first and the radical philosophy of freedom with its potentially unsettling implications proclaimed by the second: by synthesizing both polar principles within a point of metaphysical simultaneity within the Godhead that is the *Ungrund* within which both rest as androgynous pairs, God the Creator's personal freedom is saved from being logically dependent upon a moment of cancer in divine being that upsets the joyful bliss of eternity, and in a similar move, subjectivity is no longer made possible by that which disrupts the smooth placidity of substance.

These basic conceptual differences at such a foundational level of inquiry reverberate through the entire movement of the three stages in a meaningful way in each draft:

1. Not only is human freedom actually a misrecognition of blind (Spinozistic) causality, so that the movement of dialectical human temporality is an illusion, all being co-present in the self-harmonizing synchronicity of the system—here we see Schelling struggling to rearticulate his old ideas in a new format—but even the act of contracting finitude is a *necessity*, so it could not *not* have happened, deriving from the "primordial Freedom in an absolutely immediate, 'blind,' non-reflected, unaccountable way."[312]

2. The *fact* of finitude in God or of freedom in man proclaims that synchronic substance cannot be a devouring totality, but must be an open not-all plagued with fragility and inconsistency *all the way down*. The very self-positing of finite being in God

not only precludes all attempts to enclose it within a totalizing whole even within the divine understanding itself, since self-positing is equated with an absolute self-assertion, but (even more devastatingly) the emergence of God as a personal being out of its contracted material *Grund* is *uncertain*, insofar as there is no guarantee that He will come to His own by speaking the Word, unlike in the first draft where it is part of divine's substance infinite self-articulation.

3. The problematic ramifications of the second position are foreclosed by making God's free existence as an entity predetermined and guaranteed in advance through the dialectical simultaneity of freedom and determinism in a higher synthetic principle. Thus the creation of the world is an absolutely contingent act following from a volitional arbitrariness expressing God's essence as love, making divine being, rather than a turmoil-ridden drama with an unforeseeable end, a self-maintaining whole. In this sense the third draft symbolizes a kind of retreat from the second; one is even tempted to say an (unconscious) attempt to save oneself from the traumatic, horrifying implications of its philosophy of freedom. The true basis of spontaneity was, as it were, *too much* for Schelling—he had to pull back.

Not only do the existent drafts of the *Weltalter* give testament to an uncompromising tension, an endless circulation around an inassimilable kernel, both in terms of the relationship of God as person and consciousness to the eternal darkness of their ground, but it also appears as if Schelling's own philosophical career could only continue once it cut off, *repressed*, this encounter with the Real. In the turn to the Schelling₃ of the philosophy of mythology (already hinted at in the third draft of the *Weltalter*) we can glimpse a recoil from the abyssal basis of freedom as pure self-positing unleashed in the second in the same way that the earlier *Realphilosophie* of Hegel is later abandoned in order to embrace a consoling triadic dialectics: just as Hegel tries to save the absolute from a diremptive wound that can never be healed, here Schelling attempts to save the essence of God and nature from the insoluble deadlock of drives eventually engendered by the self-institution of finitude and negativity he stumbled across in the *Potenzenlehre* of the second draft and already implicit in the eruptive logic of the *Grund* in the *Freiheitsschrift*; in both there is an attempt to retreat from the notion of a barred organic whole, a metaphysics of the not-all, as forced upon us by the philosophy of freedom whose first outlines we see already in Kant, substantiating Žižek's claim that both Hegel and Schelling *repress* the unacknowledged truth, the *Grundlogik*, of German Idealism.[313] By referring to the Godhead as *das Überexistierende* that summons the blind rotatory movement of drives, the third draft strives to save reality from the irredeemable conflict that it is faced with in the contraction of finitude: instead of the latter being absolutely self-positing as a moment in the movement from the potentiality of freedom in its abyssal eternity to its actualization, God in some strong sense now precedes the *Grund* of His existence, assuring His protection from the non-coincidence to self announced by the dependence of light on darkness: there is "an activity performed at a safe distance."[314] This becomes even more evident in the late philosophy of mythology, where the entire theoretical edifice becomes grounded on the distinction between the *Was* and the *Daß* of God. The transcendence of the *Daß* from the flux of the *Potenzen* not only allows for an implicit, yet self-articulating teleological movement intrinsic to the antagonisms of finitude of the latter so that there are stages that unfold throughout nature and then human history that ultimately pave the way for the final revelation of God, but it also makes any appearance of ontological disarray merely a "perceptual illusion" generated by a self-harmonizing scheme deduced by negative philosophy (in Žižek's words, this is Schelling's regress to pre-modern essentialism). Complementing negative philosophy, Schelling envisages a form of positive philosophy, one of whose primary tasks is to find and explicate these stages in nature and history: that is to say, "to function as a kind of 'transcendental empiricism,' and to 'test' the truth of rational construction in actual life,"[315] thereby subsuming the restless negativity at the heart of reality as revealed specifically in the second draft into a mere secondary feature of God's plan within the spectacle of the absolute's own self-development, deflating it to a mere ephemeral phase in an overarching cosmic dance towards revelation. The absolute *yearns* for self-disclosure once it has *willed* it, so that all things in creation move towards it, even if unknowingly: here, not only is nature's unpredictable catastrophism and widespread murder and extinction[316] no longer indicative of a lack of a totalizing principle, but man, denied the right to be an autonomous writer in the drama of divine being, is reduced to a mere actor or puppet who follows a pre-written script (a *telos*) given by the very structure of the *Potenzen* themselves for the joy of its author in His distant, cold kingdom of divine eternity, the non-rational *Daß of* God being, after all, distinct from and existing over and above the *Was* of God. But in the movement from Schelling$_2$ to Schelling$_3$ we should not just draw our attention to how in the latter there is absolutely no room for subjectivity with the very technical sense of the word that we have been using. What is much more revealing is how concerned Schelling$_3$ is to establish God as that which guarantees the consistency and internal coherence of nature *and* history, previously jeopardized, *for us and God Himself*: there is a frantic obsession to demonstrate the existence of the Other of the Other in the Real when the inconsistencies and frailty of order have already been pushed upon us. The third stage in Schelling's thought is nothing but a reaction formation against his radical philosophy of freedom.

Leaving aside the possible theological implications of Žižek's reading of Schelling—which deserve to be evaluated in their own right—due to his outright rejection of theosophy as ultimately nothing but a mytho-poetics of the Symbolic's coming into being, what Žižek's Schelling unearths in his frenzied attempt to develop a philosophical program able to battle Hegelian Absolute Idealism is the not-all nature of the absolute. Trying to give an account of the emergence of finitude and driven on by the alchemical intuition that there is an identity between the highest and the lowest, the self-begetting of God and the self-caused birth of the subject in its freedom, he delves into the nocturnal site out of which the human self is born and experiences the terror of the failure of positive being to ground itself, its "self-lacerating rage" (*sich selbst zerreißende Wut*), which acts as the vanishing mediator between nature and culture by opening up the possibility for the self-assertion of freedom from within the Real and its vicissitudes. This not only by definition prevents the completion of the project of the *Weltalter* insofar as it precludes any possibility of the reconciliation promised by the Third Age, the Future wherein *Grund* and existence become reconciled in redemption, which would merely just institute a triadic dialectics similar to that of Hegel's mature system—it also brings Schelling's philosophy to a halt, a standstill, as it comes upon metaphysical implications revealed by the split nature of subjectivity. Only ever successfully completing the first, preliminary part of his mytho-poetic ages of the world, his description of the eternal Past, Schelling remains forever unable to proceed; it is this which causes him to fade slowly from the public eye, where he was once a star and the leader of one of the greatest intellectual movements the world has ever witnessed, because he came too close to its true horrifying core.

9.2 That Which Is in Schelling More than Schelling Himself—Žižek

Schelling's failure to finish the *Weltalter* is not due to his lack of conceptual prowess or an earth-shattering, existential strife: it results from *an encounter with the Real*, an encounter that is philosophically meaningful. Because there is an inassimilable kernel within its symbolic space tearing it apart, its discourse is riddled with harrowing tension: unable to bring this encounter to its complete symbolization, Schelling's *Weltalter* falls to the ground and is only able to save itself through an unconscious disavowal that takes the form of an insistence on the existence of the Other of the Other. By consequence, it has to be interpreted psychoanalytically so that its truth or cause can finally be integrated into its symbolic space, and its place as the concluding step of German Idealism's formative *Grundlogik* can be firmly established. If this can be accomplished, then we will be permitted to say that, retroactively, Schelling's project fell to the ground not only in the sense of a purely negative collapse, but also as the condition of the possible opening of a new beginning, following the double connotation of the German *zugrunde gehen*. The failure of the *Weltalter*, the fact of its incompletion, turns out to be a *triumph* of human reason:[317] its apparent limitations—the feverish frenzy of the work, the inconsistency brought forth by its conceptual unrest—are actually expressive of an underlying ontological and metaphysical intuition that we can catch a glimpse of through the interstices of its discourse. Žižek's claim is that if we pass through the negative determination at the heart of the work, the non-coincident in-itself we witness can become a for-itself.

The "victory" that Žižek perceives in the *Weltalter* is in its gestures
towards philosophical logic underlying the birth of consciousness and its
wider metaphysical implications. The strangeness and density of the *Weltalter*
project are not due to its out-of-jointness with the modern tradition,
but due to the fact that it comes too close to its disavowed essence. The
anxiety-inducing reverberations that shake one's body when one reads the
descriptions of "Schelling's grandiose 'Wagnerian' vision of God in the
state of a endless 'pleasure in pain,' agonizing and struggling with Himself,
affected by an unbearable anxiety, the vision of a 'psychotic,' mad God"[318]
are so difficult because they make us approach the very kernel not just
of our existence as subjects but also the nature of the world at large. This
experience of reading its drafts is properly "traumatic" in the meaning Lacan
gives to this term drawing upon its etymological origins in ancient Greek:
they bring forth a devastating encounter by which the symbolic support of
our personality is "wounded" or "pierced," during which the coherence of
our identity is torn apart as it comes upon its truth.[319] The effect is twofold.
Firstly, both Schelling's own inability to finish the project, his heap of lost
manuscripts, and the subsequent necessity to "invent" a solution to continue
his philosophical career *and* its neglect in the philosophical community as a
whole could thus be seen as nothing but a *recoil* from the Real of our being
as finally explicitly brought into the open within his texts. It is thus Schelling
who, in an attempt to give a death-dealing materialist response to Hegel's
"pan-logicism," most fully experiences out of all the representatives of the
modern tradition the "incomprehensible basis of reality," that mysterious
X that forever haunts transcendentally constituted reality (the Real as a
"kink" in the Symbolic), precedes it (the Real as pre-symbolic immediacy
lost due to language), and in some modality conditions its very possibility
(the Real [Я] as auto-disruptive substance [N ≠ N] whose self-laceration
creates the space for free experience). In an attempt to articulate the
irreducibility of freedom, Schelling plunges headfirst into the paradoxical
character of subjectivity—not only into the denaturalized state of unruliness
we must posit as prior to the emergence of phenomenal reality and culture,
the pulsating cauldron of chaotic, heterogeneous forces that first make
possible the gesture of infinite withdrawal into the nocturnal irreal self of
the world, but the very ambiguity of the latter as an absolute self-positing

act. Secondly, the originality of this narrative of German Idealism that Žižek allows us to construct is its implicit claim that the *Weltalter* is *the* text of modernity and that its incompletion, fragmentation, and unpopularity are philosophically rich in meaning, perhaps even *necessary* reactions to its truth. Not only does this contribute to elevating Schelling to his rightful place in history of philosophy after having long been overshadowed by Hegel, it also (and more importantly) calls us to own up to other elements of our being that may be more difficult to bear, even too difficult to bear, by one of their greatest theorists.

Žižek's work on Schelling is so crucial for understanding his philosophy as a whole, not only because it provides us the resources we need to show the coherence of his reading of the modern philosophical tradition, but also because it allows us to demonstrate the profound level of philosophical scrutiny and methodological rigor inherent in his apparent heterodoxy. If the self-development of the former's account of subjectivity is characterized by a recoil from the parallax ontology of transcendental materialism at the core of the *cogito*'s self-positing, the traces of which we can see in the negative contortions of its symbolic space through its entire history, it is only by reconstructing his psychoanalytical interpretation of Schelling as the culmination of German Idealism that we can truly legitimate and assess this claim. Although such a recoil from this traumatic Real may be evident in Descartes's reification of the subject as a thinking *thing*, Kant's attempt to ontologize "this I or he or it (the thing) that thinks" or more strongly his inability to delve into obscure foundations of unruliness and diabolic evil, or in Hegel's mature system as a covering up of the madness of the night of the world, it is only by recourse to Schelling that he can retroactively posit such a self-deploying disavowed knowledge that deepens itself through the trajectory of the tradition and that leads to its eventual culmination in psychoanalysis.[320] What makes Schelling such an important outlier to this sustained recoil, however, was his ability (for a relatively brief period of time) to completely immerse himself within the frenzy, horror, and pandemonium that are the true origin of subjectivity in such a way that he brings to the fore the entire latent *Grundlogik* of modern philosophy of the subject preceding him and that is surpassed only by psychoanalysis' thematization of the unconscious and *Todestrieb*. His own turning away from this insight and the various inconsistencies that lace his texts must be seen as symptomatic of a greater tendency within the movement (and in humans in general) towards the development of defense mechanisms in the face of an inability to integrate the psychoanalytical truth the Real tries to force upon us. If Schelling's own recoil—a return to a pre-modern essentialism—is so severe, it is because he, as the one who experienced the horror of the metaphysical implications of subjectivity most strongly, needed a defense mechanism more radical than the rest. In their "very failure, [the *Weltalter*] are arguably the acme of German Idealism and, simultaneously, a breakthrough into an unknown domain whose contours became discernible only in the aftermath of German Idealism."[321]

Žižek thus sees his philosophy not only as an attempt to *reactualize* the German Idealist tradition, but also as *immanently participating* within its own self-deployment. He understands his project as a remodulation of its surface logic by clinically working through what he perceives as its internal tension, so as to construct the self-effacing, transcendental materialism that has been its unconscious truth.[322] He is not merely performing an act of hermeneutical retrieval, but (more strongly) taking these ideas into what he considers to be their dialectical "completion" from which they have been hindered by the tradition itself. For Žižek, it is Lacan who gives us the methodological tools we need to "rehabilitate" its fundamental concepts, but which amounts to something more than a mere *application* of psychoanalytical concepts to various texts in the history of philosophy. The approach is much more provocative. By enacting a kind of therapeutic space *within* key texts of the middle-late Schelling as the culminating point of German Idealism, the wager of Žižek's philosophy is that, by being open to their own inner movement, he can bring forth that which is in Schelling more than Schelling himself: the extimate, traumatic core lodged deep within his spirit and soul and from which Schelling withdrew into philosophical "paralysis" by integrating (*constructing*) the originally inassimilable theoretical potential and unsettling metaphysical consequences of the second draft of the *Weltalter*. The relationship of Žižek to Schelling as the endpoint of German Idealism is therefore structurally identical to that of Lacan to Freud. As Miller puts it:

The Four Fundamental Concepts of Psychoanalysis appears to be
a tribute to Freud, since the four concepts are taken directly
from his work. Just as Lacan at that time calls his institute the
"Freudian School," in his seminar he uses the term "Freudian
concepts" just to prove that he is not a dissident. But within
this "tribute" he tries to go beyond Freud. Not a beyond
Freud which leaves Freud behind; it is a beyond Freud which
is nevertheless in Freud. Lacan is looking for something in
Freud's work of which Freud himself was unaware. Something
which we may call "extimate," as it is so very intimate that
Freud himself was not aware of it. So very intimate that this
intimacy is extimate. It is an internal beyond.[323]

But how is Žižek able to accomplish such a feat, seeing that Schelling
himself *fought against this*?

9.3 A Mytho-Poetics of Creation and the Seducing Hand of Fantasy

The answer lies in the second draft, where Žižek sees a distinctively *Hegelian*
structure that enables him to develop a metapsychological reading of the
text, preventing its underlying ontology from succumbing to philosophical
commitments that he rejects and identifies as in opposition to the
unconscious *Grundlogik* of German Idealism. In fighting against what he
perceives to be the limitations and threat of Hegelian logic, Schelling, in
the end, only radicalizes its perverse truth, yet is unable to contain the
monster that he unleashes. After developing an astonishing philosophy of
freedom, Schelling immediately recoils from its implications by positing
a principle of mediation that enables the neutral coexistence of *Grund*
and existence through their mutual grounding in what Schelling in the
Freiheitsschrift refers to as the *Ungrund*, that which in itself is ungrounded
and thus simultaneously precedes both and is neither one nor the other.
Because Schelling here understands the freedom of unconscious decision
(*Entscheidung*) that separates *Grund* from existence as a return to the
primordial origin of all reality that is the abyss of freedom itself, its
conceptual edifice displays a structure of quaternity, which is articulated

in his thinking largely through a systemization and reconceptionalization of thinkers like Jakob Böhme and Franz Baader, and is thereby able to sidestep the implication of freedom as a cancerous upsurge of pure self-assertion. But insofar as the second draft displays freedom as a kind of self-positing activity that identifies *Grund* (the will-to-contraction, the No) and existence (the will-to-expansion, the Yes), Žižek jumps at this slight "slip" in Schelling's text, seeing in this discursive inconsistency a possibility of "formalizing" the conceptual movement of the work by "purifying" it of all extraneous theosophic commitments through traces of Hegelian logic he sees operative within it. It is in this sense that Žižek's philosophy is a hybridism of Schellingian ontology and a Hegelian quadruple dialectics of non-reconciliation.

For Žižek, Hegel is the superior logician because he has no need to posit a principle of mediation outside of the internal dynamic of *Grund* and existence. There is no possible return to (or even initial existence of) a state of "originary" health, as typified by the abyss of freedom as independent from the antagonism of the dual principles, for there is nothing that has not always already succumbed to the restlessness of the negative. Although textbook Hegelianism presents the third moment of the logic as a synthesis of two previous incompatible conceptual polarities by means of a *cancellation* of the falsehood and a *preservation* of the truth contained in each and thereby bringing them into a higher, more comprehensive dialectical standpoint (the banal reading of the equivocal character of the word "*Aufhebung*") Žižek thinks this picture misses the true philosophical innovation that we see in the movement from one stage to another.[324] The third moment itself is only the second insofar as it hegemonically usurps the position of the first through positing itself as such—which is, in a way, a mere amplification of an already existing interruption in the immanence of the first's logical field, an amplification that destroys its sway from within, but without ever leaving its fold. The dialectical movement from (i) immediacy → (ii) negation → (iii) negation of negation is superior not only because there is no return to the first (something irreducibly different and operatively new emerges, irreversibly reconfiguring the entire [onto]logical apparatus through its self-positing) but also because there is no need to posit something outside the self-movement of negativity to explain the entire logical process: "[t]here is thus no reversal of negativity into positive greatness—the only greatness is 'negativity' itself."[325] In other words, the negativity of the second is entirely inscribed within the first, arising from within its closed immediacy as a kind of tension or contradiction, and is in this regard not separate or distinct from it insofar as there is nothing but the dialectical register of the first. Yet because the second presents us with an internal limit (it itself has no substance of its own) and is thus by definition non-coincident with the first and its operational principles, it is in the same breath minimally distinguished from it, thus engendering a fissure in the logical self-closure of the field in a movement that makes the entire order inconsistent and ill at ease, which in turn opens up a foothold for the possibility of change.[326] For Hegel, it is this deadlock of real internal limit—an inassimilable kernel—that ultimately serves as the springboard for all dialectical change by creating the space necessary for the unpredictable self-founding of a new order, but of itself it only becomes explicit in the aftermath of the third as it overthrows the primacy of the first through the paradoxical causality of a retroactive positing of presuppositions (*Setzung der Voraussetzungen*). There is something like an internal parasitic logic that re-totalizes the entire dialectical framework, so that instead of witnessing a return to the first, an initially subordinate moment degrades its own genetic conditions *into its own subordinate moment* by means of the unforeseeable and destructive power of negativity, which now reigns supreme.[327]

With the self-positing of the third (the second positing *itself*, counting itself, thus *making itself the third by a self-doubling*), negativity is finally fully "brought to life," but in such a way that its dark pre-history in the vicissitudes of the previous stage as a purely negative real limit necessarily vanishes from sight, for the contingency of its self-positing has been immanently overcome. But even if the stark remodulation of the (onto)logical field within which it occurs, a remodulation that effectuates itself by establishing itself as the supreme category, covers up its steps like an experienced criminal used to getting away with his crime, in the same breath it sets the stage for a new (relatively closed) immediacy and thus the possibility of new unforeseeable dialectical change. But we must recognize that this self-positing always comes too late: its upsurge may posit itself at the logical beginning of the movement as necessary, *it may make itself the primary principle*, that to which the movement had always tended, but this only becomes visible after the fact and is thus plagued by a devastating belatedness. There is no way notionally to deduce the act of self-positing because, as free, it impossible to predetermine its arrival or even be aware that it could occur at all.[328] The reversal characteristic of the third moment *befalls being*, for "every dialectical passage or reversal is a passage in which the new figure emerges *ex nihilo*."[329] What we often miss in the necessity of the dialectical movement and what is even obfuscated by it is the fact that every movement of its self-articulation is, in fact, *constituted by a series of a contingent acts* brought on by negativity, contingencies that only retroactively gain the status of necessity by *making themselves necessary*.[330] The passage from tension to victory is never ontologically guaranteed—and it is precisely this ambiguity intrinsic to the restlessness of negativity that constitutes the Real of the *Weltalter*. If it was Hegel who gave the former the most profound philosophical articulation in its raw purity in his *Science of Logic*, it was Schelling who *was the first to stumble upon the full range of its metaphysical implications* (to which we shall return).[331] What is more, this also lets us explain why Hegel could have stopped dead in his tracks in his mature thinking of a triadic relationship between logic, nature, and spirit despite already having at his disposition such a sophisticated account of a metaphysically contingent retroactive restructuring of being from within. Although the inner movement he describes in the *Logic* gives perfect expression to the quadruple dialectics already hinted at in the night of the world of his *Realphilosophie*, the problem is that the categories it describes, like Lacan's mathemes, do not supply us with any horizon of meaning. As such, they must be supplemented with the "concrete" symbolic content of the philosophies of nature and spirit, thus creating space in which Hegel could phantastically recoil from his breakthrough insight into the subject as a self-instituting gap in being and its stark consequences for our understanding of the self and the world. Hence why the *Weltalter* is so crucial for grasping the true importance of subjectivity as a contingent, world-changing event: it gives us mytho-poetic content that comes closer to grasping the matter at hand than Hegel's account of the particular sciences does, which rather obfuscates it (just as many empirical accounts continue to do today when faced with the explosion of the Ideal out of the Real).

The immediate problem facing Žižek here is the fact that *all* of
Schelling's middle-late works present themselves as a theogony, an
account of the birth of God, based on the anti-dialectical structure of the
quaternity, where the last movement is *not* the expression of something
logically irreducible and operatively new immanently emerging from within
a system, but a "return" to the first as a kind of direct contact with and
raising up to a higher power of a dormant force that is simultaneously the
primordial and unfathomable origin of all things. Each text repeats the same
movement, although the drafts of the *Weltalter*—in contradistinction to the
Freiheitsschrift—abruptly end before historical time. As the first, the abyss
of God's freedom as the impenetrably dark source of divine and created
reality rests in the absolute joy of eternity, a blind existence, where it wills
nothing because it is the pure virtuality wherein everything is potentially
contained, though does not determinately exist. Yet without distinction
and duality, the eternal nature as freedom remains unrevealed and thus
lacks the fullness of self-knowledge. In order to achieve this, God (who
is here not yet a person) must somehow contract finitude and difference,
limit His freedom, if He is to have an Other through which He can reveal
Himself, thereby establishing the distance necessary to Himself to become
a subject capable of owning freedom as a predicate instead of merely being
freedom as a pure virtuality. He breaches this pure virtuality by instituting
the conflict of *Grund* (the No, the darkness of materiality, the contractive
energy that holds all together) and existence (the Yes, the light of spirit, the
expansive structures that give order to the rulessness of the *Grund*) within
Him, so that He can beget Himself as a self-conscious being and eventually
decide to bestow upon His own *Grund* the status of an independent and
productive being, thus becoming God the Creator and allowing this same
conflict constitutive of his inner life to be mirrored in all living things. Hence
Schelling can say at the end of the *Freiheitsschrift* that nature is the first
revelation of God.[332] But with the highest creature, man, something new
emerges in creation as the principles become separable, which leads to the
possibility of the *free* conquering of the dark principle by the light if humans
choose to live their lives in imitation of God's spirit as the perfect unity of
Grund and existence and, by consequence, to the possibility of a complete
revelation of God to Himself insofar as humans then become the image of

God (*imago dei*). With the forward march of history, the goal of creation will be attained when evil is completely vanquished, for this will have meant that we, like God, will have achieved the holy unification of the light and dark principles, insofar as we will have made ourselves subjects capable of owning freedom as a predicate by autonomously choosing the Yes and thus overcoming our separation from God by returning to Him. Material being, which we will have then "divinized" in showing how it is capable of the good in and through us, and personal God will then be reconciled and love—which presents itself as the fourth, the positive counterpart at the end of the system corresponding to the *Ungrund* as its absolute beginning—will prevail: as nature *yearns* for the spoken Word, humanity *longs for* for the destruction of the antagonism of principles in the Future, which proves itself to be a paradoxical "return" to the Past, since once the Present has begun, its beginning is always already lost, so that the only way the *Ungrund* can reemerge is if the world ends in a Future that is to come. The pure virtuality that contains everything potentially may be irretrievable, but redemption—as love—awaits as a point to which the world tends, for this tendency towards its own annihilation as we know it is part of its metaphysical structure. The inner life of all being thus follows a series of fourfolds that are modelled after the structure intrinsic to the life of God:

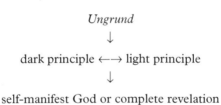

Ungrund
↓
dark principle ←—→ light principle
↓
self-manifest God or complete revelation

But how is Schelling able to maintain such a narrative within the second period *even in face of a structure that apparently forecloses its very possibility*?

That which enables Schelling to sustain such a narrative in face of a structure that compromises the dynamic of the quaternity paradoxically coincides with his insight into a parallactic dialectics of restless negativity. The success of Schelling's reaction formation goes hand in hand with the intensity of his plunging into the abyssal origins of subjectivity, since the latter constitutes some kind of primordial trauma whose repression is simultaneous with the transcendental constitution of reality so that it is only to be expected that such a two-way tension would emerge. Given that the origins of the Symbolic withdraw in their founding gesture, if Schelling is to describe the interior involutions of the Real, and in what sense they could bring forth the conditions of the possibility of an absolutely free subjectivity (either human or divine) Schelling must have recourse to a mytho-poetic medium to talk about that which forever precedes and can never enter the light of consciousness and language. If the subject is "the primordial Big Bang" of experiential reality,[333] how are we to grasp what occurred only nanoseconds prior to it? The issue is not the Real-as-excess as that which logically *precedes* and *exceeds* symbolization, which spectrally haunts all synthetic constitution, but the very moment in which the Symbolic upsurges; and because such an event is a structurally impossible object of discourse, any discourse that attempts to account for it is by the same token plagued by this very impossibility. Faced with this impasse, we are forced to fall back into mythology to explain that which transcends the bounds of ideality as its core:

> Does not this step involve "regression" to a version of New Age mythology? When, at the key points of their theoretical edifice, Freud and Lacan also resorted to a mythical narrative (Freud's myth of the primordial father in *Totem and Taboo*, his reference to Plato's myth of androgynous primordial man in *Beyond the Pleasure Principle*; Lacan's myth of "lamella" in his *Four Fundamental Concepts of Psycho-Analysis*), they were driven by the same necessity as Schelling: the need for the form of mythical narrative arises when one endeavours to break the circle of the symbolic order and to give an account of its genesis ("origins") from the Real and its pre-symbolic antagonism.[334]

Although mythology is *rationally justified* insofar as we have, as it were, deduced the necessity of the non-deducible and now need a new manner to investigate it, it does not come without its risks: the pre-symbolic act at the very founding gesture of language—the vanishing mediator between nature and culture that cannot be found in either—is that which we can "access" through a kind of self-reflexive speculative fabulation that stages "the birth from darkness into light,"[335] but in such a way that we cannot guarantee a priori that such an endeavour will not be plagued by defence mechanisms, unconscious fantasies and wishes, especially given its essentially traumatic nature. To search for our origins, we must plunge into the abyss, but it can lead us astray: the mytho-poetics of speculative fabulation can just as much help us narrate the pre-history of the Symbolic and the always already lost act that institutes it, the trauma that is the lacerating cut of pure self-positing in its full horror, as it can nourish psychoanalytical defences against it when we approach the ontological catastrophe at our nativity as human subjects. It is exactly here at this juncture of interplay of mytho-poetic fabulation and phantasmic interference within Schelling's second period that Žižek intervenes, using the resources of Lacanian psychoanalysis to traverse its fantasy and thereby restructure its conceptual space so as to bring forth that which is in Schelling so intimately that it is most properly characterized as extimate. But how can Žižek accomplish such a feat? Before we can directly answer this question, it is necessary to summarize the two intertwined levels active in the rational mythology of the *Weltalter* project in order to locate the unsolved tension from which psychoanalysis offers us a way out.

Within the stillborn drafts of the *Weltalter*, Schelling divides the passage from the eternal Past to the Present into three distinct stages. Because Schelling's text simultaneously operates in a theosophic and metapsychological mode, I will quickly summarize Žižek's presentation of each stage. Instead of outlining the various conceptual distinctions and internal differences that occur within the three existent drafts of the *Weltalter*, I will only be dealing with Žižek's own exegesis, which focuses on the second draft, since as we have seen he largely dismisses the importance of the other two versions.

1. In the absolute beginning prior to God's contraction of material being and the annular rotation of drives, there is a joyous nothingness, a pure potentiality that exists in timeless, inexhaustible rapture. God is not a yet a "He," but merely an impersonal, anonymous "it": knowing no conflict, God knows not even itself as radical freedom. For Žižek, in contemporary terms this would be equivalent to the pure void that exists before the vacuum fluctuation declared by quantum cosmology, a

nothingness that must be declared positively charged because from its (auto)disturbance "something" emerges. What is of utmost importance here is the irreconcilable contrast between this stage and the next: the joyous void of divine non-being is breached by the contraction of finitude and the self-diremption of perfection that it entails. Metapsychologically, this sundering of heavenly symmetry is thus structurally identical to the disruption of the oceanic unity of child and mother that supposedly precedes the Oedipus complex, or the smooth, placid functioning of cyclical nature, which is skewered by the advent of human subjectivity.

2. After the contraction of material being, we have what Žižek calls "Schelling's grandiose 'Wagnerian' vision of God." Within Schellingian cosmogony, this is so "terrifying" because, instead of the endless joy of divine eternity, we have a God as subject who finds Himself caught within the self-lacerating rage of matter. There is a sense in which God the Almighty is in infinite pain because his freedom has been lost within the torment-ridden movement that is coincident with the moment when the blind rotation of drives falls into an erratic, uncontrollable oscillation. As such, God is comparable to a helpless animal stuck in a trap.[336] To exemplify this point further, Žižek compares this stage to the unfathomable chaos that occurs after the vacuum fluctuation at the origins of the universe: the contraction of matter into an infinite point of absolute singularity, an incomprehensible upheaval within which the logic of our known physical universe breaks down. In terms of a metapsychology, it can be read as a mytho-poetic description of the ontological short circuit within the instinctual schemata of nature occurring before the eruption of human subjectivity. This moment of ontological standstill coincides with the pre-personal realm of anarchic self-experience seen in the night of the world and expresses the first beginnings of psychotic withdrawal of nature into an irreal self that severs the *Innenwelt* from *Aussenwelt*.

3. Finally, we have God who is able to speak the Word and thus
    overcome the deadlock that he found Himself lodged within
    by becoming a full-fledged subjectivity. Ejecting the materiality
    that He had contracted, pushing it out of him like some kind of
    foreign body, he bestows upon this now excremental product
    its own independent existence and thus becomes God the
    Creator. For Žižek, this corresponds in physics to the primordial
    Big Bang itself: the beginning of our material universe as the
    self-expansion of the initially infinitely dense point of matter.
    Metapsychologically, in the Word we see the unconscious
    decision (*Entscheidung*) that separates *Grund* and existence for
    the first time. The Symbolic erupts as an attempt to discipline the
    unruliness of the previous stage, which has immanently disrupted
    the primacy of organism's autopoietic schemata. The schismatic
    split that characterizes the essence of the psychoanalytical
    experience and the actual freedom of the *cogito* is posited as such
    for the first time as a response to the complete denaturalization
    that is the zero-level of the subject. In both the theosophy of
    creation, the physics of the Big Bang, and the metapsychology
    of the birth of subjectivity, this stage is something unpredictable
    that founds something new (God the Creator, material reality, the
    universe of meaning).

The existent drafts of the *Weltalter* find themselves confronted with
the same problem as the *Freiheitsschrift*, that is, the arbitrariness of the
beginning: why does God speak the Word? If the act of unconscious decision
cannot be deduced according to notional necessity (were it able to be,
Schelling would fall back into the perceived threat of Absolute Idealism
that he is fighting against) *there is no guarantee* that God, after contracting
material finitude, will be able to assert His freedom by making it a predicate
of Himself: that is, *there is no guarantee* that the subject will be able to
liberate itself from the deadlock of the drives within which it finds itself, in
other words, their unruliness. Attempting to articulate a radical philosophy
of freedom, Schelling in the second draft has no possible recourse to an
explanatory principle capable of saving God or human being from possible
infinite diremption: he is unable to foreclose the possibility that both could

have become completely lost to themselves at a now inaccessible point in the vicissitudes of their dark pre-history. What is so terrifying here is that, instead of the light of consciousness and the universe of meaning, *there could have been nothing but the agonizing rotation of drives in their frantic disorder, nothing but the ontological mayhem/madness wherein being would be irrevocably laid to waste in its own breakdown and catastrophism.* If being awakens in a moment of primordial trauma, how could one be certain that its defense formation (subjectification through the Symbolic) would work? That it would solve its antagonism? If freedom is to be irreducible, it must posit itself entirely by its own activity from within the clutches of unbreakable determinism, but this comes at a price—and it is exactly around this problematic of the breach of symmetry necessary for a suitable "foundation" of freedom and its alarming metaphysical implications that the existent stillborn drafts circulate and ultimately falter, each offering a different spin irreconcilable with the others.

For Žižek, however, the psychoanalytical tension of the *Weltalter* drafts displays a much more complex structure than that of a mere attempt to cover up the dialectical contingency at the heart of the unconscious decision and its wider implications. What intensifies the problem at hand is that the entire investigation has the fundamental structure of fantasy.[337] In the articulation of the absolute beginning, we insert ourselves as a pure gaze into the Real that is prior to our own conception, just as if we were to imagine ourselves as spectators in our funerals watching our friends react to our death—and if we read the mytho-poetic introspective analysis that leads Schelling to such a discussion with this in mind, then we must conclude that it too exhibits the psychoanalytical traits associated with such fantasy constructions, complete with all of the problems that go along with them. For both endeavour to describe the impossible: a linguistically ordered field of experience where there is none, a world of thought where no thinking could possibly exist, the first merely in a "subjective" sense (I cannot witness my own funeral because my own personal ego will never exist after my death in order to be able even to see such events unfolding as I may imagine them), but the second in an "objective" sense (not only is there *no one* there to witness the emergence of a world of signification, since consciousness presupposes someone has already emerged, but thought itself as *logos* has yet even to appear on the scene). When put in this manner, the question that poses itself is how the second, "objective" fabulation can be saved from the various kinds of illusions that may play themselves out in the first, "subjective" mode of fabulation such as those that occur in our daydreaming. In this respect, it is understandable how Schelling could have fallen into a trap: because we can only retroactively posit the material origins of subjectivity from within the Symbolic and the Imaginary and these origins represent the unthinkable basis of thinking itself,[338] the descriptions of this natal darkness can serve as a mere screen upon which we project fantasmatic supplements to satisfy unconscious desires. Not only does the very nature of the investigation jeopardize it (since we can structurally never reach the act that brings consciousness into existence, speculation has reached its limit and must pass into dramatic mytho-poetics) but it could easily be abolished through a reduction to the narcissistic orbit of the Imaginary or succumb to various symbolic levels of defence that would prevent the subject from performing its description, even in a self-reflexive mytho-poetic medium. By protecting us from the traumatic Real of our being, something that we of course all want, these supplements can lead us away from the truth for which we are searching. But it is precisely here that the strength of psychoanalysis shows itself: as a discourse about discourse, in short, a discourse whose aim is to understand the inherent limitations plaguing all discourse (itself thus included), it is able to bestow upon such theoretical investigation an extra level of self-reflexivity that could help it from falling into such traps: "the way to avoid this utopian reduction of the subject to the impossible gaze witnessing an alternate reality from which it is absent is not to abandon the topos of alternate reality as such, but to reformulate it so as to avoid the mystification of the theosophic mytho-poetic narrative which pretends to render the genesis of the cosmos."[339] Thus, by focusing on the ambiguity of inserting ourselves as a pure gaze into the absolute beginning that we must retroactively posit, that is, the very impossibility of the endeavour itself to succeed in its task, Žižek is able to find a way to entirely cut off the theosophic character of Schelling's text and read it exclusively as a metapsychological account of the emergence of Symbolic from the meaningless Real. Man's inclusion within the divine theo-cosmogonic drama ultimately proves to be an extraneous feature of the operative logic of the *Weltalter* drafts, a code to be deciphered, many features of which can be ignored as a mere phantasmal projection accidentally adjoining itself to an exploration of the abyssal origins of subjectivity. One of Žižek's most provocative claims is that one can see such a phantasmal projection in the attempts to cover up its most groundbreaking insight: the destructive self-movement of negativity in reality that leads to and is radicalized in the self-positing of subjectivity. In this way, we can say that paradoxically *"it was [Schelling's] very 'regression' from pure philosophical idealism to the pre-modern theosophical problematic which enabled him to overtake modernity itself."*[340] But now the question imposes itself upon us: what is revealed when we purify the odyssey that is the *Freiheitsschrift* and the *Weltalter* from its mytho-poetic phantasmagoria?

Notes

294. See Žižek, *The Ticklish Subject*, p. 55; and *The Parallax View*, p. 166.

295. Žižek, *The Indivisible Remainder*, p. 8.

296. Schelling, *Freiheitsschrift*, p. 276.

297. Ibid., p. 278.

298. Žižek, *The Indivisible Remainder*, p. 105.

299. Ibid., p. 92.

300. Ibid., p. 103.

301. Ibid., p. 106.

302. Žižek, *Less Than Nothing*, p. 234.

303. Žižek, *The Indivisible Remainder*, pp. 35–39.

304. Schelling, *Weltalter II*, p. 4.

305. Žižek, *The Indivisible Remainder*, p. 38.

306. Ibid., p. 92.

307. Wirth, "Translator's Introduction," in *Weltalter III*, pp. ix–x.

308. Hegel, *The Phenomenology of Spirit*, p. 9.

309. Žižek, *The Indivisible Remainder*, pp. 20–21.

310. Schelling, *Freiheitsschrift*, p. 281.

311. Schelling, *Weltalter II*, p. 121.

312. Žižek, *The Indivisible Remainder*, p. 38.

313. Ibid., p. 92.

314. Ibid., p. 37.

315. Ibid., p. 39.

316. Schelling, *Weltalter II*, p. 121.

317. Žižek, *The Abyss of Freedom*, pp. 3–4.

318. Žižek, *The Indivisible Remainder*, p. 24.

319. See Laplanche and Pontalis, *The Language of Psychoanalysis*, trans. D. Nicholson-Smith (London: Karnac Books, 1988), pp. 465–69; and also Lacan, *The Seminar of Jacques Lacan, XI: The Four Fundamental Concepts of Psycho-analysis, 1963–1964*, ed. Jacques-Alain Miller, trans Alan Sheridan (London: Vintage, 1998), p. 51.

320. Žižek, "Liberation Hurts"; and *The Ticklish Subject*, p. 48.

321. Žižek, *The Abyss of Freedom*, pp. 3–4.

322. Žižek, *The Indivisible Remainder*, p. 92.

323. Miller, "Context and Concepts," in *Reading Seminar XI: Lacan's Four Fundamental Concepts of Psychoanalysis*, ed. Richard Feldstein, Bruce Fink, and Maire Jaanus (Albany: SUNY Press, 1995), pp. 7–8.

324. Žižek, *Less Than Nothing*, pp. 300ff.

325. Ibid., p. 198. Compare with pp. 292ff. and 304.

326. Ibid., pp. 293–94.

327. Ibid., p. 234.

328. Ibid., p. 285.

329. Ibid., p. 231.

330. Ibid., p. 213.

331. Ibid., p. 274.

332. Schelling, *Freiheitsschrift*, p. 284.

333. Žižek, *The Ticklish Subject*, p. 31.

334. Žižek, *The Indivisible Remainder*, p. 9.

335. Schelling, *Freiheitsschrift*, p. 239.

336. Žižek, *The Indivisible Remainder*, p. 23.

337. Ibid., p. 22.

338. Žižek, *Less Than Nothing*, p. 645.

339. Ibid., p. 273.

340. Žižek, *The Indivisible Remainder*, p. 8.

Chapter 10
Radicalizing the Subject
Substance *Gasping for Breath*, the Metaphysics of Quantum Mechanics, and the Žižekian Unconscious

Although Žižek's transcendental materialism relies upon Schelling to explicate the origins of subjectivity, Hegel is nevertheless omnipresent in Žižek's work. Perceiving a strictly Hegelian structure of self-relating negativity in the second draft of the *Weltalter* that identifies *Grund* and existence in a manner inconsistent with its surface structure of quaternity, Žižek offers a psychoanalytical reconstruction of Schelling's aborted masterpiece by showing how Hegelian dialectics is its unconscious truth. Demonstrating this complex and nuanced hybridism of Hegelian logic and Schellingian ontology at the heart of Žižek's philosophy does not merely help us see its originality and singularity; it also enables us to shed light on in what sense his philosophy is a revisionist metaphysics of the subject. The existence of subjectivity not only attests that nature is at best a fragile not-all whose disruptive wounds are more primordial than its positive being. More drastically than this, the absolute, instead of being a fully subsisting reality that exists by means of a self-explanatory surplus, is at its most basic level only minimally indistinguishable from the void of nothingness, whereby the subject becomes one of the names of the eternal disturbance of this void by means of which there is something rather than nothing. This also leads us into a discussion of the paradoxical causality explicit in the self-begetting

of the Žižekian subject and its repercussions for our understanding of the
unconscious.

10.1 From the Psychoanalytical Purification of the Theosophic to Substance *Gasping for Breath*

Žižek does not articulate his own solution to the problematic of how he is
able to purify the odyssey that is the *Freiheitsschrift* and the *Weltalter* from its
mytho-poetic phantasmagoria. The issue at hand is how he can formalize
Schelling's philosophy by purifying its theosophic content (the illusion of
an originary oceanic bliss and its crucial role in covering up the intrinsically
dialectical structure inherent to the *Grund* by means of a quaternity) by
traversing its fantasy. To do this, Žižek relies on the primordiality of the
psychoanalytical experience and the irreducibility of negativity in Hegelian
logic, the traces of which he sees in the second draft's descriptions of the
three stages involved in the movement from the Past to the Present. The
resources offered by both allow us to internally reconfigure its conceptual
movement by removing this distorting fantasy element through a
philosophical reconstruction of the abyssal origins of the subject by tarrying
with the Real of Schelling's texts. It is this revamped version of the *Weltalter*'s
investigations into the spectral, never-present beginnings of the Symbolic
that enables Žižek to draw out the full metaphysical implications of the
paradoxical nature of psychoanalytico-Cartesian subjectivity.

   According to psychoanalytical experience, the zero-level fact in the
passage from the Past to the Present has to be the second stage,[341] that
is, the self-lacerating rage of matter. Because Žižek identifies the subject
with the non-coincidence of substance, its alienation from itself,[342] this
self-lacerating rage is equivalent to what Lacan refers to as the "organic
dehiscence" exhibited in the mirror stage that forms the basis of the
ontogenesis of personality.[343] But if we are to mytho-poetically explain
how such a dismemberment forms the meta-transcendental conditions
for the possibility of subjectivity's self-positing, we cannot understand it
as a haphazard feature of nature that falls upon it like an alien blow from
nowhere—rather, its pure contingency must itself emerge from some kind
of immanent, self-effacing possibility *always already implicit within it*.[344] As
that which metapsychologically corresponds to the eternal calm of the pure

immanence of substance preceding the deadlock of drives and the struggle to speak the Word, the joyous nothingness of divine eternity is therefore merely a part of the ego's fantasy of desired fullness, a narcissistic and reactive attempt to secure the false status of nature as all in order to protect us from the dark truth implicit in the psychoanalytical experience: *that one cannot draw a metaphysical distinction between substance as a nothingness that rejoices in the oceanic bliss of non-experience and the unruly basis of human subjectivity that "disrupts" this unity.* For Žižek, the transcendental materialist logic of which we see premonitions in the second draft thus allows us to add precision to the late German Idealist attempts to think substance as subject: the model of subjectivity as a disease within the vital fold of being needs to be slightly modified, for there was *never* a state of metaphysical harmony and innocence that the going-haywire of human unruliness could have brought into ruin once and for all. This is exactly why Žižek feels justified in proclaiming the superiority of Hegelian logic and violently remodulating Schelling's middle-late ontology to get rid of its notion of absolute indifference, for in positing an initial state of health, Schelling demonstrates a tendency—a tendency only encouraged by the abyssal void of the Real-as-origin—to construct a rampant fantasy whose imaginary support (certain theosophic details) could protect him from his own insight into the restless movement of negativity in the interior life of being and at the core of the subject's pure act, a fantasy that in itself is filled with holes and inconsistencies as shown by the endless proliferation of stillborn drafts of the *Weltalter* in an attempt to secure it.

That the subject is synonymous with the irrevocable self-sundering of substance does not mean that before the advent of complete denaturalization in our constitutive excess there was no internal obstruction within the former's immanent ebb and flow. If the human being is an irreversible blockage in the vital fold of being, it must represent an amplification of an already existing potentiality in nature. We can see this in various forms—natural disasters, deformed animals, mass extinction, black holes, all of which point to ways in which the originary "harmony" of the world is predicated upon disorder, eruptive disarray, and its inability to sustain itself in perfect symmetry. Knowledge in the Real is never perfect:

The most unsettling aspect of such phenomena is the
disturbance caused in what Lacan called "knowledge in the
Real": the "instinctual" knowledge which regulates animal
and plant activity. This obscure knowledge can run amok.
When winter is too warm, plants and animals misread the
temperature as a signal that spring has already begun and so
start to behave accordingly, thus not only rendering themselves
vulnerable to later onslaughts of cold, but also perturbing the
entire rhythm of natural reproduction.[345]

These examples of destruction in nature must, however, be seen in their raw
conceptual materiality. Rather than being justified by Žižek's rhetoric, they
point to one of the major achievements of Žižek's dialectics: its ability to
think through the philosophical implications of what is normally seen as a
mere contingent breakdown of all-present order or a short-lived calamitous
outburst of pandemonium in the otherwise smooth flow of things. Žižek
refuses such a thesis: for him, contradiction and non-coincidence are to be
seen as at the very basis of reality to such an extent that *reality's logical closure
upon itself is unable to sustain itself and is constitutively torment-ridden with
fracture points*. Rather than being a totalizing weave that is and thus embraces
all things in its soft, calming touch, despite things seeming otherwise in
experience (just as turbulent eddies are only possible given the oneness of
the ocean that persists through them), substance is dirempt and constantly
risks bursting at its seams due to its own internal fragmentation. These
wounds in the absolute do not exude the vital blood of substance in such a
way that they will, after a brief moment of cosmic fright, heal themselves and
once again be subsumed within the economy of a symphonized sexualized
dance of lack and plenitude, life and death: substance does not engage in a
ritual of bloodletting to gain strength, as if conflict, although internal to the
system, only existed so that through its conquering substance could express
again and again its infinite, almighty power. On the contrary, the wounds
of substance are those places where it *touches the void*. Torn apart from the
inside out, substance in its auto-laceration is in danger of dissipating into
nothingness, of no longer being capable of holding itself together. Here one
must think of the fundamental presupposition of Schellingian philosophy:
were substance (God) all, were there from the very beginning nothing but

a balanced movement, a pure, all-devouring totality, no subjectivity or experience would be possible.[346] In this sense, Žižek is not merely trying to radicalize this insight by reactualizing Schelling's metapsychology so that it does not succumb to its theosophic tendencies, but more primordially *trying to make it internally consistent.* According to Schelling's own words, if we posit an initial state of health, we cannot explain how subjectivity could emerge. Perfection is only an imaginary, fantasmatic extension of the existential horizon of our broken finitude, that is, *a reaction formation,* a reaction formation within which we encounter again and again the insupportable negativity that tears apart the world, for after all, *the repressed always returns.* As the greatest thinker of subjectivity, we begin to grasp why there would be such an immense conflict within Schelling's middle-late period between the irreconcilable extremes of a radical philosophy of freedom and an equally radical philosophy of a theo-cosmogonic drama of divine being seeking self-manifest revelation. They go hand in hand: traumatic insight elicits protective defences, but the latter can never be completely successful.

Accordingly, Žižek psychoanalytically modifies Schelling's descriptions of the Past as that elusive X that forever haunts and precedes consciousness so that the real encounter (the horror of substance as subject) can be freed from its imaginary, fantasmatic surface (the theosophic odyssey) and brought into explicit mythologico-symbolization. This has severe consequences. First and foremost, we must remember that at the level of logic, Schelling's mytho-poetic narrative of the Past does not primordially present a *chronology* of the absolute, even if it is derived from phenomenological experience by the alchemical identification of the highest and lowest and can thus be used to explain the onto*genesis* of the individual subject by means of reason by analogy. The "stages" Schelling refers to are purely logical and organized according to priority: the category of linear temporality only emerges with the Present as that which mirrors the structural relations intrinsic to the inner life of God. Consequently, there is no sense in which the joyous nothingness *temporally* precedes God as subject caught in the throes of the self-lacerating rage of matter. However, insofar as freedom as a predicate of a subject *exists* (stage three), the abyss of freedom as pure potentiality—a freedom that is not yet posited as such—must be said to *logically* precede the rotation of drives prior to full-fledged subjectivity (stage two). Žižek follows the argument thus far, but then makes a crucial change in an attempt to draw out a truth hidden in Schelling's descriptions of the passage from one moment to the other. Given that there is no temporal separation between the descriptions of the joyous nothingness of non-experience and the infinite, agonizing oscillation of the potencies, or substance and subject, they are, in essence, *two sides of the same coin.* The "passage" is nothing but a logical conversion:

> Let us step back for a moment and reformulate the primordial contraction in terms of the passage from a self-contented Will that wants nothing to an actual Will which effectively wants something: the pure potentiality of the primordial Freedom— this blissful tranquillity, this pure enjoyment, of an unassertive, neutral *Will which wants nothing*—actualizes itself in the guise of a *Will which actively, effectively, wants this "nothing"*—that is, the annihilation of every positive, determinate content. By means of this purely formal conversion of potentiality into actuality, the blissful peace of primordial Freedom thus changes into pure contraction, into the vortex of "divine madness" which threatens to swallow everything, into the highest affirmation of God's egotism which tolerates nothing outside of itself. In other words, the blissful peace of primordial Freedom and the all-destructive divine fury which sweeps away every determinate content are one and the same thing, only in a different modality—first in the mode of potentiality, then in the mode of actuality.[347]

The ultimate paradox of the shift from the bliss of divine eternity, freedom as pure potentiality, to the annular rotation of drives in the *Grund* that serves as the stepping-stone to freedom as the predicate of a subject is that *there is no movement at all—Grund is always already the Ungrund, the "closed" circle of nature is always already the scene of the possible emergence of freedom.*[348] If we equate freedom with negativity, then we see that the *Ungrund* is no longer that which neutrally grounds the conflict of the polar principles in order to know itself and reveal itself to itself through them, but rather becomes synonymous with the devastating negativity at the heart of being, the places where it *risks touching the void*, and that even when it remains non-posited as such, is always already present within the palpitations of the latter like a cardiac arrest waiting to happen: *the ground is always already minimally ungrounded, ridden with tension, bursting at the seams.* We see this clearly in the dialectic of the ontogenesis of the subject. Although the movement from (i) the rapture of symmetry that is substance to (ii) the harrowing madness of the drives in the unruliness of the infant appears to be due to the grotesque excess of life that is human being as an unfortunate accident, the matter is more complicated. In the first stage freedom (negativity) is always already there as a logical possibility, but remains for the most part non-posited in the general economy of the dynamics of substance, though it shows its head constantly, so that we just have a relatively closed and blind annular rotation of drives; in the second, however, it finally successfully posits itself in a significant manner (although not as such) as the self-lacerating rage of matter, but in such a way that its rawness risks devouring itself. It needs to be tamed, disciplined, gentrified. The decisive moment comes with (iii) the act of decision through which freedom as subject (inner limit of substance) is converted into freedom as the predicate of a subject (self-relating negativity), an act that is not only notionally non-deducible because it is, in itself, radically free, but also one that withdraws in its very gesture of self-positing. When this occurs, negativity, instead of being a single part in the totality of material being, turns itself into an independent center that hegemonically dominates the whole to which it once belonged, which in turn forces the negativity always already contained in the first moment finally to become fully explicit. Freedom is not in direct contact with the *Ungrund* as that which neutrally grounds the conflict of the polar principles as indifference, nor is it a resurgence of the primordial abyss of freedom: it is *nothing but* this movement in which the second (the negativity of being), relating to itself, counting itself, usurps the position of the first (being) and thus institutes a mere formal reconfiguration of the whole.[349] As pure negativity, full-fledged self-standing freedom (self-relating negativity) does not emerge out of nowhere within a harmonious play of forces, *because its existence attests that there is freedom (negativity) all the way down.* As Žižek says, "the only greatness is 'negativity' itself."[350]

What the psychoanalytico-Cartesian subject thus shows us is that the idea of extra/pre-subjective nature as the self-harmonizing *Grund* of all

things, a causally closed play of forces caught within a blind necessity, is
a pure fantasy: the beginning is not a solid, inert density, but a seething
mass of heterogeneous matter lacking overarching symmetry and balanced
movement. Matter is not some kind of impenetrable or irreducible "real
stuff" that persists beyond conscious representation and follows eternal
laws—at its very core, matter constantly dematerializes itself by opening up
its flesh to the void of (virtual) non-being to the point where it is no longer
matter but something more: that is, a full-fledged *subject*. The self-operative
logic of nature as *Grund* consequently demonstrates that the immanence of
substance is not a permeating weave of positive being, a never-ending sea
whose fullness encompasses all: it is plagued constitutively by the possibility
of self-fragmentation, since irrevocable zones of (virtual) non-being
shattering the ordered reality of the world and its causal closure always
threaten to erupt and turn it into a chaotic pandemonium of disordered,
anarchic forces combating for rulership—a state that would, in fact, *bring
substance itself to its untimely end*, for a substance that has globally turned
"into a dispersed floating of *membra disjecta*"[351] is no longer a substance
at all. The self-lacerating rage of matter thus takes on a new meaning.
The libidinal frenzy of the unruliness of human nature does not merely
represent a single case of the diseased breakdown of the ontological, but
rather the inability of substance to posit itself as all: substance is destined
towards auto-destruction; the "ground fails to ground,"[352] for it is always
on the verge of passing over into hemorrhaging conflict and ravaging
antagonism. In this regard, substance is constitutively weak, a precarious
all whose fragility is not only always struggling to keep itself together as the
contractive energy of all things, but also always capable of the new and the
unpredictable at any cosmic moment due to its negativity, for what will be
is not necessarily causally contained in what was. Here we see the extremely
Hegelian logic that Žižek extracts from Schelling in the second draft: it is
the failure of the first moment (the self-actualization of substance and the
indivisibility of its causal self-enclosure, its closed annular rotation) that
leads to/is the second (the unruliness of human nature, the unbearable short
circuit in the rotation of drives), whose vicissitudes in turn set the stage for
the third (the self-positing of the subject through this rupture in the fold
of being, which opens up an autonomous logical space that attempts to

suture the hole). The essence of the third moment is the self-negation of the previous one, which gives it a fully developed notional self-reflexivity in such a way that by guaranteeing the identity of *Grund* and existence Žižek is able to foreclose the possibility of a theosophic quaternity from within the conceptual fabric of Schelling's text. In this sense we can finally comprehend two controversial claims put forth by Žižek: first, that that "the founding gesture [the subject as the vanishing mediator] 'repressed' by the formal envelope of the 'panlogicist' Hegel is *the same* as the gesture which is 'repressed' by the formal envelope of the 'obscurantist' Schelling,"[353] for both reveal in their own way the "unacknowledged" *Grundoperation* of German Idealism; and, second, that "to articulate clearly the *Grundoperation* of German Idealism [...] necessitates reference to Lacan; that is to say, our premiss is that the 'royal road' to this *Grundoperation* involves reading German Idealism through the prism of Lacanian psychoanalytical theory."[354] It is in this respect that Žižek's philosophy is a hybridism of Hegelian logic and Schellingian ontology, for it is a mere attempt at the thematization of its unconscious *Grundlogik*.

The metaphysical basis of freedom is the irremovable possibility of negativity from within any self-totalizing, self-enclosed system. There are always unavoidable ruptures and breaks within the logical fold of the world, but these are not mere contingent features of the otherwise harmonious symphony of the infinity of being: the activity of the first moment always already "possesses" its own failure as exhibited in the constant proliferation of negativities that can never be fully subsumed within its dynamics, indicating that substance is constitutively minimally non-coincident to itself. Monstrosities and ontological abortions are an inescapable effect of substance's functioning, for function now shows itself to be one with dysfunction. In terms of Žižek's "reactualization" of Schelling, it is here that its most textually violent moment is located. It proclaims that the only way to save the Schellingian legacy is to say that nature as a full, rich creative potency inherent in the dark womb of the world is an illusion. Nature was always already a sickly creature, whose collapse coincides with its own conditions of (im)possibility. It is not only that nature never knew a moment of eternal happiness and joy, but that the dull, inarticulate pressure of its own gasping for breath (spirit, we remember, comes from the Latin *spiritus*, "breath," and is related to *spirare*, "to breathe") precedes the very positivity of its being. Substance can only *be* substance—nature can only *be* nature—insofar as it is *always already* internally torn apart by a constitutive moment of auto-laceration that is the site of spirit/subject: "incompleteness [is] already in itself a mode of subjectivity, such that subjectivity is always already part of the Absolute, and reality is not even thinkable without subjectivity."[355]

If the ontological dislocation attested to by emergence of the subject is always already a part of the absolute, then the passage from nature to culture is a mere logical conversion—it only requires a certain gesture or incitation to be brought to the fore while nothing changes at the level of "positive" being. Full-fledged subjectivity, and hence the symbolic universe of meaning that emerges as a belated response, may be an unpredictable event whose result institutes a new age of the world, but its ontological basis demonstrates that there is no ultimate opposition between us and the world. The idea of a unified, self-penetrating substance only comes *après-coup* as part of a fantasy that helps the subject protect itself, for without such a fantasmatic support of fullness we risk losing our very subjective consistency in face of the tragic incompletion of the world. The fiction of "Nature" is, in many ways, unavoidable: we unconsciously create it to save ourselves from recognizing the true basis of subjectivity and its stark implications, namely, the fact that the world, constitutively ravaged by the *Ungrund*, is metaphysically imbalanced and thus not-all:

> True "anthropomorphism" resides in the notion of nature
> tacitly assumed by those who oppose man to nature: nature as
> a circular "return of the same," as the determinist kingdom of
> inexorable "natural laws," or (more in accordance with "New
> Age" sensitivity) nature as a harmonious, balanced Whole
> of cosmic forces derailed by man's *hubris*, his pathological
> arrogance. What is to be "deconstructed" is this very notion
> of nature: the features we refer to in order to emphasize man's
> unique status—the constitutive imbalance, the "out-of-joint,"
> on account of which man is an "unnatural" creature, "nature
> sick unto death"—must somehow be at work in nature itself,

although—as Schelling would have put it—in another, lower power (in the mathematical sense of the term).[356]

But here we must be careful. Insofar as the subject is *an immanent event within the world*, that is, insofar as through it being has "gained" the power to look upon itself by internal reflection due to a maximization of this constitutive self-sabotaging tendency within nature and symbolization occurs as a means to deal with this trauma, one cannot conclude that symbolization is a mere defence mechanism constitutive of the *human* ego. The illusionary world of the Symbolic into which we withdraw to save ourselves from the trauma that is the very essence of our freedom *is simultaneous with being's own recoil from itself as it achieves self-disclosure.* Awakening into the nightmare that is the psychoanalytical horror of substance as subject in all of its ambiguity, the primordial reaction of the world opening its eyes for the first time is that of hellish panic, a panic whose ultimate fate is the necessity of an ontological passage through madness *which we enact* as symbolic subjects by (re)constituting reality in an ontologically solipsistic, eternally nocturnal space of signifiers, a universe of meaning. If the self-revelation of being to itself leads to an originary madness, then not only should we understand the proliferation within the latter of self-composing dream-like images, a rhapsody of social and political phantasmagoria that function as the fabric of our own identities, as events in being, but *also this very fiction of ontological completion we witness in accounts of "Nature."* Through us, in a moment of fantasy, being sees itself as perfect—or as having been possibly perfect were it not for our intervention—by living out the impossibility of its own illusionary fullness, a fantasy that is a complete perversion of the typical narrative of God reaching full self-consciousness only by means of human activity. In this sense, if the theological implications of quantum mechanics, wherein particles can cheat the universe by coming into and out of existence before they are "symbolically" registered, are that we must "posit a God who is *omnipotent, but not omniscient,*"[357] then Žižek's metaphysics compels us to posit a God (nature, the absolute) that is neither omnipotent nor omniscient, yet somehow persists in being. But how?

10.2 *Eppur si muove*: Ontological Dislocation and the Metaphysics of the Void

At this conceptual conjuncture, Žižek takes an additional step in his psychoanalytical reconstruction of German Idealism that simultaneously brings into complete culmination its unconscious, disavowed *Grundlogik* and leads him into a profoundly new variety of metaphysical thinking that is uniquely his own. If in order to explain the emergence of the subject out of substance we have to proclaim that the latter, rather than being an indivisible oneness that weaves all things into an all-encompassing fabric, is predicated upon a site of auto-laceration, then the subject—as a name for this gap in substance that "sets it in motion"—has in turn to be more fully investigated, for we have not yet seen how ontological dislocation could be a creative force. We cannot stay at the level of substance qua nature: the ordered universe that compromises cosmological, geological, and biological time is so ravaged by negativity that the subject in its various vestiges does not merely indicate the places where substance in its trembling and uneasy auto-articulation *risks touching the void*, that is to say, is *in danger of no longer holding itself together*, but also the places where *the void threatens to (re-)erupt*. In this regard, the dynamic processes of the world are not just dependent upon (potential) disarray, but suggest that substance cannot be the last metaphysical word, since it appears on a second glance that the world itself is a response to something more primordial, something that is constantly trying to show its ugly head: ultimately "there is no Substance, only the Real as the absolute gap, non-identity, and particular phenomena (modes) are Ones, so many attempts to stabilize this gap."[358]

Risking anachronism,[359] Žižek sees a way to reinterpret the German Idealist attempt to think substance as subject through quantum mechanics that sheds light on this problematic. As quantum mechanics teaches us, any metaphysical investigation into the foundation of substance qua nature (the basic material constituents of reality) has a paradoxical result. Instead of coming upon a dense field of fully constituted realities that form the ultimate building blocks of the universe, "the more we analyze reality, the more we find a void":[360] rather than encountering entities complete in themselves, we see irreducibly indeterminate states lacking being in any traditional sense and from which "hard" reality can only emerge if there is a collapse of the wave function;[361] "normal" laws of linear temporality and causality break down as we encounter particles that retroactively "choose" their paths along virtual chains of possibilities and others that can even cheat the universe, coming in and out of existence without the latter even knowing.[362] But this not only drastically challenges any sharp distinction between nature and culture,[363] but also attests that the micro-universe of quantum particles is strangely "less" than that of the macro-universe that constructs itself from its vicissitudes, in a way that is remarkably similar to how the Kantian subject can only construct a unified world of appearances from the inconsistent fragments of sensation. In an uncanny logical short circuit, it would appear that not only is there no bottom-up causality at the level of experience (transcendental constitution is more real than what Kant calls "a rhapsody of perception,"[364] since it founds a coherent field of reality), but even the most fundamental level of the universe is metaphysically more chaotic and constitutively less ontologically complete than the ordered macro-level physical world that science, as according to classical models, describes. Substance is not a given, but an achievement: it is as if *all reality is transcendentally constituted*, as if nature itself emerges out of this field of quasi-entities. But just as we had to explain the ontogenesis of unruliness, we must also explain the emergence of these ontologically incomplete realities that serve as the basis for the ordered universe, since they cannot be a brute, arbitrary given. The emphasis of the key philosophical question is thus shifted from how the subject can emerge out of the Real qua substance (thought from being) to how the subject can emerge out of the Real qua void (something from nothing), for the more strictly speaking ontological question of ontogenesis thus proves to be irreducibly entangled with the most fundamental of metaphysical questions.

The more we analyze reality the more we find a void, because once we reach the level of quanta our conventional conceptions of the ordered cosmos just stop working. Not only do we here recognize that "there simply *is no basic level*," that "divisions go on indefinitely," whereby "the quantum level marks the beginning of the 'blurring' of 'basic' full reality,"[365] but also that "[o]ne should thus reject the 'positive' ontology that presupposes some zero-level of reality where things 'really happen' and dismisses the higher levels as mere abbreviations, illusory self-perception, and so forth. There is no such zero-level: if we go 'all the way down,' we arrive at the Void."[366] This has a surprising consequence, one whose full metaphysical implications quantum mechanics thus summons us to accept: namely, that the closer we get to the origin of all things, the more ontologically incomplete reality is, the less distinguishable its fundamental constituents are from the void, thus forcing us not merely to proclaim that the void is "the only ultimate reality,"[367] but more drastically still that "'all there is' is, precisely, not-All, a distorted fragment which is ultimately a 'metonymy of nothing.'"[368] In short, what we experience as hard, full reality is at its core a mere vibration of nothingness lacking any true ontological depth, since there exists a certain radical *indistinction* between being (a structured physical universe) and the void (a structureless zone without any dense ontological determination in any traditional sense).[369]

But if the building blocks of the world are nothing but variations upon nothingness, then why do they emerge in the first place? And what prevents the universe from imploding upon itself in some kind of triumphant suicidal gesture, leaving us with nothing but the "eternal peace" of the void? Why something rather than nothing? Žižek hints that the answer is to be found in the very tension between the void and this field of quasi-entities that, the further we push them, the more indistinguishable they appear from nothingness itself—using the Higgs field as an example. Physical systems tend towards a state of lowest energy. In another vein, if we take energy away from a system, we should eventually expect to reach a vacuum state where the total energy count would be zero. Yet certain phenomena tell us that "there has to be something (some substance) that *we cannot take away from a given system without raising that system's energy*—this 'something' is called the Higgs field: once this field appears in a vessel that has been pumped empty, and whose temperature has been lowered as much as possible, its energy will be further *lowered*."[370] Incredibly, once a physical system's energy has been lowered to the point where it it is on the brink of zero, this "something" appears, a "something" that requires *less energy than nothing*. Consequently, "'nothingness (the void, being deprived of all substance) and the lowest level of energy paradoxically no longer coincide, that is, it is 'cheaper' (it costs the system less energy) to persist in 'something' than to dwell in 'nothing,' at the lowest level of tension, or in the void, the dissolution of all being."[371] But here we should radicalize this paradox by extending it to the ultimate metaphysical level of reality. It is not merely that we cannot bring any physical system to a zero-level of energy without the Higgs field positing itself: what the latter suggests is that *nothingness is minimally "inconsistent" with itself and that it is this very "inconsistency" that is responsible for the emergence of something out of nothing.* The rapture of void, the bliss of an eternity freed from all tension, does not merely come at too high a price for us as creatures living in this world, but is, strictly speaking, impossible. Metaphysics is thus starkly remodulated:

> What if we posit that "Things-in-themselves" emerge against the background of the Void of Nothingness, the way this Void is conceived in quantum physics, as not just a negative void, but the portent of all possible reality? This is the only true consistent "transcendental materialism" which is possible after the Kantian transcendental idealism. For a true dialectician, the ultimate mystery is not "Why is there something rather than nothing?" but "Why is there nothing rather than something?"[372]

Although Žižek makes use of the Higgs field mainly as an image, in *Less Than Nothing* his expansive engagement with quantum mechanics sheds new light on its precise conceptual role in his own thinking. Not only does this engagement enable him to draw out underlying ontological implications from quantum mechanics' fundamental insights, but it more strongly gives us sufficient resources from which we can extract a more strictly speaking metaphysical argument from his discussion of the Higgs field, which attests to how Žižek potentially supplies quantum mechanics with a wider, non-naturalistic foundation while simultaneously founding a new alternative in metaphysics argumentatively independent from its framework. As that which (theoretically) controls whether forces and particles behave differently, the Higgs field has two modes: it is either "switched off" (inoperative) or "switched on" (operative). While in the first, given that the system is in a state of pure vacuum, forces and particles cannot be distinguished, in the second symmetry between particles and forces are broken so that differentiations among them can occur. However, the paradox lies precisely in the following: what is so unique about the Higgs field is that it is favorable for it to be "switched on" (operative), for if a system is in a state of pure vacuum "the Higgs field still has to spend some energy—nothing comes for free; it is not the zero-point at which the universe is just 'resting in itself' in total release—the nothing has to be sustained by an investment of energy."[373] Because the pure vacuum requires the expenditure of energy, in order to solve this paradox we are forced to substitute it with another by "introduc[ing] a distinction between two vacuums":

> first, there is the "false" vacuum in which the Higgs field is
> switched off, i.e., there is pure symmetry with no differentiated
> particles or forces; this vacuum is "false" because it can only
> be sustained by a certain amount of energy expenditure.
> Then, there is the "true" vacuum in which, although the Higgs
> field is switched on and the symmetry is broken, i.e. there is
> a certain differentiation of particles and forces, the amount
> of energy spent is zero. In other words, energetically, the
> Higgs field is in a state of inactivity, of absolute repose. At the
> beginning, there is the false vacuum; this vacuum is disturbed
> and the symmetry is broken because, as with every energetic
> system, the Higgs field tends towards the minimization of
> its energy expenditure. This is why "there is something and
> not nothing": because, energetically, *something is cheaper than
> nothing.*[374]

What is crucial to note with the Higgs field is that the two vacuums whose existence it posits are not by any means equal: rather than encountering a mere polarity, a two-sided principle that brings together a delicate dance of opposites like light and day, life and death, fullness and lack, into equilibrium, we see a *constitutive imbalance.* Once we apply this principle cosmologically as a metaphysical principle, instead of having an eternal repetition of creation (breaking of the symmetries) and its destruction (return to the void), reality and its disappearance into the abyss, we come across a "displaced One, a One which is, as it were, retarded with regard to itself, always already 'fallen,' its symmetry always already broken."[375] As such, there is nothing but creation or reality because the "pure" vacuum wherein one would expect absolute repose is "false," that is, *stricto sensu* impossible—*it structurally must have always already passed over into and became the "true" vacuum*; and although this would appear to make the "false" vacuum theoretically superfluous (it never had, or could, exist) "this tension between the two vacuums [is to] be maintained: the 'false vacuum' cannot simply be dismissed as a mere illusion, leaving only the 'true' vacuum, so that the only true peace is that of incessant activity, of balanced circular motion—the 'true' vacuum itself remains forever a traumatic disturbance."[376] But why? *For the precise reason that without this primordial antagonism we could not explain the minimal distinction between the void and its vibrations, between the nothing and the ontologically incomplete realities barely distinguishable from it—in short, how the symmetries between particles and forces could have been broken in the first place.* Were we only to have the "true" vacuum, then finitude, materiality, and ultimately experience would be a mere illusion, for there would be no difference between the symmetry of the void and its disturbance, leaving nothing but a nirvana-like principle of nothingness to which all things are reducible. But once we witness the irreducibility of the antagonism within the void itself between its two modes, reality becomes less a seeming that we have to break through than an intrinsic part of the void that necessarily arises as a response to the primordial metaphysical trauma that is the perturbation of the "true" vacuum and whose essence is thus preserved. Even if nothing and the metonymy of nothing is all there is, this presupposes that the latter does not logically collapse into the former although the exact boundary between them is blurred. Hence, the reason Žižek can say that if "[t]he answer to 'Why is there Something rather than Nothing?' is thus that there *is* only Nothing, and all processes take place 'from Nothing through Nothing to Nothing,'" then "this nothing is not the Oriental or mystical Void of peace, but the nothingness of a pure gap (antagonism, tension, 'contradiction'), the pure form of dislocation ontologically preceding any dislocated content,"[377] thus radically changing our very notion of nothingness itself.

The Higgs field thus not only offers us an interesting naturalistic explanation of the world when used in cosmology, but more strongly hints at a new variety of metaphysics. Fleshing out its broad consequences, Žižek is not only able to offer a new account of the emergence of things that is inspired by though independent from quantum mechanics, but can also radicalize his ontology of the subject, thereby weaving metaphysics and

ontology into a dynamic, self-articulating whole. For him, the primordial
fact from which metaphysics must begin is the fact that nothingness *is*.
Drawing upon insights gained by contemporary science, however, he says
that in order to explain the mere existence of things, we must posit that
nothingness necessarily fails "to be," for any attempt to have a purely
vacuous void paradoxically costs more energy than things existing against
the background of this void. Here we encounter "the primacy of the inner
split,"[378] whereby irresolvable conflict is at the origin of all things: the
absolute is nothing but this fragile de-substantialized process that "arises"
out of the self-splitting of a positively charged void, a split that befalls it
from within through its own failure "to be" what it is without that very split.
There is no primordial fullness, no positive hard reality that self-unfolds
according to a creative principle of actualization;[379] there is nothing but a
pure ontological dislocation of which we can only say *eppur si muove* ("and
yet it moves"). But insofar as this gap cannot be mediated with the absolute,
it presents itself as "the non-dialectical ground of negativity," so that
"[t]he old metaphysical problem of how to name the nameless abyss pops
up here in the context of how to name the primordial gap: contradiction,
antagonism, symbolic castration, parallax, diffraction, complementarity,
up to difference."[380] But the name that is perhaps best suited to this is *the
subject*. This would inscribe this metaphysics of the void into the legacy of
the German Idealist attempt to think substance as subject, while bringing
us simultaneously beyond it and into a new sphere, a new materialism.[381]
If German Idealism has taught us that epistemic ambiguities in idealism
(how can the subject overcome its own synthetic mediation of the world and
reach the latter *an sich*?) occur because our division from being is identical
with being's own division to itself, quantum mechanics calls us to radicalize
this notion of the subject even further and claim that it exhibits the same
structure as the split responsible for all things:

> This, perhaps, is how one can imagine the zero-level of
> creation: a red diving line cuts through the thick darkness
> of the void, and on this line, a fuzzy something appears, the
> object-cause of desire—perhaps, for some, a woman's naked
> body (as on the cover of this book). Does this image not
> supply the minimal coordinates of the subject-object axis, the

truly primordial axis of evil: the red line which cuts through
the darkness is the subject, and the body its object?[382]

If in Žižek's strictly metaphysical thinking the emphasis shifts from how
the subject can emerge out of the Real qua substance (thought from being)
to how the subject can emerge out of the Real qua void (something from
nothing), it is because there is no radical difference between the creation
of the world and the creation of the world of meaning. Both exhibit the
same catastrophic cutting, so that the primary question becomes that of the
originary catastrophe itself rather than just one of its specific "instantiations"
in human freedom. The fact that the answer for both (the Real is always
already subject) is identical proclaims that there is only the Real of the
gap, that the splitting precedes what is split. Žižek's paradoxical conclusion
is that if the subject is "the primordial Big Bang,"[383] it cannot merely be
that of the universe of meaning, *but must also be that of all that there is.* The
great lesson to be drawn from the metaphysical archaeology of the subject
is that "[w]hat, ultimately, 'there is' is only the absolute Difference, the
self-repelling Gap":[384] although substance qua nature proves itself to be
not-all (traces of which we see in German Idealist accounts of negativity
and most radically in contemporary science), so that we must posit the
logical precedence of the void to which its indivisibility is always already
contrasted and thus impossiblized, nevertheless just like substance qua
nature this originary void in itself also proves to be split—a split that is not
merely a mere catastrophic cut, but a rupturing antagonism imbued with an
"energetic" or "energizing" force, a force that is somehow less than nothing.
This has two drastic consequences. First, the complex order of the cosmos
may at some point in time be reduced to unimaginable chaos (being nothing
but a heterogenous play of powers) but never to a nirvana-like nothingness,
for before the moment at which an absolute zero would be reached the
void would, as it were, break its own symmetry in advance and prevent its
own repose. We cannot escape the fragile and macabre dance of the not-all:
non-coincidence is the pulsating heart of all reality, a heart whose diastoles
and systoles may whimper under their own weight and threaten to collapse
upon themselves at any moment in one great and final apocalyptic turmoil,
yet cannot, because this turmoil costs the universe less energy than the pure
virtuality of the void. Second, if thinking substance as subject reveals that

nature itself is anything but a powerful, creative source, a pure affirmation displaying ontological closure à la Spinoza, then the void in being imposed upon us by the metaphysical archaeology of the subject demonstrates something much more radical than the fact that the human subject is not a mere accidental breakdown of the natural order, but actually depends upon an inborn negativity that impossiblizes its attempt at a self-articulating totality from the outset ("we should accept that nature is 'unnatural,' a freak show of contingent disturbances with no inner rhyme or reason"[385]). It further demonstrates that it is not the human subject that is the ultimate ontological catastrophe, but *reality as such*:

> There is nothing, basically. I mean it quite literally. But then how do things emerge? Here I feel a kind of spontaneous affinity with quantum physics, where, you know, the idea there is that [the] universe is a void, but a kind of a positively charged void—and then particular things appear when the balance of the void is disturbed. And I like this idea spontaneously very much, that the fact that it's not just nothing—things are out there—it means that something went terribly wrong, that what we call creation is a kind of a cosmic imbalance, cosmic catastrophe, that things exist by mistake.[386]

However, if what we call creation, the primordial Big Bang, is some kind of cosmic mishap, then this mishap must in some sense have been unavoidable. The ontological catastrophe that is creation *is a necessity* because nothingness itself fails "to be" nothingness and through its failure never ceases to create "something"; and since this "something" is paradoxically less than nothing, the infinite proliferation of ontologically incomplete quasi-entities is only minimally distinguishable from the purely vacuous void itself. The world does not find its origin in a willed creation, an impersonal emanation from a sphere of consummate being overflowing in itself, or the uncontainable productivity of substance qua nature as absolute power—no, the world comes to be in an originary disaster, a primordial metaphysical cataclysm that *is always already occurring*, it being impossible to pinpoint a logical moment within which nothingness could have succeeded at "being" itself. Yet the split that is the subject in both its modes should not be considered a loss, but rather *a liberation*. Ontological catastrophe is paradoxically "*a deprivation, a gesture of taking away which is in itself a giving*, productive, generative, opening up and sustaining the space in which something(s) can appear,"[387] even if these something(s) only exist because ontological catastrophe is uncannily less than nothing.

The veritable horror of substance as subject—ontological catastrophe—revealed through the metaphysical archaeology of the psychoanalytico-Cartesian subject is therefore twofold. At the first level, it indicates that nature was always already a sickly creature, its rhythms always already disordered, unsteady, broken. Within the "passage" from drives to desire, substance to subject, no positive content is added, nothing changes at the level of the Real qua Real. What the subject imposes upon us is the realization of the constitutive contingency that lies at the centre of creation, the fragility of the seemingly ordered cosmos that has arisen before us, so that the immanent causality of nature is seen to be predicated upon its potential internal breakdown. On the second level, the metaphysical archaeology of the subject tells us that if we remain here, we have not gone far enough. If we are truly to understand how the not-all of substance could sustain itself in its own precarious being and, more fundamentally, how it could have emerged in the first place, we must radicalize the subject understood as an underlying dysfunctioning of substance's dynamics. If, as Žižek maintains, experience is revelatory of the fact that reality must be not-all, then it also contains a still deeper truth: reminding us that substance fails to ground itself, that it is riddled with holes, that it opens up the logical space of the substance and its contrast, the void, forcing us to explore the latter. We have thus come full circle: an ontological account of the emergence of the subject (the arising of representation out of being) has morphed into a discussion concerning the ultimate metaphysical structure of the world (the upsurge of "something[s]" out of nothing), because the two questions are seen to be intimately linked, the former automatically leading to the latter. And falling upon this intuition, Žižek asks what if the same structure is at play at both levels, so that the answer to the latter will prove to be similar to that of the former, namely, that the movement from the Real of void to creation is not as initially problematic as it may appear because the Real of void shows itself to be always already tainted by the Real of gap. Ontological catastrophe is the zero-level of reality because there is a necessity of the primordial void of which mystics speak to be disturbed, a necessity that is not due to the notional necessity of right-wing Hegelian theology (in order for the Idea to actualize itself as infinite freedom, it must sacrifice itself in nature so that it can fully return to itself in spirit after arising from its own ashes) or the conditional necessity of the late Schellingian quaternity (if the *Ungrund* were to become self-manifest to itself, then it would have to arbitrarily limit its primordial freedom in the kabbalistic act of contracting finitude) but a necessity that derives from the impotence of the void "to be" a purely vacuous void, a necessity that is synonymous with the absolute non-coincidence of nothingness to nothingness that is motor of all things. The language of catastrophe is in this sense completely justified, for creation does not present itself as intrinsically beautiful and creative or purposeful, but rather as a monstrous seat of ontological abortions and terrors devoid of sense though from time to time capable of miracles. Rather than the world being given to us by the self-overflowing exuberance of the Good or the personal hand of God, it moves from nothing through nothing to nothing due to the self-repelling gap of the void, the internal split of a positively charged nothingness, which denies all positivity to that which it sets in motion: "[p]erhaps this gap separating the two vacuums is then the ultimate word (or one of them, at least) that we can pronounce on the universe: a kind of primordial ontological dislocation or *différance* on account of which, no matter how peaceful things may appear *sub specie aeternitatis*, the universe is out of joint and *eppur si muove*."[388]

10.3 The Act of Uneasy Self-Begetting: *Entscheidung* and the Paradoxical Self-Positing of Freedom

By plunging into the abyssal origins of subjectivity Žižek is not just led to a new, disquieting form of transcendental materialism that offers an original account of the relationship between the Real and the Ideal, with stark implications for our understanding of substance, the emergence of order, and even the beginnings of the cosmos. He is also led to develop a theory of the unconscious that challenges both the traditional Freudian and Lacanian accounts, and even the one developed by Schelling that he draws upon. This theory deserves to be highlighted in some detail because it is revelatory of one of the most difficult and provocative aspects of Žižek's philosophy:

that is, the pure act at the origin of the subject that is simultaneous with the ontological passage through madness that forces upon us the rational necessity of speculative fabulation to embark upon a metaphysical archeology of the subject.

Schelling's account of the birth of subjectivity is more than a theory of the meta-transcendental state of affairs that must be in place if subjectivity is to arise out of nature with a triumphant cry, for central to Schelling's ontogenetic narrative is that the former, though providing necessary conditions for the birth of the subject in/out of nature, does not supply its sufficient conditions. To explicate the moment of ontological judgement that institutes the pure difference between *Grund* and existence and with it the entire universe of human meaning (the Present), Schelling must concern himself with the very moment of unconscious decision (*Entscheidung*) by which subjectivity paradoxically liberates itself out of the immanent field of being to which it once "belonged" in a moment that is a self-caused immaculate conception insofar as this self-positing, which cannot be deduced according to notional necessity, is an arbitrary act of pure freedom. What is of paramount importance is the root of the term, which in English displays a similar play on words: *Entscheidung* as *Ent-Scheidung*, decision as de-scission. Since the German suffix *-ung* refers to a process, *Entscheidung* designates a "de-scissioning" at the basis of self-consciousness and language as that which, by creating the Present, banishes the Past into the abyssal dregs of forgotten and inaccessible time. What Žižek focuses on is precisely the formal structure of the act itself, its activity of *severing* the Real into the parallax of the unconscious drives of nature and phenomenal reality, whereby the act itself is primordially repressed as necessary for the dawning of full-fledged subjectivity and becomes an impossible object for any discourse. Recognizing that the *Entscheidung* itself is that which originarily constitutes the conscious/unconscious distinction, Žižek argues that one of the fundamental breakthroughs of the *Weltalter* is its demonstration that drives themselves are, strictly speaking, *nonconscious*: if the very conscious/unconscious distinction only occurs with the utterance of the Word (there cannot be a *ground* without a *grounded*: prior to the grounded, the ground cannot be posited as ground as such, for it is merely a self-subsisting, semi-closed system of materiality, rather than the *ground of existence*) then it would be philosophically fallacious to call this energetic rotation of energy the unconscious proper or the true foundation of subjectivity, even if it incites (or to put it differently negatively carves up the room for) the latter's founding gesture. The result is that the Žižekian-Schellingian subject of the unconscious is radically non-coincident with *both* the id-forces of the body in its primary mode (the Real of *Triebe* can only be unconscious as a secondary effect of the self-positing of the act of de-scission[ing] as such) and the more-than-conscious matrix of the Symbolic (the self-generating play of language and culture only emerges *after* the founding gesture that marks the beginning of transcendental self-reflexivity). That is, the unconscious is *the very gap, the irreconcilable parallax*, between both registers: it is synonymous with the subject itself as the impossible in-between that binds together materialism (being) and idealism (thought) in their non-relationality by protruding out of yet being simultaneously spectrally present in both. As an irreducible, self-positing negativity that institutes the realm of culture and eternally separates it from nature, the subject of the unconscious is the true site of freedom.

Here lies the challenge to Freud and Lacan, who broadly could be said to have respectively located the unconscious in the biological movement of instinctual energy and the alienating effects of language. For Žižek one must presuppose a more primordial level of unconscious activity than that of the biologically closed libidinal energetics within the corpo-Real of the body or that which emerges through the split between the subject of enunciation and the enunciating subject caused by the unpredictable reverberations of meaning within the infinite web of language: namely, an act that exploits the libidinal frenzy of the Real of the human body, the unruliness represented by the *Todestrieb*, to ground the self-generation and self-proliferation of the automatic machinery of language as a reaction formation. In this sense, Žižek's reactualization of the Schellingian unconscious is an attempt to sublate both the traditional Freudian and Lacanian accounts within a higher dialectical unity by showing their dependence on another, more fundamental conceptual level. His original addition to psychoanalysis is the formation of a conception of "the subject [which] at its most elementary is indeed 'beyond the unconscious': an empty form deprived even of unconscious formation encapsulating a variety of libidinal investments."[389]

Here again we see just how much Žižek's account of the subject is highly reliant upon his "modification" of the *Weltalter* in a way that challenges his so-called Hegelianism.

Žižek's controversial wager is that there is something more primordial within Schelling's descriptions of the birth of the subject out of the utter twilight of pre-personal being than an account of the self-transformation of the "unconscious" spirit of nature as it rises towards the openness of self-revelation. In a move similar to psychoanalysis' claim that the material processes of our organs *cannot* be, strictly speaking, unconscious (physiological stimuli and reflexes are of a radically different nature),[390] Žižek levels out the richness of the Schellingian account of nature to a mere material autopoiesis that is unable to explain the true seat of personality. This is also why Žižek is so adamant that the unconscious is not to be equated with the set of irrational drives that structurally oppose and yet affect the self-transparency of rationality as we see in various forms of *Lebensphilosophie.*[391] What Schelling's account of decision as the metapsychological event par excellence proclaims is that there is no point of positive juncture between nature as *Grund* and the subject of the unconscious, insofar as decision takes over/usurps the logically primary position of the *Grund* through its own self-positing freedom, but in a manner that its self-positing is more fundamental than, and even erases, its dark pre-history: the libidinal-material chaos within nature does not come close to establishing the unconscious proper because the latter is never completely subsumable within the dynamic movement of natural history or laws, for it institutes itself into the fabric of being by means of a self-caused immaculate conception. If freedom is to be truly free, then we must not be able to deduce it according to notional necessity; it is as if, when substance risks touching the void in the painful oscillation of drives constitutive of the unruliness of the human organism, the subject *creates itself out of nothing, with all the paradox that entails*:

> In the psychoanalytical perspective, of course, this primordial act of free self-positing cannot but appear as the Real of a fantasy-construction: the status of the primordial act is analogous to that of the Freudian parricide—although it never effectively took place within temporal reality, one has

to presuppose it hypothetically in order to account for the
consistency of the temporal process. The paradox of the
primordial act is the same as that of Baron Münchhausen
pulling himself out of the swamp by lifting himself by the
hair—in both cases, the subject is somehow already here
prior to existence and then, by way of free act, creates-posits
himself, his own being.[392]

The subject's freely posited withdrawal into self is intrinsically paradoxical,
for the very act of self-positing creates the very self that is at the origin
of said positing. This is why we cannot escape the Baron Münchhausen
dilemma: the subject is miraculously present at its own birth.[393] But how? To
follow Žižek and draw upon a Hegelian logical category, when full-fledged
subjectivity emerges in being it can be said to come into existence by a
process of *recollecting* or *interiorizing* itself. This recollective interiorization
(*Er-inner-ung*) is the direct effect of the subject's uneasy self-begetting,
the aftermath of its self-caused immaculate conception in/out of matter
that exploits the immanent negativity of the latter for the institution of its
"miracle":[394] this recollection is not a mere remembering of something
in cosmic memory, an always already existing but non-actualized self
awaiting the dawning of consciousness in the world—the very gesture of
interiorization *is that which creates what is interiorized,* that is to say, the self
in which the world withdraws out of its bloody night, in such a way that
the recollected self or interiority retroactively posits itself as that which was
always at the starting point.[395] Even a self-caused immaculate conception in
being demonstrates a threatening belatedness, for it is stuck in a dialectical
contradiction that cannot be resolved: "'[r]econciliation' between subject
and substance means acceptance of this radical lack of any firm foundational
point: the subject is not at its own origin, is secondary, dependent upon
its substantial presuppositions; but these presuppositions do not have a
substantial consistency of their own and are always retroactively posited."[396]
*The only successful ontogenesis is one that underlines the very impossibility, the
upper limit, of ontogenesis as such:* what is essential is not a transition (whether
it be understood in terms of teleological development or the potential
productivity of breakdown, as we see in the night of the world) but the
pure difference that is the full-fledged subject (which is responsible for "the

madness of the passage to the Symbolic itself"[397]) which institutes a "gap which makes impossible any account of the rise of the New in terms of a continuous narrative."[398]

But we must be very attentive to the conceptual movement if we are not to lose its radicality. Insofar as the chaotic oscillation of drives we witness in unruliness only becomes the *Grund* of existence after the act of decision, drives only become unconscious in the aftermath of the act itself. Due to the latter's irreducible self-positing, consciousness and the Real of drives qua unconscious both emerge in one magical brushstroke that retroactively constitutes its own evolutionary past—covers up its contingency—by subsuming the ontogenetic pre-history of the subject as part of its own self-effectuation through the paradoxical causality of the Freudian *Nachträglichkeit*/Lacanian *après-coup*/Hegelian positing of presuppositions. Here, however, we notice the difficulty of the Real-as-origin: since the abyssal beginning of the subject—the act of decision—effaces itself in the simultaneous gesture of converting the Real of drives into the unconscious as a libidinal system and founding consciousness, the birthplace of the subject becomes a mere posit that is in and of itself never accessible in language; and, as that which only shows itself in its very withdrawal ("*sous rature*"), it is denied the right of even "indirectly" shining through the cracks of the Ideal. It can only be narrated. Although we must posit the ontogenetic condition of desire (a pre-logical antagonism in the Real-as-excess) as that which *precedes* and in a certain sense *renders possible* the self-positing of the decision, the latter proves itself to be not only superior by saying "No!" to substance, thereby setting up a new age of the world within which the Past is always already "lost" through symbolization (an act that institutes the hegemony of the Real-as-lack), *but also to be ontologically primary, despite being ontogenetically secondary*. In a paradoxical movement where the cause-and-effect chain loses its grip, the self-unfolding causality of nature as substance is "torn apart" in the upsurge of freedom as self-relating negativity, which demands primordiality at all costs, *even making being infinitely non-coincident to itself*. It must be remembered, however, that this movement from *Grund* to subjectivity, from the breakdown of nature into a writhing mass of heterogeneous forces to the abyss of unconscious decision, must be described at the level of mytho-poetics. At the level of the

Real, we are not warranted to make certain claims we have been forced to make: when the subject asserts itself at the beginning of its own pre-logical genesis (posits its own presupposition), it is not actually giving birth to itself (which implies a poietic production or genesis) in some kind of temporal loop, but *directly creates itself at the instant of its own upsurge.* The example of Baron Münchhausen's pulling himself up out of the swamp by his own hair expresses the intrinsic difficulty posed to any transcendental materialist account of the subject, for the subject does not exist before the very act of self-positing that it nonetheless paradoxically enacts—hence why it all happens in one magic brushstroke. *The subject has no history except at the level of speculative fabulation (rationally justified mythology), for it is only after the subject's self-positing that we can raise the question of its origins*: "what escapes our grasp is not the way things were before the arrival of the New, *but the very birth of the New,* the New as it was 'in itself,' from the perspective of the Old, before it managed to 'posit its presuppositions,'"[399] which is why Žižek can say that the true arche-fossil for correlationism is not occurrences in cosmological or geological time before the transcendental, but *the very transcendental itself.*[400]

In this sense, the difficulty of the task of speculative fabulation finds itself reflected upon itself: that is to say, doubled. Not only do there exist psychoanalytical defence mechanisms to cover up the abyss of unconscious decision at the "heart" of subjectivity by means of fantasy constructions, but because the only way we have access to the latter is through a mytho-poetic ontogenesis of the subject's dark pre-history in the ontological vicissitudes of being, there is always the tendency to swap the real trauma (the pure contingency of the act as absolute spontaneity) for a fake (the painful oscillation of drives in the human infant that shows nature's sickness unto death in humanity). Even Schelling has a tendency to make us forget that the *Grund*, "this monstrous apparition with hundreds of hands, this vortex that threatens to swallow everything, is a lure, a defence against the abyss of the pure *act*,"[401] which is why psychoanalysis is so important. Although this secondary trauma must still be considered as having explanatory merit—it is, after all, a necessary condition for the primary trauma—the point is to pierce through one trauma (ontological catastrophe as the immanent breakdown of substance) to arrive at a more primordial one (ontological catastrophe as the pure difference that *severs being in two*). The "repressed spectral 'virtual history' is not the 'truth' [...] but the fantasy that fills in the void of the *act* [...] the secret narrative that tells its story is purely fantasmatic,"[402] which is why:

> Schelling's fundamental move is thus not simply to ground the ontologically structured universe of *logos* in the horrible vortex of the Real; if we read him carefully, there is a premonition in his work that this terrifying vortex of the pre-ontological Real itself is (accessible to us only in the guise of) a fantasmatic narrative, a lure destined to distract us from the true traumatic cut, that of the abyssal act of *Ent-Scheidung*.[403]

This is why Schelling's inability to complete his middle-late project of an ontology of freedom is of such paramount importance to Žižek, for "[t]he repeated failure of his *Weltalter* drafts signals precisely Schelling's honesty as a thinker—[not only] the fact that he was radical enough to acknowledge the impossibility of grounding the act or decision in a proto-cosmic myth," but also that he was "compelled to posit an uncanny act of *Ent-Scheidung* (decision or separation), an act in a way more primordial than the Real of the 'eternal Past' itself."[404]

Focusing on the necessary posit of the convulsing labyrinth that is the pre-symbolic Real-as-excess in human unruliness, and plunging ourselves into it, we risk forgetting the abyss of the Real-as-origin that stares us in the face. The painful oscillations of the *Grund* in unruliness merely defer us from the true terror that is the pure act instituting the Symbolic's infinitely self-reflexive play of signifiers in which we live and which guarantees that it possesses no direct connection to the extra-notional world. Because this act absolutizes the short circuit between the *Innenwelt* and *Aussenwelt*, we can only encounter its abyssal origins in their very gesture of withdrawal. It is not nature, even in its mode of self-erasure ($N = N$), that is the first revelation,[405] but rather, *the void within which the Entscheidung spins*—and we can only catch glimpses of the latter as the impossible in-between negatively tying together nature and culture, the Real and the Symbolic, and thereby hope to develop a comprehensive theory of subjectivity inclusive of a new, paradoxical form of metaphysics from within the mytho-poetics of the subject's slow, unsteady, and painful "emergence" out of the vicissitudes of being. But all of this has an interesting implication. If the Symbolic is a self-organizing system that freely constitutes the fabric of experience without any contact with objective reality, then this suggests that, from within its ontologically solipsistic dance of cybernetic ciphering, *we can break through the impenetrable dusk of psychosis* as we (in a reflexive albeit fabulative gesture) see it as the madness it is in a careful reconstruction of its trauma. Here, however, we encounter one of the most fundamental and perhaps paradoxical conclusions of Žižek's parallax ontology. It must be recalled that the trauma at the birthplace of the human subject is not only coincident with its freedom:[406] that is, its withdrawal from one's natural environment into an irreal, virtual self,[407] but its exploration necessarily demonstrates the structure of fantasy as we insert ourselves as a pure gaze in the moment of our own birth.[408] Not only can materialism only justify itself in "the shadow cast by [self-grounding] idealism's insurmountable incompleteness,"[409] but more radically, if we follow the true horror of substance as subject at the core of the latter, then we are forced to conclude that a metaphysics is only possible *as a form of "successful" psychotic thinking*,[410] a thinking that, from within the clutches of idealism as an insurmountable ontological psychosis and using the very energy and internal limitations of this psychosis, manages to succeed in achieving the impossible coincidence of subjective and objective reality: that is to say, in developing a comprehensive metaphysics of the Real. A cure to our correlationist imprisonment being excluded from the outset, philosophy has no hope of offering a therapy. What is more, if such a form of thinking is to be truly successful, not only must we find a way to overcome the realism-idealism debate within idealism, but we must also do so from the side of realism by writing the great epic of being as the eternal Past to come to terms with the ontological passage through madness at the latter's foundation, a task that requires a self-conscious *mythologizing, fictionalization,* or *retrospective narration* and is only achievable by entering the abyss of the spectral Real-as-origin and fending off the thrust of unconscious desires that try to protect us from it in order to draw out its stark metaphysical consequences. Only a scientific, psychoanalytically guided fabulation allows one to catch sight of the vanishing mediator that enacts the withdrawal into the night of the world. But how is a radical subjective idealism capable of such a feat? And as what brand of metaphysics should we baptize it?

Notes

341. For a discussion of the passage, see chapter 9.

342. Žižek, *The Ticklish Subject*, pp. 88–89.

343. Lacan, "The Mirror Stage as Formative of the *I* Function," *Écrits*, p. 96/77.

344. See chapter 4.

345. Žižek, *Living in the End Times*, pp. 350–51. I capitalize "the Real" for consistency.

346. Schelling, *Weltalter III*, p. 219.

347. Žižek, *The Indivisible Remainder*, p. 23.

348. Johnson, *Žižek's Ontology*, p. 92.

349. Žižek, *Less Than Nothing*, p. 197.

350. Ibid., p. 198. Compare with pp. 292ff. and p. 304.

351. Žižek, *The Ticklish Subject*, p. 33.

352. Johnson, *Žižek's Ontology*, p. 92.

353. Žižek, *The Indivisible Remainder*, p. 92.

354. Ibid.

355. Žižek, *Less Than Nothing*, p. 905.

356. Žižek, *The Indivisible Remainder*, p. 220. See also p. 223.

357. Žižek, *Less Than Nothing*, p. 923.

358. Ibid., p. 377.

359. Ibid., p. 947.

360. Ibid., p. 925.

361. Ibid., p. 724.

362. See, ibid., pp. 918–19; and *The Indivisible Remainder*, pp. 220–31.

363. See chapter 5.

364. Kant, *The Critique of Pure Reason*, A 156/B195.

365. Žižek, *Less Than Nothing*, p. 726.

366. Ibid., p. 730.

367. Ibid., p. 726.

368. Ibid., p. 641.

369. Ibid., p. 60.

370. Žižek, *The Puppet and the Dwarf: The Perverse Core of Christianity* (Cambridge: MIT Press, 2003), p. 93.

371. Ibid.

372. Žižek, *Less Than Nothing*, p. 925.

373. Ibid., p. 944.

374. Ibid., pp. 944–45.

375. Ibid., p. 949.

376. Ibid., pp. 949–50.

377. Ibid., p. 38.

378. Ibid., p. 386.

379. Žižek, *Living in the End Times*, p. 232.

380. Žižek, *Less Than Nothing*, p. 950.

381. Ibid., p. 60.

382. Ibid.

383. Žižek, *The Ticklish Subject*, p. 31.

384. Žižek, *Less Than Nothing*, p. 378.

385. Ibid., p. 298.

386. *Žižek!*, dir. Atra Taylor (Zeitgeist Video, 2007).

387. Žižek, *The Puppet and the Dwarf*, p. 93.

388. Žižek, *Less Than Nothing*, p. 377.

389. Žižek, *Living in the End Times*, p. 311.

390. Freud, "Instincts and Their Vicissitudes" (1915), *SE*, XIV, p. 118.

391. See Žižek, *The Indivisible Remainder*, pp. 28 and 174.

392. Ibid., p. 19.

393. Ibid.

394. Žižek and Daly, *Conversations with Žižek*, p. 59.

395. Žižek, *Less Than Nothing*, p. 235.

396. Žižek, *Living in the End Times*, p. 229.

397. Žižek, *Less Than Nothing*, p. 331.

398. Ibid., p. 273.

399. Ibid.

400. Ibid., p. 644.

401. Žižek, *The Fragile Absolute*, p. 70.

402. Žižek, *Less Than Nothing*, p. 273.

403. Ibid., p. 275 (taken initially from *The Fragile Absolute*, p. 73).

404. Ibid., p. 274.

405. Schelling, *Freiheitsschrift*, p. 284.

406. Žižek, *Less Than Nothing*, p. 265.

407. Žižek, *The Ticklish Subject*, p. 35.

408. Žižek, *The Indivisible Remainder*, p. 22.

409. Johnston, *Žižek's Ontology*, p. 19.

410. Here I am playing with Henri Maldiney's reading of Hegel's *Phenomenology* as a "successful depressive thinking" and taking up certain gestures already hinted at in Jean-Christophe Goddard's interpretation of this passage. Compare Maldiney, *Penser l'homme et la folie*, p. 27; and Goddard, *Mysticisme et folie. Essai sur la simplicité* (Paris: Desclée de Brouwer, 2002), pp. 83–84. I return to these points in chapter 12.

III
Overcoming Idealism

Chapter 11
From Radical Idealism to Critical Metaphysics
How Idealists Write Being's Poem

Žižek's transcendental materialism understands itself as an uncanny variation on the late German Idealist theme of providing an ontogenesis of the subject consistent with transcendental idealism. But being more than a rethinking of its central problems, it presents itself as a highly rigorous psychoanalytical reconstruction of its unconscious *Grundlogik*, which reveals itself as a disavowed insight into the identification of subjectivity with an immanent rupture in being so devastating that not only does being lose all direct access to itself, but we must actually posit ontological dislocation as the primary metaphysical fact. In so doing, however, it would appear that there is a potentially fatal inconsistency in Žižek as he oscillates between an inconsistent idealism (the Hegelian notional or symbolic Real-as-lack) and a self-sabotaging materialism (the Schellingian pre/extra-symbolic Real-as-excess). What is more, pointing to the immense difficulty of describing the emergent parallax of being and thinking—the ontological passage of madness—*from within the ontological solipsism of thinking itself*, Žižek argues for the necessity of a form of thinking that would enable being and thinking to be fully reconciled *from the side of being itself* through the mytho-poetic narrativization of the moment of parallax. If radical idealism can succeed at overcoming itself and writing being's poem, it will prove itself capable of being maximally idealistic and realistic in a single gesture that leaves behind the speculative throes of correlationism by rendering correlation itself immanent to the absolute, thus becoming a *critical* metaphysics that has much to offer today to the so-called speculative turn.

11.1 Lacan and the Prison-House of the Symbolic

As an account of the subject's own immaculate self-begetting from within the material flux of being as that which institutes the genesis of the Symbolic, Žižek's transcendental materialism is an attempt to explicate the ontological origins of a self-grounding idealism wherein ontology has been rendered seemingly impossible. Insofar as the Symbolic is able to generate meaning without external reference, it refuses all forms of realism: access to a Real outside of the correlation being/language is proclaimed a naïve position to be rejected due to the immense linguistic power that constructs our reality. Yet even if our entrapment within the self-referential, masturbatory play of signifiers is absolute, the ontological solipsism that it entails is precisely that: namely, an *ontological* solipsism whose very existence suggests that this very inability is somehow *internal to the interior play of forces constitutive of being.* The issue at hand is that "the transcendental standpoint is in a sense irreducible, for one cannot look 'objectively' at oneself and locate oneself in reality; and the task is *to think this impossibility itself as an ontological fact*, not only as an epistemological limitation."[411] In this minimalist sense, images and words cannot be seen as mere parasites that contingently latch themselves onto being and disturb its otherwise smooth flow, but must be negatively indicative of some self-sabotaging tendency always already at work in its heart of hearts: "[t]he symbolic order is not a cause which intervenes from the outside, violently derailing the human animal and thus setting in motion its becoming-human."[412] In other words, to account for the very "consistency" of the Symbolic we are called upon to write the great metaphysical epic of that forgotten eternal Past preceding our coming into the world as speaking subjects.

Such a conceptual move, however, poses an epistemological problem. Within the Lacanian registers, the Real necessarily appears as a lack. As soon as the Symbolic emerges as a self-replicating, self-evolving differential system that transcendentally constitutes the condition of the possibility of phenomenal reality, any direct contact with the Real qua ontological field is lost. The Lacanian thesis is a variation of structuralist linguistic idealism: it is not only that concepts do not need to adequate themselves with objects subsisting in a world that exists despite me; more radically, the free ciphering of the Real by the Symbolic means that signification has *nothing* to do with objective reality in itself, for signifiers only participate in an endless chain of self-relation that precludes access to the "outside" world. There is no room possible for a realist epistemology within Lacan because the very link between signifier and extra-linguistic object is cut. And although Žižek remains unsatisfied with taking such a theoretical edifice as a given and seeks to understand the ontological/meta-transcendental event that it must imply (thus recognizing the ultimate need for giving an account of the Symbolic if psychoanalysis is to find a proper scientific footing) the constraints that Lacan himself bestows upon discourse make Žižek's project appear intrinsically problematic. Doesn't the Real in itself prior to or outside of language remain essentially unknowable (because it is always already constituted by a subject, therefore produced by it, and never without its taint)? Isn't the pre- or extra-symbolic Real an impossible concept, for only that which can be spoken in language exists?

Nevertheless, Žižek offers more than another sophisticated form of structuralist linguistic idealism. If Lacanian psychoanalysis proclaims that the Real can only appear as a lack within the ciphering activity of language, Žižek attempts to break out of the correlationist circle of language by showing that the very inconsistencies of thinking offer a solution to the problem of how we are able to reach the Real even if we are trapped within the play of appearance appearing to itself. Because the Real we encounter in thinking the world is never "simply subjective, [whereby] it would present a case of the hollow playing of the subject with itself, and we would never reach the level of objective reality,"[413] thinking's inability to close in on itself shows that the pre/extra-Symbolic must insist within it. However, such a formulation does not directly address the minimal transcendental conditions of the possibility of attaining an access to the Real "it itself" from within the Symbolic. Adrian Johnston's formulation of the paradoxical materialism-idealism relation is highly revealing of the deadlock Žižek faces: "materialism [...] formulates itself vis-à-vis the deadlocks internal to radical transcendental idealism. On this account, materialism is philosophically tenable only as the spectral inverse of idealism, accompanying it as the

shadow cast by idealism's insurmountable incompleteness."[414] The problem
is the following: even if the immanent "breakdowns" of solipsistic self-
enclosure—the internal obstructions of language's psychotic dance—
represent the inability of the subject to posit itself as an autocratic all
hallucinating its world, *they only point to a negative experience of the Real and
do not suffice to offer a positive articulation of the ontological qua ontological.*
Of course ciphering sometimes runs into knots, but this very blockage can
only be understood in the Symbolic *by the Symbolic* and in such a way that
we never leave its prison. How could a kink in the Symbolic be revelatory
of the pre- or extra-symbolic Real that somehow unpredictably upsurges
within its sphere? Even given the paradoxical mode of the double-feature
of inclusion/exclusion, internal/external, and presence/absence that defines
the Real, it is still, formally speaking, *a lack*, nothing more than a notional
antagonism in its ciphering code. It is unclear how this logical torsion,
an internal hindrance in ideality, could serve as a foundation for a new
materialist metaphysics, for there is no such thing as an outside or Other to
symbolic mediation to which we can have access: "the Lacanian Real—the
Thing—is not so much the inert presence that 'curves' the symbolic space
(introducing gaps and inconsistencies in it), but, rather, *the effect* of these
gaps and inconsistencies."[415] If it is understood as the alien presence of
some extra-ideal presence within synthesis, it can only be understood as
such insofar as it is posited as such—or, as Fichte says, insofar as there is a
transference of the productive activity of the subject to the not-I, but such
a *transference*, although enabling us to give a consistent account of why
representations often fail due to some "alien presence" that obstructs them
(the necessity of a realist moment in a critical idealism), never leaves the
constraints of a subjective idealism. We appear stuck in the most rampant
form of correlationism.

Even if the Real can negatively show itself through an internal tension
pressurizing the Ideal from within, we can never reach the ontological as
such. There is always the correlation language/being wherein being itself
is reduced to that which is constructed in the symbolic field of discourse,
regardless of there being elements that appear within the latter that it cannot
control. We may forever approach it as the negative magnitude contorting
our notional apparatus as produced by the latter's very inconsistency, but

this never leads to any knowledge of the Real in itself. From within the originary psychosis of a self-grounding idealism, there can be no overlapping of subjective and objective reality, for the very emergence of the subject as an ontological lacuna has as its founding gesture an irreconcilable rupture between the *Innenwelt* and *Aussenwelt*. Despite this, however, Žižek embarks upon an exploration of how a structuralist self-enclosed system preventing any direct engagement with the Real could have arisen by using the very fact of the Symbolic as a manner of proceeding. If the Symbolic is an *ontological* solipsism, then the lack of access to being we have must be understood as an event in being. In this sense, the Real-as-lack must ultimately open onto a metaphysics of the Real as that which *precedes* and *exceeds* the Symbolic and the Imaginary. But Žižek's Lacanian commitments would seem to render such a move unjustifiable. It is uncertain how he can balance his own radical idealism with his other materialist tendencies—indeed, his attempt to inscribe the former within the latter, to make the epistemic limitations of linguistic idealism synonymous with being's non-coincidence to self, appears to intensify the problem. How can a "negative materialism" based on the *infinite* conflict between mind and body found a new metaphysics? If we take as our starting point the (non-)relation between system (materialism) *and* freedom (idealism) as revealed by the psychoanalytical experience, then doesn't the logical category of the disjunctive "and" explicit in their contradiction prohibit us from delving into the retroactively posited past of the Real-as-origin to see how the latter explodes out of being as an event? How can we overcome the withdrawal into the nocturnal self of the world at the very birth of subjectivity so as even to see this withdrawal for what it is?

11.2 The Hegelian Real-as-Lack: The Painful March of Ontological Solipsism

The problem at hand is how to understand the separate theses that (i) the inconsistency of thinking methodologically justifies an overcoming of the realism-idealism debate from within idealism and (ii) given the fact that the Symbolic is always already minimally outside itself we can embark upon an explication of its origins without ever leaving it. Endeavoring to give Lacanian psychoanalysis the support it needs—a comprehensive metaphysics—it is perhaps to be expected that Žižek falls into such a theoretically difficult position. Lacan argues that we are stuck in language and, accordingly, that access to the ontological is impossible. Yet such a claim, if it cannot account for the *ontological genesis* of that which in the first place impossiblizes *our access to the ontological*, risks being merely a dogmatically asserted statement. This tension between the two major theoretical roles that the Real must assume—a notional lack and a symbolically excessive activity that is independent to all forms of correlation or access conditions—explains the constant oscillation in Žižek's position as he wavers between his strictly Lacanian and larger metaphysical and ontological commitments, even if the latter are always mediated by the former. Although most of his comments on Schelling, for instance, bespeak the possibility and necessity of delving into the Real-as-excess,[416] understood as the pre-symbolic antagonism that gives rise to the transcendental matrices of the subject (the "orgasm of forces") he often refers to the purely fantasmatic character of such inquiry due to the impossibility of reaching the absolute beginning of language[417] and its necessary mytho-poetic component given its resistance to rational speculation,[418] often without acknowledging the problem that this could appear to pose to the endeavor of establishing the ontological grounding of the subject. Given that he identifies "the key question" of philosophy as that of "how thought is possible in a universe of matter," so that we should focus our efforts on "the very rise of representation or appearing out of the flat stupidity of being" if we are to avoid "a regression to a 'naive' ontology of spheres or levels,"[419] the conceptual contours of this problematic deserve to be investigated in full. This is further necessitated by the fact that many fundamental Žižekian concepts directly exhibit this tension-ridden simultaneity of two opposed directions between the Real-as-lack and the Real-as-excess. His discussions of the night of the world in *The Ticklish Subject*, for instance, have a tendency to treat the Real as the other side of transcendental imagination, and hence as a logical rather than an ontological concept (Žižek warns us that "it is crucial to 'close the circle': we never exit the circle of imagination"[420]), although he also bestows upon the notion a clear metaphysical reach by locating the destructive force of understanding preceding its synthesizing powers within the originary event of substance's auto-destruction (equating it with an ontological *"tearing apart"* or *"dismembering"*[421]). This latter utilization of the concept—which he presents as a reworking of Kant's theory of unruliness—is then used to displace the mature Hegelian dialectical triad and argue for its inability to explain the passage from nature to culture,[422] thereby further intensifying its speculative reach. How can he move from one register to the other?

Despite this uncertain wavering between the purely logical and metaphysical or ontological value of Žižek's reading of the night of the world, other categories that Žižek extracts from Hegel show why he, as a rule, would generally have a preference for Hegel over Schelling, even in face of the obvious debt to the latter in his own transcendental materialism. The Hegelian concept "tarrying with the negative," for instance, intrinsically displays the structure of the Real-as-lack and is thus, strictly speaking, completely compatible with Lacanian epistemology, whereas the categories he finds in Schelling pose a more immediate problem. Emerging out of Hegel's critique and extension of the Kantian thing-in-itself, tarrying with the negative is an attempt to show that the latter, as a theoretical posit, is superfluous. Objects give themselves to consciousness, but it is an illegitimate move to say that, beyond their appearing, there is an inner core of the thing that is hiding, ever out of reach of the transcendental ego's limited synthesizing powers, because even this infinite elsewhere of subject-independent interiority is itself only possible from within the manifold field of phenomenal experience: that is, *it is itself an appearance.* This becomes most evident in the experience of non-coincidence between our concepts and that which they "represent." Within the inconsistency of the immanent structure of knowledge exhibited by these types of encounters, the object "in itself" shows itself through the form of a negative determination that burdens experience. We could say that what we come across here is the raw positivity of the object that obstructs our idealization and forces us to adapt to it, but only with the qualification that this positivity is revealed within the shadows cast by idealization's failure in such a way that *it can only be brought forth or posited retroactively* by means of a modification of the matrix of concepts that constitute our mediation of the world so that the original paradox or blockage disappears. In the aftermath of this epistemic remodulation, we see that what we initially experienced as an internal or structural deformation of ideal space was the negative refraction of the object's "true" nature such that the Real, less than a solid thing that obstructs ideality from the outside, is a pure effect. This has two implications: firstly, we do not need to overcome the split between phenomenal appearance and the thing-in-itself because this very split arises from within appearance itself, so appearance is "always more than appearance," as it were. Secondly, the noumenon as a "transcendence" that gives itself of itself to experience is reduced to a mere defence against the potential horror of the immanent, uncontrollable flux of pure appearance, for if a transcendent object *causes* our representations, then our representations are guaranteed to constitute a minimally smooth fabric. As an illusion of a place wherein all contradiction is always already resolved in a reality complete unto itself, the noumenon helps bestow a sense of order and unity to the structure of experience even where it does not of itself display any, thereby taking the edge off of ideal fragmentation. The infinite (the perfect ontology of the noumenal extra-subjective being) only emerges as a response to the radical finitude of phenomenal reality (ideal obstruction in our dealings with reality), whereby "every positive figure of the In-itself is a 'positivization' of negativity, a fantasmatic formation we construct to order to fill in the gap of negativity"[423]: there is only the restlessness of the negative, the incessant internal fracturing of experience due to idealism's intrinsic limitations and inability to posit itself as a complete all, which always leads to symbolic dismemberment, so that noumena, now understood as the negativity of phenomena, their internal inconsistency, "designate the In-itself *as it appears to us, embedded in phenomenal reality* [...] there is no mysterious gap separating us from the unknown, the unknown is simply unknown, indifferent to being-known."[424] In other words, what is on the other side of the screen of consciousness is not another reality, but *"the same reality we find in front of the screen"*: Žižek tells us to think of the illusion of a theatre stage, where what is responsible for the illusion is not the machinery backstage to which we have no access while the play is going on, but the very theatre stage itself, for even if the backstage and its mechanics are visible not only do we realize that the secretive reality normally "beyond our grasp" is exactly the same as the one being staged, but the deceptive effect is nevertheless still produced;[425] in other words, *thinking itself produces the illusion that it has no access to being due to the transcendental framework through which it (only haphazardly) grasps (fragments of) the latter.* The issue is not that thinking cannot comprehend being, but that, since it is inscribed within the latter, thinking can obtain no transcendent gaze upon it by which it can totalize it into a complete system. Thinking is necessarily incomplete—there is an irremovable lacuna in every truth-claim—because it can never get rid of the subjective gaze, a gaze that, while making knowledge finite, simultaneously renders it possible in the first place. Following this train of thought to its logical conclusion, we must assert that not only can we never know the system of the world, but if thinking itself is a part of the world, and there is only one world, there is no god's-eye point of view from which the world can never turn back upon itself and close itself. The gaze of the subject is a non-suturable gap in being—this is what it means to say that "phenomenalization, appearance, 'illusion,' split, finitude, Understanding, and so on, [...] are inherent to the life of the Absolute itself."[426]

Through its own subjective movement, thought comes to realize that there is an outside to thinking *posited from within as that which insists and persists as the extimate core of all discourse.* That is to say, thought is a constant struggle insofar as its struggle *with itself* is never a mere masturbatory play, but is simultaneously a struggle *with the outside world.* Its operationally and epistemologically closed ciphering of the world is capable of knowledge because the very inside-outside distinction becomes *intra-discursive,* that is, *immanent to thinking itself because it is sustained by the activity of thinking, so that there is a paradoxical coinciding of the purely subjective and the purely objective:* "[e]very tension between Notion and reality, every relationship of the Notion to what appears as its irreducible Other encountered in the sensible, extra-notional experience, already is an intra-notional tension i.e., already implies a minimal notional determination of this 'otherness.'"[427] Although we are trapped in idealization and the Real-as-lack is our doomed fate, there is no need to mourn the loss of some kind of immediate being in itself, some Oedipal womb of nature from which we have fallen: what Hegel shows is that, from within the level of the logical self-articulation of the reflective notional constructs of thinking themselves and the symbolic space of self-generating meaning they engender, we can "reach" objective reality because there is no significant gap between thinking and being *at the level of thinking.* The Symbolic is that which opens up access to being: we provide a freely developed notional construct that creates the norm for an intelligible field, a field that then may fall into inconsistency when said notional construct fails to render its corresponding phenomenal reality consistent, but inasmuch as the failure of said notional construct enables us to modify it we thus can be said to slowly and patiently track truth over time. Once we have seen that "[t]he opposition between idealistic and realistic philosophy is therefore without meaning,"[428] we can develop a metaphysics *critically* rather than *dogmatically*. This dissolves the worry regarding how we can have access to the world from within the clutches of subjective thinking. To say that the Real is a product of thought is not to lapse into a Berkeleyan form of idealism wherein reality is simply created by the subject: "the Real is not some kind of primordial Being which is lost," but rather "*what we cannot get rid of*, what always sticks on as the remainder of the symbolic operation."[429] As an aftereffect of this symbolic operation, it ensures that we have an *indirect* but *methodologically secure* entry point into the world by means of the inconsistencies that our notional apparatus generates in the freely determined self-generation of the universe of meaning, inconsistencies that unexpectedly let us develop an objective discourse.

But the limits of idealism entail that idealism is always already more than itself—thought itself is utterly incapable of positing itself as a self-enclosed positivity that simply creates its own universe of meaning; it becomes contaminated, as it were, by a constitutive "outside" as soon as it tries to posit itself in its own self-determining freedom, so that it must constantly struggle with this outside. This constitutive failure on behalf of thinking successfully to posit itself as all guarantees that there is a subject-independent reality that we experience and can speculatively describe:

> There is a Real not because the Symbolic cannot grasp its external Real, but because the Symbolic cannot fully become *itself*. There is being (reality) because the symbolic system is inconsistent, flawed, for the Real is an impasse of formalization. This thesis must be given its full "idealist" weight: it is not only that reality is too rich, so that every formalization fails to grasp it, stumbles over it; the Real *is* nothing but an impasse of formalization—there is dense reality

"out there" *because* of the inconsistencies and gaps in the symbolic order.[430]

With this insight gained Žižek, like Hegel, discovers an *epistemological* foothold—the productive space of ideal inconsistency (in the quote above Žižek is talking about our access to the Real *from within the Symbolic* rather than its *ontological* constitution)—from within which he can find the resources required to develop a new metaphysics. It is less idealism that poses a problem for the latter than the traps that it (unconsciously) creates for us as we attempt to catch a glimpse what "lies beyond" phenomenal reality: the inevitable and necessary symbolic dismemberment of a self-grounding idealism that fails to fully become itself not only creates the possibility of error, but since the first showing of the Real is always an internal deformation of ideal structure (a pure negative form lacking content), it itself risks being riddled with a thick layer of fantasmatic projections and unconscious desires. *That which allows idealism to overcome itself also can hinder the speculative process.* Yet, despite this, the Real-as-lack and the Real-as-excess do not stand in opposition to one another. Although the former is always epistemologically superior or primary, being the transcendental condition of the possibility of access to the latter, we are nevertheless capable of attaining that which is pre- or extra-Symbolic not only *despite* but more primordially *by dint* of the Symbolic's clutches. This is why, on Žižek's reading, Hegel's *Science of Logic*, while never leaving the matrix of self-thinking thought, can coincide with metaphysics and describe pre-subjective reality in its raw categorial purity and dialectical movement. Ontological solipsism is only apparent, for materialism justifies itself in the cracks of a radical idealism: the very condition of possibility of discourse means that discourse is always more than itself, even if that means that its very possibility coincides with its impossibility. Fichte refers to such a theoretical position—a critical idealism brought to fruition—as a real-idealism or an ideal-realism.[431] Although his own position may fail to execute this adequately, it can serve nevertheless as the most consequent description of a true, successful idealism. As Žižek correctly points out, "[t]he irony of the history of philosophy is that the line of philosophers who struggle against the sophistic tradition ends with Hegel, the 'last philosopher,' who, in a way, is also the ultimate sophist, embracing the self-

referential play of the Symbolic with no external support of its truth."[432]
Hegel can accomplish this *prima facie* paradoxical feat because he is able to
demonstrate that accepting the impossibility of leaving the "correlationist
circle" does not fall into a naïve idealism whereby objective reality is
reduced to nothing, but rather shows how even the self-referential nature
of thinking itself always already depends upon and is entangled with the
world, thereby attesting that the split between knowledge in itself and for
us exists not because we are separated from the world, but because we are
a part of it: "the very limitation of our knowing—its inevitably distorted,
inconsistent character—bears witness to our inclusion in reality."[433] In this
respect, idealism (reflection, notional constructs, language as such) creates
the space of reasons in virtue of which things can present themselves to us
as they are in reality in itself. This presenting, however, requires a stage upon
which their theatrical appearance can be performed, a stage that produces
the illusion of a backstage to which we do not have access. Instead of merely
separating us from the world, the reflexivity of the Ideal thereby allows
objects to have meaning for us as something more than objects to be used
by specialized biological or natural needs. We *symbolize* them, grant them
a place in discourse, a discourse whose failures make it seem as if a world
out there directly attacks our concepts and theoretical models when, in fact,
we never exit discourse at all, for only its self-sustaining matrix can sustain
phenomenal reality as a universe of meaning. This signifies, moreover, that
to pose the question of being *qua* being, there must be a *difference* between
us and being, for being *qua* being can only show itself to a finite thinker for
whom there exists a distance within which being can be phenomenalized
or phenomenalize itself by means of notional constructs. It is important
to note, however, that in order to get being right, we must also be able to
get it wrong, the minimal condition of which is satisfied by the ontological
madness that is the basic structure of ideality as that which prevents us
from having a direct "immersion" in the world and as such opens up the
possibility of replicating being within itself; the self-stipulating norms
of discourse internally guide the constitution of phenomena while their
inconsistency demonstrates that we are capable of objectively describing
them simply through the process of thinking only thinking itself. In this
regard, Hegel's monumental achievement is the critical proof that one of

the effects of the Symbolic's self-enclosure is that, in point of fact, it allows things to appear *intelligibly* through the reflective mediation of language. All we have to do is take the appropriate attitude toward the inner limitations of phenomenal reality as such. Paradoxically, a realist epistemology does not make a realist. This is why the choice between idealism and realism is false for the idealist.

11.3 A Call for a *Critical* Metaphysics

At this juncture we must underline one important feature of this argument for a self-grounding idealism that intrinsically contains an irreducibly real moment. If the Symbolic freely constitutes phenomenal reality "with no external support of its truth,"[434] then this suggests that from within its ontologically solipsistic dance of cybernetic ciphering, *we can break through the impenetrable dusk of psychosis* as we find, in an innovative theoretical gesture, a secure foothold from which to found a new science of being. But this means that we should not merely overcome radical idealism *from within idealism* (an epistemological sublation of the correlation): we must also overcome it *from the side of being* by showing how the ambiguities of idealism are in fact a part of the world's fundamental structure through an account of how being comes to appearance/thinking/phenomenalization (an ontological inscription of the correlation). If we can succeed, then realism and idealism will have become intimately dialectically linked. Not only would this entail a strong theory of thinking insofar as the latter would be inscribed within the fold of being as an irreducible event rather than as a mere illusory feature, but also a profoundly rich metaphysics inclusive of both realism and idealism given that both would now reciprocally ground one another (in realistic *and* idealistic terms) in a completely self-sufficient and self-reflexive whole. That is to say, we would have a new variation on the late German Idealist theme of the unification of system and freedom: or, in other words, another take on the Kantian heritage and how it radically changes the field of philosophizing. In this respect, whereas much of contemporary philosophy's understanding of idealism fails to take it seriously, often equating it with a form of Berkeleyanism (a tradition that runs from Kant's first critics to Lenin[435] and taken up once again by Moore[436] and most recently by Meillassoux[437]), one of the greatest strengths of Žižek is his nuanced vision of the world that is able to use idealism's resources not only to overcome its own apparent limitations from within, but also to demonstrate how, if this self-overcoming is successfully executed, our understanding of being is simultaneously remodulated. Idealism and realism, transcendentalism and metaphysics, are not mutually opposed if you think them through in relation to one another, for the former forces us to come to grasp what it means for thinking *to exist* in an irreducible manner, a fact that has stark consequences for our understanding of the world at large.

After a long period in contemporary philosophy where there was a general disdain for speculation, what distinguishes Žižek so radically from others who have also raised the question of the possibility of a new metaphysics (perhaps most notably Deleuze and Badiou) and those who are now active in establishing this possibility is his call for a *critical* metaphysics and its superiority over a mere return to *dogmatic* philosophizing as a means of overcoming the heritage of what has recently come to be known since Meillassoux's *After Finitude* as correlationism.[438] For Žižek, the urgent call for a philosophy that can combat the apparent speculative throes of the irreducibility of the correlation in our knowledge of the world (if the intelligibility of any specific empirical truth-claim depends upon the subject for whom such a truth-claim has meaning in the first place, how can we even speak about that which occurred before the existence of such a subject without falling into ontic nonsense?) does *not* have its origin in paradoxes concerning "ancestral" statements concerning what the universe must have been like prior to humanity, as Meillassoux would like us to believe,[439] this having been proven to be an intrinsic possibility opened up by the logical space of the correlation as such, but rather what the universe must be like if something like humanity and its transcendental constituting powers are to arise at all. The issue is how the Real could have come to appear to itself—and although this may appear to risk an anthropomorphization of nature ("[w]e should apply here something like a weak anthropic principle: how should the Real be structured so that it allows for the emergence of subjectivity [...]?"[440]), one should proceed cautiously. Žižek's metaphysical archaeology of the psychoanalytical subject is an attempt to think the intersection of the Real and the Symbolic, the coldness of being and the fervor of humanity, because if images and words, and by implication thinking, *exist, they must exist in the world*. The universe is inclusive, not exclusive, of humanity: a true speculative philosophy should comprehend both the Real in its pure non-correlationality (the nonhuman) *and* how correlation comes to pass in being (the human). Perhaps unexpectedly, the price we pay for this theoretical gain of re-inscribing humanity into nature, that is, the latter's minimal anthropomorphization, is a simultaneous *denaturalization of nature* and a *dehumanization of humanity*. Not only is nature now reduced to "a freak show of contingent disturbances with no inner rhyme or reason,"[441] but even if humanity still retains a certain qualitatively distinct status in contradistinction to other things in virtue of its autonomy, what we normally take as the great and sublime achievements of thinking are, in fact, grounded in a mere virtual re-compensation for our traumatic disruption from the Real. What thus makes Žižek's speculative real-idealism/ideal-realism (to borrow that German Idealist leitmotif) so penetrating and deserving of attention today is its ability to combine a profoundly idealist epistemology with a dynamic realist metaphysics in one single gesture, which shows us one path that contemporary metaphysics could take: namely, a *critical* one. In this regard, if Meillassoux's critique of correlationism is a call to station ourselves *after (Kantian) finitude*, it must be recalled that this is precisely what Schelling and Hegel did in their own critique of correlationism *avant la lettre*.

Žižek is able to balance the real and ideal poles in such a nuanced way because of his precise and original take on the breakthrough inaugurated by transcendental philosophy, a breakthrough that for him presents itself as the unthought (Lacanian) cause at the heart of German Idealism. One of his central claims is that if we read Kant closely, we see hints that what truly fascinates him is not how the subject brings forth its own universe of meaning as a new kind of metaphysical agent capable of guaranteeing the universality and necessity of experience/empirical truth, the two being identical for Kant, but "something quite different," something that sets the stage for the "few decades [of German Idealism that] represent a breathtaking concentration of the intensity of thinking" within which "more happened than in centuries or even millennia of the 'normal' development of human thought."[442] Commenting on Kant's description of the Copernican revolution (the experiment of seeing "if he might not have greater success if he made the observer revolve and left the stars at rest"[443]), which Kant identifies with his own transcendentalist position, Žižek notes:

> The precise German terms (*"die Zuschauer sich drehen"*—not so much turn around another centre as *turn or rotate around themselves*) make it clear what interests Kant: the subject loses its substantial stability or identity and is reduced to the pure substanceless void of the self-rotating abyssal vortex called "transcendental apperception."[444]

What initially appears as a rampant subjectivism wherein the ego reigns above the world proves on closer inspection to be something infinitely more complex, for the self-grounding field of phenomenal reality only exists because it itself revolves around the positively charged void of I. The breakthrough of transcendental idealism is precisely the discovery of this zone of negativity *within the subject*, that X that can never be fully appropriated into transcendental constitution and yet somehow engenders its very possibility, whereby it shows itself to be not so much a displacing of the substantial unity of reality from the external world to the conceptual forms of cognitive construction (a subjective Ptolemaic *counterrevolution* against Galileo's de-centering of the medieval world of teleology[445]) as the opening up of a new understanding of being, that is, of the radical ontological incompletion of reality, the breakdown of substance, provoked by the meta-transcendental conditions of thought as such. As the late German Idealist reappropriation of the subject demonstrates, what is truly unique in transcendental idealism is that the real *and* ideal poles are unsettled *in one brush stroke*: linked to the *Todestrieb* that destroys the homeostasis of nature and *das Unbehagen in der Kultur* that prevents our second nature from becoming a new substantialist order, the "objectal status" of the subject is that which is "no longer" ontological and "not yet" symbolic because it cannot be contained in either register in its pure form;[446] it is what Žižek sometimes refers to as *the absent centre* that, by protruding out of all ontological and symbolic structures, negatively ties them together in its very undecidability. Here, and only here, the real and the ideal poles intersect, so that both are given their equal due because of an unapproachable X, a *je ne sais quoi*, that relates them in their very non-relationality and whereby one leads to the other: "[w]e can also see in what way two lacks overlap in this impossible object: the constitutive lack of the subject (what the subject has to lose in order to emerge as the subject of the signifier) and the lack in the Other itself (what has to be excluded from reality so that reality can appear)."[447]

Although the transcendental (our subjective position) *objectively* exists in the world, it nevertheless appears to itself in its first mode as merely *subjective*. To overcome itself and pass over into a metaphysics, it must do so from within; it does so by drawing attention to the fact that, beneath the correlation of (the conscious) subject and reality, "there is the more primordial correlation of the subject (of the unconscious) and its Real/impossible objectal counterpoint, S-*a*."[448] Although this may seem to be just another correlation (as Heidegger only institutes the correlation being/*Dasein* as more originary than that of consciousness/world, doesn't Žižek do something similar?) this is a false appearance. Rather than being a strict correlation in Meillassouxian terms this binary points towards *the emergence of correlation within being*: "this impossible/Real object is the very mode of inscription of the subject into trans-subjective reality; as such, it is not transcendental but (what Derrida would have called) arche-transcendental, an attempt to circumscribe the 'subject in becoming,' the trans-subjective process of the emergence of the subject."[449] Žižek's wager, one that he shares with the entirety of post-Kantian idealism as a *critical* metaphysics fighting against any *dogmatic* breed thereof, is that if we are to truly break free from correlationism, no return to a "naïve" realism is possible. Not only is the latter always open to critique insofar as it could remain correlational in a hidden way (isn't its specific image of reality related to a subject?[450]), so that the specific nature of the correlation, namely the *ideal* conditions of the possibility of intelligibility of any theory, should always be thematized before embarking on speculation, but more primordially it fails to give us of a grasp of how thought is situated/comes to pass in being and, therefore, the very *ontological* conditions of the possibility of its own status *as a theory*. Concerning the latter, merely explaining subjectivity as a purely contingent emergence amongst others à la Meillassoux bodes no better: "one should locate traces of this contingency in a kind of umbilical cord which links the subject to its pre-subjective

Real, and thus breaks the circle of transcendental correlationism."[451] In this manner, we should search for how the transcendental hints towards its dark beginnings (the pure act of the Real-as-origin and the unruliness of drives in the Real-as-excess that precedes it), the emphasis being on the ontogenetic process of becoming more than on the specificity of the transcendental constitution of reality for us, so that the fundamental issue is no longer so much how can we attain knowledge of the absolute (this already being accomplished by the first methodological step, as for instance in Hegel) but how does our subjective viewpoint fit into it as something that objectively exists: "[t]he true question is therefore how I (as the site where reality appears to itself) emerge in 'objective' reality (or, more pointedly, how can a universe of meaning arise in the meaningless Real)."[452] With this, we have come full circle and hit upon the great merit of Žižek's philosophy. Having already overcome idealism from within, and having opened up the space for a speculative philosophy, he can develop a theory that is capable of being maximally realist *and* idealist and therefore best suited as a self-explanatory theory of the metaphysical "totality" of the world, insofar as it can simultaneously supply the ontological conditions of the possibility of its own status as a theory *and* the ideal conditions of possibility of its own intelligibility in one sweeping move, thus making the theory itself extremely self-referential in its structure. In short, the theory displays complete systematic self-enclosure: *it explains itself as a theory in both the real and ideal registers in such a manner that both depend upon and mutually ground one another in a self-articulating whole; it has succeeded at developing "a concept of the world or the Real which is capable of accounting for the replication of reality within itself."*[453] What Žižek teaches us, a lesson already brought to the fore in late German Idealism but since forgotten, is that radical idealism is not a closure to the absolute. It is rather a new approach towards it, a new way of relating to it—and to see it as such merely requires a parallax shift in perception.

11.4 Being's Poem: Speculative Philosophy and the Mytho-Poetic Parallax Shift

If Žižek is right to say that the founding gesture of idealism is an ontological passage through madness, then it would not go far enough if we were to admit that the opposition between realism and idealism has been already resolved *at the level of* idealism. Something is missing, for the real event that immediately precedes the autarchy of the Ideal, and whose exploration would enable this opposition to be also resolved *at the level of realism* (thus radicalizing and guaranteeing what Fichte referred to as a real-idealism or ideal-realism), *is an impossible object of discourse*. Conceding that notional antagonism can indeed be spectrally expressive of objective reality, and thus enable us to speculate about reality within ideality, to fully explain how we can have contact with the world where there is properly speaking no contact at all we must nevertheless acknowledge that we can never even indirectly reach the exact moment at which being begins to exist in the modality of the Ideal. The difficulty is much more severe than that the Real is always already minimally symbolized, since the Real-as-origin expresses two fundamental theoretical problems. First, insofar as its abyss of unconscious decision represents a pure self-instituting difference that unpredictably splits the world into two new logically irreconcilable registers, it cannot be deduced from the auto-movement of the Real; there is no "transition," but only a self-caused "leap" that forever evades complete conceptual or natural dialectic mediation. Second, because this act withdraws in the very gesture of giving birth to the Symbolic, it lies *stricto sensu* "beyond" the grasp of the latter and can never appear within it, not even negatively. It is in this precise manner that the subject is neither Real nor Symbolic and is only expressible through a series of paradoxical avatars unable to bestow content upon it (the disjunctive "and," the "in-between," the "abyss of freedom," the "vanishing mediator," and so on). A philosophical discourse about the subject is thus intrinsically paradoxical because the latter is "a non-provable presupposition, something whose existence cannot be demonstrated but only inferred through the failure of its direct demonstration."[454] In short, *it can only be investigated at the level of mytho-poetics*. But what intensifies the problematic of such a metaphysical archeology of the subject is that without such a mytho-poetic narrativization of its impossible Past we would be unable fully to explicate how the Symbolic can in fact relate to reality in itself, for without it we cannot perform the parallax shift of "transposing the tragic gap that separates the reflecting subject from pre-reflexive Being into this Being itself," whereby "the problem becomes its own solution: it is our very division from absolute Being which unites us with it, since this division is immanent to Being."[455] In other words, the real *and* the ideal sides of overcoming idealism are intimately connected and cannot be discussed in isolation from one another: in order for idealism to completely surmount its own apparent limitations, it must be able to come full circle and show how, from within realism, its own ambiguities are not merely epistemological but *also ontological*; it must show what it means for thinking to be a part of the world, a manner in which the world relates to itself, no matter how paradoxically.

In creating itself by an act of immaculate conception, the Real-as-origin of the pure act at the birth of full-fledged subjectivity retroactively takes over what we come to know as the Real-as-excess of the drives. In a contradictory moment in which cause-and-effect relations are torn apart, the effect becomes greater than and autonomous from its cause, even going so far as to write a virtual possibility into the eternal dregs of the Past that never existed prior to its having been written there through an act of positing of its own presuppositions. *The subject creates its own past in the same instance in which it begets itself out of nothing,* so that the true "arche-fossils" are not ancestral statements concerning what occurred billions of years ago before the emergence of the thinking subject or life itself, but the objectal status of the subject:

> what Lacan asserts is precisely the irreducible (constitutive) discord, or non-correlation, between subject and reality: in order for the subject to emerge, the impossible object-that-is-subject must be excluded from reality, since it is this very exclusion which opens up the space for the subject. [...] The true problem of correlationism is not whether we can reach the In-itself the way it is outside of any correlation (or the way the Old is outside its perception from the standpoint of the New); but the true problem is to think the New itself "in becoming." The fossil is not the Old the way it was in itself, the true fossil is the subject itself in its impossible objectal status—the fossil is myself, the way the terrified cat sees me when it looks at me. This is what truly escapes correlation, not the In-itself of the object, but the subject as object.[456]

Because the objectal status of the subject escapes any straightforward causal explanation and lies outside of all correlation insofar as it is responsible for its very upsurge, the only way to reach it is by means of a mytho-poetics of speculative fabulation. And given that this realistically non-deducible and idealistically inaccessible zone coincides with that very place in which the subject is inscribed within being as one creature amongst others (and is thus that which would enable us to pass *without any immanent obstacle* from the real pole to the ideal pole and vice versa) the parallax shift from the negative limitation of knowledge to the positive structure of the absolute itself requires more than mere rational ideal discourse. Only then can we "relate the In-itself to the split in the subject,"[457] for "what Lacan calls the *objet a*, the subject's impossible-Real objectal counterpart, is precisely such an 'imagined' (fantasmatic, virtual) object which never positively existed in reality—it emerges through its loss, it is directly created as a fossil."[458] In this sense, Žižek's philosophy is paradoxical precisely because it attempts to think the unthinkable, that is, the *cogito ergo sum* as "I am that impossible piece of the Real where I cannot think"[459] that uncannily corresponds to that space within which the meaningless Real contingently awakens and opens its eyes for the first time. In so doing, the metaphysical archaeology of the subject it offers endeavors to demonstrate that what the subject "loses" in order to become a subject coincides with what is excluded from reality so that reality can appear to itself, in such a way that the Real is thereby transformed from being a primordial being to which we have lost access due to its symbolization into something of which we cannot shake ourselves, no matter how hard we try, because through a mere formal reversal *the gaze of the subject is seen to be the gaze of the world upon itself*, the ambiguities and difficulties of the former being always already those of the latter: what we see is that "the narrative [we are telling] is not merely the subject coping with its division from Being, it is simultaneously the story Being is telling itself about itself," so that realism and idealism are no longer in opposition, but stand in a self-sufficient totality inclusive of both as immanent to the life of substance. The system of being and thinking has closed upon itself in one final self-referential gesture.

In Žižek, we must narrativize the movement from being to thinking if we wish to reconcile the two and completely escape the speculative throes of correlationism, since at the level of content there is always a minimal "non-dialectizable" difference of one to the other (a division) that prevents such a move in purely rational discourse. But we must highlight the precise logical structure of this solution if we are to come to terms with the originality, daringness, and potential problems of Žižek's position. Given that the exact real event that instigates being's coming into appearance/thinking/phenomenalization is the primordial *ontological* trauma that is the subject as object, we must in a mytho-poetic register (the subject in its objectal status being forever elusive) show that this trauma is not a mere accidental, haphazard occurrence in the personal history of an individual subject, but rather reveals itself as a constitutive, yet disrupting part of a greater trauma within being itself. But this (Žižekian) dialectical reconciliation is not a complete sublation of the opposition between realism and idealism, a complete break with the paradoxes of correlation, for the problematic nature of the latter is something that must be accounted for rather than explained away. As with all dialectical movement, "reconciliation is a reconciliation with the irreducibility of the antinomy, and it is in this way that the antinomy loses its antagonistic character,"[460] so that in this case, reconciliation only truly occurs when we realize that *there is no reconciliation (a complete solution) possible* because what we take as *our* finitude should be inscribed into the thing itself (being) as *its* non-coincidence to self; and although this reconciliation can only thus come to pass at the level of mythological form, and never at that of content, instead of focusing on the impossibility of idealist representation to capture that which is being described, namely the objectal status of the subject, the solution paradoxically "shifts the focus to how (as Lacan put it) *the signifier itself falls into the Real*, that is, how the signifying intervention (narrativization) intervenes into the Real, how it brings about the resolution of a real antagonism,"[461] thus working against its own impossibility: "the narrative path directly renders the life of Being itself."[462] Though we can never "exit the circle of imagination"[463] to capture the abyss of unconscious decision at its real origin, by writing being's poem we can see, due to a mytho-poetic parallax shift, that the poem we are writing coincides with the one that being is writing about itself. The human eye is never merely human: it is identical with the world itself "gaining" the power to see itself, so that our apparently purely epistemological limitations are intimately linked to the ontological grounding of our notional apparatus. But is such a mytho-poetic narrativization a sufficient basis for a new speculative philosophy? As we will see in the next chapter, delving into this question leads us to three potentially fatal issues with Žižek's critical metaphysics, all emerging from its fundamental concept of ontological catastrophe as the vanishing meditator between the Real and the Ideal. Does Žižek have the resources necessary to combat them? And if so, at what price?

Notes

411. Žižek, *Less Than Nothing*, p. 239.

412. Ibid., p. 562.

413. Žižek, *The Abyss of Freedom*, p. 45.

414. Johnston, *Žižek's Ontology*, p. 19.

415. Žižek, *The Puppet and the Dwarf*, p. 66.

416. See Žižek, *The Ticklish Subject*, p. 55; and *The Parallax View*, p. 166.

417. For example, Žižek, *The Indivisible Remainder*, pp. 22–23.

418. See, for instance, ibid., p. 9.

419. Žižek, *Less Than Nothing*, p. 905.

420. Žižek, *The Ticklish Subject*, p. 33.

421. Ibid., p. 31.

422. Ibid., pp. 79ff.

423. Žižek, *Less Than Nothing*, p. 282.

424. Ibid., p. 283.

425. Ibid., pp. 374–75.

426. Žižek, *The Ticklish Subject*, pp. 88–89.

427. Žižek, *Tarrying with the Negative*, p. 20.

428. Hegel, *The Science of Logic*, p. 124.

429. Žižek, *Less Than Nothing*, pp. 645–46.

430. Ibid.

431. Fichte, *Science of Knowledge*, p. 247.

432. Žižek, *Less Than Nothing*, pp. 76–77.

433. Ibid., p. 390.

434. Ibid., p. 77.

435. References to such are scattered throughout Lenin's *Materialism and Empirio-Criticism* (Peking: Foreign Languages Press, 1972).

436. See Moore, "Refutation of Idealism," *Mind* 12 (1903).

437. This is at the heart of Meillassoux's critique of correlationism via the arche-fossil in *After Finitude: An Essay on the Necessity of Contingency*, trans. Ray Brassier (New York: Continuum, 2008).

438. For a similar in spirit account of the distinction between *critical* and *dogmatic* metaphysics, see Gabriel, *Das Absolute und die Welt in Schellings*, p. 8. For the basic definition of "correlationism," see Meillassoux, *After Finitude*, pp. 4–6.

439. Meillassoux, *After Finitude*, pp. 9–13.

440. Žižek, *Less Than Nothing*, p. 905.

441. Ibid., p. 298.

442. Ibid., p. 8.

443. Kant, *Critique of Pure Reason*, B xvi.

444. Žižek, *Less Than Nothing*, p. 631.

445. Meillassoux, *After Finitude*, pp. 118–19.

446. Žižek, *The Ticklish Subject*, p. 36.

447. Žižek, *Less Than Nothing*, p. 645.

448. Ibid., p. 642.

449. Ibid.

450. Ibid.

451. Ibid., pp. 642–43.

452. Ibid., p. 924.

453. Gabriel and Žižek, "Introduction: A Plea for a Return to Post-Kantian Idealism," in *Mythology, Madness and Laughter*, p. 13.

454. Žižek, *Less Than Nothing*, p. 730.

455. Ibid., p. 15.

456. Ibid., p. 644.

457. Ibid.

458. Ibid., p. 645.

459. Ibid.

460. Ibid., p. 950.

461. Ibid., p. 16.

462. Ibid.

463. Žižek, *The Ticklish Subject*, p. 33.

Chapter 12
The Deadlocks of Ontological Catastrophe
The Cases of *Naturphilosophie*, Anton-Babinski Syndrome, and *Tarte à la crème*

Žižek's theoretical philosophy aims to be a *critical* metaphysics capable of simultaneously overcoming radical idealism *from within idealism* (an epistemological sublation of the correlation) and *from within realism* (an ontological inscription of the correlation). However, at this juncture three potential problems emerge from various directions. The first direction is that of Schelling's *Naturphilosophie*. Not only does Schelling proclaim that, insofar as the subject is anything but an ontological catastrophe, thought is inscribed within being in such a way that we have no need to overcome radical idealism from within itself, it also challenges Žižek's own psychoanalytical reactualization of Schelling. The second direction is that of the skeptic, who can invent a thought experiment to demonstrate that it is perhaps impossible to develop any positive metaphysics from within a differential system of signifiers without any external reference. The third direction is that of the very basis of ideality itself understood as a psychotic withdrawal into the night of the world, the overcoming of which demands the seemingly impossible task of developing a paradoxical form of "successful" psychotic thinking capable of penetrating the impenetrable dusk of its own psychosis. How does Žižek stand up to such critiques? Is his radical idealism truly capable of providing us with a comprehensive metaphysics?

12.1 The Schellingian Real-as-Excess: Iain Hamilton Grant, *Naturphilosophie*, and the Interior Involutions of Being

But is mytho-poetics the only option here? Although Žižek follows Hegel's defence of radical idealism as capable of a speculative account of extra-notional reality, a potentially fatal problem arises internally within Žižek's own position as soon as we take a closer look at Žižek's other major interlocutor: *Schelling*. Ultimately unsatisfied with Hegel's mature account of the passage from nature to culture, Žižek turns to Schelling to explicate the genesis of the Symbolic. What Hegel missed was the paradoxical essence of this very movement, a dialectical movement that causes dialectics *to collapse upon itself*. With the birth of subjectivity, we see a snag in substance that prevents the absolute from self-actualizing itself so that, instead of being the Idea completely returning to itself out of its otherness in nature, which would present us with a reconciliation of nature and spirit in the Idea, nature's complete self-sublation in spirit, culture is actually a mere secondary ("virtual, artificial, symbolic, not substantially natural"[464]) response to the primordial ontological trauma that lies at the core of the human being. For Žižek, this means that culture is the always failed attempt at reconciliation: the Idea is nothing other than this very act of its own returning to itself, this movement being constitutive of that to which is returned;[465] for it to reach its end would herald its death. Representing a recoil into a psychotic, irreal space, not only do the subjective and objective/mind and world thereby fall into infinite conflict with one another, but it becomes impossible to explain why the Ideal emerges. According to Žižek it is Schelling who, fighting against the perceived threat of Hegelian Absolute Idealism, gives the most detailed account of this immanent self-sundering of being into its real and ideal poles in his account of the *Grund* as the ever elusive, eternal Past of consciousness, and the pure act of unconscious decision underlying the birth of the universe of human meaning. Schelling's position is paradoxical: from within a solipsistic space (transcendental idealism) he tries to develop a philosophical language capable not only of piercing the primacy of the Real-as-lack and explaining its monstrous pre-history within pre-symbolic antagonism (materialism), a logically prior but directly unreachable modality of the Real that *precedes* and *exceeds* the Symbolic, but also of describing the inexplicable self-positing of subjectivity (idealism). After all, even if we can be said to have access to both the ancestral past of the Real prior to subjectivity and the Real that surrounds us "outside" of language through the very inconsistency of our notional apparatus, the methodology of which Hegel offers us through an analysis of the dialectic of phenomenal appearance and the very structure of symbolic thought, nevertheless the precise moment in which the subject institutes itself into being poses a problem to such a self-overcoming of radical idealism, because it is a leaping point in the Real into a new age of the world that is always "beyond" the Symbolic as its irretrievable origin. Because Schelling realizes the impossibility of a purely speculative account of the subject's emergence, and thus the necessity of a mytho-poetics, it is he and not Hegel who most adequately realizes the quadruple logic of dialectics at the core of German Idealism.

But even with his highly methodological psychoanalytical construction of the unconscious *Grundlogik* of German Idealism, for anyone who is familiar with Schelling's vast corpus it is unclear how Žižek can appropriate Schelling for his own project without potentially destabilizing his most fundamental theoretical category: that of the ontological catastrophe. Although the two major concepts Žižek utilizes—denaturalized unruliness (the dark pre-history of subjectivity in the vicissitudes of being) and the unconscious decision (the separating *Ent-Scheidung* whose effect is the institution of a metaphysically disjunctive "and")—are meant to explain how we get entrapped in the Symbolic and the matrix of idealization, Žižek's own writings on Schelling do not seem fully to take into account the possibility that the latter might not be able to be so easily translated into the framework that he sees as basic to the entire tradition. His division of Schelling's thinking into three distinct stages—the Schelling$_1$ of a quasi-Spinozistic philosophy of absolute indifference, Schelling$_2$ of a radical materialist ontology of freedom, and Schelling$_3$ of the philosophy of mythology and revelation—already hints at an irremovable tension. It is uncertain that the materialism-idealism relationship we see in the Schelling of the *Freiheitsschrift* and the *Weltalter* can be read as a mytho-poetics of the birth of a radical transcendental idealism in the manner Žižek suggests. When we look at Schelling's thought, even as Žižek himself presents it, we are tempted to say that, if Hegel is able to show that the absolute opposition between idealist and realist philosophy is without meaning *from within idealism,* Schelling could be said to do the same *from within realism and without needing to pass through the former.* This is further supported by the fact that Schelling never gives us a dialectical analysis of phenomenal appearance or the structure of symbolic thought in the way Hegel does and describes his own idealism in the *Darstellung* as "real" or "objective," for its principal idea is not to use thought's inconsistencies to find a new starting point for speculative philosophy, but rather to directly investigate the origins of thought itself from its dark nonconscious ground,[466] a point repeated by the "higher realism" of the *Freiheitsschrift*[467] and the emergence of ideality in the *Stuttgarter Privatvorlesungen* out of minerals.[468] The argument that Schelling$_2$ is an ephemeral rupture risks succumbing to arbitrariness, since now we find a manner to unify the central problematic of the *Naturphilosophie* and the "theosophic" philosophy of freedom. Given that one of the key tools for the development of Žižek's own metaphysics is the extracting of an unconscious *Grundlogik* underlying German Idealism, if Schelling's philosophy turns out to be more continuous than Žižek's analysis lets on, then his psychoanalytical construction of the German Idealist tradition could be jeopardized.

For Schelling, we do not just "tarry with the negative." The X that eludes consciousness, one of the centrepieces of Schelling's thought, is never just a mere formal limit: it is an attempt to express the subject-independent interiority of nature to which we have access despite the mediating activity of consciousness *precisely because the subject and its ideational capacities are a part of nature, one way through which nature relates to itself as ground.* Schelling refuses to separate the ontological in-itself of precognitive or extra-symbolic reality from the epistemological sphere of idealist representations, arguing that the two must be intimately connected if philosophy is to find a secure basis. If there is an *identity* between the Real and the Ideal, the problem of their relation to one another is relegated to a metaphysical or naturephilosophical level rather than a strictly epistemic or idealist one. Whereas in the middle-late period this idea of identity is expressed by the notion of the *Mitwissenschaft* ("co-science") of creation, it is more clearly for our purposes articulated in the earlier *Ideas for a Philosophy of Nature,* where Schelling argues for the necessity of a dialectically positive interactivity between mind and matter if transcendental idealism is to have a proper founding, which goes in the face of both the Hegelian proof of the insignificance of an opposition between idealistic and realistic philosophy *and* a Žižekian metaphysics of the disjunctive "and":

> For what we want is not that Nature should coincide with the laws of our mind *by chance* (as if through some *third* intermediary), but that *she herself*, necessarily and originally, should not only *express*, but *even realize*, the laws of our mind, and that she is, and is called, Nature only insofar as she does so.
>
> Nature should be Mind made visible, Mind the invisible Nature. Here then in the absolute identity of Mind *in us* and Nature *outside us*, the problem of the possibility of a Nature external to us must be resolved. The final goal of our further research is, therefore, this idea of Nature.[469]

It is exactly this problematic that reverberates throughout the entirety of Schelling's thinking, even when he attempts to outline the tension-ridden oscillations of the Yes and the No, the light and the dark principles, constitutive of the self-operative logic of the *Grund*. Rather than offering some kind of paradoxical eruptive logic balancing materialism and idealism through their infinite conflict, Schelling's philosophy can very easily be read as a passionate attempt to show that the forces underlying human spiritual-transcendental activity are nothing more than the already existent potencies of nature arisen to a higher "power" through nature's auto-development. If the starting point of Žižek's transcendental materialism is a self-grounding idealism (which shows his distinctive Lacanian-Hegelian presuppositions), Schelling's own transcendental materialism is a self-articulating realism (which shows how Schelling has been influenced by the evolutionary dynamism of natural scientists such as Kielmeyer), the stark point separating them being that whereas in the former materialism is always a *spectral materialism* developed in the cracks of idealism, in the latter idealism becomes, as it were, a mere *conditioned* phenomenon. In this strict sense, if Schelling's philosophy is an account of the self-unfolding of the powers of nature according to their inner movement, it is because it is a *speculative* realism understood in its original etymological meaning: deriving from the Latin *speculari* (to watch over), it is a realism that attempts to, through a scrutinizing surveillance, account for the immanent pulsations of the universe as it transforms bodies of matter into the complex field of living being and eventually thought as ideal self-mediation, so that the Real is not only always excessive to the Ideal, that which can never be brought into it due to nature's raw productivity, but the latter also loses its theoretical primacy insofar as nature in the stirrings of its nocturnal ground itself becomes the true a priori.

It is interesting to bring up this aspect of Schelling's philosophy, not just because it could be a weak point in Žižek's psychoanalytical reading, but also because it is a specific manner in which Žižek's metaphysical problematic enters into direct debate with the current speculative turn. In this regard, Iain Hamilton Grant's own transcendental materialism is in *complete* opposition to that of Žižek, so that contrasting the two allows us simultaneously to bring to the fore both the daring character of the latter's position and its potential internal limitations. Taking up Schelling's diagnosis that modern philosophy exhibits an agonizing deficiency—*that nature does not exist for it*[470]—Grant puts forward the argument that this diagnosis is just as sound today as ever: "[i]nsofar therefore as the antithetical couple 'Plato-Kant' that lay at the heart of the immediate postkantian context continues to organize metaphysics, contemporary philosophy is importantly and immediately postkantian."[471] Through a careful reconstruction of Schelling's philosophical career with an eye towards its explicit naturephilosophical content and the natural scientific context that surrounded and inspired it, Grant's thesis is that by following its spirit, we may finally find a way to leave behind us the Kantian heritage insofar as Schelling offers us, instead of a two-world metaphysics that results in an "eliminative practicism" (the irreducibility of culture to nature), a "one-world physics capable of the Idea."[472] We cannot cut the world in two, for there is no great divide: even to understand culture as culture, we have to understand its genesis from its ground within nature, for culture itself is originally natural. There is no absolute split between the Real and the Ideal, mind and matter, the dead movement of inanimate objects and the life of organic being—there are only the unconditioned, groundless powers of nature as a pulsating all that creates specific bodies and their various, innumerable, and unpredictable organizations according to its own cryptic inner process. According to Grant, Schelling's revolutionary thesis is that the only way we can explicate ideality is to see it as just one specific expression of nature's productivity, one among many possible products of nature as a priori. There is just a difference of degree and not of type between, say, atoms, chemicals, and free ethical subjects, insofar as there is a *natural* history of mind to which we must have recourse to explain its apparent autonomy. Far from being an idealism that grounds itself from within the infinite self-reflexivity of thinking "with no external support of its truth,"[473] Schelling's idealism is a naturephilosophical investigation into the interior involutions of being, the latter being equally inclusive of thought's transcendental activity as the somatic constitution of physical bodies. Nature is a dark dynamicity that brings philosophy far away from the practico-concrete sphere of an anthropocentric universe into the enigmatic palpating powers that gave birth to it in their antagonism and the forgotten aeons of the abyssal dregs of cosmic time that have preceded us. In this manner, Grant is taking Schelling literally at his word:

> A great work of the ancient world stands before us as an incomprehensible whole until we find traces of its manner of growth and gradual development. How much more must this be the case with such a multifariously assembled individual as the earth! What entirely different intricacies and folds must take place here! Even the smallest grain of sand must contain determinations within itself that we cannot exhaust until we have laid out the entire course of creative nature leading up to it. Everything is only the work of time, and it is only through time that each thing receives its particular character and meaning.[474]

Although Grant and Žižek are reading Schelling in different, largely incommensurable ways—the former by a remarkable reconstruction of Schelling's naturephilosophical and scientific context, the other by a violent psychoanalytical overhauling of the entire German Idealist tradition—the fact that they both fall upon the same figure to elaborate their own materialist position is extraordinarily thought provoking. First and foremost, it suggests that the role of Schelling in Žižek's thinking poses a potential problem for the latter's own transcendental materialist ontology of the subject, and not merely for external reasons: *it challenges the latter's very notion of a metaphysics of the disjunctive "and."* The great contribution of Schelling's *Naturphilosophie* was to enact a complete displacement of the human subject, for it imposes upon us the counterintuitive task of a *geology of morals* that fights against any complete separation of the human (the realm of free acting) from the natural (the realm of necessity). The stark implications of this, as Grant himself notes, were clearly perceived by Eschenmayer, a Fichtean natural scientist, who after reading the *Freiheitsschrift* fell into a paroxysm of horror due to its primary soul-wrenching implication: "your essay on human freedom seems to me a complete transformation of ethics into physics, a consumption of the free by the necessary, of feeling by understanding, of the moral by the natural, and above all a complete depotentiation of the higher into the lower order of things."[475] Commenting on this passage, Grant writes:

> We can imagine Eschenmayer's shock: why does this work on the subject of freedom contain so much geology? Why is the *turba gentium* [...], the world-disorder or species-riots, presented as the ground of freedom? [... B]ecause the consequences of the dependence of transcendental physics on dynamic naturalism impose upon Schelling's reconditioned transcendentalism the demand that the All be grounded in the "subject of nature itself," i.e., in the forces. Accordingly, the more disorderly the phenomenon, the darker and more abyssal the ground. This is why the inquiry into *human* freedom must (a) specify the attachment of this power of infinite evolution to a finite phenomenon (human), and (b) consider the ground of such a freedom as derivative of the "self-operation of the ground" or the "will of the deep" in the geological series: the potentiating series through which such a freedom must (repeatedly) evolve must therefore present the *expression of geological potencies* in practical intelligence.[476]

In this respect, when Žižek claims that it is Schelling who gives the most detailed description of the ontogenesis of subjectivity in the philosophical tradition—which makes him the father of dialectical materialism and contemporary philosophies of finitude—he is in many ways completely justified, but in so doing he risks opening himself to the criticism that he misses how Schelling proceeds in this endeavour as well as its larger philosophical consequences, which presents two immediate major problems in his own usage of Schelling. First, if Grant is correct, Schelling rejects from the outset the very idea of a self-enclosed transcendental framework and its concomitant mind-body dualism, the ontological emergence of which is, according to Žižek, the fundamental philosophical obsession of the middle-late Schelling. If the unconscious *Grundlogik* of German Idealism is constituted by the dynamic of a self-grounding idealism and a spectral materialism grounded in the former, then Schelling's precise place within it would seem to be uncertain. Second, if Žižek's transcendental materialism assumes the birth of the I out of the not-I as an *impossible* event with no true precursor in the ancestral past of the pulsating fires of the heavens, the sluggishly slow evolution of geological formations, or even the forces of evolution in biological life-forms (none of its apparent brethren come close to its pure difference), in such a way that the self-positing of freedom literally cuts the absolute in two in an inexplicable manner, then we must conclude that Schelling's own metaphysics does not automatically result in a metaphysics wherein substance is split at its core, and thus ontological dislocation is the primordial fact. Contra Fichte, Schelling explicitly claims that there *is* a continuity between the I and the not-I, that the passage is one of a transition, not a leap. If psychoanalysis is to work in a therapeutic setting, an encounter with the Real can only truly be brought forth if all the intended meanings of the subject have been understood for what they are; otherwise a psychoanalytical interpretation does not work, because it does not hit the cause (which is why Lacanian analysts rarely offer interpretations). Moreover, even if we agree that Žižek is right to contend that the theosophical content of the middle-late Schelling is a mythological component that we can formalize in order to render its content more explicit (which Grant's work also implicitly does, given that he does not explicitly deal with the theological aspect of the *Freiheitsschrift* or the *Weltalter*), it is uncertain that he can so easily get rid of the naturephilosophical implications of these texts. But the stakes are much higher than those of the philological-textual fidelity of an interpretation in this case: if Schelling's

philosophy presents a framework incompatible with the one Žižek sees in it
and his own psychoanalytical reconstruction extensively relies upon this for
its own argumentative vitality, Žižek's own development of a metaphysics of
the Real by an engagement with Schelling is not only potentially misguided,
but could also lose sight of various other resources explicit in Schelling that
could be used to rethink the materialism-idealism relationship.

Elaborating on Grant's argument, we see that Schelling completely
bypasses the problem of the materialism-idealism relationship because
idealism is never a purely self-referential play. The whole concept of a
"spectral" materialism just has no place here; speculative philosophy has a
stricto sensu non-idealistic foundation. As Grant succinctly puts it, what is
at stake is the "impersonal coincidence of the transcendentally generated
universal and self-generating nature [... and] Schelling's hypothesis
is, in other words, that there is a naturalistic or physicalist ground of
philosophy,"[477] a ground that does not implicate an eliminative materialism
wherein all is reduced to empirically observable bodies—somatism—but in
such a way that genuine philosophy "consists in the dynamic elaboration
of the identity of nature *and* Ideas."[478] In this manner, if one reads Žižek's
own transcendental materialism alongside that which Grant develops from
his own reactualization of Schelling, one is presented with an alternative
to Žižek's own metaphysics of the not-all, one not centred in the Ideal as
being's irreconcilable self-division, but rather one based upon the fragile
productivity of nature as it contingently and continually takes on new
forms (and destroys others), a productivity that in no way has man as
its summit, but will create new creatures (and monsters) without end
because there is no stasis, but only a restless movement of the depths, a
beautiful and macabre dance of great delicacy and improvisation whose
actors simultaneously whimper and laugh under its weight. Lacanian
psychoanalysis prohibits this Schellingian move because it would require
that the chain of signification constitutive of human language be not based
on an operationally closed system with no natural grounding, but could
actually open up onto the world as it is in its own interior involutions
because it would be, as it were, *one with it.* Although we philosophize about
nature by "following a procedure of successive unconditioning performed
by thought-operations about nature," a process that allows us to "arrive

at a conception of '*nature as subject*,'" this investigation is never a mere reconstruction within the ideal series of the Real, but is rather a movement of the Real itself, for "such a philosophical system does not therefore seek a fixed point from which to gain leverage on an external world, nor to rise above it, but is itself a 'genetic' [...] movement in and on this world, unconditionally."[479]

Schelling expresses this identity most daringly when he says that "to philosophize about nature means to create nature."[480] "Mental" activity is always already a part of nature and therefore a part of its own auto-development by being one of its emergent attributes, but nature, being the truly and absolutely a priori, is unconditional and thereby guarantees that thought is never limited to the mere ideational or physiological constraints of conditioned particulars insofar as it is an expression of nature's productivity rather than embodied in the fixity of one of its products. In this way, for Schelling, we are primordially "connected" with nature as the pre-Symbolic, insofar as the Real and the Ideal remain identified at an essential level, the consequence being that the subject is *not* a dialectically non-sublatable in-between that exists as the psychotic withdrawal of the world into self. Accordingly, Žižek's reliance upon Schellingian ontology risks problematizing his own position, for if Žižek draws upon Schelling as a partner for the elaboration of the impossible genesis of the transcendental out of an orgasm of forces within the pre-symbolic Real, this immediately draws our attention to other possibilities of understanding the subject that do not present the latter as an irrevocable moment of ontological catastrophe in the flux of material being. This would force us to rethink the very nature of the psychoanalytical experience and the essence of the disjunctive "and" that is central to Žižek's own parallax ontology—and in this manner, not only does its theoretical first principle begin to tremble, but the very primacy of the Lacanian psychoanalysis that serves as its starting point is put into question. It is highly revelatory that to make use of Schelling for his project in the first place Žižek can only focus on two works (the *Freiheitsschrift* and the second draft of the *Weltalter*) because of their apparently disavowed Hegelian structure as that which would enable one to extract from them a self-operative logic establishing the primacy of the Real-as-lack through the abyss of unconscious decision.

We can begin to see why Žižek's proclamation that his project is *Hegelian*, but never *Schellingian* (despite the fact that the *Freiheitsschrift* and the *Weltalter* contain the most vivid description of the emergence of the Symbolic), is multilayered. First and foremost, Žižek takes radical idealism as the only true beginning for philosophy insofar as we can only interact with the world through the medium of thought, making correlationism basic to our experience. If the cracks within ideality epistemologically enable us to develop a spectral materialism, then the irreducibility of the Real-as-lack paradoxically does not prohibit us from having access to being as the Real-as-excess because this very concept thereby becomes internal to our notional apparatus. In this manner, Žižek is quite justified in saying that his project is Hegelian given that—on his own reading of Hegel at least—it strictly speaking shares this identical starting point and draws from it the exact same consequences, a move that in turn allows him to avoid the problem of expressing too strong a reliance on and debt to Schelling, which could potentially bring his own thinking uncomfortably close to everything he denies: the non-Freudian unconscious (in its Bergsonian, Jungian, Deleuzian, etc., forms), "pre-modern" cosmology, or Romantic theories of nature. Yet, this does not by any means solve the ambiguity of the Hegel-Schelling relationship in his thinking, for as we have seen, what is crucial to Žižek's own reading of Schelling is that Schelling's own theoretico-epistemological framework, at least in the second period of his thinking, *is unknown to itself the same as that of Hegel*. Although Žižek has to do great violence to Schelling to extract a Hegelian dialectical structure of negativity in his texts, nevertheless the interpretation he presents is extremely internally consistent and methodologically sound. If the thoroughness of a position like Grant's is a challenge to Žižek, then Žižek's own reading of Schelling is equally a challenge to Grant's and other canonical and non-canonical interpretations that exist. The game goes both ways—and because the conceptual terrain within which both operate is vastly different, it is not evident how we are to decide upon the favourability of one interpretation over another. However, one has to underline that this oscillation between Schelling and Hegel is not so much an inconsistency or sleight-of-hand gesture on Žižek's part, the reason being that what interests him is less the specific differences between the historical thinkers of the tradition, but an unconscious truth that can be seen to deploy itself through them. Accordingly, not only is there absolutely no contradiction in saying that Žižek's philosophy is a hybridism of Hegelian logic and Schellingian ontology insofar as it is precisely this hybridism that can retroactively be seen to be the traumatic core at the formative heart of the tradition itself, but reflecting upon the intrinsic ambiguity of the Hegel-Schelling relationship helps us reveal the originality and daringness of Žižek's critical metaphysics.

12.2 Anton-Babinski Syndrome: Slavoj Žižek's Paradoxical Overcoming of Idealism

Although Žižek's appropriation of Schelling could be perceived as highly problematic, insofar as the latter may not so easily fit into the proto-structuralist framework Žižek sees as operative in German Idealism, another problem immediately arises that potentially hits the core of his overcoming of radical idealism. Even if we accept the legitimacy of his reading of Schelling, it is unlikely that Žižek's own Hegelian attempt to show the insignificance of any absolute opposition between idealist and realist philosophies *from within idealism* would satisfy a realist. If we never leave the clutches of idealism, then any knowledge that we possess would never be able to reach the absolute in its pure non-correlationality to the subject. We are always entrapped in the masturbatory play of signifiers in their incessant sliding. Moreover, the Real-as-excess as what *precedes* and *exceeds* consciousness is an explicitly *impossible* concept. Even Žižek's "materialist" response to idealism has as its fundamental task to bring to the fore this intrinsic impossibility: remodulating the Schellingian act of unconscious decision, its seeks to show how the shift from the Real-as-excess (pre-symbolic antagonism) to the Real-as-lack (symbolic imprisonment) is the ultimate ontological parallax by a speculative fabulation of the always lost and inaccessible moment of the auto-disruption of the noumenal realm. At its best, realist metaphysics appears to be reduced to mythology.

Žižek's overcoming of idealism articulates itself in two distinct moments. First, since the Real-as-lack is the logical zero-level of any philosophy due to the insurmountability of the Symbolic, to arrive at some kind of knowledge of an "extra-"notional zone of experience (the Real-as-excess) would appear a priori foreclosed. However, the very inconsistency of our notional apparatus allows us to develop knowledge of reality in itself, for as soon as we "apply" a category to the world and it shows itself as inadequate, we see that the field of appearing is *always more than appearance*, whereby the noumenal now appears as the self-limitation of the phenomenal. Our experience of the world is not a full-blown hallucination: we can use these experiences of breakdown to our advantage in order to explore a world that only seems to be infinitely "beyond" our reach. The Real-as-excess becomes an intra-discursive category, so that epistemic limitations of knowledge negatively demonstrate our inclusion into and thus capacity of understanding the world at large, rather than our imprisonment in a socially constructed universe of discourse. It is precisely because of this that Žižek says that "the true problem is not how to reach the Real when we are confined to the interplay of the (inconsistent) multitude of appearances, but, more radically, the properly Hegelian one: *how does appearance itself emerge from the interplay of the Real?*"[481] Second, given that we are in some sense a part of the absolute, our failure to reach it has to coincide with a failure of the absolute itself. Žižek's wager is that if we do fail in reaching the absolute in thought, this cannot be due merely to the finitude of our notional apparatus: "[i]f we can *think* our knowledge of reality (i.e., the way reality appears to us) as radically failed, as radically different from the Absolute, *then this gap (between the for-us and the in-itself) must be part of the Absolute itself*, so that *the very feature that seemed forever to keep us away from the Absolute is the* only *feature which* directly *unites us with the Absolute.*"[482] The point is not to "'overcome' the gap [...] but to take note of how *this gap is internal to* [*the Absolute*]":[483] arguing that our inability to overcome our entrapment in the Symbolic and find our place within being *is already the very lost object we are looking for*, Žižek turns epistemological limit into positive ontological condition by inscribing the limitation of knowledge into the world as an event immanent in the latter: that is, *by making it an (auto-)limitation of the absolute itself*. If idealism is some form of ontological solipsism, then it must be revelatory of a zone wherein the absolute is irrevocably non-coincident to itself. In another vein, this means that any radically self-grounding idealism is always already a materialism, the two being nothing more than supplementary views on the same underlying reality; moving from one to the other just requires a certain switch of perspectives, a parallax shift, whose very possibility we can only explain by making the very irreconcilable split between idealism and materialism the imperceptible truth of both. Žižek's name for that which can strangely mediate between them because it is neither idealistic nor materialistic yet is included in both as excluded ("include me out!") is the subject as an insurmountable ontological and symbolic lacuna. Consequently, the Symbolic is always already more than itself because it points to its dark origins in being's passage through madness—and even if the precise moment in which the world withdraws into its nocturnal, irreal self is forever lost in the universe of meaning it brings forth, we are nevertheless justified in mytho-poetically fabulating the act of decision that induces our collective psychosis, because the Symbolic can never do away with its origins.

Although the undecidable ambiguity of the Real is a problem Žižek inherits from Lacan, a problem similar to that faced by many forms of idealism, Žižek throughout his writings remains true to his great master's attempt to desubstantialize the Real, but with an important twist, a twist that accentuates the theoretical challenge of his critical metaphysics. What most clearly distinguishes Žižek's project from that of Lacan is his refusal to take our lack of access to the Real as a brute fact and his subsequent endeavour to inscribe it within being. The question arises, however, of whether Žižek's account of this emergent ontological parallax is even philosophically possible, given his epistemological commitments. Since phenomenal reality emerges only *after* being has sundered itself, whereby our access to the Real must be mediated by transcendental constitution, Žižek's double claim that the internal inconsistency of idealism is that which allows us to overcome it from within and that our inability to reach the thing itself is already that which we are looking for poses two important difficulties to his project that, for many, may not be adequately resolved or seem outright problematic. On the one hand, to switch epistemological limit into positive ontological condition by a mere parallax shift of perspective appears in many ways to be a mere sleight-of-hand argument. Given that this precise moment where our division from the absolute coincides with the self-division of the absolute (so that the story we are telling about being is simultaneously the story that being is telling to itself) can only be narrativized at the level of mytho-poetics, which reconciles substance and subject at the level of form and never at the level of content, it is unclear that the claim that the problem its own solution does the argumentative work it purports to do. To put it bluntly, since this precise moment defies any proper speculative explanation, it merely covers up the underlying issue that we are facing: that is, *how we could have access to being in the first place.* On the other, it is unclear that we can really collapse the distinction between realism and idealism by making the very distinction itself *intra-conceptual* or *intra-discursive* insofar as this move fails to sufficiently provide the conditions under which we could develop a truly speculative account of reality in itself that is not always already entrapped within the ambiguities of symbolization. In both cases, a realist would be quick to argue that we have done everything but leave the correlationalist circle, that we are stuck in a constituted world *for us.* For the former, it could not be said that we have some kind of "access" to reality through the immanent obstructions of the Symbolic as that which indicates the spectral presence of an extra-notional reality posited from within it, for the Real *is a mere effect of the Symbolic.* Does this go far enough in establishing the groundwork for a new metaphysics?

If we call the Real an *internal* limit or limitation of the Symbolic, we must be careful, because the Real is not so much a limit in the sense of a border that separates two distinct yet commensurable terrains, or a limitation in the sense of a restricting condition coming from an exterior force that one ought to overcome. Rather, the adjective "internal" is of utmost importance here because it stresses that the Real is completely immanent to the Symbolic's very idealizing activity in such a way that there is no outside except an outside that is paradoxically posited as inside. If the Symbolic functions within a *psychotic* withdrawal from the world, not only does it *freely (re)constitute reality according to an autonomous, self-referential play or ciphering,* but any obstruction that occurs within it would only be due to its freedom. In its first guise, the Real is nothing other than "a purely formal parallax gap or impossibility," "the rupture or gap which makes the order of discourses always and constitutively inconsistent and non-totalizable,"[484] so that even if we are permitted to call this negative encounter with the Real a "positive running up against" the exterior world that operates as if it "touches the Real,"[485] in the same breath we must qualify this statement insofar as this can only be brought forth in the aftermath of symbolic distortion, that is, *après-coup*. *This recognition of an indirect confrontation with a constitutive outside internal to the Symbolic is in itself just another symbolization*: any "materialism" that could be developed by means of it will always already be entrapped within its ambiguities, so that this "materialism" is nothing but a mere retroactive adjustment of ideality to accommodate for its internal inconsistencies, for it is only from within the Symbolic that we see the Real as the residue of a failed attempt to synthesize an "extra"-notional reality. As Adrian Johnston puts it:

> It's not that there is no Real that isn't immanent to the Symbolic. Instead, the non-immanent Real is accessible exclusively through the deadlocks and inconsistencies immanent to the Symbolic [...]. The Real-as-presupposed [the Real-as-excess as posited in/by the Symbolic] actually exists "for us" only insofar as it indirectly shines through the cracks in the façade of Imaginary-Symbolic reality, insofar as it is asymptotically approached by the *parlêtre* along the fault lines of this reality's inner conflicts.[486]

But "...indirectly shines through..." is a misleading metaphor: *nothing* breaks through the prison of language. As Žižek says, "we do not touch the Real by way of breaking out of the prison of language and gaining access to the external transcendent referent [...]. We touch the Real-in-itself in our very failure to touch it."[487] This is what Žižek emphasizes when he posits an ontological passage through madness at the beginning of the Symbolic, for once it has occurred there is no contact with the world that is possible. If we take Lacan and Žižek at their word, we can *never* truly liberate ourselves from the psychotically self-sustaining construction of reality that is the Symbolic's autonomous idealization. Even if the latter does not equate to an omnipotent, non-limited hallucination of our world of experience—a Godlike primary process—nevertheless there is no escape from our collective hallucination of reality: impenetrable in its density, omnipresent in its extension, nothing is left untouched by this tenebrous realm of transcendental phantasmagoria within which we live and breathe as speaking subjects. The light of being is unable to radiate through the holes of the all-encompassing web of the Symbolic.

Here the case of Anton-Babinski syndrome should be evoked as a possible skeptical argument against Žižek's overcoming of radical idealism. A rare medical phenomenon, the syndrome is a symptom of brain damage (usually from a stroke) in the occipital lobe. What is so peculiar is that people who suffer from it, although cortically blind, *claim that they can see*. In their speech and general behaviour there is often, at first, no sign of blindness—family members and the medical team typically only begin to notice something is amiss when the patient begins to stumble into various physical objects in their path, whether it be tripping over a coffee table in front of him, walking into a wall, or describing things that are not really there. Not only do patients continue to *refuse* to admit their blindness despite all the inexorable obstructions in the all-out hallucination of their own visible field of experience, but, more primordially, it is clear that no amount of tarrying with the negative offered by the latter's internal short-circuiting would ever enable them to develop a "spectral" vision of the world in itself of which they have been deprived through organic devastation. To deal with the incomprehensible agony caused by such constant disturbances in their psychotically self-sufficient and imagined perception of subjective reality, those who suffer from Anton-Babinski syndrome actually find ways of giving support to its free generation by falsifying their memories, a process that in the medical community is called *confabulation*. In other words, even if a patient, realizing their condition, were to think that they are actually in the process of developing a sound mental map of the physical universe that is around them through the aid of their mishaps as a means of retroactively readjusting their imaginary field, and this not only with the hope of learning to navigate within it, but also to overcome their blindness by making the absolute opposition between a hallucinated world produced in the void of blindness and a vision of objective reality caused by retina input *without meaning within their hallucination*, it must be concluded that they could never assure themselves that this "spectral" seeing captures the world nor whether it is not just another hallucination that has been produced to save themselves from the psychological trauma of their own blindness. Lost in visual madness, they can never indirectly see the world shine through the inconsistencies of their hallucination.

But isn't this precisely the same situation we find ourselves in with respect to Žižek's attempt to break the correlationalist circle? The only possibility for an ontological grounding of the psychoanalytico-Cartesian subject being a phantom-like vision of the world building itself within the internal obstructions of the Symbolic's ciphering of the world, it would seem that just as it is impossible for those suffering from Anton-Babinski syndrome to spectrally construct a vision of the world that has been lost to them due to their lack of sight, so it is impossible that one could achieve some kind of paradoxical coincidence of the subjective and the objective capable of positive truth from within the nocturnal night of the world. If the self-overcoming of radical idealism proves insufficient to ground a new speculative philosophy, then the only alternative left is a pure mytho-poetic fabulation of the obscure origins of the Symbolic, the latter's ontological solipsism always already pointing beyond itself to an inaccessible material event that haunts it but that remains forever inaccessible. Unable to sublate the opposition of realism and idealism *from within idealism*, we could still, by writing being's poem, provide a mythological account of how our division from being is the same as being's division to itself, thereby hinting towards how this opposition is always already reconciled *from within realism*, making the problem itself moot: we must tell a story that inscribes our failure to reach the absolute in the absolute itself, so that which appears to keep us from the absolute is in actuality the only thing that ties us to it. Our madness is being's own. But if such a medium of expression presents itself as the rational necessity of a non-rational discourse to explain discourse as such, then just as those suffering from Anton-Babinski syndrome create false memories to guarantee the consistency of their self-sufficient hallucination, so too does all speculative fabulation risk always being nothing more than a *con*fabulation. What complicates this philosophical issue is the fact that in all mytho-poetic narratives where the very "origins" of the Symbolic in the Real are at stake, the event in question that institutes the movement from one to the other "never effectively took place within temporal reality, [although] one has to presuppose it hypothetically in order to account for the consistency of the temporal process."[488] The result is that the event of the decision that violently separates *Grund* from existence *potentially never occurred*: it could be nothing but a fantasmatic, retroactive posit necessary for the internal consistency of our universe of meaning, so that the distinction between philosophy and fantasy/defence mechanism risks being blurred. As a consequence, Žižek's Schellingian "obscurantist idealist" manner of "deducing" this act from the pre-Symbolic could only be true insofar as it gestures towards the fundamental horror underlying subjectivity, just as the empirically false memories unearthed by those with false memory syndrome (being seduced, child sexual abuse) often merely reveal an underlying deadlock haunting a patient (that there is no sexual relationship). In this regard, not only is it unclear how we could truly test one mytho-poetic fabulation against another so as to guarantee their scientificity, but whether they have any metaphysical or ontological merit as such.

Given that our freedom means that we are forever stuck within a constitutive psychosis, the withdrawal of the world into the eternal darkness of its irreal self, the very category of truth here has been so starkly modified that Žižek's own philosophy risks undercutting the very ground it seeks. The subject is reduced to a mere spinning in the void of freedom, a void whose very emergence appears to render itself inexplicable and problematize any knowledge of the "outside" world. A realist will not only always find the reduction of the thought/being opposition to an *intra-conceptual* distinction an insufficient basis for a positive knowledge of the ontological and its vicissitudes, but will also reject myth as a speculative science insofar as correlationism has been preserved rather than overcome, for without the prior self-overcoming of idealism, the best mytho-poetics can do in the framework of a radical subjective idealism is to reconcile substance and subject at the level of mere mythological form rather than that of content. If idealism is co-incident with an ontological passage through madness, how could we develop a form of linguistic thinking able to overcome the psychotic withdrawal from objective reality that appears to be its very meta-transcendental condition of possibility to describe its event in being?

12.3 Fichte's Laughter, Henri Maldiney, and the Necessity of a "Successful" Psychotic Thinking

Spinning in the void of freedom—isn't this the Fichtean position? Does Žižek truly succeed in overcoming the theoretical impossibility forced upon us by the pure I and develop what Fichte thought was contrary to reason: namely, a transcendental materialist account of its emergence out of the not-I? Or is it not Fichte who, by refusing to fall upon the speculative potential opened up by the *Anstoß* and sticking to the internal dynamics of subjectification, ultimately has the last laugh in the history of post-Kantianism as a paradoxical attempt to develop a new metaphysics in the wake of idealism? Could he have uncannily predicted this dilemma? Perhaps it is in this precise sense that we should read Fichte's incomprehension of his critics, an incomprehension designed not so much to show his disgust at the childish laughter of established scholars at the apparent absurdity of his position ("Fichte, do you really think that air and light are a priori transcendental conditions of human freedom?") as to directly express by public ridicule his own laughter at the absurdity of their position ("Established scholars, you really think you can break free of correlationism and develop a speculative philosophy?"):

> I tell them that I have given here an a priori deduction of air and light. They answer me: "Air and light a priori, just think of it! Ha ha ha! Ha ha ha! Ha ha ha! Come on, laugh along with us! Ha ha ha! Ha ha ha! Ha ha ha! Air and light a priori: *tarte à la crème*, ha ha ha! Air and light a priori! *Tarte à la crème*, ha ha ha! Air and light a priori! *Tarte à la crème*, ha ha ha!" et cetera ad infinitum.
>
> Stunned, I look around me. Where did I lose my way? I thought that I had entered the republic of scholars. Have I fallen into a madhouse instead?[489]

For Fichte, true madness is not the psychotic withdrawal at the founding gesture of subjectivity, but rather rejecting its implications—in short, *acting as if it never happened*. If the ontological solipsism of the Ideal reduces all reality to a mere image, so that all "is transformed into a fabulous dream, without there being any life the dream is about, without there being a mind which dreams; a dream which hangs together in a dream of itself,"[490] rather than bemoaning the loss of being, we should realize the implications of this inexplicable leap into freedom, that is, that the phenomenal world "*absolutely creates itself* [...] in a genesis out of nothing."[491]

Just like the Fichtean transcendental *Wissenschaftslehrer* is able to come to the realization that life as we know it is nothing but a void doubled in on itself, *a dream of a dream*, so too the Žižekian transcendental materialist is able from within the throes of originary psychosis to see this psychosis for what it is. But he does not stop there. While the *Wissenschaftslehrer* proclaims that the only thing left for us to do is to actively create, through the infinity of imagination, the groundless images necessary to fully actualize our freedom in concrete striving, the transcendental materialist pauses for a moment at this insight: if we can see that our life is a *dream of a dream*, if we can understand *psychosis as psychotic*, then there must be a minimal level of distance possible, as it were, between us and the transcendental (re)constitution of reality as a collective hallucination—and it is precisely this distance that enables us to thematize the entire process for what it is both in terms of the internal dynamics of subjectification and its wider inscription within being. In short, the theoretical gesture at the heart of Žižek's project is the following: if we can recognize our symbolic entrapment *as entrapment*, then our idealist psychosis is not only non-coincident with itself, but must in certain instances be "unable" to fully lock us within its cage. The very reason why we even know that there is a free transcendental constructionism fabricating our world of experience in the first place is that this constructionism fails and is unable to absolutely create itself: radical idealism fails to be radical idealism because it is haunted by seemingly non-ideal constraints, so that in this immanent failure it opens up the space for a new form of materialism insofar as it demonstrates that the Symbolic is always already minimally outside itself. In this sense, the Real-as-lack, as that which was apparently at the very root of the realist objection to being able to overcome correlationism from within idealism, is of irreducible importance since it enables us to enact a metaphysical archaeology of the subject, and thus mytho-poetically fabulate a picture of its emergence from a pre-symbolic antagonism that sets the stage for the free idealization of the world. For otherwise, we cannot explicate how we can see psychosis as psychotic in the first place. It is the only possible Archimedean point from which we could be saved from confabulation by a constant tarrying with its traumatic piercing. Yet a speculative fabulation is merely that—*a fabulation*: recognizing the limits of rational inquiry for describing the exact moment of withdrawal into self at the commencement of the universe of meaning, it supplements it with a mythology that is consciously aware of the intrinsic inaccessibility of its object. Even if such a medium is justified by means of the Symbolic's own failure, which shows itself in a parallax shift of perspective as a disruptive ontological occurrence, we must concede that the actual narrative cannot truly articulate the miraculous advent of subjectivity in the Real. By delving into the impossible, the best it gives us is a sideways glance into the always absent origin.

The scientific legitimacy of mytho-poetics relies, for its theoretical force, largely on Žižek's solution to the realism-idealism debate from within idealism. To embark upon a mythologico-metaphysical archeology of the subject is to try to come to terms with the unfathomable zone in between the pure Real and the Symbolic that lies paradoxically in both and neither. But to describe the passage from one to the other is *stricto sensu* impossible because such a passage that can be nothing other than an unpredictable event that arises *ex nihilo* within the Real itself and which simultaneously is always already withdrawn from the very logical space that could rationally investigate it. But to see this as an impossibility in the Real ("the leaping point") and not just of the Symbolic (its "origin" in unconscious decision) presupposes that the question has changed from how we can gain access to the Real through the Symbolic to the ambiguous genesis of the latter out of the former. But has Žižek given us an adequate foothold from within which we can escape correlationism and answer this? Henri Maldiney, a little known French phenomenologist who rethinks human transcendence through the experience of psychosis, can give us some useful if controversial resources to draw out the intrinsically paradoxical nature of this inquiry.

Discussing the introduction to Ludwig Binswanger's case studies on schizophrenia,[492] Maldiney outlines a peculiarity in the former's phenomenological method. Rejecting the possibility of understanding schizophrenia *directly*, either through positivistic methodology or an immediate experience (what the person says being inadequate to express their illness), one has, as Biswanger notes, to "let oneself be carried by the very nature of things," that is, presuppose an inner, self-articulating structuration of the phenomenon that will reveal itself through a careful description as that which lets its phenomenological essence mediate itself to us. In this sense, there is a distinction to be made between (the) *phenomenal* experience (of schizophrenia) and (the) *phenomenological* experience (of schizophrenia as the object of a science). But this presupposition is, in fact, a Hegelian presupposition: "let oneself be carried by the very nature of things" is a literal repetition of the definition of science in the Preface of *The Phenomenology of Spirit*, where it is said that, in the dialectical method, we must let ourselves sink into the content at hand, thereby "letting it move spontaneously of its own nature."[493] We must always presuppose an interior life of the object whose essence will then be freely and spiritually internalized/mediated/idealized by the concept. Even if this presupposition appears harmless, it has a strange consequence in this context because of the specific object under investigation by the phenomenologist: "[i]t is not enough to bear witness to the incompatibility between science and psychosis. For their very incompatibility here is due to an extremely close proximity," for given that the phenomenological aims to be the (self-) thematization of the phenomenal, their very distinction risks dissipating into nothing as a certain undecidability emerges.[494] *The task of the phenomenological science of psychosis is to let psychosis live in its fullness, to show its true meaning.*

It is this methodological ambiguity that in turn enables Maldiney to reap a wealth of resources from the experience of psychosis. For Maldiney, the similarity that Hegel's dialectical method in *The Phenomenology of Spirit* bears to Binswanger's phenomenological approach to schizophrenia and thus, by implication, to his own to psychosis is not just limited to how they define their way of proceeding. Rather, it can also be seen at the *very level of the investigation of their objects*, so that there exists an extremely close proximity between the two levels of investigation that is constantly in danger of conflating them, but with an important twist. In the case of a phenomenology of psychosis, by letting psychosis speak the fullness of its essence *by letting oneself be carried away by the in-dwelling logic underlying its phenomenality*, what is at stake is not merely to understand how a psychotic crisis is a singular event responsible for the existential demise of an individual, but more primordially how this demise is revelatory of a failed transcendence and thus continues to participate in the very ambiguity and enigma at the heart of transcendence itself, even if in an out-of-joint manner, for "[i]ts dramatic testifies (*pathei mathos*) to that which is irreducible in man."[495] If this is the case, then we can question psychosis in order to bring to the fore the various existentialia operative in the very process of subjectification and temporalization central to human existence: "[w]hether his illness [*maladie*] is organic or vesanic, for man it is first of all a human trail; and it is only possible to understand the latter if one first of all knows what it means 'to be man.'"[496] In this sense, the experience of psychosis as a *failed* transcendence is beneficial for coming to terms with what a *successful* transcendence would be, by opening up the room for its (self-)thematization. In other words, if there is a certain ambiguity between the phenomenal (psychosis) and the phenomenological (its scientific essence) in this case, it is because the latter shows us that the former is always a possibility for us, an intimate potential of being human, so that the advent of the Real (in the sense of Maldiney) at the core of the subject is indifferent to the success or failure of the latter.

The *Phenomenology*, however, does not present us with a failed transcendence whose very failure highlights irreducible features of the drama of existence, as in Biswanger's case studies or Maldiney's own work on psychosis. But neither does it present us with a straightforwardly successful transcendence (if such a thing even exists) for the movement of consciousness it depicts is identical to the fundamental structure of depression, so that the question itself emerges as to how the *Phenomenology* can even arrive at dynamic unity and stability *if the consciousness it describes is intrinsically depressive in nature*:

> The principle of *Aufhebung*, "to abolish and to preserve," is consistent with the general scheme of depressive existence. Its double meaning agrees with, amongst other things, the double dimension of the depressive dramatic as explained by psychoanalytic theory, according to which the "relation to the object" serves to signify being-in-the-world with the same unilaterality that we see in Hegel. From the psychoanalytical perspective, depression is constituted by an uncertain relation to the primordial object, to which the subject remains attached even though it has been detached from it. Compelled, after the loss of the primordial object, to search for another, in the quest for a new object it is always in search of the lost object. But each object giving way to another object, those who suffer

from depression are forced to persevere in this indefinite
path—a circle without beginning and end, a circle in which
their thinking is ensnared, has become their only horizon.[497]

For Maldiney, the primordial lost object that the *Phenomenology* searches for
is "in reality existence" itself:[498] that is, human transcendence as a capacity
of welcoming the completely unexpected and utterly new as revealed to
us in the very flesh of sensation wherein subject and object are constituted
after the fact by means of a single movement in the flux of a pure appearing
that knows no bounds and no a priori. Maldiney relates this not only
to the originary impression (*ursprüngliche Empfindung*) that Hölderlin
identifies at the origin of his poetry, a primordial experience that demands
a complete transformation—an asubjective becoming-other—wherein the
world emerges at each moment as something never seen before,[499] but
also to the pure present that is the true place within which subjectification
and temporalization take place.[500] As a result, the key to understanding
transcendence is not ideational-conceptual mediation (the gnosologic: the
encyclopedia, the systematic), but rather sensibility (the pathic: the eruption
of the unpredictable, being held out into the Open), which leads Maldiney
to claim that the present is ecstatic—not in the sense analyzed by Hegel,
but as an event that is "an outpouring, a gushing, of the new. All of this is
just to name the ORIGINARY. It is the originarity of the present which founds
at each moment the reality of time; and it is its novelty that renders time
irreversible."[501] Because Hegel's critique of sense certainty excludes any
access to this primordial self-giving outside of conceptual mediation, *it is
as if the very source of all unity and stability has been obstructed.* The paradox
is that, although consciousness has lost its primordial object, which should
lead to psychopathology, "the Hegelian *Aufhebung* reproduces—in its own
register—the transcendence of existence; but it can only *reproduce* it (in
terms of a substitute of an *Ersatz*)—and this is the decisive characteristic—
because existence has already been *lost.*"[502] It is in this manner that the
Phenomenology exhibits a contradictory existential form of "successful"
depressive thinking.

The problem is only intensified when one takes into account the
methodological ambiguity Maldiney emphasizes in any phenomenology of
psychosis between the phenomenal and the phenomenological, insofar as in

the *Phenomenology* this ambiguity is expanded from the distinction between the phenomenal and the phenomenological to the distinction between the phenomenal and phenomenological *and the investigator within which this distinction is enacted, so that the in-dwelling phenomenological essence of the phenomenality they investigate can be brought forth.* Since the phenomenal here is conscious experience in its depressive existence, the investigator, by assuming the phenomenological attitude, is performing an ideal reconstruction of his or her own consciousness with said structure (which is simultaneously a self-construction of a depressive consciousness within the concept) into a scientific knowledge that is the system of experience. In this sense, the phenomenological level cannot be isolated from the phenomenal any more than it can in the phenomenology of psychosis, but now with an important precision to be made: the phenomenal experience is here the direct self-experience of the consciousness that goes through the odyssey that is the *Phenomenology*, but in such a way that it is as if phenomenal experience becomes *phenomenological to itself, thematizes itself,* in an act of gaining distance from itself, for the investigator who is exploring what it means to be a depressive consciousness is implicated in the very process. In short, there is ultimately no distinction between us and the object of investigation, because we are participating in the very thing that we are investigating. Accordingly, if the *Phenomenology* reveals that the fundamental structure of consciousness is a depressive structure, for those who embark upon it it is simultaneously a transformation of the mode of existing in transcendence that is depression into a unique style of living, wherein the same structure we see in the psychopathological state of depression is made into that which bestows upon consciousness a profound and never-ending source of energy while resting all the while depressive. If the phenomenology of psychosis brings to the fore various existentialia operative in the very process of subjectification and temporalization so that we see a successful transcendence in its contours, the *Phenomenology* offers a therapeutic realization of a similar kind of vitality that the latter provides, but *within its very failure.* To say that the *Phenomenology* is a form of *successful* depressive thinking is thus to say that it has apparently immanently overcome depression without ever leaving its clutches on existence *by encountering the crisis head-on and coming out strong.*

Consequently, we see three structural levels of depression in Hegel's *Phenomenology*: the basal depressive structure of consciousness—the loss of the primordial object—which is the zero-level of its transcendence as such (originary depression or depression$_0$, failed transcendence); the psychopathological response that brings a particular person to an existential standstill, which we see in psychiatry (clinical depression or depression$_1$); and lastly the dialectical system of experience that, although depressive, is somehow successfully so, since even if its trial insists in experience it becomes a positive basis for a newfound energy and dynamism rather than a catalyst for decay (a form of successful depressive *thinking*, which is not a successful *depression* and is different in nature from depression$_1$). Following a suggestion taken up by Jean-Christophe Goddard, we can expand the idea as follows: it is not merely that the *Phenomenology* is a paradoxical form of successful depressive thinking, but more radically, it sketches a form of *successful psychotic thinking in general.*[503] Insofar as the event to which we are exposed by being held out into the Open in the pathos of sensation is the utterly new and unpredictable of which we can say nothing in advance, to give oneself over to it in its pure self-outpouring must itself be a form of originary psychosis, so that we see two possible responses: either from within an originary psychosis inflicting human transcendence as such we learn to be successfully psychotic or we opt for a path that would end in a pathological response to this primordial experience at the core of our being by levelling out its trauma instead of using it as the ground for the very impetus of one's subjective life in the world (a capacity Maldiney refers to as *transpassibility*).

Just as Hegel's *Phenomenology* could be described as an attempt to develop a form of successful depressive thinking, so too it could be ventured that Žižek's transcendental materialism may be an attempt to develop a form of successful psychotic thinking, but psychosis taken here not in Maldiney's unique understanding of it, but in the technical definition that Žižek instills it with as the world's withdrawal into its nocturnal self. Taking as its object the thematization of the inner structure of psychosis, which, since "madness signals the unconstrained explosion at the very core of human being,"[504] *can only be done in and through psychosis*, it seeks to use psychosis to pierce through its own impenetrable dusk by letting it move spontaneously of its own nature, that is, by reconstructing it ideally and scientifically in the concept through a mytho-poetic medium. But if the entirety of the Symbolic is some kind of virtual recompensation for this loss of objective reality, then this originary psychosis, essential to what it is to be a subject, must be primordially repressed if it is to be successful. We must forget that the very fabric of culture is nothing but the deluded ravings of the asylum, since otherwise we are confronted with the very monstrosity—ontological catastrophe, the passage of being through madness—that it was meant to cover up. This is precisely why the psychoanalytical experience is of irreducible importance for Žižek, for we could only hope to get beyond the various defence mechanisms underlying the constitution of our fantasmatic reality and catch a glimpse of their abyssal origin if this reality were wrought with piercing holes: if in our everyday lives we are completely lost in the transcendentally hallucinated world fabricated by the Symbolic, then only the upsurge of the Real as indicative of the infinite disharmony between mind and body can enable us to gain the necessary distance towards our self-loss in psychosis and thereby render possible its free (albeit mythological) internalization within the concept. But the Real not only opens up the space necessary for speculative fabulation as a faculty for explicating how we got "trapped" in ontological solipsism; it also lets us find a way, from within our constitutive psychosis, to minimally overcome this very entrapment. As that which is irreducible to the autonomous construction of the world of experience, the Real creates a realist moment within idealism itself. With these two elements achieved, we could be said to have developed a form of successful psychotic thinking: that is to say, a thinking that, from within its own psychosis, would not be limited by the latter in the same way that a form of successful depressive thinking would not be limited by its depression and would have gained a vitality similar to successful transcendence, despite its remaining depressive in structure.

A successful psychotic thinking—such an expression is intrinsically ambiguous and reveals the insurmountable difficulty any radical idealism has to overcome its own limitations. If our starting point is a self-grounding subjective idealism, we can never truly get "behind" it from within the universe of ideality, even if this idealism is wrought with fracture lines, inner tension, and agonizing cracks, for its symbolic (re)constitution of

reality functions with no need of an "external support of its truth."[505]
Instead of representing that by which the light of being sneaks in despite
the correlationalist prison, these can only indicate a torsion, an immanent
implosion, from within ideal self-enclosure. By thematizing these places of
non-coincidence we can perhaps come to terms with our entrapment and
see it for what it is (namely, an entrapment). Yet it is not clear we can hope
for much more if these skeptical reflections hold true: a successful psychotic
thinking *does not* result in any strict overcoming of the epistemological
constraints psychosis imposes upon us; it is *only from within* the Symbolic
that we see the Real as the residue of a failed attempt of synthesis, thereby
rendering it *always already* minimally symbolized, idealized, *always already*
necessarily lost, there being nothing but the Symbolic and its self-referential
play. The paradoxical overlapping of the purely subjective and the purely
objective is precisely that: *paradoxical*. It does not allow for any encounter
of the pure Real within the Symbolic, but is rather cognizant of the fact
that, since the Real is an impossible concept, any attempt to describe its
extra-notional character must be done from within its clutches. Knowledge
of reality in itself becomes reduced to a retroactive readjustment of
the Symbolic. We see this most clearly in the very expression itself. If
a successful psychotic *thinking* is not a successful *psychosis* (a cure) but
still exhibits the fundamental structure of psychosis, just as a successful
depressive thinking in no way means that depression has been left behind
and is always searching for the lost object, what we have attained would
be at best the upper limit of the dialectic of appearance as such, which
has finally collapsed upon itself in one great final cry giving voice to a
contradictory combination of absolute power and utmost impotence. In
recognizing the very limit of ideal synthesis, even if we are in a certain
sense minimally beyond it (the "realist" moment) we can only admit the
limit as an impasse with no beyond or content (even the "real" moment
is completely determined by the throes of idealist entrapment). But is this
sufficient to establish a new metaphysics? To speak metaphorically, it is as if,
on Žižek's account, in radical idealism we see the four walls that surround
us as a barrier not due to some window to the outside by which we know
this site as the prison that it is (the ontological solipsism of the constitutive
psychosis of the Symbolic) and could envisage an escape, but rather

due to their very shaking we feel that we are incarcerated in an infinitely claustrophobic space from which we will never emancipate ourselves. From the cracks in the wall there may seep through faint, trembling voices, but in the painstaking process of reconstructing their mumbled words they risk becoming identical with those voices that we hallucinate in our solitude. And even if we succeed at spectrally envisioning this outside by a careful translation of their garbled noise into structured speech, could we be said finally to have liberated ourselves by making the very distinction between liberty and imprisonment void?

If a successful form of psychotic thinking is an intrinsically paradoxical concept, it is perhaps because radical idealism is itself intrinsically paradoxical. To say that we can *never* reach reality, that we are *forever* stuck within the human universe of meaning, is not merely problematic to ordinary natural and scientific consciousness because it goes against our basic intuitions, but in a more primordially discomforting way: for it proclaims an originary withdrawal from objective reality at the very foundation of what it is to be human, thus potentially reducing the world of experience to the rampant free play of phantasmagoria. For someone who adheres to such a radical idealism, it would appear that even if the inconsistency of our notional apparatus may always be insufficient for a realist to overcome the ambiguity of a successful psychotic thinking, and thus to find resources to establish a strong realism from within idealism itself, we can still embark upon a speculative fabulation of ontological catastrophe as the necessary condition of the possibility of the subject. For we must nevertheless be able to explicate the fact that we can see our life as a *dream of a dream*, our ontological *psychosis as psychotic*, for the Symbolic fails to posit itself as all, and must therefore be always already minimally outside itself. Just as Schelling declares that many things take place before the beginning proper, so Žižek contends that a lot happens in the indemonstrable Real-as-origin haunting the Symbolic. The abyss of unconscious decision vibrates with an immense energy, and when we catch a glimpse of this impossibility in a mytho-poetics of the Symbolic's genesis, we simultaneously see a glimmer in the corner of our eye of why idealism is such an explosive event in being, despite the ontological solipsism of idealism itself. But such an epiphany is limited by the very impossibility of its object, for we have fallen into a new age of mythology that has been rationally justified. Yet language is always more language (this is the major consequence of the Real), and if ontology and metaphysics have been rendered impossible, insofar as we can see this fact for what it is, we must have the right to investigate it in a non-rational discourse, no matter what the status of idealism's self-overcoming.

Although a transcendental materialism developed *après-coup* in the enclosed terrain of a radical idealism may always leave the realist unsatisfied as to its very possibility, turning epistemological limit into positive ontological condition via a mytho-poetic narrativization of being's self-division does allow us to make minimal ontological claims that go beyond mythological imagery. If the Symbolic does present itself as quasi-full-blown constructionism of reality that cuts all ties with an extra-notional, extra-linguistic outside, then the very founding gesture of the Symbolic's self-containment must be structurally homologous with that of psychosis understood as a withdrawal from social reality into an irreal self, and thus must attest to an originary madness at the very ontogenetic basis of human subjectivity. In this respect, were one to refuse the move to mythology as a means of overcoming radical idealism as a mere confabulation that assures the consistency of its order by the production of false memories, the latter would nevertheless reveal a deadlock haunting subjectivity: *the deadlock of ontological catastrophe*. If the Symbolic exists, then the world is, at best, a fragmented totality whimpering under its own weight—a totality that, unable to posit itself as all, in the case of at least one creature (man) is forced to withdraw into a nocturnal irreal self due to a primordial moment of metaphysical trauma in its heart of hearts, thereby establishing the primary role of dislocation in ontology. Even if we might not be able to say more without writing a great fabulative epic, many details of which may succumb to confabulation and fantasmatic figures, the mere existence of a radically self-grounding idealism would not only demonstrate that reality split itself into two irreconcilable logical zones insofar as thought must exist, but more primordially that ontological catastrophe, whereby being is infinitely divided from itself and doomed to wander in a world of images that are images of nothing, is irreducible in the transcendental explanation of the conditions of the possibility of experience and the Symbolic. Idealism declares that *something must have gone horribly wrong* in the life of the absolute: for no God, no divine nature, could have wanted this to be our fate, since for both, our fate is tied up with theirs.

Notes

464. Žižek, *Less Than Nothing*, p. 314.

465. Ibid., pp. 234–35.

466. Schelling, *Darstellung*, I, 4, p. 106.

467. Schelling, *Freiheitsschrift*, p. 232.

468. Schelling, *Stuttgart Seminars*, pp. 216ff.

469. Schelling, *Ideas for a Philosophy of Nature*, trans. Errol E. Harris and Peter Heath (Cambridge: Cambridge University Press, 1995), pp. 41–42.

470. Schelling, *Freiheitsschrift*, p. 236.

471. Grant, *Philosophies of Nature after Schelling*, pp. viii–ix.

472. Ibid., p. ix.

473. Žižek, *Less Than Nothing*, p. 77.

474. Schelling, *Weltalter II*, pp. 121–22.

475. Schelling, "Briefwechsel mit Eschenmayer bezüglich der Abhandlung 'Philosophische Untersuchungen über das Wesen er menschlichen Freiheit'," *Schellings sämmtliche Werke*, I, 8, p. 150; translation taken from Iain Hamilton Grant, *Philosophies of Nature after Schelling*, p. 202.

476. Grant, *Philosophies of Nature after Schelling*, pp. 202–3.

477. Ibid., p. 2.

478. Ibid., p. 62.

479. Ibid., pp. 1–2.

480. Schelling, *First Outline of a System of the Philosophy of Nature*, trans. Keith R. Peterson (Albany: State University of New York Press, 2004), p. 14.

481. Žižek, *The Parallax View*, p. 106.

482. Žižek and Woodard, "Interview," *The Speculative Turn: Continental Materialism and Realism*, pp. 412–13.

483. Ibid., p. 413.

484. Ibid., p. 409.

485. Cf. Johnson, *Žižek's Ontology*, p. 148.

486. Ibid., p. 152.

487. Žižek, *Less Than Nothing*, p. 959.

488. Žižek, *The Indivisible Remainder*, p. 19.

489. Fichte, *Fichte: Early Philosophical Writings*, pp. 347–48. Also quoted by Žižek, "Fichte's Laughter," in *Madness, Mythology and Laughter*, p. 160, but with a different interpretation than what I offer here.

490. Fichte, *The Vocation of Man*, p. 64. For my discussion, see chapter 6.

491. Fichte, *Wissenschaftslehre 1805*, pp. 127–28.

492. Maldiney, *Penser l'homme et la folie*, p. 9.

493. Hegel, *Phenomenology of Spirit*, p. 36; cited by Maldiney, *Penser l'homme et la folie*, p. 263.

494. Goddard, *Mysticisme et folie*, p. 83.

495. Maldiney, *Penser l'homme et la folie*, p. 7.

496. Ibid., p. 263.

497. Ibid., p. 27.

498. Ibid., p. 29.

499. Ibid., p. 288.

500. Ibid., p. 36.

501. Ibid., p. 35.

502. Ibid., p. 30.

503. Goddard, *Mysticisme et folie*, pp. 83–84.

504. Žižek, "Fichte's Laughter," in *Madness, Mythology and Laughter*, p. 162.

505. Žižek, *Less Than Nothing*, p. 77.

Bibliography

Boothby, Richard. *Freud as Philosopher: Metapsychology after Lacan.* New York: Routledge, 2001.

Descartes, René. *Meditations on First Philosophy.* Trans. Donald A. Cross. Indianapolis: Hackett Publishing, 1993.

Fichte, Johann Gottlieb. *Gesamtausgabe der Bayerischen Akademie der Wissenschaften.* Ed. R. Lauth, Hans Jacob, & H. Gliwitzky. Frommann: Stuttgart-Bad Cannstatt, 1964. Division III: Briefe, Vol. I.

Fichte, Johann Gottlieb. *Fichte: Early Philosophic Writings.* Trans. Daniel Breazeale. Ithaca: Cornell University Press, 1988.

Fichte, Johann Gottlieb. *Foundations of Natural Right.* Ed. Frederick Neuhouser. Trans. Michael Baur. Cambridge: Cambridge University Press, 2000.

Fichte, Johann Gottlieb. *The Science of Knowledge.* Ed. and trans. Peter Heath & John Lachs. Cambridge: Cambridge University Press, 1982.

Fichte, Johann Gottlieb. *The Science of Knowing: Fichte's 1804 Lectures on the Wissenschaftslehre.* Trans. Walter E. Wright. Albany: SUNY Press, 2005.

Fichte, Johann Gottlieb. *The Vocation of Man.* Trans. Peter Preuss. Indianapolis: Hackett Publishing, 1987.

Fichte, Johann Gottlieb. *Wissenschaftslehre 1805.* Ed. H. Gliwitzky. Hamburg: Felix Meiner, 1984.

Fink, Bruce. *The Lacanian Subject: Between Language and Jouissance*. New York: Princeton University Press, 1995.

Freud, Sigmund. *The Standard Edition of the Complete Psychological Works of Sigmund Freud*, translated from the German under the General Editorship of James Strachey, in collaboration with Anna Freud, assisted by Alix Strachey and Alan Tyson. London: Hogarth Press and the Institute of Psychoanalysis, 1953–1974.

Freud, Sigmund. "The Aetiology of Hysteria." *SE*, III, 187–222.

Freud, Sigmund. "Instincts and Their Vicissitudes." *SE*, XIV, 117–40.

Freud, Sigmund. "Neurosis and Psychosis." *SE*, XIX, 149–53.

Freud, Sigmund. "The Loss of Reality in Neurosis and Psychosis." *SE*, XIX, 183–87.

Freud, Sigmund. "Construction in Analysis." *SE*, XXIII, 255–70.

Gabriel, Markus. *Das Absolute und die Welt in Schellings Freiheitsschrift*. Bonn: University Press, 2006.

Gabriel, Markus, & Slavoj Žižek. "Introduction: A Plea for a Return to Post-Kantian Idealism." *Mythology, Madness and Laughter: Subjectivity in German Idealism*. New York: Continuum, 2009. 1–14.

Goddard, Jean-Christophe. *Mysticisme et folie. Essai sur la simplicité*. Paris: Desclée de Brouwer, 2002.

Grant, Iain Hamilton. *Philosophies of Nature after Schelling*. New York: Continuum, 2006.

Hegel, G. W. F. *The Difference between Fichte's and Schelling's System of Philosophy*. Trans. H. S. Harris & Walter Cerf. Albany: SUNY Press, 1977.

Hegel, G. W. F. *Frühe politische Systeme*. Frankfurt am Main: Ullstein, 1974.

Hegel, G. W. F. *Lectures on the History of Philosophy: Medieval and Modern Philosophy*. Trans. E. S. Haldane & Frances H. Simson. London: University of Nebraska Press, 1995.

Hegel, G. W. F. *The Encyclopedia Logic: Part 1 of the Encyclopedia of Philosophical Sciences with the Zusätze.* Trans. Theodore F. Geraets, W. A. Suchting, & H. S. Harris. Indianapolis: Hackett Publishing, 1991.

Hegel, G. W. F. *Hegel's Philosophy of Nature.* 3 vols. Trans. M. J. Petry. London: Humanities Press, 1970.

Hegel, G. W. F. *Phenomenology of Spirit.* Trans. A. V. Miller. London: Oxford University Press, 1977.

Hegel, G. W. F. *The Science of Logic.* Trans. George di Giovanni. Cambridge: Cambridge University Press, 2010.

Jacobi, Friedrich Heinrich. "Idealism and Realism." *Kant's Early Critics: The Empiricist Critique of the Theoretical Philosophy.* Ed. Brigitte Sassen. Cambridge: Cambridge University Press, 2000. 169–75.

Johnston, Adrian. *Žižek's Ontology: A Transcendental Materialistic Theory of Subjectivity.* Evanston: Northwestern University Press, 2000.

Kant, Immanuel. *Anthropology from a Programatic Point of View.* Trans. Robert B. Louden. *Anthropology, History, and Education.* Ed. Günter Zöller & Robert B. Louden. Cambridge: Cambridge University Press, 2007. 227–429.

Kant, Immanuel. *The Critique of Pure Reason.* Trans. Paul Guyer & Allen W. Wood. Cambridge: Cambridge University Press, 1998.

Kant, Immanuel. *Lectures on Pedagogy.* Trans. Robert B. Louden. *Anthropology, History, and Education.* Ed. Günter Zöller & Robert B. Louden. Cambridge: Cambridge University Press, 2007. 434–85.

Kant, Immanuel. *Kant on Education.* Trans. Annette Churton. Boston: D. C. Heath, 1900.

Kant, Immanuel. *Critique of Practical Judgment. Practical Philosophy.* Trans. and ed. Mary. J. Gregor. Cambridge: Cambridge University Press, 1999. 133-309.

Kant, Immanuel. *Religion within the Limits of Reason Alone.* Trans. T. M. Greene & H. H. Hudson. New York: Harper & Row, 1960.

Lacan, Jacques. "Clefs pour la psychoanalyse (entretien avec Madeleine Chapsal)." http://www.ecole-lacanienne.net/documents/1957–05–31.doc. May 16, 2010.

Lacan, Jacques. *Écrits*. Trans. Bruce Fink. New York: W. W. Norton. 2006.

Lacan, Jacques. *The Seminar of Jacques Lacan, XI: The Four Fundamental Concepts of Psycho-analysis, 1963–1964*. Ed. Jacques-Alain Miller. Trans. Alan Sheridan. London: Vintage, 1998.

Lacan, Jacques. *Le séminaire, Livre IV: La relation d'objet et les structures freudiennes, 1956–1957*. Ed. Jacques-Alain Miller. Paris: Seuil, 1994.

Lacan, Jacques. *Le séminaire, Livre XVII: L'envers de la psychoanalyse, 1969–1970*. Ed. Jacques-Alain Miller. Paris: Seuil, 1991.

Lacan, Jacques. *The Seminar. Book XX. Encore, On Feminine Sexuality, The Limits of Love and Knowledge, 1972–3*. Ed. Jacques-Alain Miller. Trans. Bruce Fink. New York: Norton, 1998.

Laplanche, Jean, & Jean-Betrand Pontalis. *The Language of Psychoanalysis*. Trans. D. Nicholson-Smith. London: Karnac Books, 1988.

Lenin, Vladimir. *Materialism and Empirio-Criticism*. Peking: Foreign Languages Press, 1972.

Leupin, Alexander. *Lacan Today: Psychoanalysis, Science and Religion*. New York: Other Press, 2004.

Lévi-Strauss, Claude. *Structural Anthropology*. Trans. Claire Jacobson & Brooke Grundfest Schoepf. New York: Basic Books, 1963.

Maldiney, Henri. *Penser l'homme et la folie*. Grenoble: Éditions Jérôme Milion, 2007.

Meillassoux, Quentin. *After Finitude: An Essay on the Necessity of Contingency*. Trans. Ray Brassier. New York: Continuum, 2008.

Miller, Jacques-Alain. "Context and Concepts." *Reading Seminar XI: Lacan's Four Fundamental Concepts of Psychoanalysis*. Ed. Richard Feldstein, Bruce Fink, & Maire Jaanus. New York: SUNY Press, 1995. 3–15.

Moore, G. E. "Refutation of Idealism." *Mind* 12 (1903): 433–53.

Schelling, F. W. J. *Ages of the World.* [*Weltalter II*]. *The Abyss of Freedom/Ages of the World.* Trans. Judith Norman. Ann Arbor: University of Michigan Press, 2008. 113–82.

Schelling, F. W. J. *The Ages of the World: Third Version (c. 1815) [Weltalter III].* Trans. Jason M. Wirth. Albany: SUNY Press, 2000.

Schelling, F. W. J. "Briefwechsel mit Eschenmayer bezüglich der Abhandlung 'Philosophische Untersuchungen über das Wesen er menschlichen Freiheit'" *Schellings sämmtliche Werke,* ed. K. F. A. Schelling. Division 1. Vol. 8. Stuttgart and Augsburg: J. G. Cotta'scher Verlag, 1856–1861. 145–89.

Schelling, F. W. J. *Darstellung meines Systems der Philosophie. Schellings sämmtliche Werke,* ed. K. F. A. Schelling. Division 1. Vol. 4. Stuttgart and Augsburg: J. G. Cotta'scher Verlag, 1856–1861. 105–212.

Schelling, F. W. J. *Einleitung in die Philosophie.* Ed. Walter E. Ehrhardt. Stuttgart-Bad Connstatt: Frommann-Holzboog, 1989.

Schelling, F. W. J. *First Outline of a System of the Philosophy of Nature.* Trans. Keith R. Peterson. Albany: SUNY Press, 2004.

Schelling, F. W. J. *The Grounding of Positive Philosophy.* Trans. Bruce Matthews. New York: SUNY Press, 2007.

Schelling, F. W. J. *Ideas for a Philosophy of Nature.* Trans. Errol E. Harris & Peter Heath. Cambridge: Cambridge University Press, 1995.

Schelling, F. W. J. *Philosophical Investigations into the Essence of Human Freedom [Freiheitsschrift].* Trans. Priscilla Hayden-Roy. *Philosophy of German Idealism.* Ed. Ernst Behler. New York: Continuum, 2003. 217–84.

Schelling, F. W. J. *Stuttgart Seminars. Idealism and the Endgame of Theory.* Trans. Thomas Pfau. Albany: SUNY Press, 1994. 195–268.

Schelling, F. W. J. *System of Transcendental Idealism.* Trans. Peter Heath. Charlottesville: University Press of Virginia, 2001.

Spinoza, Baruch de. *Ethics and Selected Letters.* Ed. Seymour Feldman. Trans. Samuel Shirley. Indianapolis: Hackett Publishing, 1982.

Verene, Donald Philip. *Hegel's Recollection: A Study of Images in the Phenomenology of Spirit.* Albany: SUNY Press, 1985.

Wirth, Jason. "Translator's Introduction." *The Ages of the World: Third Version (c. 1815)*. Albany: SUNY Press, 2000. vii–xxxii.

Zimmerman, Rainer E. *Die Rekonstruktion von Raum, Zeit und Materie. Moderne Implikationen Schellingscher Naturphilosophie*. Frankfurt am Main: Lang, 1998.

Zimmerman, Rainer E. *System des transzendentalen Materialismus*. Paderborn: Mentis, 2004.

Žižek, Slavoj. *The Abyss of Freedom. The Abyss of Freedom/Ages of the World*. Cambridge: MIT Press, 2008. 3–89.

Žižek, Slavoj. "The Big Other Doesn't Exist." *Journal of European Psychoanalysis*. Spring-Fall 1997. http://www.lacan.com/zizekother.htm. January 7, 2013

Žižek, Slavoj. "Cartesian Subject versus Cartesian Theater." *Cogito and the Unconscious*. Ed. Slavoj Žižek. Durham: Duke University Press, 1998. 247–74.

Žižek, Slavoj. *How to Read Lacan*. New York: W. W. Norton, 2007.

Žižek, Slavoj. *The Indivisible Remainder: On Schelling and Related Matters*. New York: Verso, 2007.

Žižek, Slavoj. "Fichte's Laughter." *Mythology, Madness and Laughter: Subjectivity in German Idealism*. New York: Continuum, 2009. 122–167.

Žižek, Slavoj. *Less Than Nothing: Hegel and the Shadow of Dialectical Materialism*. London: Verso, 2012.

Žižek, Slavoj. *Living in the End Times*. New York: Verso, 2011.

Žižek, Slavoj. *The Fragile Absolute: Or, Why Is the Christian Legacy Worth Fighting For?* London: Verso, 2000.

Žižek, Slavoj. "Liberation Hurts: An Interview with Slavoj Žižek (with Eric Dean Rasmussen)." http://www.electronicbookreview.com/thread/endconstruction/desublimation. February 23, 2010.

Žižek, Slavoj. *The Parallax View*. Cambridge: MIT Press, 2009.

Žižek, Slavoj. *La Parallaxe*. Paris: Fayard, 2008.

Žižek, Slavoj. *The Puppet and the Dwarf: The Perverse Core of Christianity*. Cambridge: MIT Press, 2003.

Žižek, Slavoj. *Tarrying with the Negative: Kant, Hegel, and the Critique of Ideology*. Durham: Duke University Press, 2003.

Žižek, Slavoj. *The Ticklish Subject: The Absent Centre of Political Ideology*. New York: Verso, 2000.

Žižek, Slavoj, & Glyn Daly. *Conversations with Žižek*. Cambridge: Polity, 2004.

Žižek, Slavoj, & Ben Woodard. "Interview." *The Speculative Turn: Continental Materialism and Realism*. Ed. Levi Bryant, Nick Srnicek, and Graham Harman. Melbourne: re.press, 2011. 406–15.

Žižek! Dir. Atra Taylor. DVD. Zeitgeist Video: 2007.

76122013R00181

Made in the USA
Middletown, DE
10 June 2018